Interfaces of Morphology

studia grammatica 74

Herausgegeben von
Manfred Bierwisch,
Hans-Martin Gärtner
und Manfred Krifka

unter Mitwirkung von
Regine Eckardt, Göttingen,
Paul Kiparsky, Stanford

Holden Härtl (Ed.)

Interfaces of Morphology

A Festschrift for Susan Olsen

Akademie Verlag

Bibliografische Information der Deutschen Nationalbibliothek

Die Deutsche Nationalbibliothek verzeichnet diese Publikation in der Deutschen Nationalbibliografie; detaillierte bibliografische Daten sind im Internet über http://dnb.d-nb.de abrufbar.

Ein Wissenschaftsverlag der Oldenbourg Gruppe

www.akademie-verlag.de

Umschlagentwurf: hauser lacour
Druck: Concept Medienhaus, Berlin
Bindung: Buchbinderei Klotz, Jettingen-Scheppach

Dieses Papier ist alterungsbeständig nach DIN/ISO 9706.

ISBN 978-3-05-006056-9
eISBN 978-3-05-006379-9

Contents

Holden Härtl
Introduction 7

Gisbert Fanselow
Morphological mismatches in discontinuous noun phrases 11

Werner Frey
On indefinite NPs participating in the German predicate complex 27

Andrew McIntyre
English particle verbs are complex heads: Evidence from nominalization 41

Sophie Repp
D-Linking vs. degree: Inflected and uninflected 'welch' in exclamatives and rhetorical questions 59

Karin Pittner
Reflexivization and intensification in syntax and lexicon 91

Markus Egg
Don't mince your words: In defense of lexical integrity 107

Claudia Maienborn & Sascha Geldermann
'Expertengeprüft' und 'vom Experten geprüft': Zur Semantik von Nomen-Partizip II-Komposita und ihrer präpositionalen Partner 127

Holden Härtl
Arguments of non-heads 163

Angelika Wöllstein
Aspekte des Absentivs: 'Wir sind Sue gratulieren' – Zum Problem der Lokalisierung im Absentiv 179

Elisabeth Löbel
Semantische Kongruenz 201

Ilse Zimmermann
Selektion und Interpretation morpho-syntaktischer Einheiten 217

Nicole Dehé & Allison Wetterlin
Secondary stress in morphologically complex words in Faroese: A word game 229

Heinz Vater
On participles of German verbs borrowed from English 249

Heike Tappe
Morphological code-mixing: The case of Zulu agreement in English 263

Lothar Peter
English – synthetic, analytic and synthetic again? Are we going round in circles? The cases of the reduced auxiliaries 'have' and 'will' 287

Heike Zinsmeister
Corpus-based modeling of the semantic transparency of noun-noun compounds 303

Claudia Olk
Why say 'yes' in Joyce? Molly Bloom's 'yes because' in the "Penelope" episode of *Ulysses* 323

Introduction*

Holden Härtl

The ability to create as many new words as we need or like is surely one of the central characteristics of the human language faculty; but we have to admit that we have not got an exactly clear picture about its nature. This is indicated by the large amount of open questions in the field—which are sometimes disturbingly fundamental. One example is the debate if there is such a thing as "word" at all, which scholars like Haspelmath (2011) strongly doubt; see also Jacobs (2011) for further discussion. Another issue, which has been in the focus of research for quite a while, concerns the precise locus of word-formation in the language system. And in order to complicate matters a bit further, the latter question can be addressed from various perspectives: First, we can ask generally if word-formation is part of grammar or not. Some have maintained a "lexicalist" view here, the standard text is Chomsky (1970), assuming that word-formation—mainly because of its idiosyncrasy—is anchored in the mental lexicon and is, thus, not part of core grammar. Second, once one has accepted certain grammatical regularities of word-formation, their specific positioning within the grammatical system needs to be determined. Here, a prominent approach is the "integrative" one, where principles of word-formation are fused with the domain of syntax (cf. Selkirk 1982), while others have argued for a "separatist" viewpoint, assuming a distinct morphological component (cf. Di Sciullo and Williams 1987). The latter stance embodies, in fact, an updated lexicalist approach, now enriched with grammatical principles in their own right. A somehow mediating perspective instrumentalizes certain semantic-lexical as well as linking principles to be the basis for the formation and interpretation of (complex) words (cf. Bierwisch 2009, Lieber 2009), thus implementing a semantic-lexical system without having to accept a separate morphological component in the narrow sense.

Against this background the current volume brings together studies from a broad disciplinary spectrum to contribute to an investigation of lexical creativity and flexibility from the perspectives of system-theoretical and cognitive-scientific linguistics as well as computer linguistics and literary science. All contributions are dedicated to Susan Olsen on the occasion of her birthday—and nothing would be better suited as a Festschrift for her than a (self-picked) bunch of flowers of different varieties. Sue Olsen has always viewed the mental lexicon as based on a formal system that combines an inventory of morphological units according to lexicon-specific rules of grammar. At the same time, Sue Olsen has been cautious to link lexical issues to the domains with which the lexical system interfaces, like

* Acknowledgements: I wish to thank Heike Tappe for comments on an earlier version of this Introduction. I am also deeply indebted to Marco Benincasa, Janine Bothur, Sven Kotowski, Friederike Kreter, and Laura Sievers for their valuable help with the preparation of this volume.

syntax or semantics, and integrated insights and data from these domains into her analyses. It is this "interface view" combined with her competence as a classically trained linguist with a strong and broad background in grammar theory that has made Sue's work so insightful and stimulating for other researchers in the field. Moreover, Sue's research goes far beyond the narrow scope of core grammar and her awareness of cognitive-scientific and conceptual-ontological layers of language description is constantly visible in her linguistic work as well as her teaching.

Sue Olsen is a true, enthusiastic linguist. She started her academic career in Vermont, at the renowned Middlebury College, where she obtained a Master's degree in German Linguistics. She completed her doctoral dissertation on *seem/scheinen* in 1980 at the University of Cologne; her advisor was Heinz Vater. She had taken up positions as assistant professor in Cologne as well as in Bloomington (Indiana) before she was offered a position as associate professor at Bloomington, which she left shortly after to accept an offer from Stuttgart. She then followed an offer for a full professorship for English Linguistics at the University of Leipzig in 1996 before she received a "Ruf" to the prestigious Humboldt-Universität in Berlin, where she has been working since 2002.

Her research covers a broad array of topics including, e.g., general problems of word-formation, the grammar of complex verbs and compounds, the locative alternation as well as the syntax of noun phrases and aspects of lexical and conceptual semantics. A key element in Sue Olsen's work is the strong empirical basis of the argumentation as well as a cross-language perspective, which connects her work to the broader framework of investigations into linguistic universals. Sue Olsen's linguistic work is associated with various DFG projects, whose research foci also hint at the broadness of her academic specialties, ranging from a semantic-morphological description of particle verb formation in German and English to an implementation of thematic relations in a model of language production. Further, Sue Olsen was the speaker of the interdisciplinary doctorate program *Universalität and Diversität: Sprachliche Strukturen und Prozesse* at the University of Leipzig. Most impressively, however, are Susan Olsen's publications, which attest the high standards of her work in a remarkable way and we can only consider a couple of milestones here, like Sue's well-known *Wortbildung im Deutschen* (Olsen 1986), her work on the syntax of the determiner phrase in German (Olsen 1991), her papers on complex verb formation and compounding (Olsen 1998, 1999, 2000, 2001, 2010) or her remarkable commitment in the latest *HSK* volume on word-formation (Müller et al. to appear).

The papers in this volume relate to various aspects of Susan Olsen's work and, in particular, the above-mentioned interface perspective towards morphology. Investigations into grammatical interfaces can give us important insights into the internal architecture of the language domains involved as well as the sharpness of their boundaries. One of the classical domains often postulated to be adjacent to morphology is syntax. Here, *Gisbert Fanselow* opens the discussion with an examination of discontinuous noun phrases of the type *Geld habe ich keines* ('money I have none') and the morpho-syntactic as well as the semantic-pragmatic conditions underlying these construction. *Werner Frey* examines the positioning of indefinite argumental noun phrases in the predicate complex and explores the implications of an incorporation analysis for these configurations. *Andrew McIntyre* studies the syntactic interface as well and argues, based on data from nominalizations and reduplication cases like *writer downer*, for an analysis of particle verbs as complex heads. *Sophie Repp* examines the distribution of uninflected, exclamative *welch* as in *Welch eine Freude!* (*What a joy!*) in German in contrast to the inflected, interrogative form and links them to different types of speech acts, employing a semantics of degree. In her analysis of reflexives, *Karin Pittner* explores how the notions of reflexivization and intensification are connected and how the latter concept is mirrored in syntactic as well as word-internal composition. Word-internal aspects also play a role in the contribution by *Markus Egg*, in which he advocates the validity of the *Principle of lexical integrity* and implements it into a semantic underspecification framework. Egg's contribution bridges to the domain of semantics, where *Claudia Maienborn* and *Sascha Geldermann* explore compounds involving participles of the type *expertengeprüft* ('expert-tested') and—focusing on their compositional semantics—contrast them with their phrasal counterparts (i.e., *vom Experten geprüft*, 'tested by experts'). Also against the background of the discussion about the boundary between syntax and morphology, *Holden Härtl* examines lexical-semantic conditions of compound-external realizations of arguments of non-heads, i.e., constructions of the type *Fahrgemeinschaft nach Italien* ('ride_community to Italy', *ride sharing to Italy*). Individual morphological-grammatical categories are studied in the following section, which is opened by *Angelika Wöllstein* with a discussion of the so-called *Absentive*, as in *Meine Frau ist einkaufen* ('my wife is (away) shopping'), and an analysis of the category as the predication of a location. The contribution by *Elisabeth Löbel* is devoted to the phenomenon of semantically determined agreement, e.g., gender agreement as in *Das Mädchen*$_{\text{i-NEUTER}}$ *spielte mit ihrer*$_{\text{i-FEMININE}}$ *Puppe* ('the girl played with her doll'), and the underlying grammatical conditions. *Ilse Zimmermann* discusses compositional properties of lexical units in Russian and the realization of morphosyntactic features for case, number, tense, and mood, for which she implements an operation of "delayed" semantic interpretation. Aspects of language comparison as well as language contact come into play in the next section, where *Nicole Dehé* and *Allison Wetterlin* report on data from experimental studies on stress patterns in morphologically complex word in Faroese. Furthermore, *Heinz Vater* investigates German participles borrowed from English like *geforwardet* ('PARTICIPLE-PREFIX_forward_AFFIX') and describes different configurations thus defining three subclasses of these items. In a related context, *Heike Tappe* discusses instances of lexical as well as grammatical-morphological code-mixing between Zulu and English and analyzes data from a large empirical study in this domain from a broader socio-linguistic perspective. Focusing on aspects of language change in English and the case of auxiliaries, *Lothar Peter* investigates arguments for a cyclic development in the occurrence of synthetic and analytic language means. The section concluding this volume adds text-oriented viewpoints from the fields of information technology and literary science: *Heike Zinsmeister* relates the semantic classification of noun-noun compounds to corpus-based evidence and illustrates how contextual as well as family-size factors can be used to predict co-occurrence patterns. Closing the discussion, *Claudia Olk* investigates lexical creativity as is reflected in the numerous usages of the particle *yes* in the "Penelope" episode of *Ulysses* and analyzes its semantic ambivalence against the background of Derrida's work, thus explaining even paradoxical uses of *yes*.

Bibliography

Bierwisch, M. (2009): Nominalization – Lexical and Syntactic Aspects. In: A. Giannakidou and M. Rathert (eds.), *Quantification, Definiteness, and Nominalization* (Oxford Studies in Theoretical Linguistics 24). Oxford: Oxford University Press, 281–320.

Chomsky, N. (1970): Remarks on Nominalization. In: R. A. Jacobs and P. S. Rosenbaum (eds.), *Readings in English Transformational Grammar*. Waltham, MA: Blaisdell, 184–221.

Di Sciullo, A. M. and E. Williams (1987): On the Definition of Word. *Linguistic Inquiry Monographs* 14. Cambridge, MA: MIT Press.

Haspelmath, M. (2011): The Indeterminacy of Word Segmentation and the Nature of Morphology and Syntax. *FoliaLinguistica*45(1): 31–80.

Jacobs, J. (2011): Grammatik ohne Wörter? To appear in: S. Engelberg, A. Holler and K. Proost (eds.), *Sprachliches Wissen zwischen Lexikon und Grammatik. Institut für Deutsche Sprache*. Jahrbuch 2010. Berlin/New York: de Gruyter.

Lieber, R. (2009): A Lexical Semantic Approach to Compounding. In: R. Lieber and P. Štekauer (eds.), *The Oxford Handbook of Compounding*. Oxford: Oxford University Press, 78–99.

Müller, P., I. Ohnheiser, S. Olsen and F. Rainer (eds.) (to appear): *HSK Word-Formation: An International Handbook of the Languages of Europe*. Berlin/New York: de Gruyter.

Olsen, S. (1986): *Wortbildung im Deutschen*. Stuttgart: Kröner.

Olsen, S. (1991): Die deutsche Nominalphrase als Determinansphrase. In: S. Olsen and G. Fanselow (eds.), *DET, COMP und INFL. Zur Syntax funktionaler Kategorien und grammatischer Funktionen*. Tübingen: Niemeyer, 35–56.

Olsen, S. (1998): Prädikative Argumente syntaktischer und lexikalischer Köpfe – Zum Status der Partikelverben im Deutschen und Englischen. *Folia Linguistica* 31: 301–329.

Olsen, S. (1999): Verbpartikel oder Adverb? In: J. Rehbein and A. Redder (eds.), *Grammatik und mentale Prozesse*. Tübingen: Stauffenburg, 223–240.

Olsen, S. (2000): Compounding and Stress: A closer look at the boundary between morphology and syntax. *Linguistische Berichte* 181: 55–69.

Olsen, S. (2001): Copulative Compounds. A Closer Look at the Interface between Morphology and Syntax. In: G. Booij and J. van Marle (eds.), *Yearbook of Morphology 2000*. Dordrecht: Kluwer, 279–320.

Olsen, S. (2010): New Impulses in Word-Formation. Sonderheft *Linguistische Berichte* 17. Hamburg: Buske, 253–281.

Selkirk, E. (1982): *The Syntax of Words*. Cambridge, MA: MIT Press.

Morphological mismatches in discontinuous noun phrases*

Gisbert Fanselow

1. Introduction

It is a well-known fact that the parts of a discontinuous noun phrase in German often take a form different from the one they would have in a continuous construction (cf., e.g., Haider 1985). The data constellation (1) represents a typical instance of such mismatches: in a continuous noun phrase, the quantifier *kein* 'no' is inflected in its weak form (1)a, which must not show up in the corresponding discontinuous construction (1)d. The discontinuous construction (1)c is fine with the strong form *keines,* which cannot be used in the continuous counterpart (1)b.

(1)	a.	Ich habe kein Geld. 'I have no money.'	[continuous NP, weak inflection of Q]
	b.	*Ich habe keines *Geld.*	[continuous NP, strong inflection of Q]
	c.	Geld habe ich keines.	[discontinuous NP, strong inflection of Q]
	d.	*Geld hab ich kein	[discontinuous NP, weak inflection of Q]

Such observations have often been cited as evidence against the claim that discontinuous noun phrases are formed by extracting a subconstituent out of the noun phrase (cf., e.g., Haider 1985, Fanselow 1988 and, more recently, Ott 2011 for such a view), but mismatches of that kind could also be captured in a model in which discontinuity can be a result of movement, but in which the exact morphological shape of a word is computed/checked at a very late point in the derivation, after movement. In the present paper, I would like to argue that this second view is at least as successful as the first one.

One line of reasoning deals with the fact that morphological mismatches seem to come in two varieties. There is a purely formal type of feature mismatch (as shown in (1)), but there is also a kind of mismatch that appears to be confined to certain semantic/pragmatic contexts. As an example for the latter, consider (2). The parts of a discontinuous noun phrase can also differ in their number specification in German, as illustrated by (2)a in which a plural left part of the discontinuous noun phrase is combined with a singular right part; cf. Fanselow and Ćavar (2002) for a discussion, among others.

* The research reported here has been supported by DFG grant FA 255/5. For helpful discussion of some of the issues dealt with here I would like to thank Caroline Féry and Denisa Lenertovà.

(2) a. Zeitungen lese ich nur eine.
newspapers read I only one
'I only read one newspaper.'
b. *Ich lese nur eine Zeitungen.
c. Ich lese nur eine Zeitung.
'I read only one newspaper.'

We will show how the mismatches in (1) and (2) differ, and discuss whether these differences are due to different derivations of these discontinuous constructions. The data seems to imply that the computation of the morphological form of a phrase must follow movement at least in some cases. A brief discussion of how linear order and morphological 'repair' interact concludes the paper.

2. Adjective form

Let us begin with a brief sketch of the standard analysis of the changes illustrated in (1). They are due to the laws of adjectival inflection in German. Adjectives are inflected in either a strong or a weak form, and the choice among these options depends on the nature of the determiner, the inflection of other adjectives in the construction, and the presence or absence of an overt noun. I will not attempt to present a theoretically sophisticated analysis here (which can, e.g., be found in Olsen 1990, 1991a), and will confine myself to some remarks on how the relevant generalizations relate to the position a noun phrase occupies in a tree.

If there is a determiner that bears strong morphology (such as the definite determiner), the adjective (if present) must be inflected in the weak form (3)a, if there is no determiner (or if the determiner has weak morphology), the adjective bears strong inflection (3)b.

(3) a. Sie kauft die polnischen Gänse.
she buys the Polish.acc.pl.weak geese
b. Sie kauft polnische Gänse.
she buys Polish.acc.pl.strong geese

In the continuous noun phrase (4)a, the quantifier *keine* bears strong inflection, hence the adjective *polnischen* appears in its weak form. In the discontinuous counterpart (4)b both *keine* and the adjective *polnische* are strongly inflected, however. This follows from the assumption that the form of inflection the adjective takes is computed in its *surface* position. In (4)a the adjective is c-commanded (governed) by a strongly inflected quantifier in the (largest) nominal projection it appears in. In (4)b, on the other hand, the (largest) nominal projection in the left periphery of the clause contains no strongly inflected quantifier, so that the strong form of the adjective must be chosen.

(4) a. Sie kauft [keine polnischen Gänse].
she buys no.strong Polish.acc.pl.weak geese
b. [*Polnische Gänse*] kauft sie [*keine*].
Polish.acc.pl.strong geese buys she no.strong

For the computation of the form of the adjective in (4)b it does not matter what structural context the adjective would be in in the corresponding continuous noun phrase (4)a. Why is the determination of form for the adjective in (4)b not influenced by the quantifier *keine*?

Some have proposed to capture this fact by the assumption that discontinuous noun phrases are not formed by moving a subpart of the noun phrase to the left. Rather, such models assume that *polnische Gänse* and *keine* each are complete noun phrases of their own that are generated independently of each other (Fanselow 1988, Kuhn 1999, Ott 2011). Their relation is mediated by binding, predication, or a topic comment-relation. In such a theory, it is no wonder that the presence of *keine* is irrelevant for the form constitution of *polnische Gänse* in the left periphery, because the two expressions are part of different phrases.

The need for inflecting the adjective strongly in (4)b would, however, also be accounted for if the computation of morphological properties is a late process that follows movement and does not employ any "reconstruction" mechanism. The presence of *keine* in the noun phrase which *polnische Gänse* originated in would then no longer be visible when the form of *polnische* is determined in (4)b. We will not attempt to decide between these options at the moment.

An identical pattern of differences between continuous and discontinuous constructions can be observed for sequences of adjectives in which, often, only the leftmost adjective bears strong morphology, as in (5)a. When the formation of a discontinuous noun phrase removes a weak adjective from the c-command domain of a strong one, the former must bear strong morphology, as in (5)b.

(5) a. Rotem polnischen Wein vertrauen wir nicht.
red.sg.dat.strong Polish.sg.dat.weak wine trust we not
'We do not trust red Polish wine.'
b. Polnischem Wein vertrauen wir nur rotem.
Polish.dat.sg.strong wine trust we only red.dat.sg.strong
'We only trust red Polish wine.'

The changes in (1) are due to a different rule. *Ein* ('a') and *kein* ('no') differ from other determiners in having both weak and strong forms (in that respect, they inflect like adjectives). In the nominative/accusative, *ein* and *kein* are inflected weakly unless the noun phrase they appear in has no overt noun, cf. (6)a–d. When an adjective is present, it is inflected strongly, and triggers weak inflection on the quantifier (6)e–f.

(6) a. Ich habe kein Geld.
I have no.acc.weak money
b. *Ich habe keines Geld.
I have no.acc.strong money
c. Ich habe keines.
I have no.acc strong
d. *Ich habe kein.
I have no.acc.weak
e. Ich habe kein estnisches Geld.
I have no.acc.weak Estonian.acc.strong money
f. Ich habe kein estnisches.
I have no.acc.weak Estonian.acc.strong

The paradigm in (1) follows from this generalization if the computation of the strong/weak distinction is a surface matter in this context as well: The noun phrase in which *keines* in (7)a–c appears has no overt noun, hence the strong form must be chosen ((7)a,c). However, when a strong adjective accompanies the quantifier, the latter has, again, weak morphology.

(7) a. Geld habe ich [$_{\text{NP}}$ keines –].
money have I no.acc.strong
b. *Geld hab ich [$_{\text{NP}}$ kein –].
money have I no.acc.weak
c. Estnisches Geld hab ich [$_{\text{NP}}$ keines –].
Estonian.acc.strong money have I no.acc.strong
d. Geld hab ich [$_{\text{NP}}$ kein estnisches –].
money have I no.acc.weak Estonian.acc.strong

It should be stressed that such morphological changes are not an idiosyncrasy of German. There is, e.g., an alternation of adjectival inflection in Hungarian, too. The adjective must be fully inflected when it is detached from its head noun in Hungarian discontinuous noun phrases, just as in German. We will present and discuss more examples from different languages below; cf. also Fanselow and Féry (accepted).

(8) a. láttam nagy bicikliket. [Hungarian]
saw.I big bike.pl.acc
b. bicikliket láttam nagyokat.
bike.pl.acc saw-i big.pl.acc

3. Number

Fanselow and Ćavar (2002) propose that the construction illustrated in (2), repeated here as (9), should be analyzed roughly along the lines just discussed for alternations of adjectival form. Closer inspection reveals, however, that we are confronted with a different phenomenon.

(9) a. Zeitungen lese ich nur eine.
newspapers read I only one
'I only read one newspaper.'
b. *Ich lese nur eine Zeitungen.
c. Ich lese nur eine Zeitung.
'I read only one newspaper.'

In (9)a, the two parts of the discontinuous noun phrase differ in their number specification: the left part bears plural marking whereas the right part is singular. Fanselow and Ćavar (2002) take this to be an adjustment of form comparable to the one discussed in the previous section. Their argument goes as follows: Singular count nouns normally cannot appear without a determiner in German, cf. (10).

(10) a. Anna liest ein Buch.
Anna reads a book.sg
b. *Anna liest Buch.
c. Anna liest Bücher.
Anna reads books.pl

In discontinuous constructions such as (9)a, a singular count noun appearing alone in the left periphery of a clause would find itself in a constellation in which it has no accompanying (c-commanding) determiner. If surface constellations matter (as the discussion in the preceding section has suggested), such a construction should be ungrammatical, because singular count nouns need an accompanying determiner within their (largest) nominal projection. Fanselow and Ćavar (2002) suggest that the constellation can be repaired, however, either by 'replacing' the offending singular by a plural (as in (9)a), or by inserting a determiner as in (11)b as already proposed by Riemsdijk (1989). They implement this idea in an optimality-theoretic framework.

(11) a. Ich habe keinen Wagen.
I have no car
b. Einen Wagen habe ich keinen.
a car have I no

Again, it is worth being pointed out that constructions such as (9)a can be found in quite a number of languages[1], such as Dutch (12), Romanian (13c)[2] (cf. also Giurgea 2006), or Spanish (14). These languages also disallow the use of singular count nouns without determiners, a fact that seems to support the analysis of Fanselow and Ćavar (2002). However, we find number mismatches in discontinuous noun phrases also in languages that lack a determiner system such as Gujarati (cf. (15)).

---

[1] The data cited here have been collected in the context of the DFG-funded research project on discontinuous noun phrases, cf. Fanselow and Féry (accepted) for acknowledgements.

[2] Note that there is also a change in the morphology of the right part in the Romanian example that is reminiscent of the facts concerning German *ein* and *kein* discussed in the preceding section.

(12) Boeken heb ik nog geen één geschreven, maar artikelen al een heleboel.
books have I still no a written but articles already a lot
'I have still not written any book, but already a lot of articles.'

(13) a. Am cumpărat un disc.
I-have bought a CD
b. Am cumpărat unul.
I-have bought one
c. Discuri am cumpărat unul.
CDs have.I bought one
d. *Am cumpărat unul disc(uri).
have.I bought one CD(s)

(14) libros he leido solamente uno.
books have-I written only one

(15) ChopaDi-(o) meN vaanchi chhe matra ek.
books-(PL)-FEM I-ERG read-PST be-PRS only one
'Books, I have read only one.'

Data such as (15) reduce the initial appeal of the proposal of Fanselow and Ćavar, because it shows that the need for morphological repair cannot be the *only* trigger for number mismatch constructions. In addition, their proposal also overlooks a number of facts about German that render the repair analysis incorrect.

First, the adjustment of form with respect to the strong/weak distinction is mandatory, and (therefore) happens independently of the semantic and pragmatic properties of a discontinuous noun phrase. The number mismatch construction, however, is only possible with the numeral interpretation of *ein* and sometimes with the negative quantifier *kein*. Recall that German *ein* functions both as an indefinite determiner and as a numeral (as evidenced by the two English translations 'a' and 'one' for *ein*). The dialogue in (16) is fine, in which the context question forces the numeral interpretation of *ein* in (B).

(16) A: Wie viele Bücher hat er geschrieben?
'How many books has he written?'
B: Bücher hat er nur eins geschrieben.
books has he only one written
'He has only written one book'
B': Bücher hat er kein einziges geschrieben.
books has he no single written
'He has not written a single book.'

The situation is different in (17), where the context question favors the indefinite determiner reading of *ein*. Answer B is ungrammatical in this context, which suggests that number mismatch is forbidden for indefinite determiners. (17)B', B"show that the fronting of the object is not to be blamed for the inacceptability of (17)B: object fronting and noun phrase discontinuity do not make the construction unacceptable, only number mismatch does[3].

(17) A: Ist er auch ein Autor?
is he also an author
B: *Ja, Bücher hat er eins geschrieben.
yes, books has he a written
B': Ja, Bücher hat er eine ganze Menge geschrieben.
yes, books has he a whole lot written
B": Ja, Bücher hat er geschrieben.
yes, books has he written

The number mismatch construction differs from determiner doubling as in (11)b in this respect. (18)a is fine when *ein* is destressed and *langweiliges* ('boring') is accented, i.e., when *ein* is not a numeral. (18)b is ungrammatical in such contexts (but it would be fine if both *ein* and *langweiliges* were stressed, allowing *ein* to be read as 'one').[4]

(18) a. Ein Buch hat er ein langweiliges geschrieben.
a book has he a boring written
'He wrote a boring book.'
b. *Bücher hat er ein langweiliges geschrieben.
books has he a boring written

This suggests that determiner doubling is indeed a kind of repair construction that provides a singular count noun in the left periphery with an (expletive) article, but the shift to plural morphology in (18)b does not fulfill such a function.

Second, the pragmatic functions of number mismatch constructions seem to be restricted. A number mismatch construction is fine when the plural noun phrase can be construed as a topic. It is difficult to use it in a constellation in which the plural noun phrase is a corrective focus, as (19) shows. The left part of a discontinuous noun phrase can be a corrective focus (19)a/B), but not if it does not agree in number with the right part (19)b/B.

(19) a. A: Er hat drei Bücher gekauft.
he has three books bought
B: Nein! Zeitungen hat er drei gekauft.
no! newspapers has he three bought
b. A: Er hat ein Buch gekauft.
he has a book bought
B: Nein! *Zeitungen hat er eine gekauft.
no! newspapers has he one bought

3 (17)B is acceptable when *eins* is stressed and is therefore interpreted as a numeral.

4 The addition of *nur* 'only' does not improve (18)b. However, it seems as if the article interpretation of *ein* is somewhat more acceptable when *ein* is combined with a PP rather than an adjective, as in ?*Geschenke hab ich leider nur eins für Deine Tante dabei* ('presents have I unfortunately only one for your aunt with me', *Unfortunately, I only have a present for your aunt*). I cannot offer an explanation for this difference.

One might want to make the morphological differences between the first and the second sentences in the dialogue responsible for the drop in acceptability in (19)b, but this idea cannot be on the right track, because differences involving the strong-weak inflection do not matter, as shown in (20).

(20) A: Er hat kein Wasser.
he has no.weak water
B: Nein! Bier hat er keines.
no! beer has he no.strong

Similar facts hold in verum focus and wide focus constructions, cf. also below. Notice furthermore that singular count nouns can appear as left parts of discontinuous noun phrases to quite some extent, as was already observed by Kniffka (1996) and van Hoof (2006), perhaps with some dialectal variation. A quick internet search[5] yielded 16 hits for the search string "Fahrrad hab ich keines", and one can easily find further examples such as (22)[6]. A good context for such sentences is one in which the content of the fronted noun is given as in (23), but the other pragmatic functions compatible with discontinuous noun phrase are also fine.

(21) Fahrrad hab ich keines.
bike.sg have I no
'I have no bike.'

(22) Hausmeister hab ich keinen gesehen.
caretaker.sg have I no seen

(23) Haben Sie eine Festplatte eingebaut?
have you a hard disk.sg built in?
'Have you built in a hard disk?'
Nein, Festplatte habe ich keine eingebaut.
no, hard disk have I no built in
'No, I haven't built in a hard disk.'

These observations undermine the proposal of Fanselow and Ćavar: there is, apparently, no need to repair noun phrases in the left periphery that lack an article but are projected from singular count nouns.

---

5 Google search on August 9, 2012.

6 The question arises why such constructions were often rated as ungrammatical in the literature. Part of the answer may be found in Fanselow and Frisch (2006). In a rating experiment, discontinuous noun phrases with singular count nouns as their left part were more acceptable when the noun was morphologically ambiguous between a singular and a plural reading as in (i) *Piloten liebt sie keinen* ('pilot(sg/pl) loves she no.sg', *she loves no pilot*), as compared to (ii) *Kapitän liebt sie keinen* ('captain.sg loves she no'). Modifying their analysis, one might claim that the left part of a discontinuous noun phrases is always temporarily processed as a complete full noun phrase in left-to-right parsing. While the processing of (i) runs smoothly under this view, the reaction to the initial string of (ii) is a perception of ungrammaticality (because complete singular count noun phrases may not lack an article). Such a negative initial assessment contributes to a lowered overall acceptability according to assumptions made by Fanselow and Frisch (2006) and others.

Combinations of nouns and numerals in discontinuous noun phrases behave in a particular way in other languages, too. Consider Russian and Ukrainian in this respect (cf. Féry, Paslawska and Fanselow 2007, Fanselow and Féry, accepted). In both languages, low numerals such as three require a form of the noun different from the one that appears in constructions with higher numerals, such as five, or quantifiers. The low numeral *tri* constructs with a singular noun in (24)b rather than with the plural in Russian, and the low numeral *try* combines with an accusative (rather than a genitive) noun in Ukrainian (25)a.

(24) a. pjat' knig [Russian]
five book.gen.pl
b. tri knigi
three book.gen.sg
c. knig on kupil tol'ko tri.
book.gen.pl he bought only three
'He bought only three books.'

(25) a. Marija maje try krisla. [Ukrainian]
Mary has-got three chairs.acc
'Mary has three chairs.'
b. Marija maje bahato krisel.
Mary has-got many chairs.gen.pl
'Mary has many chairs.'
c. Krisel Marija maje try.
d. Krisla Marija maje try.

In a discontinuous construction the special rules for low numerals can be ignored, however, as (24)c and (25)c show—the noun may take the form it would have when constructed with a high numeral or quantifier.

There is evidence that the singular marking of the noun in examples such as (26)a can be analyzed as an exceptional marking of a low numeral, too. Note that the slight change of construction in (26)b leads to a plural marking of the noun—it is therefore not the semantics that triggers singular marking in (26)a. I propose that the singular marking in (26)a is a lexical exception of the simple numeral *ein* that can be ignored in discontinuous constructions in German just as in the Slavic languages.

(26) a. Im Durchschnitt isst jedes Kind jeden Tag eine Birne.
in the average eats each child each day one.acc pear.sg
'On average, each child eats one pear a day.'
b. Im Durchschnitt isst jedes Kind jeden Tag eins komma null Birnen.
in the average eats each child each day one.acc point zero pear.pl
'On average, each child eats one point zero pears a day.'

4. Three levels of syntactic integration

As we have remarked above, sentences such as (1), (3), and (5) have been used as arguments for the view that both parts of a discontinuous noun phrase must fulfil the formal constraints of complete, independent noun phrases. This, in turn, figured as an argument in favor of a theory that generates the two parts of discontinuous noun phrases independently of each other (cf. Haider 1985, Fanselow 1988, Ott 2011, among others).

The status of (21) and (22) constitutes a problem for such a view. Singular count nouns cannot be used as independent noun phrases. One might object to this by citing examples such as (27) that could show that the need for an article only holds for referential but not for predicative singular noun phrases in German. However, constructions such as (27) are quite restricted; as a rule, the article must be present even in predicative constructions (cf. (28)a vs. (28)c), and the contrast between (28)b and (28)a is hard to explain if one assumes that the parts of a discontinuous noun phrase must always be able to figure as a single, complete noun phrase, too.

(27) Ich bin Lehrer.
I am teacher

(28) a. *Das ist Hub.
this is hub
b. Hub ist das keiner.
hub is this no
'This is no hub.'
c. Das ist ein Hub.
this is a hub

One way of explaining (28)b thus lies in assuming that discontinuous noun phrases can indeed arise from the extraction of a nominal projection out of a complete noun phrase. The morphological facts in (1), (3), and (5) then simply show that the strong-weak distinction is computed after movement.

Notice that the value of the strong-weak dimension is adjusted in discontinuous noun phrases with singular count nouns, too. If (28) and the facts discussed below argue for a movement analysis of (28)b, the data in (29) shows that the morphological shape must be determined after movement.

(29) a. Sie traut keiner polnischen Zeitung.
she trusts no.dat.strong Polish.dat.weak newspaper
'She trusts no Polish newspaper.'
b. *Sie traut keiner polnischer Zeitung.
she trusts no.dat.strong Polish.dat.strong newspaper
c. *Polnischen Zeitung traut sie keiner.
d. Polnischer Zeitung traut sie keiner.

One further argument for the conclusion concerning the movement nature of at least some discontinuous noun phrases comes from cases that show so-called partial fronting effects.

Puig-Waldmüller (2006) observed that discontinuous noun phrases can also be formed in wide focus contexts; cf. also Fanselow and Lenertovà (2011). For example, the dialogue in (30) illustrates a discontinuous noun phrase appearing in a VP-focus context. (30) is not an utterance about books or an utterance with books in focus (as one would expect if *Bücher* is generated independently of *ein paar gekauft*). So, only part of the focus appears at the left edge of the clause.

The constraints on this subcase of discontinuous noun phrases seem identical to the overall constraints on subpart of focus fronting (cf. Fanselow and Lenertovà 2011). The construction, therefore, should have the same analysis as standard subpart of focus fronting, *viz.* attraction of some projection by an unspecific edge feature (in the sense in minimalist syntax) of a Comp node.

(30) What have you done downtown?
Bücher hab ich ein paar gekauft
books have I a few bought
'I have bought a few books.'

The construction in (30) may even give rise to cases in which an idiomatic noun phrase is split up, as in (31).

(31) Schöne Augen hat sie mir noch keine gemacht.
beautiful eyes has she me yet no made
'She has not yet made eyes at me.'

(31) involves the idiom *schöne Augen machen* ('beautiful eyes make', *to make eyes at someone*). The idiomatic reading is not lost when only part of the idiom is fronted, in particular, when a discontinuous noun phrase is created in the negated version of the idiom.

Because of the options that follow from the unspecific nature of attraction to Spec,Comp in German, parts of idioms can be fronted quite easily in German. For a movement derivation of discontinuous noun phrases, (31) poses no particular problem. Note again that the adjective shifts from the weak (32) to the strong form (31) in the discontinuous constructions.

(32) Sie hat mir noch keine schönen Augen gemacht
she has me yet no beautiful.weak eyes made

Since parts of idioms are meaningless, it is difficult to see how the idiomatic interpretation of (31) could be computed if discontinuous noun phrase formation always involved the generation of two independent noun phrases[7].

Wide focus interpretations for discontinuous noun phrases as in (30) or (31) are impossible when there is a number mismatch in the construction. Thus, while (33)a–b can answer a question such as *Why are the kids angry at their grandmother?*, (33)c does not sound acceptable in this context (while it would be fine as an answer to *How many gifts did she*

[7] At least, Fanselow's (1988) idea that the noun phrase at the left edge binds an empty pronominal within the right noun phrase (as introduced in Olsen 1991b) does not capture (31) because meaningless elements cannot bind other elements. It is not clear whether Ott's (2011) approach can be modified in such a way that it could also deal with split idioms.

bring?). If the principled availability of a wide focus interpretation is a diagnostics for movement as effected by an unspecific edge feature, we have to conclude that (33)c is not generated in this way.

(33) a. Geschenk hat sie keins mitgebracht.
gift has she no.sg brought
'She brought no gift.'
b. Geschenke hat sie keine mitgebracht.
gifts has she no.pl brought
c. Geschenke hat sie für jeden nur eins mitgebracht.
gifts has she for everyone only one brought
'For everyone, she only brought one gift.'

We conclude that discontinuous noun phrases with number mismatches are not generated by moving a constituent out of a larger noun phrase to the left edge—rather, we assume that this construction involves two independently generated noun phrases, with one being the topic of the clause they appear in. Cf. Fanselow (1988) and Ott (2011), among others, for specific proposals of this kind. This means that run-off-the mill discontinuous noun phrases such as (34) have in fact two analyses—extraction out of a noun phrases and generation of two independent noun phrases.

(34) Bücher liest er viele.
books reads he many
'He reads many books.'

Constructions with number mismatch show the syntactic connectivity effects discussed by Riemsdijk (1989) and Ott (2011) as well. Thus, anaphoric binding can be reconstructed, as shown in (35)–(37): the anaphor embedded in the noun phase at the left edge sitting in Spec,CP can easily be bound by the subject sitting in TP. In this respect, the number mismatch construction resembles left dislocation as in (38)–another construction that, arguably, involves two noun phrases generated independently of each other.

(35) Bücher übereinander$_i$ haben sie$_i$ nur eins geschrieben.
books about each other have they only one written
'They only wrote one book about each other.'

(36) Geschenke füreinander$_i$ haben sie$_i$ nur eines gefunden.
gifts for each other have they only one found
'They found one gift for each other.'

(37) Geschenke für sich selbst$_i$ hat sie$_i$ nur eines gefunden.
gifts for herself has she only one found

(38) Bücher übereinander$_i$, die haben sie nicht geschrieben.
books about each other these have they not written

Such data is particularly interesting because the reconstruction of binding relations is not possible in all constructions that superficially resemble discontinuous noun phrases. In particular, reconstruction seems not possible in free topic constructions. Consider the following data in this respect:

When a noun phrase is embedded in a PP, it can be serialized discontinuously provided that the preposition is doubled as in (39)a; cf. Fanselow and Ćavar (2002) and Ott (2011) for different analyses. The noun and the quantifier agree in Case in this construction, just as in normal discontinuous noun phrases. However, many speakers also tolerate structures such as (39)b, in which the noun at the left edge bears nominative Case and is not preceded by a doubled preposition.

(39) a. In Schlössern hab ich noch in keinen gewohnt.
in castles.dat have I yet in no.dat lived
'I have not yet lived in any castles.'
b. Schlösser hab ich noch in keinen gewohnt.
castles.nom have I yet in no.dat lived

Arguably, *Schlösser* is an independent topic in (39)b, probably base-generated in Spec,CP. The degree of syntactic integration is low (there is no Case agreement), which leads to the expectation that there should also not be any connectivity effects for binding. This prediction is borne out, as the contrast in (40) shows.

(40) a. In Häusern von sich selbst hat er noch in keinen gewohnt.
in houses.dat of himself has he yet in no.dat lived
He has not yet lived in any of his own houses.
b. *Häuser von sich selbst hat er noch in keinen gewohnt.
houses.nom of himself has he yet in no.dat lived

5. A left/right asymmetry

I want to conclude this paper with a brief discussion of an interesting parallel between the formation of discontinuous noun phrases and deletion operations. It has been observed by Nolda (2007), among others, that an adjustment of the strong-weak feature also takes place in forward deletion contexts such as (41).

(41) Otto hat drei Bier getrunken und Fritz eins/*ein.
Otto has three beer drunk and Fritz one.strong one.weak

While this may suggest that the strong-weak distinction is always fixed at the last possible moment in the derivation of a sentence, a consideration of backward deletion shows this is not true; cf. (42), also taken from Nolda (2007). Backward deletion follows the complete determination of morphological form, or is invisible to the process determining the strong-weak feature.

(42) Otto hat ein ___ und Fritz hat drei Bier getrunken.
Otto has one and Fritz has three beer drunk

At a certain level of abstraction, (41) resembles German discontinuous noun phrases such as (43) more than (42): the noun is to the left of the quantifier/determiner in (41) and (43).

(43) Bier hat er eines getrunken.
beer has he one drunk

In backward deletion, there is no re-adjustment of morphological form, and this may coincide with the absence of 'repair' in discontinuous noun phrases in which the noun appears on the left rather than the right side. Such structures are more or less inexistent in German, but consider the following Ukrainian data instead. We have already discussed the pattern in (44)a–d, which illustrate optional adjustment of Case in discontinuous noun phrases with a left nominal part; cf. (44)c. But such an adjustment seems impossible when the numeral appears at the left edge in the discontinuous construction as in (44)e.

(44) a. Marija maje try krisla. [Ukrainian]
Mary has-got three chairs.acc
'Mary has three chairs.'
b. Marija maje bahato krisel.
Mary has-got many chairs.gen.pl
'Mary has many chairs.'
c. Krisel Marija maje try.
d. Krisla Marija maje try.
e. Try maje Marija krisla/*krisel.

(42) and (44)e share the property that the noun appears in the right part of the construction. Such failures of adjustment can be observed in more languages (Bulgarian, Russian, Nogai) and have been cited as evidence for a principled distinction between two types of discontinuous noun phrases, e.g., in Fanselow and Féry (2006). If correct, the parallelism with forward vs. backward deletion would also suggest that deletion operations should figure prominently in the derivation of discontinuous noun phrases, too.

However, we do not observe a failure of adjustments in structures such as (44)e in all languages (Estonian is a case in point). Furthermore, the cases of adjustment failures that I know of all involve the expression of number in one or the other way. In the present paper, I have tried to explain such number related effects away by assuming that they involve a partially integrated syntactic topic. Perhaps, it is natural to expect that special forms related to a partially integrated topic do not occur when the noun does not occupy a topic position, as in (44)e, a point already made by Féry et al. (2007). This would undermine the argument for a syntactically different treatment of (44)c–d and (44)e, and would also render the parallelism with deletion constellations spurious.

Bibliography

Fanselow, G. (1988): Aufspaltung von NPn und das Problem der 'freien' Wortstellung. *Linguistische Berichte* 114: 91–113.

Fanselow, G. and D. Ćavar. (2002): Distributed deletion. In: A. Alexiadou (ed.), *Theoretical approaches to universals*. Amsterdam: John Benjamins, 65–107.

Fanselow, G. and C. Féry (2006): *Prosodic and morphosyntactic aspects of discontinuous noun phrases from a comparative perspective.* Manuscript, University of Potsdam.

Fanselow, G. and C. Féry (eds.) (in preparation): *Discontinuous noun phrases*. Cambridge, Cambridge University Press.

Fanselow, G. and S. Frisch (2006): Effects of Processing Difficulty on Judgments of Acceptability. In: G. Fanselow, C. Féry, M. Schlesewsky and R. Vogel (eds.), *Gradience in Grammar*. Oxford: Oxford University Press, 291–316.

Fanselow, G. and D. Lenertovà (2011): Left peripheral focus. *Natural Language and Linguistic Theory* 29: 169–209.

Féry, C., A. Paslawska and G. Fanselow (2007): Nominal split constructions in Ukrainian. *Journal of Slavic Linguistics* 15: 3–48.

Giurgea, I. (2006): Split DP topicalization and the role of interfaces. *Online Proceedings of IATL 22*: http://english.huji.ac.il/IATL/22/.

Haider, H. (1985): Von 'sein' oder 'nicht sein': Zur Grammatik des Pronomens 'sich'. In: W. Abraham (ed.), *Erklärende Syntax des Deutschen*. Tübingen: Narr, 223–254.

van Hoof, H. (2006): Split topicalization. In: M. Everaert and H. v. Riemsdijk (eds.), *The Blackwell companion to syntax*. Oxford: Blackwell, 408–462.

Kniffka, G. (1996): *NP-Aufspaltung im Deutschen*. Hurth: Gabel.

Kuhn, J. (1999): The syntax and semantics of split NPs in LFG. In: F. Corblin, C. Dobrovie-Sorin and J.-M. Mandarin (eds.), *Selected papers from the Colloque de Syntaxe et Sémantique à Paris (CSSP 1997)*. The Hague: Thesus, 145–166.

Nolda, A. (2007): *Die Thema-Integration. Syntax und Semantik der 'gespaltenen Topikalisierung' im Deutschen*. Tübingen: Stauffenburg.

Olsen, S. (1990): AGR(eement) in the German Noun Phrase. In: C. Bhatt, E. Löbel and C. Schmidt (eds.), *Syntactic Phrase Structure Phenomena in Noun Phrases and Sentences*. Amsterdam: Benjamins, 37–47.

Olsen, S. (1991a): AGR(eement) und Flexion in der deutschen Nominalphrase. In: G. Fanselow and S.W. Felix (eds), *Strukturen und Merkmale syntaktischer Kategorien*. Tübingen: Narr, 51–69.

Olsen, S. (1991b): Die deutsche Nominalphrase als Determinansphrase. In: S. Olsen and G. Fanselow (eds.), *DET, COMP und INFL: Zur Syntax funktionaler Kategorien und grammatischer Funktionen*. Tübingen: Niemeyer, 35–56.

Ott, D. (2011): *Local Instability*. Unpublished Diss., Harvard University, Cambridge, MA.

Puig Waldmüller, E. (2006): *Wörteri stehen da einigei. On nominal split topicalization in non-standard Viennese German*. MA thesis, Universität Pompeu, Fabra.

van Riemsdijk, H. (1989): Movement and regeneration. In: P. Benincà (ed.), *Dialect variation and the theory of grammar*. Dordrecht: Foris, 105–136.

On indefinite NPs participating in the German predicate complex

Werner Frey

1. Resultatives

It is known for quite some time that compared to other arguments in German, resultative arguments, among which directional argumental PPs belong (Wechsler and Noh 2001), show a special behavior (e.g., Steinitz 1989, Frey 1993). For example, they do not allow any other element to stand between them and the predicate:

(1) a. weil Hans die Tische (alle) sauber (*alle) gewischt hat
since Hans the tables all clean all wiped has
b. Otto hat den Tisch (vorher) sauber (*vorher) gewischt.
Otto has the table before clean before wiped
c. weil Paul die Sachen (zum Glück) unter das Klavier (*zum Glück) gelegt hat
since Paul the things fortunately under the piano put has
d. *Paul hat unter das Klavier die Sachen gelegt.

It would be too hasty to try to account for the ungrammaticality of (1) by the stipulation that resultatives cannot scramble. To see this consider first the following example:

(2) Maria schaut sich gerade was ganz genau an.
Maria looks at REFL currently something to a hair's breadth PRT

In (2), a w-indefinite precedes a manner adverbial. This is noteworthy, since w-indefinites do not scramble, as can be seen in (3)b, d, f:

(3) a. dass wer was lesen will
that someone something (to) read wants
b. *dass was wer lesen will
c. dass wen was empörte
that someone-Acc something-Nom shocked
d. *dass was wen empörte
e. dass sie in einem Park was lesen will
that she in a park something (to) read wants
f. *dass sie was in einem Park lesen will

It can be shown (cf., e.g., Lenerz 1977, Frey 2003) that the base positions of the arguments of a transitive verb like *lesen* is Nom < Acc. For a psych verb like *empören*, it is Acc < Nom. Furthermore, it is established that in a clause with a transitive verb the base position of a locative adverbial is between the arguments: Nom < Adv_{loc} < Acc. Thus, the data in (3)b, d, f demonstrate that a w-indefinite cannot be reordered in the middle field. Therefore, in the literature (e.g., Haider 2010 among many others) it is assumed that w-indefinites cannot be scrambled.

In view of the fact that w-indefinites cannot scramble, (2) demonstrates that the base position of a manner adverbial is lower than the base position of a direct object. In fact it, can be shown that the base position of a manner adverbial is lower than the base positions of all the arguments of transitive, ditransitive and intransitive verbs, and lower than the base position of an adverbial of any other type (cf., e.g., Frey 2003). Now, given that manner adverbials have such a low base position and that manner adverbials like *langsam* or *kräftig* cannot be scrambled, the examples in (4) are of interest. These data illustrate that the base position of resultatives is even lower than the base position of manner adverbials.

(4) a. Paul hat (*langsam) alles (langsam) unter das Klavier (*langsam) gelegt.
Paul has slowly everything slowly under the piano slowly put
b. Otto hat (*kräftig) die Tische (kräftig) sauber (*kräftig) gewischt.
Otto has forcefully the tables forcefully clean forcefully wiped

Note that the behavior of the resultative PP in (4)a is due to its status as a resultative, other PPs behave differently:

(5) a. Maria wird jeden auf dieses Problem nachdrücklich hinweisen.
Maria will to everyone this problem emphatically point out
b. Otto hat über die Euro-Krise sehr leidenschaftslos gesprochen.
Otto has about the Euro crisis very dispassionately talked

There is evidence that resultatives are not just standard sentence constituents with a very low base position in the middle field but that they are part of the Right Sentential Bracket (*rechte Satzklammer*, cf. Helbig and Buscha 1986, Abraham 1986, Frey and Tappe 1992, as well as Neeleman 1994 for Dutch), i.e., there is evidence that they constitute a complex predicate with the main verb of the clause. The following data are instructive:

(6) a. Gelesen hat Max heute was ganz genau.
read has Max today something very accurately
b. Gesprochen hat Max erst gestern über dieses Thema.
talked has Max only yesterday about this subject
c. Gekocht hat Maria bei diesem Wetter die Suppe nackt.
cooked has Maria in this weather the soup naked
d. *Gewischt hat Paul die Tische sauber.
e. Sauber gewischt hat Paul die Tische.
f. *Gelegt hat Paul die Sachen unter das Klavier.
g. Unter das Klavier gelegt hat Paul die Sachen.

In German, the main verb may positioned in the prefield without other sentence constituents, (6)a, b, c. For many syntacticians, an example like (6)a is disturbing, since it is not easy to maintain that in this case a VP which is partially emptied by scrambling of the object and the adverbial is moved. In (6)a, the w-indefinite object, which cannot be scrambled, remains in the middle field. Thus, (6)a suggests that *gelesen* by itself constitutes a maximal projection, which can be moved to the prefield. Frey and Tappe (1992) take such preposing data as evidence that the verbal complex of, say, (6)a has the structure in (7):

(7) $[_{V} [_{VP}$ gelesen] hat]

The θ-grid of the complex predicate *gewischt hat* is derived by percolation of the θ-role of *gewischt* (see also Neeleman 1994, Haider 2010). Corresponding structures are to be assigned to the verbal complexes in (6)b, c.

However, at this moment another point is more relevant for our considerations. The examples demonstrate that with the preposing of the predicate to the prefield, a DP-object and a manner adverbial, (6)a, a prepositional object, (6)b, and a depictive adverbial, (6)c, respectively, may stay behind. In contrast, (6)d, f show that a resultative may not be left behind; in order to get a grammatical sentence the resultative has to accompany the predicate to the prefield, (6)e, g.

For understanding the data in (6), a semantic peculiarity of resultatives is likely to be relevant. Resultatives express a predication on an argument, which becomes true as a result of the event denoted by the main verb. The same does not hold for the object and the manner adverbial in (6)a, for the prepositional object in (6)b, and for the depictive in (6)c. Thus, it is reasonable to assume that the main verb and the resultative together express a predication on an argument. In other words, the resultative and the verb together take an argument, i.e., they form a complex predicate (Helbig and Buscha 1986, Abraham 1986, Frey and Tappe 1992, Neeleman 1994).

Under this assumption, resultatives are not sentence constituents base generated in the middle field, but are base generated in the Right Sentential Bracket as part of the predicate complex. Structures like the following would have to be assigned:

(8) a. $[_{V} [_{VP} [_{AP}$ sauber] gewischt] hat]
b. $[_{V} [_{VP} [_{PP}$ unter das Klavier] gelegt] hat]

It follows that the reason for the ungrammaticality of (6)d, f is the same as for (9)b, e. In all these cases a non-maximal part of the complex predicate is positioned in the prefield.

(9) a. weil er morgen das Buch gelesen haben wird
since he tomorrow the book read have will
b. *Haben wird er das Buch morgen gelesen.
c. Gelesen haben wird er das Buch morgen.
d. weil er den Artikel zu verstehen versucht hat
since he the article to understand tried has
e. *Versucht hat er den Artikel zu verstehen.
f. Zu verstehen versucht hat er den Artikel.

See, for example, Haider (2010) for evidence that *gelesen haben wird* in (9)a obligatorily forms a complex predicate, and *zu verstehen versucht hat* in (9)d optionally forms a complex predicate. (10) gives the structures of the verbal complexes in (9)a and (9)d.

(10) a. $[_{V} [_{VP} [_{VP}$ gelesen] haben] wird]
b. $[_{V} [_{VP} [_{VP}$ zu verstehen] versucht] hat]

Structures like in (8) or (10) also allow deriving the following examples:

(11) a. Sauber hat Paul die Tische gewischt.
  b. Wohin hat Paul alles gelegt?
  where has Paul everything put
  c. Zu verstehen hat er das Buch versucht.

Thus, the left branch of a complex predicate is a maximal projection, which can be moved to the prefield. Crucially, it cannot be scrambled, though. Alternatively, instead of, say, (7), (8)b and (10)b, the following structures are assumed in the literature (Neeleman 1994, Truckenbrodt 2012).

(12) a. [$_V$ [$_V$ gelesen] hat]
  a. [$_V$ [$_V$ [$_{PP}$ unter das Klavier] gelegt] hat]
  b. [$_V$ [$_V$ [$_V$ zu verstehen] versucht] hat]

Given these structures, it seems that the prefields in (6)a, (6)g, and (9)f are filled with Vs, although the prefield is a position for maximal projections. To account for such fillings of the prefield, proponents of those structures have to adopt the proposal of Riemsdijk (1989), who claims that, due to a process of regeneration, these fillings of the prefield do not violate structure preservation.

As for another piece of evidence that resultatives belong to the verbal complex we can observe that they may be included in the so-called *Oberfeldformation* (Bech 1955), (13)a, b:

(13) a. dass Hans die Tische hat sauber wischen können
  that Hans the tables has clean wipe can
  b. dass Paul die Sachen hat unter das Klavier legen können
  that Paul the things has under the piano put can
  c. $^?$dass Hans mit Maria hat über das Thema sprechen können
  that Hans with Maria has about the topic talk can

The special status of resultatives, in particular of directional PPs, also shows up in prosody (cf. Truckenbrodt 2012). In all-new-sentences, a non-pronominal subject and a non-pronominal object both receive phrasal stress as indicated in (14). (Truckenbrodt (2012) marks stress by underlining. The last stress is strengthened to the strongest of the clause, marked by double underlining.)

(14) [What happened while I was gone?]
  Ein <u>Mann</u> hat ein <u>Buch</u> gekauft.
  a man has a book bought

Normally, only given XPs do not receive phrasal stress.

(15) What did she do?
  a. Sie hat ein <u>Buch</u> gekauft.
  b. Sie hat einem <u>Kind</u> ein <u>Buch</u> vorgelesen.
  she has to a child a book read

Now, interestingly, when a direct object is followed by a directional PP, the PP need not carry phrasal stress. In (16), the PP *an einen Freund* does not carry phrasal stress, although it is not contextually given.

(16) [What happened while I was gone?]
Heute hat$_1$ ein Junge eine Geige [$_V$ [$_{VP}$ [$_{PP}$ an einen Freund] geschickt] t$_1$].
today has a boy a violin to a friend sent

Truckenbrodt (2012) proposes to account for the pattern in (16) by assuming that the directional PP conflates with the verb *schicken* and then, in turn, yields a new predicate with *hat*. Because the PP is part of a V-constituent, which is mapped to a prosodic word, it does not receive phrasal stress.

In this section some data were presented which suggest that, despite constituting a maximal projection, resultatives in German build a complex predicate with the main verb of the clause. To be sure, complex predicate formation of the kind envisaged in this section violates traditional assumptions about structure preservations: Phrases do not normally become parts of heads. However, there is independent evidence that in German inside a 'standard' verbal complex a maximal projection appears. (6)a gives a pretty clear indication that the predicate by itself may constitute a maximal projection which can be moved to the prefield (Frey and Tappe 1992). Similarly, as seen in (11), resultatives by themselves may be moved to the prefield; they even can bear wh-morphology, cf. (11)b.

2. Incorporated indefinites

In German, the phenomenon of complex predicate formation seems to be more wide-spread than assumed up to now. To see this, consider (17). These examples show that non-specific indefinites, in contrast to other nominal arguments, may follow a manner adverbial.

(17) a. Otto hat heute sehr heftig einen Kollegen beschimpft.
Otto has today very heavily a colleague-ACC berated
b. Sie hat heute ganz wunderbar Mozart-Sonaten gespielt.
she has today marvelously Mozart-sonatas played
c. $^{??}$Otto hat heute sehr heftig jeden Kollegen beschimpft.
Otto has today very heavily every colleague berated
d. $^{??}$Sie hat heute ganz wunderbar die letzte Mozart-Sonate gespielt.
she has today marvelously the last Mozart-sonata played

As indicated in the preceding section, there is evidence that manner adverbials are base generated adjacent to the verbal complex. Thus, the examples in (9) suggest that (non-specific) indefinites, in contrast to non-indefinites, may be part of a complex predicate.

That indefinites following a manner adverbial belong to the verbal complex is confirmed by the following observation. (18)a, b demonstrate that if the indefinite follows a manner adverbial, it cannot be left behind when the main verb is moved to the prefield. This makes sense if an indefinite following a manner adverbial belongs to the complex predicate. An indefinite may also precede a manner adverbial. In this case, the main verb may be moved to the prefield alone, (18)c, d:

(18) a. *Beschimpft hat Otto heute sehr heftig einen Kollegen.
b. *Gespielt hat sie heute ganz wunderbar Mozart-Sonaten.
c. Beschimpft hat Otto heute einen Kollegen sehr heftig.
d. Gespielt hat sie heute Mozart-Sonaten ganz wunderbar.

Thus, the phenomena exhibited in (17)a, b and (18)a, b constitute evidence that in German indefinites may be part of the predicate. These data are reminiscent of what is nowadays discussed under the name pseudo-incorporation. Pseudo-incorporation has been reported to exist for a number of languages, most prominently, Hindi (e.g., Dayal 2011), Hungarian (Farkas and Swart 2003), Dutch (Booij 2008), and Niuean, an Oceanic language (Massam 2001). It refers to the combination of a nominal phrase and a verb which forms a verbal predicate that, on the one hand, does not have the status of a (complex) word, but, on the other hand, is different from a standard VP in that the (pseudo-)incorporated nominal constituent is subject to certain restrictions which do not old for any regular sentence constituent.

In the literature, it is reported that pseudo-incorporation can only affect NPs but not DPs. The same holds for complex predicate formation with a nominal phrase in German. This was already demonstrated in (17)c,d and is further illustrated in (19).

(19) Max hat heute wunderbar viele/fünf/*alle/*die meisten Lieder/*jedes Lied gesungen.
Max has today marvelously many/five/all/the most songs/every song sung

That quantificational and referential phrases are ruled out in complex predicate formation in German gives further support that we are dealing here with an instance of pseudo incorporation. Note that what are usually called indefinite determiners in German may be preceded by the definite determiner, (20)a, and that the indefinite nominal phrases in question may appear as predicates in the *be*-construction, (20)b.

(20) a. die vielen Lieder/das eine Lied
the many songs/the one song
b. Meine Nachbarn sind fünf Studenten.
my neighbours are five students

In passing, we may observe that there are indefinite NPs which obligatorily build a complex with their predicates (cf. Meinunger 2000); in the middle field they have to be adjacent to the predicate, (21)b, c, and they cannot be left behind by movement of the predicate to the prefield, (21)d.

(21) a. weil er hastig Butter nahm
because he hastily butter took
b. *weil er Butter hastig nahm
c. *weil sie Butter alle nahmen
d. *Genommen hat er Butter.
taken has he butter
e. Butter hat er hastig genommen.

In the last section we have seen that obligatorily incorporated resultatives and participle verb forms may be moved to the prefield. Therefore, it is not surprising that the obligatorily incorporated indefinite in (21)e may be too.

Let us come back to incorporated NPs in general. Unlike incorporated nouns (like the noun in *Rad fahren* ('to cycle')), incorporated NPs allow modification—for example, a restrictive relative clause, (22)a, in contrast to a non-restrictive one, (22)b, is possible. In the literature, it is taken as a kind of defining property of pseudo-incorporation that in contrast to the incorporation of a noun, it allows modification of the nominal constituent by a complex constituent (Massam 2001). Furthermore, incorporated NPs in German are marked for case, e.g., (17)a, and for number, e.g., (17)a, b. That incorporated NPs in German are case marked and do not show number neutrality is not that surprising given that in German attributive adjectives are marked for case and number and NPs in the predicative *be*-construction also are marked for number, cf., e.g., (20)b.

(22) a. Max hat (laut) ein Lied, das er seit langem kennt, gesungen.
Max has loudly a song which he for a long time knows sung
b. Max hat (*laut) ein Lied, das ja jeder nur zu gut kennt, gesungen.
Max has loudly a song which PRT everyone only too well knows sung

Note, finally, that indefinites may be included in the Oberfeldformation:

(23) als Max heute piano hat ein Lied/$^{?}$dieses Lied singen sollen
when Max today piano has a song/that song sing should
'when Max today was obliged to sing a/that song piano'

In sum, the morpho-syntactic hallmarks of pseudo-incorporation in German are the absence of a determiner in the nominal phrase and the restriction that in the middle field such a phrase has to occur in a special position which is adjacent to the verb.

In addition, pseudo-incorporated NPs seem to behave phonologically in a special way. In section 1, it was hinted at the fact that resultatives, unlike standard sentence constituents, do not need to receive phrasal accent, albeit they are not given, cf. (16). (24)a demonstrates that the indefinites preceding a manner adverbial get phrasal accent. The accent on *ein italienisches Lied* is not strengthened to the strongest of the clause since an adverbial follows. Instead the main predicate receives the main accent of the clause. In (24)b, *ein italienisches Lied* follows the manner adverbial, i.e., it is pseudo-incorporated. This indefinite may remain without phrasal accent.

(24) What happened today?
a. Hans hat einer Kollegin ein italienisches Lied laut vorgesungen.
Hans has a colleague an Italian song loudly sung
b. Hans hat einer Kollegin laut ein italienisches Lied vorgesungen.

To conclude this section let us draw an obvious consequence for subcategorization. If the thesis of this section is on the right track it follows that German verbs which take a nominal argument do not necessarily subcategorize for a DP but just for a nominal argument. This requirement can be fulfilled by a NP. Such an NP has to incorporate into the predicate which triggers the (dynamic) existential closure of the variable (van Geenhoven 1998);

otherwise a representation would result with an unbound variable. It follows, furthermore, that an indefinite which is not integrated but is a regular sentence constituent has to be a DP. Either we assume that such an indefinite DP has an empty D-head which triggers the dynamic existential binding of the 'referential' argument of the noun (or the introduction of a discourse referent), or we treat the so-called indefinite articles as being ambiguous between having the syntactic status of an adjective-like element or of an existential D-element.

3. Some related phenomena

In this section, some phenomena will be discussed which find an explanation under the assumption that in German there exists the phenomenon of NP-incorporation. Let us start with the different status of grammaticality of the sentences in (25).

(25) a. Er hat ein Lied—eines von Schubert—sehr laut gesungen.
he has a song one by Schubert very loudly sung
b. *Er hat sehr laut ein Lied—eines von Schubert—gesungen.

In a German clause, following each sentence constituent there is a so called parenthetical niche, i.e., a position which can host a parenthetical. Interestingly, such a niche is not available following the indefinite in (25)b. The idea immediately comes to mind that the reason is that the indefinite in (25)b is part of the verbal complex. This is confirmed by the fact that following a resultative or a verbal form, we also do not find a parenthetical niche:

(26) a. *Max hat alles unter den Flügel—den Steinway—gelegt.
Max has everything below the piano the Steinway put
b. weil Max (, übrigens freiwillig,) das Buch (, übrigens freiwillig,) gelesen(*, übrigens freiwillig,) hat
since Max by the way voluntarily the book read has

Thus, inside the verbal complex there are no parenthetical niches. Given this observation, the ungrammaticality of (25)b constitutes further evidence for our assumption that in German NPs following a manner adverbial are necessarily incorporated into the verbal complex.

The next phenomenon I would like to consider shortly concerns the possibility of so called DP-PP-split; see (27)a, and, among others, de Kuthy (2002) for discussion. With the DP-PP-split construction it seems that the PP-complement of a DP is moved to the left. However, this evaluation of the phenomenon is likely to be wrong. First, note that the construction is not possible with any old DP, (27)b.

(27) a. Von Peter hat Maria einen Freund/Freunde beschimpft.
of Peter has Maria a friend/friends berated
'Maria has berated a friend/friends of Peter.'
b. *Von Peter hat Maria fast jeden Freund/die meisten Freunde beschimpft.
of Peter has Maria nearly every friend/most friends berated

Furthermore, leftward movement of an adjunct out of a nominal constituent is not possible:

(28) *Von Peter hat Maria einen Hund geschlagen.
of Peter has Maria a dog beaten

If (27)a would involve movement of a PP out of a DP, (27)b and (28) should be grammatical, too. Therefore, another explanation for (27)a should be sought. Under the perspective of the present article it is telling that the construction is possible if the object follows a manner adverbial, (29)a, but it is not possible if the object occurs to the left of a manner adverbial, (29)b.

(29) a. Von Peter hat Maria lauthals einen Freund/Freunde beschimpft.
of Peter has Maria full-throatedly a friend/friends berated
b. *Von Peter hat Maria einen Freund lauthals beschimpft.
c. *Von Peter hat wer einem Freund schwere Vorwürfe gemacht.
of Peter has someone to a friend heavy reproaches addressed
d. *Von Peter ist heute ein Freund mit Maria ausgegangen.
of Peter is today a friend with Maria went out

(29)c, d indicate that the ungrammaticality of (29)b is not due to a freezing effect induced by scrambling, as some authors would assume (e.g., Müller 1998). In (29)c the presumed base position of the PP would be inside a non-scrambled indirect object, in (29)d it would be inside a non-scrambled ergative subject.

According to the thesis of the present paper, the data in (27) – (29) suggest that the presumed DP-PP-split is only possible if the nominal argument which is the licensing source for the PP is pseudo-incorporated. Its valence is inherited by the newly constructed verbal complex. Under this perspective, the PP in (27)a is not an argument of the object, but it is an argument of the complex predicate *einen Freund/Freunde beschimpfen*. Like in the other examples of incorporation of an indefinite NP, the indefinite's external 'referential' variable is identified with the pertinent argument variable introduced by the main predicate. This variable is bound by dynamic existential closure triggered by the predicate. The indefinite's internal argument variable is inherited by the complex predicate (cf., e.g., Haider 2010 on valence inheritance in clause union constructions). This means that *von Peter* in (27)a is a sentence constituent. We expect that it can also appear in the middle field:

(30) Maria hat von Peter heute einen Freund beschimpft.

Note that the indefinite may be positioned in the prefield, (31)a. However, it may not appear inside the middle field, (31)b.

(31) a. Einen Freund hat Maria heute von Peter beschimpft.
b. *Maria hat einen Freund heute von Peter beschimpft.

Again, these data are expected. As observed in section 1, incorporated XPs may be moved to the prefield. However, these XPs may not appear in the middle field. The indefinite may be included in the Oberfeldformation:

(32) a. weil Maria heute von Peter hat einen Freund beschimpfen müssen
since Maria today had to berate a friend of Peter
b. *weil Maria heute einen Freund hat von Peter beschimpfen müssen

(32) confirms that in the split-construction the indefinite belongs to the verbal complex whereas the PP is a regular sentence constituent.
Note, finally, that in the split-construction the main verb cannot be moved to the prefield without the indefinite.

(33) a. *Beschimpft hat von Peter Maria heute einen Freund.
b. Einen Freund beschimpft hat von Peter Maria heute.
c. *Von Peter beschimpft hat Maria heute einen Freund.

These data are again expected. In the so-called split-construction the indefinite is part of the verbal complex. Only the constituents on the left branches of the verbal complex can be moved to the prefield, cf. section 1.

Another issue to be shortly discussed is the fact that 'weak definites' (Carlson et al. 2006) occupy the same position as incorporated indefinites. Consider the following examples:

(34) a. Hans hat gestern intensiv die Zeitung gelesen.
Hans has yesterday intensively the newspaper read
b. Hans hat gestern die Zeitung intensiv gelesen.

(34)a has a 'weak' reading; this means, for example, that the sentence allows an interpretation according to which Hans could have read different newspapers although *die Zeitung* is in the singular. In contrast, (34)b does not have a 'weak' reading, thus, it is not appropriate to describe a situation in which Hans has read more than one newspaper. Carlson et al. (2006) observe that in English, weak definites share different properties with bare singulars. It is therefore of interest for us that in German weak definites seem to have the same distribution as pseudo-incorporated indefinites.

The last phenomenon I would like to mention concerns a notorious problem of German syntax. Under very special conditions, the subject of a non-ergative may appear as part of a V-projection in the prefield. It must be a non-specific indefinite, (35)a,b, and if there appears an object in the clause, the object also has to be positioned in the prefield and it has to be non-specific too, (35)c,d. In contrast, the subject of an ergative verb appearing in a V-projection in the prefield is not subject to any of these restrictions, (35)e.

(35) a. Ein Linguist gesprochen hat hier noch nie.
a linguist spoken has here yet not
b. *Dieser berühmte Linguist gesprochen hat hier noch nie.
this famous linguist spoken has here yet not
c. *Ein Linguist t_1 gehalten hat [eine/die Laudatio]$_1$.
a linguist given has an/the encomium
d. Ein Linguist eine/*die Laudatio gehalten hat hier noch nie.
a linguist an/the encomium given has here yet not
e. Eine/die geeignete Taktik eingefallen ist dem Trainer heute Nachmittag.
a/the appropriate tactic occurred has to the coach this afternoon

In light of the data in (35), it is tempting to speculate that the subject of a non-ergative verb may only appear inside a V-projection in the prefield if it forms a complex predicate with the verb, i.e., if it is pseudo-incorporated into the main predicate. Under this assumption,

(35)b is bad because a referential DP cannot be part of a complex predicate. (35)c is bad because the indefinite subject cannot enter complex predicate formation here. Pseudo-incorporation is only possible with a phrase which is adjacent to the predicate. However, in (35)c the trace of the object stands between the transitive subject and the verb. (35)d with the definite object is ungrammatical, since the definite DP cannot become part of the predicate thereby blocking complex predicate formation of the indefinite subject with the verb. The variant with the indefinite object is possible, though. The non-specific indefinite object can be pseudo-incorporated in a first step such that the indefinite subject can be pseudo-incorporated in a second step.

4. Concluding remarks

This contribution has the rather modest objective to simply initiate a discussion whether German also knows the phenomenon of pseudo-incorporation, which has been proposed to exist in different languages. It hinted at some phenomena involving indefinite NPs which suggest that for the description of German the existence of pseudo-incorporation indeed also has to be assumed. The paper did not make any proposal as to which syntactic analysis is assigned to pseudo-incorporated structures, since the syntactic analysis of complex predicate formation with a phrasal category is unclear. Obviously, the phenomenon does not fit standard assumptions about phrase structure. For example, Booij (2008) suggests that pseudo-incorporation is assigned the category V'. However, V' is not expected to occur in a head-position. Frey and Tappe (1992) and Truckenbrodt (2012) assume that in German the verbal complex, i.e., V, may contain on the left branch maximal predicative projections like VPs, PPs, APs, or NPs. However, the theory does not foresee that a head should dominate a maximal projection. What seems to be clear, though, is that the pseudo-incorporated phrase is base-generated in its position inside the complex predicate. There are no empirical or theoretical reasons to believe that movement from an argument position inside the middle field to the position inside the complex predicate could be involved. For cases of incorporation, movement of a head from its base position to the incorporated position is standardly assumed. However, it is doubtful that in languages like German or English the phenomena which may be considered as incorporation structures do involve head-movement. For example, Haider (2010) convincingly argues that no head-movement occurs in clause union structures in German but that the verbal complex is base generated, and Olsen (2000) convincingly shows that, contrary to standard assumptions, in constructions like *They close down the store* or *als Holden eine Folie auflegte* (*when Holden put on a slide*) no head-movement of the prepositions *down* and *auf*, respectively, occurs, but that the complex verbs *to close down* and *auflegen* are base-generated.

The article has not addressed other relevant issues. I will only mention one here. It concerns the question whether in German pseudo-incorporated indefinites are transparent for anaphoric reference or not. In the literature on pseudo-incorporation it once was heatedly discussed whether pseudo-incorporated NPs allow anaphoric reference to them. However, it seems that nowadays opacity for anaphoric reference is not seen any more as a crucial property of pseudo-incorporated NPs but it is envisaged that, at least in some languages, (some forms of) incorporated indefinites may give rise to anaphoric reference. Thus, the answer to the question whether in German indefinites following a manner adverbial make anaphoric reference possible or not would not give additional evidence (or counter-evidence) for the central claim of the present paper. For that reason I refrained to discuss this issue.

Bibliography

Abraham, W. (1986): Word order in the middle field of the German sentence. In: W. Abraham and S. de Meij (eds.), *Topic, focus and configurationality*. Amsterdam: Benjamins, 1–38.

Bech, G. (1955): *Studien über das deutsche Verbum infinitum.* Tübingen: Niemeyer.

Booij, G. (2008): Pseudo-incorporation in Dutch. *Groninger Arbeiten zur Germanistischen Linguistik* (GAGL) 46: 3–26.

Carlson, G. et al. (2006): Weak definite noun phrases. In: C. Davis et al. (eds.), *Proceedings of NELS 36*. Amherst, MA: Graduate Linguistic Student Association.

Dayal, V. (2011): Hindi pseudo-incorporation. *Natural Language and Linguistic Theory* 29 (1): 123–167.

De Kuthy, K. (2002): *Discontinuous NPs in German. A Case Study of the Interaction of Syntax, Semantics and Pragmatics*. Stanford: CSLI Publications.

Farkas, D. and H. de Swart (eds.) (2003): *The semantics of incorporation: From argument structure to discourse transparency*. Stanford: CSLI Publications.

Frey, W. (2003): Syntactic conditions on adjunct classes. In: E. Lang et al. (eds.), *Modifying Adjuncts*. Berlin: de Gruyter, 163–209.

Frey, W. (1993): *Syntaktische Bedingungen für die semantische Interpretation.* Berlin: Akademie Verlag (studia grammatica 35).

Frey, W. and H. T. Tappe (1992): *Zur Interpretation der X-bar-Theorie und zur Syntax des Mittelfeldes - Grundlagen eines GB-Fragments.* Unpublished manuscript, SFB 340, University of Stuttgart.

Haider, H. (2010): *The syntax of German*. Cambridge: Cambridge University Press.

Helbig, G. and Buscha, J. (eds.) (1986[9]): *Deutsche Grammatik. Ein Handbuch für den Ausländerunterricht.* Leipzig: Enzyklopädie.

Lenerz, J. (1977): *Zur Abfolge nominaler Satzglieder im Deutschen.* Tübingen: Narr

Massam, D. (2001): Pseudo noun incorporation. *Natural Language and Linguistic Theory* 19: 153–197.

Meinunger, A. (2000): *Syntactic aspects of topic and comment.* Amsterdam: Benjamins.

Müller, G. (1998): *Incomplete category fronting*. Dordrecht: Kluwer.

Neeleman, A. (1994): *Complex predicates*. PhD dissertation, Utrecht University.

Olsen, S. (2000): Against incorporation. In: J. Dölling and Th. Pechmann (eds.), *Prosodie—Struktur—Interpretation. Festschrift für Anita Steube*. Universität Leipzig: Linguistische Arbeitsberichte Berichte 74: 149–172.

Truckenbrodt, H. (2012): Effects of indefinite pronouns and traces on verb stress in German. In: T. Borowsky et al. (eds.), *Prosody matters: essays in honor of Elisabeth Selkirk*. Sheffield, UK/Bristol, USA: Equinox, 487–513.

Riemsdijk, H. C. van (1989): Movement and regeneration. In: P. Benincà (ed.), *Dialect variation and the theory of grammar; Proceedings of the GLOW workshop in Venice*. Dordrecht: Foris, 105–136.

Steinitz, R. (1989): V^u, I^y und I^z: Überlegungen zum Prädikativ. *Linguistische Studien, Reihe A, 194*. Berlin: Akademie-Verlag, 210–234.

Van Geenhoven, V. (1998): *Semantic incorporation and indefinite descriptions*. Standford: CSLI Publications.

Wechsler, S. and B. Noh (2001): On resultatives and clauses: parallels between Korean and English. In: G. Fanselow (ed.), *Elements of Slavic and Germanic grammars: a comperative view*. Frankfurt/M.: Peter Lang, 235–253.

English particle verbs are complex heads: Evidence from nominalization

Andrew McIntyre

1. Introduction[1]

There is much literature and little consensus on the structure of particle verbs (otherwise known as phrasal verbs, verb-particle constructions) such as *take out*. One approach in the literature is sometimes called the *complex head approach* (e.g., Dehé 2002, Farrell 2005, Haider 1997, Harley and Noyer 1998, Johnson 1991, Neeleman 2002, Olsen 1997, 2000, Stiebels and Wunderlich 1994, Toivonen 2003, Zeller 2002). It claims that the verb and particle can, under certain circumstances, form what might variously be called a compound, a morphological object, a complex word or a single head of the form [$_{V^\circ}$ V P]. (1) and (2) illustrate different variants of this approach, respectively modelled on Farrell's (2005) flat VP approach and Haider's (1997) VP shell approach. In both (1)a and (2)a, the particle has the same external syntax as a normal transitive PP like *into the garage*. In the (b) variants the particle verb is a complex head. In (1)b it is assumed to be inserted as a compound, while in (2)b the particle is initially inserted as a PP but incorporates into V by head movement à la Baker (1988), so that V+P form a complex head for verb movement purposes. A variant of this approach is to assume that the particle and verb in (2)b can reanalyse as morphological structures (Zeller 2002). Complex head approaches easily explain the fact that particles are the only elements in English which can appear between verbs and (non-extraposed) objects. The inability of modified particles to undergo particle shift, cf. (3), is also expected since modified elements are generally ill at ease in compounding/incorporation structures: [[$_{PP}$(*right) over] turn the cart].[2]

[1] It is a pleasure to be able to contribute to this Festschrift for Sue Olsen. Her support for my career has been of great value to me. Like several others who have written on particle verbs and then wisely moved on to more life-affirming subjects, Sue may be wondering why I still let these nasty little creatures wreak havoc in my thoughtscape. Part of the answer is a remark she once made to the effect that particle verbs are probably morphological objects, but that clear arguments for this in English are hard to come by. Whether or not this essay fills this gap, I hope that it will inspire more attempts at understanding particles in their interaction with affixation and compounding, areas to which Sue has made important contributions.

[2] Olsen (2000) objects that head movement wrongly predicts stranding of modifiers and complements: **push in the car* [$_{PP}$ *right* t$_{in}$]; **push in the car* [$_{PP}$ t$_{in}$ *the garage*]. To meet this objection one would have to assume that modified and transitive P-items, but not particles, have additional functional structure which blocks incorporation. This may be right, but its implementation is not obvi-

(1) a. She $[_{\mathrm{VP}}$ $[_{\mathrm{V°}}$ *pushed*] $[_{\mathrm{DP}}$ the car] $[_{\mathrm{PP}}$ *in*]]
b. She $[_{\mathrm{VP}}$ $[_{\mathrm{V°}}$ *pushed in*] $[_{\mathrm{DP}}$ the car]]

(2) a. $[_{\mathrm{vP}}$ She $[_{\mathrm{v'}}$ $[_{\mathrm{v}}$ $[_{\mathrm{V°}}$ *pushed*]+v] $[_{\mathrm{VP}}$ the car$[_{\mathrm{V'}}$ t_{push} $[_{\mathrm{PP}}$ *in*]]]]]]
b. $[_{\mathrm{vP}}$ She $[_{\mathrm{v'}}$ $[_{\mathrm{v}}$ $[_{\mathrm{V°}}$ *pushed in*]+v] $[_{\mathrm{VP}}$ the car$[_{\mathrm{V'}}$ $t_{\mathrm{push\ in}}$ $[_{\mathrm{PP}}$ t_{in}]]]]]]

(3) a. She pushed the car straight in.
b. *She pushed straight in the car.

However, the complex head approach does not have a mortgage on explaining these facts. Among various alternatives surveyed in Dehé et al. (2002) and Haiden (2006), one could name an approach which assumes that the particle and object form a Small Clause or comparable constituent (e.g., den Dikken 1995, Svenonius 1996). (4) gives the variant of this approach in Ramchand and Svenonius (2002). Here the word order alternation takes place entirely within the Small Clause, here conceived as a projection of a R(esult) head, which can either attract a DP to its specifier, (4)a, or trigger head movement of a particle, (4)b. This can capture data like (3) by assuming that modified particles are not analysable as heads (modulo the complication in note 2). The approach, unlike the $[_{\mathrm{V°}}$ V P] approach, readily extends to languages where some constituent intervenes between V and a pre-object particle, cf. (5) and (6).

(4) a. *push* $[_{\mathrm{RP}}$ the car $[_{\mathrm{R'}}$ R $[_{\mathrm{PrtP}}$ $t_{\mathrm{the\ car}}$ $[_{\mathrm{Prt}}$ *in*]]]]
b. *push* $[_{\mathrm{RP}}$ $[_{\mathrm{R'}}$ *in*+R $[_{\mathrm{PrtP}}$ the car $[_{\mathrm{Prt}}$ t_{in}]]]]

(5) Kari *sparka* heldigvis *ut* hunden. [Norw. Ramchand/Svenonius]
K. kicked fortunately out the.dog

(6) Hon *sparkade* inte *ut* honom. [Swedish, Toivonen 2003: 43]
She kicked not out him

The constituent $[_{\mathrm{V°}}$ V Prt] assumed in complex head analyses should not be accepted lightly. Several extant arguments for it are inconclusive. For instance, Farrell (2005: 103) sees the mere existence of cases of affixation of particle verbs as an argument for $[_{\mathrm{V°}}$ V P], but evidence for syntactic word formation (say Fu et al. 2001, Baker and Vinokurova 2008, Bruening 2012) cautions us against uncritically accepting the No Phrase Constraint. $[_{\mathrm{V°}}$ V P] is left-headed, unlike most other morphological structures in English. While it is possible that at some stage in the history of English purely syntactically generated verb-particle strings were reanalysed by language learners as morphological structures, this should not be the default assumption given that English morphology is otherwise nearly always right-headed.

I will nonetheless argue that $[_{\mathrm{V°}}$ V P] exists. After reviewing and extending an argument from the literature from quotative inversion (*"Go away dude!" shouted out Marmaduke*), I present several arguments connected with nominalizations of particle verbs. Section 3 discusses reduplicative nominalizations of the type *fixer-upper*, arguing that the outer suffix is needed because *-er* takes a whole $[_{\mathrm{V°}}$ V P] as input, and providing other remarks on this

ous. This problem is sidestepped in theories which assume that the complex head arises by base-generation or reanalysis.

pattern needed in later sections. Section 4 adduces an argument for [$_{V°}$ V P] based on the fact that event nominals with *-ing* but not with other suffixes are compatible with particles: *the {dividing/*division} up of the country.* In section 5, I mount an argument for [$_{V°}$ V P] which is based on a previously unstudied synthetic compounds of the type *house-fixer-upper*).

2. Preliminary argument: Quotative inversion

As an appetite-whetter for my main arguments for [$_{V°}$ V P], I now present an elaboration of a little-known argument in the literature. It is based on the appearance of the verb and particle in pre-subject position in quotative inversion (Collins and Branigan 1997: 4f., Toivonen 2003: 175f.):

(7) a. "Civilization is going to pieces," *broke out* Tom violently. [attested; Toivonen]
b. "Out with it" *blurted out* the Captain brusquely. [Cappelle 2010]
c. "What!?" *shouted out* John and Yuuda simultaneously. [Google]

Collins and Branigan (henceforth C&B) argue that quotative inversion has the structure in (8) (which I have updated by substituting T for Agr, *v*P for VP). Here Op is an empty operator coindexed with the quote (it being hard to defend an analysis involving movement of discontinuous quotes like that in (8)).

(8) "Why" [$_{CP}$ Op [$_{TP}$ [$_{T°}$ [$_{V°}$ shouts out]] [$_{vP}$ Bill … $t_{shout\ out}$ t_{Op}]]] "did you do that?"

C&B argue that the subject is in its initial position (here spec,*v*P) and not extraposed. An extraposition analysis makes it hard to explain why the subject cannot appear after the PP in (9)a. These contrast with *bona fide* cases of subject extraposition like (9)b, which are only possible with heavy subjects.

(9) a. *"Get lost!" shouted at him [a man].
b. "Get lost!" shouted at him [a man in a bedraggled brown suit].

The elopement of particles with verbs to pre-subject positions in (7) is all the more striking given that other verbal dependents cannot do so, cf. (10)a and (10)b. This is not predicted if we analyse (7) in terms of movement of a VP remnant to a pre-subject position. Such an analysis would also have to explain why the *to*-PP in (10)c is not part of the remnant. These problems do not arise if we assume that structures like (7) involve head movement of [$_{V°}$ V P] to a pre-subject position, an assumption which also explains why modified particles cannot appear here, cf. (10)d.

(10) a. "Get lost!", *shouted* {**at him/*loudly*} Gertrude.
b. "Get lost!", shouted Gertrude at him loudly.
c. "Get lost!", *shouted out* Gertrude to Basil.
d. "You're a crypto-lexicalist!", *shouted (*straight) out* Gertrude to Basil.

Thus, [$_{V°}$ V P] gives us the best hope of analyzing quotative inversion. The facts we have seen certainly need to be addressed by those who reject the complex head analysis.

3. Reduplication nominalizations (*fixer-upper*)

We turn now to nominalizations as a source of arguments for $[_{V^{\circ}}$ V P]. Some such arguments involve the affix reduplication phenomenon seen in (11). This construction is well-attested on the internet, though its text frequency is curtailed by its confinement to a subset of English idiolects and to colloquial style. Use in higher style levels is unlikely since purportedly 'redundant' formatives are a sitting duck for purist invective like that in Wentworth (1936).

(11) fixer-upper, taker outer, filler-inner, writer downer, taker offer, turner-overer

While we noted in the introduction that nominalization of particle verbs is not *in itself* an argument for $[_{V^{\circ}}$ V P], the appearance of the affix to the right of the particle in (11) is most plausibly explained if the particle is part of the V which undergoes affixation, since we do not find reduplication of affixes when a nominalized verb occurs with clearly phrasal arguments (*pusher of cars, travellers to Spain*). This argument holds irrespective of whether one executes *-er* affixation in a lexicalist-style derivation with realization of phrasal arguments as arguments of the derived noun (e.g., Grimshaw 1990) or in a syntactic derivation where *-er* is a syntactic head which selects a VP or larger constituent and attracts V (including $[_{V^{\circ}}$ V P]) in a head movement operation (e.g., Baker and Vinokurova 2009).

Reduplication occurs because a suffix must attach to the right of its input but for some reason must also attach to the head of its input. A single suffix cannot fulfill both requirements with left-headed input. Web-attested data like (12) give another example of the same phenomenon. The inputs to plural affixation are treated as left-headed nominal compounds in the relevant idiolects. Stump (1994) discusses a similar case of plural affix reduplication in Breton left-headed diminutives.

(12) $^{\%}$sister*s*-in-law*s*; $^{\%}$governor*s*-general*s*; $^{\%}$atourney*s*-general*s*

It is less clear why speakers' grammars feel the need to attach affixes to the head of their input in addition to the right edge of their input. Possibly this is because heads of morphological objects are stems subject to valuation by functional heads like Tense, and are in themselves not fully formed morphological words (which is not visible in weakly inflected languages like English). Derivational suffixes solve this problem in right-headed structures but cannot do so in left-headed structures where nonhead material intervenes between the suffix and the head of the input. Whether or not this is right, it clear that the inner affix is inserted for morpho-phonological reasons, since web-attested cases like (13)a speak for the semantic vacuity of the inner affix (cf. Miller 1993: 133, Cappelle 2010). Moreover, the inner affix is expendable when it would violate other constraints. Thus, a phonologically heavy affix like *-able* is better attested on the internet without inner affixation, as in (13)b, than with it (*fixable-uppable*), presumably because reduplication produces too much phonological clutter.

(13) a. break*er*-up-*ee* [one who is broken up with by their partner]; eye-putt*er*-out*ee* [one whose eye is put out]; pisser-off-ee [one who gets pissed off]
b. fix-up-able, take-out-able, piss-off-able

c. passer-by, hanger-on, runner-up
d. … an act-getter-together (act-getter-togetherer? you know, someone to help me get my act together). [Google; March 2009]

In a third response to the problem of suffixing left-headed structures, the suffix is realized only on the head of its input. This is seen in examples like (13)c, which strike me as memorized relics of a now unproductive pattern (which was replaced by reduplication in the twentieth century, Cappelle 2010). This pattern seems to be the least acceptable of the three seen so far, with the possible exception of particles ending in <er>, where the outer *-er* is prone to haplology, witness (13)d and the fact that the string "tipper-over of" yields eleven Google hits while "tipper-overer of" yields none. By contrast this strategy is usual with inflectional affixes (*I walked in*), adjectival participial suffixes (*{fallen/falling} down houses*) and the nominalizer *-ing* (see also footnote 3).

The three solutions to the problem of suffixing left-headed morphological objects (called *double affixation*, *head marking* and *external marking* in Stump (1994)) are all suboptimal: only reduplication satisfies all morphophonological requirements but is uneconomical and apt to be stigmatized sociolinguistically. It is thus unsurprising that some speakers accept none of the three strategies. For instance, a British linguistics graduate whom I asked to nominalize *take out* suggested *out-taker*, but found it 'very marginal'. He volunteered neither *taker-outer* nor *taker-out* nor *take-outer*, and rejected them all when I asked him about them.

I now discuss the account of Svenonius (2004), who does not see reduplication as a response to inflecting a left-headed $[_{V^\circ}$ V P]. He argues that *-er* merges twice because it binds both the external and internal arguments. By comparison, there is only one *-able* in the (commonest) pattern in (13)b because *-able* only binds an external argument. Unfortunately this appealing idea does not find the empirical support it deserves. We find reduplication even if the internal argument is realized (*fixer uppers of cars*) or if there is only one argument (*walker-outer*). A final point to notice is that some speakers use triple *-er* (*fix-er up-er-er*; see Cappelle 2010), though presumably the affix is not binding three arguments here.

The remarks given above (and in footnote 3 and section 5) do not capture all the complexities of the reduplication phenomenon noted in Cappelle (2010) and Walker (2009), but I hope to have at least shown that the attachment of affixes to the right of particles in (11) puts the explanatory onus on those who believe we would be better off without $[_{V^\circ}$ V P].

4. Fussy affixes: **the explanation away of problems*

This section will propose an argument for $[_{V^\circ}$ V P] which is based on data like (14) – (17). Comparison of the (a) and (b) variants suggests that the nominalization affix *-ing* is compatible with particles, while other affixes (call these *fussy affixes*) are incompatible with particles. Comparison of the (a) and (c) variants suggests that the incompatibility of fussy affixes with particles does not extend to full PPs. (In (18) the data are abbreviated; the corresponding *-ing* nominals are well-formed with particles, as in the (b) variants in (14) – (17).)

(14) a. *the division up of the country
b. the dividing up of the country (into two)
c. the division of the country into two

(15) a. *the merger in of the company
b. the merging in of the company
c. the acquisition of Rodocker's, or merger of it into our company [www]

(16) a. *the enticement in of (the) people
b. the enticing in of the people
c. the enticement of people into a hall [www]

(17) a. *the growth up of children
b. the growing up of children.
c. the growth of children into powerful adults [www]

(18) a. the shipment {*off} (of the goods) {to Europe} (last week)
b. the leakage {*out} of water {out of the tank}
c. the clearance {*out} of the goods {out of the factory}
d. the closure {*down} of nuclear power plants
e. the trial {*out} of the products
f. the explanation {*away} of the problem

The generalization emerging from these data can be stated more precisely as follows.

(19) PARTICLE-AFFIX GENERALIZATION (PAG): Verb particles, but not full PPs, are incompatible with nominalizations with the following properties:
a. The nominalization is a *complex event nominal* (Grimshaw 1990), i.e., is an event nominalization with an argument introduced in an *of*-phrase which corresponds to a direct object or unaccusative subject of the corresponding clause.
b. The nominalization contains an overt affix other than *-ing*.

The PAG as formulated in (19) does not refer to certain types of nominalizations which are found with particles. (19)a excludes agentive nominalizations like those seen in section 3 (*fixer-up-er*). (19)b confines the discussion to nominalizations with overt affixes. It says nothing about cases of conversion/zero derivation like *bailout, meltdown, stuffup*. For many speakers these do not conform to the condition in (19)a anyway ($^{\%}$*the stuffup of the concert*).

4.1. My account: [$_{V°}$ V P] is input to affixation

I will argue that the best explanation for the PAG, and thus the data in (14) – (18), has the ingredients put forth in points A to C below.

A) The verb and particle are forced from a complex head [$_{V°}$ V P] in complex event nominalizations. The old observation that verb-adjacent particle placement is obligatory in *-ing*-nominals like (20) (e.g., Chomsky 1970) is consonant with this (though this is not *in itself* an argument for [$_{V°}$ V P]). Since my account does not depend on an explanation for the obligatoriness of particle incorporation in complex event nominals, I will postpone such an explanation to section 4.3.

(20) the dividing {up} of the country {*up}

B) It follows from point A that the input to affixation in complex event nominals based on particle verbs is [$_{V°}$ V P], and not just a simple V. I will clarify this point with regard to both lexicalist and syntactic approaches to affixation.

In a traditional lexicalist approach in which nominalising affixes attach to V°, my point would be that *the {dividing/*division} up of the country (into two)* involves attachment of the affixes to *divide up*. The DP and PP arguments selected by V are realized above affixation as arguments of the derived noun (e.g., Grimshaw 1990).[3]

Now consider non-lexicalist approaches which derive nominalizations by head movement (e.g., Alexiadou 2001, Baker and Vinokurova 2009, Borer 2003, Fu et al. 2001, Harley 2008). For our purposes the various differences between these approaches are unimportant, so I will illustrate them using the simple structure in (21). The affix is a phonological spellout of a head, labelled N in (21), which selects a phrasal projection containing the arguments of V (be it VP or a larger functional projection). V undergoes head movement to N. My claim is that the V which raises to N in (21) is *divide up*, not merely *divide*.

(21) [$_{NP}$ N [$_{VP/FP}$ divide up (of) the country into two]]

C) Some fussy affixes in (14) – (18) are unproductive (say *-th* in *growth*), so we should not expect them to enter new combinations with particle verbs. Other fussy affixes are productive but impose constraints on the (types or tokens) of bases with which they combine, and it so happens that [$_{V°}$ V P] does not conform to such constraints. I elaborate on the productivity and selection restrictions of fussy affixes in section 4.2, but for now note with Harley and Noyer (1998) that *-ing* imposes no constraints on the verbs with which it can combine

---

3 That the particle is part of the input is perhaps unexpected given *[[$_{V°}$ *divide up*]-*ing*]. I must assume that *-ing* differs from reduplicating affixes like *-er* (section 3) in that it is only spelt out on the head of its input (cf. Stump's 1994 notion of *head marking*). Some varieties show overt evidence of such affixes attaching to both the stem and the whole particle verb, witness the following web attestations:

(i) %house-fixing-upping, %trash taking-outing

Such *-ing*-reduplication structures deserve more study. Noticeably many examples on Google featured incorporated nouns like (i). To me (i) is very degraded, but *house-fixing-up, trash-taking-out* are worse, despite the perfect acceptability of *taking out, fixing up* in their various inflectional and derivational uses without incorporated nouns. A perhaps related puzzle is that perfect participle affixes do not normally reduplicate (*I have walked out; folded up chairs*), but do for some speakers when adjectival participles undergo further affixation, cf. (ii) and Cappelle (2010). For varieties rejecting all such reduplications we are left with Wentworth's (1936) prescient question: "Why the evil genius of slang permits *-er*, but not *-ing* or *-ed* to be so misused [i.e., reduplicated, A.M.] is puzzling. Forms like *calling downing, thinking upping, dropped inned,* and *walked upped*, have not been observed."

(ii) %put-out-ed-ness, %grown-up-ed-ness, %screwed-up-ed-ness, %pissed-off-ed-ness and is thus called upon when no other affix is compatible with V, including cases where V is a particle verb.[4]

Putting the three points of my argument together, we can state that if particles can form complex verbs which serve as the bases of affixes, we can reduce the incompatibility of fussy affixes to their fussiness in other areas. If particles do not incorporate in nominalizations, we would expect fussy affixes to be as oblivious to particles as they are to full PPs, which is at variance with what we see in (14) – (18).

It remains to tie up some loose ends in the argument. Section 4.2 gives more detailed remarks on the constraints on the productivity and selection restrictions of fussy affixes. Section 4.3 completes points A and B by explaining why particle incorporation should be obligatory in complex event nominals. Section 4.4 describes problems with an alternative account of data like (14) – (18), which does not rely on particle incorporation, Sichel (2010).

4.2. More details on constraints on fussy affixes

The affixes other than *-ing* in (14) – (18) are not only fussy about particles. Even in the absence of particles they are either unproductive or subject to constraints limiting the (types or tokens) of bases with which they combine, while *-ing* is free of such constraints and can be regarded as an Elsewhere nominalizer (e.g., Harley and Noyer 1998). Let us apply this to the affixes individually.

The affix in *growth* is unproductive (Marchand 1969: 349). In current English *growth* is the only clear deverbal formation with this affix. Other formations are either derivationally opaque (*stealth* < *steal*), obsolete (†*spilth*) or deadjectival (*breadth, strength, width*). Since *-th* is unproductive, we should not expect it to be able to attach to *grow up*, hence (17).

Similarly, the affix in *merger* does not productively form complex event nominals. Marchand (1969: 273–281) makes no mention of an event-denoting reading of *-er* and while Ryder (1999: 294) names some *-er*-nouns which 'refer to actions or events' (*cliff-hanger, nail-biter*), none of these are complex event nominals. The only *-er*-nouns I found which admit of complex event nominal uses are *merger*, *ouster* and *waiver* (*their waiver of the restrictions*, *their ouster of the president*).

There are doubts about the synchronic productivity of most other fussy affixes in (14) – (18). This holds of *-ance, -ure* and *-ment* according to Bauer (2001: 177–181). One can certainly find many tokens of derivations with *-ment*, but new tokens since the mid-

[4] The only constraint on *-ing*-nominalizations is blocking by well-established synonymous nominalizations, as reflected in judgments like (i) (cf. Harley and Noyer 1998). Such behaviour is normal with fully productive affixes, witness the well-known blocking of *-er*-nominals like *cooker, stealer, server* in meanings equivalent to the existing forms *cook, thief, servant*. A caveat here is that *-ing*-forms like those in (i) are web-attested and fairly acceptable to me. It might be that acceptable *-ing*-forms differ subtly in meaning from their rivals (to my ear *admiring* has an eventive reading lacking in *admiration*). However one explains such cases, it is noteworthy that even stronger blocking effects like that in (ii) are overridden in the presence of particles, cf. (iii).

(i) her {admiration/*admiring} of Mary; the {destruction/*destroying} of cities
(ii) the {trial/*trying} of the products
(iii) the {trying/*trial} out of the products

nineteenth century are scarce. By contrast, *-(at)ion* is productive, but note with Bauer (2001: 183) that nearly all new formations have affixed bases, mainly with *-ize* and *-ify* (*Obamarization, Bushification*), and other formations are apt to be jocular (*chatteration*). Our expectation that *-(at)ion* should attach to particle verbs diminishes further when we note that Germanic particles are at loggerheads with its preference for Romance input (Marchand 1969: 259–261).

(22) exemplifies constraints on the use of the fussy affixes in (14) – (18). Attributing the unacceptability in current English of the formerly possible *-ment*-formations in (22)f to blocking is unconvincing, since the only competing nominalizer is *-ing*, which is an Elsewhere affix which is itself blocked by other affixes (recall footnote 4), and since *-ing*-forms like those in *their {garnishing/flustering/reviling} of them* do not evince the familiarity effects one would expect of memorized derivations capable of blocking others.

(22) a. the {trial/denial/*supplial/$^{\%}$decrial} of them
b. the {clearance/appearance/*steerance} of them
c. the {leakage/seepage/$^{\%}$drippage/*flowage/*escapage} of water into it
d. the {closure/exposure/*imposure} of them
e. their {division/decision/derision} of them / his {confiding/*confision} of the matter to a doctor
f. †astoundment, †garnishment, †dispiritment, †flusterment, †revilement, †concernment, †bailment, †securement (Marchand 1969: 331f)

4.3. Why particle incorporation is obligatory in complex event nominals

My appeal to obligatory particle incorporation in complex nominals would gain plausibility if I can name plausible factors which force it. My attempt in this direction begins with the observation that *of*-insertion arguments must be arguments of the nominalized verb, witness the well-known observation (e.g. Chomsky 1970, Sichel 2010) that *of*-insertion is excluded with ECM objects, cf. (23)a. Similarly, complex event nominalizations of unselected object resultatives like (23)b are adjudged unacceptable by Carrier and Randall (1992) (in contrast to cases like (23)c involving objects selected by V). A complication is that some speakers, myself included, accept (23)b. I surmize that in such cases the more liberal idiolects allow the verb and result predicate to reanalyse as a complex predicate which takes the *Theme*[5] as its argument, which then means that the Theme counts as an argument of V and can be linked by *of*-insertion.

(23) a. *the considering/consideration of John (to be) honest.
b. $^{(*)}$the running of pavements thin, $^{(*)}$the working of one's fingers to the bone
c. the hammering of metal flat, the pushing of the car into the garage
d. their outplaying of the home team; the river's overflowing of its banks
e. the voting {out} of the government {*out}; the working {off} of the debts {*off}

5 I use *Theme* as shorthand for whatever thematic role an argument corresponding to a transitive object or an unaccusative subject has (be it Patient, Theme of Motion, Incremental Theme, etc.), without wishing to imply that *Theme* in this sense is a grammatical primitive.

The complex predicate formation just described involves abstract incorporation (e.g. Baker 1988) in that it has no morphological or phonological reflexes, witness the separation of the derived nominal from the result predicate by the *of*-marked Theme in (23)c. English does not allow the morphological incorporation of APs and full PPs. By contrast, it does allow the morphological incorporation of complementless prepositions, whether they surface as prefixes, as in (23)d, or as particles, as in (23)e. If my reasoning is correct, the complex predicate formation mechanism just described must be at work in (23)d and (23)e, since these examples involve unselected objects. To explain the constraint on particle placement in (e), we need only assume that the incorporation spoken of must be realized morphologically *if possible*.

A remaining question is why *of*-insertion should be illegitimate with arguments which are not thematic arguments of the nominalized V. My answer begins by noting that most devices for argument realization stipulate particular thematic interpretations for the arguments they introduce. We see this with various prepositions: *to* can assign a Recipient role (*give it to them*), *with* can link Theme of Motion arguments (*The garden crawled with spiders; Off with his head!*) and *of* has a use in linking removed objects (*rob/deprive/clear/empty X of Y*). Similarly functional heads like Voice and Appl(icative) proposed in the literature assign roles like Agent or Recipient/Beneficiary to their specifiers (e.g., Pylkkänen 2002). By contrast, *of*-insertion does not stipulate particular thematic interpretations for the arguments it links, beyond insisting that the argument be *an argument of the nominalized verb*.

This account briefly laid out here is still in its infancy, but it appears to be promising as a potential explanation for a number of different facts, and makes the obligatoriness of particle incorporation understandable.

4.4. Dismissal of an alternative account: Sichel (2010)

Sichel (2010) proposed an interesting alternative explanation for data like (14) – (18) which makes no appeal to incorporation of particles and would thus nullify my argument if it were correct. Sichel suggests that the only English nominalizer capable of supporting an event structure with multiple subevents is *-ing*. The other affixes in (14) – (18) are accordingly incompatible with resultative particles, since a resultative interpretation entails multiple subevents. An immediate problem for this account is that ruling out e.g. **the enticement in of people* wrongly excludes *the enticement of people into the building*, and analogous problems affect all data in (14) – (18).

One could try to uphold Sichel's account by adding the following assumptions to it:

(24) a. Certain PPs that look like result predicates are actually adjuncts.
b. The full PPs in (14) – (18) are adjunct PPs of the type in (a).
c. Particles cannot be merged as adjunct PPs of the type proposed in (a).
d. Adjunct PPs do not create complex event structures which are illicit in event nominals with affixes other than *-ing* on Sichel's account.

The claim in (24)a is seldom discussed, but may be right, as I argued myself (2004). It is for instance supported by (25)a, in which *re-* triggers the presupposition that the settlement had been divided in some way before, but not necessarily that it had been divided into six districts. Since the PP is outside the scope of *re*-prefixation, it is presumably merged higher in the structure than the object, in an adjunct-like position. One could extend this analysis to *the (re)division of the country into two*, as per (24)b.

(25) a. The redivided a settlement it into six administrative districts.
b. Bob kicked Bill in the head, so Bill kicked Bob in the head back.
c. We had dinner at the table in *(the house).

I also concede that (24)c is reasonable. Few particles share the ability of *back* in (25)b to appear in a clearly adjunct-like position outside other PPs. Even the particle in *we had dinner in* cannot replicate this behavior, cf. (25)c, although it has a locational modifier interpretation which one normally associates with adjuncts.

However, Sichel's account cannot be salvaged using (24). The claim in (24)b makes no sense of (15), since we are dealing with an unselected object resultative construction: the object in *they merged company A into company B* does not entail *they merged company A*. If the *into*-PP in (15)c were an adjunct, one would have to allow it to merge with a semantically and argument-structurally ill-formed *merger of it*. Similar remarks apply to (18)b: in PP in *the clearing of goods out of the factory* is hardly an adjunct given that *they cleared the goods* has the irrelevant interpretation 'affirm that the goods conform to regulations' but not the relevant motion verb interpretation.

5. Synthetic compounding in particle verb nominalizations

5.1. Introduction to the data

My next argument in favour of [$_{V°}$ V P] will involve structures like (26) in which the Theme of a nominalized particle verb is incorporated to form an apparently previously unstudied kind of synthetic compound. The examples in (26) are all internet-attested and could easily be multiplied.

(26) a. trash taker outer [cf. the taker-outer of the trash]
b. house-fixer-upper, house-puller-downer, head-kicker-inner, form-filler-inner, stain-getter-outer, shoe-taker-offer, sock-putter-onner
c. water soaker-upper, title thinker-upper

Now consider the paradigm in (27). Comparison of (a) and (b) suggests that full PP complements are compatible with Themes realized as full phrases, but not with incorporated Themes. Theme incorporation is only possible if the Goal is realized as a particle, as in (27)c. (28) furnishes more examples of failed attempts at incorporating nominals with a full phrasal complement present.

(27) a. I am an inveterate and incurable *taker of people into my house.*
b. *an inveterate people-taker into my house
c. an inveterate people-taker-inner

(28) a. *a car pusher into the garage; *the ball thrower off the boat; *a bus driver south
b. *a door breaker open; *the partner shooter-dead; *the prisoner beater to death

A complication is the fact that structures with *to*-datives like (29) are attested and perfectly acceptable to at least some speakers. These differ from the PPs in (27)a, b and (28) in that the latter are *complement* PPs, while Bruening (2010) shows convincingly that there is a kind of dative *to*-PP which merges higher than Theme arguments and is thus not a complement. (Presumably speakers who reject (29) cannot use the high-merging type of dative PP in nominalizations, for reasons which are unclear to me, but not crucial here.)

(29) a gift-giver to children

A final empirical point to note is that it is sometimes possible to improve structures of the type in (28) by incorporating the PP, cf. (30). (30)b is degraded due to the very marginal status of incorporation of full PPs in English synthetic compounds, but is not as bad as (30)a, where the PP is not incorporated.

(30) a. *a bricklayer drinker under the table
b. ??a bricklayer under-the-table-drinker [Cappelle 2010]

The conclusions from the data seen thus far can be stated as follows.

(31) a. Theme arguments cannot incorporate in the presence of a full PP complement, cf. (27)b and (28).
b. Incorporation of the PP makes Theme incorporation better, cf. (30).
c. Theme arguments can be incorporated in the presence of particles in structures of the type *trash-taker-outer* in (26), (27)c.

If particle verbs are complex heads in cases like *trash-taker-outer*, we can collapse the collection of statements in (31) into a single generalization:

(32) CONDITION ON THEME INCORPORATION (CTI): In a nominalization in which a Theme and (an argument corresponding to) a syntactic complement are realized, the Theme cannot incorporate unless the other argument incorporates first.

5.2. Deriving the data

We now show that the descriptive statement in (32) can be integrated into an explanatory system, irrespective of whether one adopts lexicalist or non-lexicalist assumptions.

One can easily integrate the CTI into a lexicalist approach which assumes that only the least prominent (non-subject[6]) argument may incorporate in a synthetic compound. If the

[6] Agents do not incorporate in synthetic compounds, cf. **girl {discussion/writing/reading/analysis/collection} (of poetry)*. To my knowledge no apparent counterexample involves genuine synthetic compounding. For instance, in (i) below *Liszt* is not an incorporated Agent but a modifier (perhaps a zero-derived relational adjective) merged *above* the PP complement, witness the ability of *one* to replace the underlined string in (ii). Furthermore, *Liszt transcriptions* is not initially stressed, unlike genuine synthetic compounds like *symphony transcriptions* in (iii). Analogous arguments also apply to cases like *city employee* discussed in Bobaljik (2002).

Theme is the only argument, it is the lowest argument, and thus incorporable: *car pusher*. Structures like **car pusher into the garage* are excluded since in a lexicalist system compounding is presyntactic, with the consequence that the PP complement is merged higher in the structure than the Theme (possible structures are given in (33)a and (33)b[7]), which violates the standard pattern according to which Theme arguments are linked in higher, more prominent positions than directional PPs.

(33) a. *[$_{NP}$ [$_{N°}$ car [$_{N°}$ push-er]] [$_{PP}$ into the garage]]
b. *[$_{NP}$ [$_{N°}$ [$_{V°}$ car-push]-er] [$_{PP}$ into the garage]]
c. [$_{N°}$ car [$_{N°}$ [$_{V°}$ push-in]-er]]
d. [$_{N°}$ [$_{V°}$ car [$_{V°}$ push-in]]-er]
e. cart-overturning, problem-overlooker, tree-uprooter, law-upholder

Capturing *car-pusher-inner* in the system just described is unproblematic if one assumes that the particle and verb form a complex verb [$_{V°}$ V P]. Possible structures are given in (33)c & d. In both cases the particle is more deeply embedded than the Theme, as it should be. The structures are configurationally equivalent to those that would be needed for data like (33)e, except that these involve right-headed complex verbs rather than particle verbs. Regarding affix reduplication, recall from section 3 the claim that the inner affix is not structurally relevant and is inserted for morpho-phonological reasons.

Structures like (33)c and (33)d could be seen as a type of recursive synthetic compounding. Data like (34) have been taken to show that synthetic compounding cannot be recursive (Selkirk 1982: 37, Lieber 2004: 58). However, these data do not show what they are supposed to, since **shelf-putting* and **child giving* are bad on the relevant readings. Apart from isolated cases like *churchgoer*, synthetic compounds with nominals corresponding to syntactic PPs and dative *to* are scarcely productive: **home address sending (of books)*, **museum donation (of art)*. Expecting (34)b to be grammatical because of the existence of *give a child a gift* misses the fact that double object constructions are not found in derived nominalizations that realize the arguments phrasally (**giver (of) a child (of) a book*). While there are certain types of synthetic compounding that are subject to genuine constraints on

(i) the Liszt transcríptions of the Beethoven symphonies.
(ii) the Liszt *transcriptions of the symphonies* sound better than your *ones*.
(iii) (Liszt) sýmphony transcriptions
(iv) *symphony Liszt transcriptions

[7] Fortunately we can sidestep the issue of whether synthetic compounds have the structure [$_N$ [$_V$ N V]-*er*] or [$_N$ N [$_N$ V-*er*]]. Dismissing the former structure because there is no verb **car-push* is a common but, I believe, overrated argument. There are plenty of attestations of synthetic compounds corresponding to verb-object idioms: *hackle-raiser* (McIntyre, in prep.). Here it will not do to say that the non-head is related to *raiser* by pragmatic inferences, since such compounds are possible even for speakers for whom *hackle* is a cranberry word not usable outside the idiom chunk. Similar cases can be found with V-Particle-Object idioms:

(i) towel thrower-inner [who throws in the towel 'gives up']
(ii) steam letter-offer [that lets one to let off steam 'relax']
(iii) tab picker-upper; rear bringer upper; new-leaf-turner-over; last word getter inner; support drummer upper

recursion, such as *-ing* adjectives (**linguist-sick-making* vs. *sickmaking, peacemaking*), I submit that a ban on recursive synthetic compound nouns is poorly motivated, and would probably not have been proposed had researchers been aware of data like (33)e and cases like *car-pusher-in-er*.

(34) a. *shelf book putting/*book shelf putting; *shelf book putter/*book shelf putter
  b. *child gift giving/*gift child giving; *child gift giver/*gift child giver

We now see how the CTI in (32) could be policed in syntactic frameworks using head movement à la Baker (1988). Harley (2008) applies this to English synthetic compounds. She updates the First Sister Principle (Roeper and Siegel 1978: 208) by assuming that complements may incorporate into the heads selecting them, but specifiers may not. This approach makes correct predictions regarding our data. A standard compound like *car pusher* would be generated from the configuration in (35)a. *Car* incorporates into *push* and *car-push* incorporates into the nominalizer. (To improve legibility, (35) does not depict the head movement.) The approach excludes **car pusher into the garage* because the presence of a PP complement automatically means that the Theme must be in a specifier (be it of a Small Clause or equivalent constituent, as in (35)b, or of a verbal projection, as in (35)c), and thus cannot incorporate.

(35) a. [$_{NP}$ -er [$_{VP}$ push [$_{N^\circ}$ car]]]
  b. *[$_{NP}$ -er [$_{VP}$ push [$_{SC}$ [$_{N^\circ}$ car] [$_{PP}$ into the garage]]]]]
  c. *[$_{NP}$ -er [$_{VP}$ [$_{N^\circ}$ car] [$_{V'}$ push [$_{PP}$ into the garage]]]]
  d. [$_{NP}$ -er [$_{VP}$ [$_{V^\circ}$ push in] [$_{N^\circ}$ car]]]

If we assume that particle verbs can merge as complex heads, as in (35)d, then *car* can be merged as complement to such a head, and would thus be able to incorporate in Harley's system, so the system would be able to derive *car-pusher-in-er* (again under the proviso that the inner affix is inserted for morpho-phonological reasons and is thus structurally irrelevant).

One might see (35)d as inconsistent since *push in* is base-generated as a complex head while nominal compounds are generated by Baker-style head movement. A perhaps preferable assumption is that Theme incorporation involves not head movement, but a much simpler process of *merger of two heads in a sister configuration*, as in either of the configurations in (36)a. (36)a is empirically superior a head movement approach to the same data, since head movement predicts complement stranding, which is ill-formed in the cases at hand, cf. (36)b.

(36) a. [$_{NP}$ -er [$_{V}$ [$_{N}$ car] [$_{V}$ push]]] / [$_{N}$ [$_{V}$ [$_{N}$ car] [$_{V}$ push]]-er]
  b. *son promotion [$_{NP}$ t_{son} of a friend] 'promotion of the son of a friend'
  c. [$_{NP}$ -er [$_{V}$ [$_{N^\circ}$ car] [$_{V^\circ}$ push in]]] / [$_{N}$ [$_{V}$ [$_{N}$ car] [$_{V}$ push in]]-er]

If Theme incorporation involves direct merge rather than head movement, either structure in (36)c would work for cases like *car pusher-in-er*; configurationally parallel structures would be usable for *law upholder* and others in (33)e. To exclude **car-pusher into the garage*, we either assume that full PPs always occupy a Small Clause configuration like (35)b, in which case the Theme would not be in a direct sisterhood relation with V, or assume the structure in (35)c and that the constituent labelled V' cannot reanalyse as a V°, in which case *car* would not be sister to a head and thus unable to form a compound with it.

5.3. Appendix: Parallel German data

I now briefly present German data which confirms assumptions made in sections 5.1 and 5.2. German freely generates particle verb nominalizations with incorporated Themes like (37) (where the particles are in italics). These are analogous to English *car-pusher-inner* and similar data in (26), except that German particle verbs are head-final and do not force speakers into suboptimal solutions to the problem of suffixing left-headed structures.

(37) a. Bäume*ab*sägen 'trees.down.sawing'; Kerzen*aus*blasen 'candle.out.blowing'; Müll*weg*bringen 'rubbish.away.taking'; Reifen*auf*pumpen 'tyre.up.pumping'
b. Feuer*an*zünder 'fire lighter'; Wand*an*streicher 'wall.on.painter' (*wall painter*); Sack*auf*reißer 'bag.open.ripper' (*device for opening rubbish bags*);
c. Selbst*auf*opferung 'self-up-offering'
d. Blut*ab*nahme 'blood.from.taking' (*blood test*)
e. Vogel*ab*schießer 'bird.down.shooter' (*person/thing that takes the cake*)

In (38) we see that the CTI in (32) is valid for German. The Theme can incorporate if the particle incorporates first, cf. (32)a, but not if there is an unincorporated directional complement, cf. (32)b, which is the analogue of cases like *car-pushing into the garage* and similar cases in (28). (32)c illustrates that this problem can be avoided by incorporating the full PP, but this kind of phrasal compounding is marginal like its English counterpart in (30)b. Finally, (32)d illustrates that unincorporated full PPs are possible if the Theme is itself not incorporated.

(38) a.	das Müll*weg*werfen; 'the rubbish.away.throwing'	das Ball*rein*werfen 'the ball.in.throwing'
b.	*das Müllwerfen in die Tonne; 'the rubbish.throwing in the bin	*das Ballwerfen in den Korb 'the ball.throwing in the basket'
c.	??das Müll-in-die-Tonne-werfen; 'the rubbish.in-the-bin.throwing	??das Ball-in-den-Korb-Werfen 'the ball.in.the.basket.throwing'
d.	das Werfen des Mülls in die Tonne; 'the throwing of the rubbish in the bin'	das Werfen des Balls in den Korb 'the throwing of the ball in the basket'

Bibliography

Alexiadou, A. (2001): *Functional structure in nominals: nominalization and ergativity*. Amsterdam: John Benjamins.

Baker, M. (1988): *Incorporation. A theory of grammatical function changing*. Chicago: The University of Chicago Press.

Baker, M. and N. Vinokurova. (2009): On agent nominalizations. *Language* 85 (3): 517–556.

Bauer, L. (2001): *Morphological productivity*. Cambridge: Cambridge University Press.

Bobaljik, J. D. (2003): Auspicious compounds. *McGill Working Papers in Linguistics* 17 (2): 65–71.
Borer, H. (2003): Exo-skeletal vs. Endo-skeletal explanations. In: J. Moore and M. Polinsky (eds.), *The nature of explanation in linguistic theory*. Stanford: CSLI Publications.
Bruening, B. (2010): Double object constructions disguised as prepositional datives. *Linguistic Inquiry* 41: 287–305.
Bruening, B. (2012): Word formation is syntactic: Adjectival passives in English. Ms. Delaware.
Cappelle, B. (2010): Doubler-upper nouns. In: A. Onysko and S. Michel (eds.), *Cognitive perspectives on word formation*. Berlin/New York: de Gruyter, 335–374.
Carrier, J., and J. Randall (1992): The argument structure and syntactic structure of resultatives. *Linguistic Inquiry 23*: 173–234.
Collins, C. and P. Branigan (1997): Quotative inversion. *Natural Language and Linguistic Theory* 15: 1–41.
Dehé, N. (2002): *Particle verbs in English*. Amsterdam: Benjamins.
Dehé, N., R. Jackendoff, A. McIntyre and S. Urban (eds.) (2002): *Verb particle explorations*. Berlin/New York: de Gruyter.
den Dikken, M. (1995): *Particles*. Oxford: Oxford University Press.
Farrell, P. (2005): English verb-preposition constructions. *Language* 81: 96–137.
Fu, Jincqui, T. Roeper and H. Borer. (2001): The VP within nominalizations. *Natural Language and Linguistic Theory* 19: 549–582.
Grimshaw, J. (1990): *Argument structure*. Cambridge: MIT Press.
Haiden, M. (2006): Verb particle constructions. In: M. Everaert and H. van Riemsdijk (eds.), *The Blackwell companion to syntax, Volume 5*. Oxford: Blackwell, 344–375.
Harley, H. (2008): Compounding in Distributed Morphology. In: R. Lieber and P. Stekauer (eds.), *The Oxford handbook of compounding*. Oxford: Oxford University Press.
Harley, H. and R. Noyer (1998): Mixed nominalizations, short verb movement and object shift in English. *NELS 28*: 143–158.
Johnson, K. (1991): Object positions. *Natural Language and Linguistic Theory* 9: 577–636.
Lieber, R. (2004): *Morphology and lexical semantics*. Cambridge: Cambridge University Press.
Marchand, H. (1969): *The categories and types of present-day English word formation*. 2nd ed. Munich: Beck.
McIntyre, A. (2002): Idiosyncrasy in particle verbs. In: N. Dehé, R. Jackendoff, A. McIntyre and S. Urban (eds.), *Verb-particle explorations*. Berlin/New York: de Gruyter, 97–118.
McIntyre, A. (2004): Event paths, conflation, argument structure and VP shells. *Linguistics* 42: 523–571.
McIntyre, A. (in preparation): *Synthetic compounds: messages from a 'bandwagon-jumper-onner' and a 'two-cents-worth-thrower-inner'*. Ms. Neuchâtel.
Miller, D. G. (1993): *Complex verb formation*. Amsterdam: Benjamins.
Neeleman, A. (2002): Particle placement. In: N. Dehé et al. (eds.), *Verb-particle explorations*. Berlin/New York: de Gruyter, 141–164.

Olsen, S. (1997): Über den lexikalischen Status englischer Partikelverben. In: G. Rauh and E. Löbel (eds.), *Lexikalische Kategorien und Merkmale*. Tübingen: Niemeyer, 45–71.

Olsen, S. (2000): Against incorporation. *Linguistische Arbeitsberichte* 74: 149–172.

Pylkkänen, L. (2002): *Introducing arguments*. Dissertation, MIT, Cambridge, MA.

Ramchand, G. and P. Svenonius (2002): The lexical syntax and lexical semantics of the verb-particle construction. In: L. Mikkelsen and C. Potts (eds.), *Proceedings of the West Coast Conference on Formal Linguistics 21*. Somerville, MA: Cascadilla Press, 387–400.

Roeper, T. and M. Siegel (1978): A lexical transformation for verbal compounds. *Linguistic Inquiry* 9: 199–260.

Ryder, M. (1999): Bankers and blue-chippers: An account of *er*-formations in present-day English. *English language and linguistics* 3 (2): 269–297.

Selkirk, E (1982): *The syntax of words*. Cambridge, MA: MIT Press.

Sichel, I. (2010): Event structure constraints in nominalization. In: A. Alexiadou and M. Rathert (eds.), *The syntax of nominalizations across languages and frameworks*. Berlin/New York: de Gruyter, 151–190.

Stump, G. (1994): The uniformity of head marking in inflectional morphology. In: G. Booij and J. van Marle (eds.), *Yearbook of morphology 7*. Dordrecht: Kluwer, 245–296.

Stiebels, B. and D. Wunderlich (1994): Morphology feeds syntax: the case of particle verbs. *Linguistics* 32: 913–968.

Svenonius, P. (2004): *The Zero Level*. Ms. Tromsø.

Toivonen, I. (2003): *Non-Projecting Words*. Dordrecht: Kluwer.

Walker, J. (2009): Double *-er* suffixation in English. *Lexis, E-Journal in English Lexicology* 1: 5–14.

Wentworth, H. (1936): On Adding the Suffix of Agency, *-er*, to Adverbs. *American Speech* 11: 369–370.

Zeller, J. (2002): Particle verbs are heads and phrases. In: N. Dehé, R. Jackendoff, A. McIntyre and S. Urban (eds), *Verb-particle explorations*. Berlin/New York: de Gruyter, 233–267.

D-Linking vs. degree: Inflected and uninflected *welch* in exclamatives and rhetorical questions

Sophie Repp

1. Introduction

German has two types of *which*-phrases. Both types are formed with a *wh*-word that has the stem *welch* but one type is inflected whereas the other type is uninflected. In the inflected type of *which*-phrase *welch* is inflected for number, case, and, in the singular, for gender. Depending on the particular form required it comes as *welcher*, *welchen*, *welchem*, *welches*, *welche*. In this paper I will use the abbreviation *welchE* to refer to the inflected type irrespective of the particular form. Uninflected *welch* only ever takes the form *welch*, and I will refer to it as *welch*. Uninflected *welch* can be followed by the indefinite determiner *ein* ('a'), inflected *welchE* cannot. Adjectival modifiers that occur with inflected *welchE* carry so-called weak inflection endings. Adjectival modifiers that occur with uninflected *welch* carry strong inflection endings. This is illustrated in (1). The pattern is the normal pattern for inflection in German noun phrases (cf. Olsen 1989, 1991a, 1991b, Gallmann 1996, Müller 2004, Roehrs 2009).

(1)	a.	welch	(ein)	schön*es*	Haus
	b.	welch*es*	(*ein)	schön*e*	Haus
		welch	a	nice	house

Semantically, inflected *welchE* roughly is the equivalent of English *which*, i.e., in a *which/welchE* question, given a set of entities that have the property specified by the complement of *which/welchE*, the speaker asks the addressee to pick out the entity or entities that make the proposition true. *WelchE* phrases are d-linked (Pesetsky 1987) just like English *which*-phrases. Uninflected *welch* might be compared to English *what a* as in *What a nice dress! Welch* has been suggested to trigger the presupposition that the property denoted by its complement applies to a high degree (D'Avis 2001). Furthermore, *welch ein* has been argued to have the same meaning as German *was für ein* ('what for a'; Gallmann 1997), which ask for kinds or properties (Beck 1996). The English equivalent of *was für ein* is *what* occurring with nouns as in *What shoe size are you?*

In this paper I explore the distribution of *welch* and *welchE* in different types of speech acts. Uninflected *welch* has been claimed to occur only in exclamatives (Gallmann 1997, D'Avis 2001). D'Avis (2001: 128) discusses the examples in (2).[1] In (2)a the finite verb occurs in clause-final position, which marks this sentence unambiguously as an exclama-

[1] Small caps signal pitch accents.

tive. In (2)b the finite verb occurs in second position (i.e., in C), which is compatible both with an interpretation as exclamative and as question. Nevertheless, the question interpretation is not available, see (2)c.

(2) a. [$_{\text{CP}}$ Welch einen TOLLEN Mann [$_{\text{TP}}$ die geheiratet hat!]]
welch a fantastic man she married has
b. [$_{\text{CP}}$ Welch einen TOLLEN Mann [$_{\text{C'}}$ hat [$_{\text{TP}}$ die geheiratet t_{hat}!]]]
'What a fantastic man she has married!'
c. #Welch einen tollen Mann hat die geheiratet?
lit.: 'What a fantastic man did she marry?'

In general, the use of *welch* in questions is assumed to be dated, and even in exclamatives it has been claimed to be limited to formal registers (Gallmann 1997). Example (3)a below might be taken to illustrate an exclamative in a formal register, (3)b illustrates the question use of *welch* in literary work by Thomas Mann, i.e., predating 1945 (cited in Zifonun, Hoffmann and Strecker 1997).

(3) a. Welch eine Freude und welch Harmonieempfinden kann eine lichtvolle
welch a joy and welch feeling.of.harmony can a bright
Gruppenmeditation auslösen!
group.mediation trigger
'What joy and what feeling of harmony elated group meditation can spark!'
From a webpage on 'Astrological information exchange on the quality of time in January and February 1999'
b. Welch Unglück sollte den Herrn betroffen haben, seitdem er mich ließ?
welch calamity should the gentleman overcome have since he me left
'What calamity should have overcome that gentleman since he left me?'
From Mann, T.: *Joseph und seine Brüder* (Joseph and his brothers).

Inflected *welchE* has been claimed not to be able to occur in exclamatives and to be restricted to questions. (4) is from Wiltschko (1997: 114). (4) is unacceptable to the extent that it is hard to assign a meaningful interpretation to it as is also reflected in the English translation.

(4) *Welcher Mann!
which man
'Which man!'

In this paper I will show that in contemporary Standard German *welch* is neither generally restricted to formal registers, nor is it restricted to exclamatives. *Welch* also occurs in rhetorical questions. Furthermore, it can occur in ordinary questions but there it is indeed restricted to a non-neutral register, which, however, is not necessarily formal. I will discuss the distribution of *welch* in these two types of questions in section 4. I will also show that *welchE* can occur in exclamatives but that it makes a different meaning contribution than *welch*. Therefore the two *which*-phrases are not interchangeable and they are acceptable in different types of *wh*-exclamatives and in different contexts. The discussion of the distribution of the two *which*-phrases in exclamatives, which I will present in section 3, will show that when looking at *wh*-exclamatives one needs to distinguish between clausal *wh*-exclamatives like those in (2), and what I will call *nominal* wh-*exlamatives* here. (4) is such a nominal *wh*-exclamative: it consists only of the *wh*-phrase and lacks a finite verb. We shall see that this distinction plays a role in the distribution of *welch* vs. *welchE*. The occurrence of *welchE* in nominal *wh*-exclamatives is much more restricted than in clausal *wh*-exclamatives. The reasons are mainly pragmatic. For the semantics of *welchE* I will argue that its overall distribution follows from its d-linking characteristics. For *welch* I propose that it is a degree expression that binds the degree variable of a gradable predicate and introduces a standard degree that needs to be exceeded. This analysis is inspired by earlier proposals for *welch* (Gallmann 1997, D'Avis 2001). Overall I will argue that the most parsimonious analysis of exclamatives in German is probably one that syntactically and semantically takes them to be questions (cf. D'Avis 2001, 2002, Abels 2004). Section 2 will give a general introduction to exclamatives and the issue of exclamative-specific *wh*-phrases. Before I turn to that, however, I will say a few words about the data used for the present investigation.

Some notes on the data

Exclamatives are expressive speech acts that typically are communicated in a context that causes a surprise. Judgements about the acceptability of expressive speech acts sometimes can be very subtle because a lot depends on the ability of the person that judges the acceptability, to imagine themselves in a particular situation that would provide the appropriate emotional context. We shall see plenty of illustration for this in section 3, where I will ask the reader to retrace subtle arguments about particular contexts. With respect to *welch* there is the additional difficulty that it has been described as stylistically marked – belonging to formal registers, or being dated (see above), which might make it less accessible to intuitions. Therefore, the present study uses corpus data as a starting point, where the structures I am interested in occur in context. This makes possible a more systematic investigation of contextual factors and issues of style or rhetoric. Furthermore, potential restrictions on *welch*-phrases to occur only in certain types of speech acts – or the lack of some alleged restrictions – are easier to uncover by the use of a corpus. The data found in the corpus were evaluated with native speaker intuitions, e.g., by deciding what particular speech act type was involved. Furthermore, they formed the basis for the formation of minimal pairs in order to target more specific questions about the use of *welch* or *welchE*. In section 3, where I present the main analysis of the two types of *which* phrases, intuitions about minimal pairs will play an important role. Section 4, where I investigate speech act type restrictions will work primarily with corpus data.

The corpus used in the present study is a part of the German corpus of the *WaCky* project (*deWaC* with 1.7 billion tokens; see http://wacky.sslmit.unibo.it/doku.php for documentation). The *WaCky* project is an automatically collected web-crawled corpus for domains ending in *.de* that was POS-tagged and lemmatized (see Baroni et al. 2009). The part of the German corpus that was used for this research (*deWaC 1*) contains 268.849.871 tokens and was accessed via the corpus query processor (CQP) interface of the corpus linguistics department of the Humboldt-Universität zu Berlin (Anke Lüdeling). The limitation to only a part of the entire German *WaCky* corpus was due to practical reasons. For many issues addressed in this paper, every relevant occurrence in the corpus needed to be examined individually for context, text style, and speech act type. Therefore a limitation of the corpus size was desirable. Furthermore, since the aim of the corpus investigation was not a thorough quantitative investigation a more comprehensive survey was not necessary.

The queries in the corpus were conducted as follows. Clauses starting with *welch* or *welchE* and ending in an exclamation mark were extracted as candidate matrix exclamatives. Clauses starting with *welch* and ending in a question mark were extracted as candidate matrix questions. *WelchE* was not investigated in questions as the occurrence of *welchE* in questions is not debated. The tokens found this way were annotated individually for their 'real' speech act status as judged with native speaker intuitions (see section 4 for discussion). Clauses containing uninflected *welch* in embedded clauses were extracted as well but they were not used for the present investigation.

The set of tokens found this way was further restricted by the following criteria. With respect to the question of formal or dated style, data were annotated according to the text type they occurred in. Literary works predating 1945 were considered stylistically dated. Any text from the bible as well as sermon texts or texts discussing biblical passages or other religious works also counted as stylistically dated (unless they were from academic contexts). The reason is that such texts often adopt the style / register of the topic they discuss. Poetry, fairy tales, fantasy tales and the like, whose date of origin was not obvious, also were grouped in the same category. Any other text type was considered as potentially built on the basis of the competence grammar of a speaker of contemporary Standard German, and thus relevant for the present investigation. Passages written in dialects other than Standard High German were not included in the investigation.

Some tokens were excluded from the investigation for formal reasons: a few data contained some obvious misprint(s), including misplaced punctuation marks in the middle of a sentence, or missing punctuation marks at the end of a sentence – both of which led to a wrong segmentation of text units into sentences –, or the misprints were such that the sentence as a whole did not make sense. Furthermore, when clauses appeared several times in the corpus only one instance was considered. Even though a statistical investigation of the findings was not of interest in the present research, I report below the numbers of occurrences to give a rough illustration of the distribution of the data with respect to individual factors.

2. The semantics and pragmatics of exclamatives

Exclamations are sentences that can be used to express an expressive speech act which signals that the speaker finds a certain state-of-affairs surprising because it violates his or her expectations. Exclamations come in different forms. They can be expressed by declarative sentences or by a variety of other constructions, see (5) for some examples in English. For the non-declarative constructions it is debated whether they are exclamation-specific constructions, i.e., whether there is an exclamative sentence type (cf. Grimshaw 1979), or whether they have the same syntax and/or semantics as other, more 'basic' construction or sentence types. For instance, with respect to *wh*-exclamatives – in different languages – there is a debate as to whether they are derived from, or indeed are interrogatives (Gutiérrez-Rexach 1996, D'Avis 2001, 2002, Zanuttini and Portner 2003, Abels 2005, Roguska

2008), or e.g., free relatives (Rosengren 1997, Rett 2008, see D'Avis 2001 for convincing arguments that *wh*-exclamatives in German cannot be free relatives).

(5)
a. Wow, your apartment is big! — *declarative sentence*
b. What a big apartment you've got! — *wh-exclamative*
c. What a big apartment! — *nominal wh-exclamative*
d. The apartment you've got! — *nominal exclamative*
e. Wow, do YOU have a big apartment! — *polar exclamative*

The idea that *wh*-exclamatives might be derived from interrogatives has been fuelled by the observation that the two sentence types are formally similar in many languages. The most obvious similarity is the occurrence of a *wh*-element. *Wh*-exclamatives can be found e.g., in English, German, Italian (Zanuttini and Portner 2003), Hungarian (Lipták 2006), Icelandic (Jónsson 2010), Swedish (Delsing 2010), Catalan (Castroviejo-Miró 2006), or Japanese (Ono 2006). However, the set of *wh*-elements that occur in interrogatives in many languages does not seem to be the same as the set that can occur in exclamatives. Some languages allow only a subset of the interrogative *wh*-phrases in exclamatives. For instance, English only allows *how* and *what (a)* but not e.g., *who* or *when*. Icelandic also allows only *how* (=*hvernig*) and *what* (=*hvað*; see Jónsson 2010). Italian and Hungarian allow the entire set with the exception of *why* (Zanuttini and Portner 2003, Lipták 2006[2]). German allows all interrogative *wh*-words in exclamatives. This is illustrated in (6). Note that for a *why*-exclamative to be felicitous the main stress must fall on the *wh*-word (on the second syllable)[3]. Any other stress placement would result in a question reading or in unacceptability. In the other *wh*-exclamatives the main stress either falls on the pronominal subject, which must be realized as a strong pronoun, which is a demonstrative pronoun, or the main stress falls on another lexical element in the clause.

(6)

what:
Was	der	gegessen	hat!
what	he.DEM	eaten	has

'The stuff he ate!'

who:
Wen	der	eingeladen	hat!
who.ACC	he.DEM	invited	has

'The people he invited!'

how:
Wie	lang	der	geblieben	ist!
how	long	he.DEM	stayed	is

'How long he stayed!'

when:
Wann	der	gekommen	ist!
when	he.DEM	come	is

'At what time he came!'

where:
Wo	der	hingegangen	ist!
where	he.DEM	went.to	is

'The place he went to!'

what: for:
Was	der	für	ein	Haus	hat!
what	he.DEM	for	a	house	has

'What a house he's got!'

why:
WaRUM	der	gekommen	ist!
why	he.DEM	come	is

'The reason why he came!'

which:
Welchen	Ring	der	ausgesucht	hat!
Which.ACC	ring	he.DEM	chosen	has

'The ring that he has chosen!'

2 Lipták (2006) reports inter-speaker-variability for *miért* ('why') in Hungarian.

3 The position of the stress on *warum* may vary. It is important that it is on the second syllable here.

In many languages there are *wh*-elements that only seem to be allowed in exclamatives. For instance, in English [*what a* ...]$_{DP}$ indicates that the clause it occurs in is an exclamative (e.g., Eliot 1971, 1974, Grimshaw 1979):

(7) a. What a house he lives in! [Grimshaw 1979: 281]
b. *What a house does he live in?

Similarly, Icelandic *hvílíkur* ('what a') seems to be exclamative-specific (Jónsson 2010), as is Italian *che* ('which') if followed by an adjective (Zanuttini and Portner 2003). With respect to uninflected *welch* in German we saw in the introductory section that it seems to be exclamative-specific (and I announced that I would show in section 4 that this is not true). The relevant example was example (2), repeated below for convenience:

(8)	a.	[$_{CP}$ Welch	einen	TOLLEN	Mann	[$_{TP}$ die	geheiratet	hat!]]
		welch	a	fantastic	man	she	married	has
	b.	[$_{CP}$ Welch	einen	TOLLEN	Mann	[$_{C'}$ hat	[die	geheiratet t_{hat}!]]]
	c.	#Welch	einen	tollen	Mann	hat	die	geheiratet?

If exclamatives and interrogatives do not allow the same *wh*-phrases an account that assumes that exclamatives are, or are derived from interrogatives, needs to explain why there are exclamative-specific *wh*-phrases, and, conversely, why there are *wh*-phrases that can occur in interrogatives but not in exclamatives. With respect to the first question, D'Avis (2001), who argues that exclamatives in German syntactically and semantically are interrogatives, gives the following reason for the inappropriateness of cases like (8)c. He assumes that *welch* is a degree phrase DegP that occurs in the specifier position of the DP it occurs in (cf. Gallmann 1997). From there it takes scope over a gradable element in the NP complement. It comes with the presupposition that the gradable property (*toll* 'fantastic' in (8)) applies with a high degree. It is this presupposition that renders (8)c on the question interpretation infelicitous. (8)c asks to what degree the man that the woman married was fantastic and at the same time presupposes that that man was fantastic to a high degree. So it presupposes its answer. This is not compatible with the speaker ignorance normally associated with questions.[4] The same reasoning applies to the restriction of so-called *intensifiers* to exclamatives: *very* in *how very,* or the corresponding modifiers in *how incredibly tall*, *how enormously hungry* are not felicitous in questions as the following English examples illustrate (e.g., Eliot 1974, Grimshaw 1979):

(9) a. How very tall he is!
b. *How very tall is he?

(9) asks how tall *he* is and presupposes that he is *very* tall.

In section 3 we shall see that the semantics D'Avis (2001) suggests for *welch* matches the data from the corpus well. I will give a precise formal definition of *welch*, which will help us understand its specific meaning contribution, and which will set it apart from *welchE* but

[4] See Zanuttini and Portner (2003) for another account of exclamatives that works with the idea that exclamatives presuppose their content. See Rett (2008, 2011) for arguments against presuppositional accounts and see Abels (2010) for arguments against Rett's arguments.

also from *was für*, which, as we saw in the introduction, has been argued to be synonymous with *welch*.

With respect to the second question, viz., why some languages do not allow the full set of interrogative *wh*-phrases in *wh*-exclamatives, we need to dwell a bit longer on the issue of degrees. Most examples that I have discussed in this section involve gradable predicates: *big, tall, fantastic* (*toll* in German). As a matter of fact, it has been claimed that exclamatives – as opposed to declaratives serving as exclamations – in general make direct reference to degrees.[5] For instance, Castroviejo Miró (2006) suggests for Catalan that *wh*-exclamatives are special degree constructions. Rett (2008, 2011) suggests for English that when using an exclamative the speaker expresses that s/he expected a gradable property to be instantiated up to a particular degree, which is exceeded by the actual degree. Exclamations expressed by declaratives, in contrast, are not subject to such a degree restriction. This difference is illustrated in (10), adapted from Rett (2011: 430):

(10) a. (Wow), John arrived early!
b. How early John arrived!

(10)a is felicitous if the speaker expected that John would not arrive early and if John arrived early but not necessarily very early. For (10)b to be felicitous John must have arrived earlier than the expected degree of earliness.

Rett (2008, 2011) suggests that the degree restriction is a general characteristic of exclamatives cross-linguistically (although she focuses on English). She says that exclamatives are only acceptable with *wh*-phrases that range over degrees but not with *wh*-phrases that range over individuals or times etc. For English this seems to be correct. As we saw above, English *wh*-exclamatives only allow *how*, and *what a*, the latter receiving a degree interpretation (also see Sæbø 2010 for a proposal for the semantics of these two items). As for the semantics of the exclamative clause one can draw different conclusions from these observations. Rett (2008, 2011) suggests that exclamatives denote degree properties whereas exclamatory declaratives denote a proposition. The degree property is derived via the semantics of the *wh*-phrase ranging over degrees.[6]

Now, I showed above that German (contrary to some earlier claims) has no restrictions with respect to the kind of *wh*-phrase that can occur in an exclamative. We could explain this difference between English and German by assuming that in German, exclamatives are not degree properties but other semantic objects, e.g., sets of true propositions, like interrogatives, as proposed by D'Avis (2001, 2002) or Zanuttini and Portner (2003).[7] The degree

5 D'Avis (2002) discusses degree and non-degree readings of exclamatives. I do not look at his proposal here because it deals with embedded exclamatives. Whether or not embedded exclamatives exist is a highly controversial issue (cf. e.g., Eliot 1974, Grimshaw 1979, Huddleston 1993, Abels 2005, Rett 2011).

6 Rett's claim that exclamatives denote degree properties actually includes polar interrogatives and nominal interrogatives. Therefore she proposes that there must be a silent degree operator that occurs in these constructions.

7 Sæbø (2010) suggests for embedded exclamatives in English that the degree characteristic is part of the denotation of the *wh*-word but that the *wh*-exclamative itself just like interrogatives assigns to any world a true proposition.

restriction – assuming that it holds for German – could be encoded in the speech act operator, or in some other operator in the clause. For instance, Zanuttini and Portner (2003) assume a special widening operator, which introduces scalarity. D'Avis (2001) is not explicit about the formal side of the semantics-pragmatics interface but he says that the true proposition – which reflects the state of affairs that the speaker is surprised at – and the expected proposition are ordered on a scale such that the true proposition is ordered at a distance from the expected proposition and that the size of distance reflects the strength of the deviation from the expected proposition.

I will assume here that *wh*-exclamatives in German denote sets of true propositions but I will leave open the question of how precisely the semantics-pragmatics interface works. For simplicity I will assume that there is a speech act operator that contributes the degree characteristic that has been observed for *wh*-exclamatives. I take this to be a more parsimonious approach than for instance the assumption that all interrogative *wh*-phrases in German have a sibling that ranges over degrees and therefore might occur in exclamatives. Thus, I propose that the *wh*-phrases that occur in interrogatives have the same semantics as those that occur in exclamatives. This has the nice consequence that we expect certain characteristics of *wh*-phrases, such as the d-linking characteristic of *which/welchE*-phrases, to have comparable effects in interrogatives and exclamatives. I will show in section 3 this is exactly what we find.

The assumption that German exclamatives are (derived from) interrogatives whereas English exclamatives possibly are not also receives some indirect support from the syntax of exclamatives vs. interrogatives in English vs. German. In English interrogatives there is T-to-C movement whereas in exclamatives there is not:

(11) a. [$_{CP}$ How long [$_{TP}$ this train journey could take!]]
b. [$_{CP}$ How long [$_{C'}$ could [$_{TP}$ this train journey t_{could} take?]]]
c. *[$_{CP}$ How long [$_{TP}$ this train journey could take?]]
d. *[$_{CP}$ How long [$_{C'}$ could [$_{TP}$ this train journey t_{could} take!]]]

As already mentioned above, in German exclamatives there can be T-to-C movement or not. (12) illustrates with an example that is parallel to the English example above.

(12)	a.	[$_{CP}$ Wie	lange		[$_{TP}$ diese	Zugreise	dauern	könnte!]]
		how	long		this	train.journey	take	could
	b.	[$_{CP}$ Wie	lange	[$_{C'}$ könnte	[$_{TP}$ diese	Zugreise	dauern	$t_{könnte}$!]]]

Note that most native speakers when asked about the preferred word order for *wh*-exclamatives in German would probably go for the variant without T-to-C movement. We will see below, though, that at least for *welch*-exclamatives this preference is not at all reflected in the corpus data. Considering that matrix interrogatives in German always have T-to-C movement (embedded interrogatives do not) the assumption that German exclamatives might be closer to interrogatives than their English counterparts is at least not implausible. With this much in hand let us now turn to *welch* and *welchE* in German exclamatives.

3. *Welch* and *welchE* in exclamatives

I begin this section with a rough description of the distribution of *welch/welchE*-exclamatives that we find in the corpus. Recall that the corpus query was for sentences with clause-initial *welch/welchE* ending in an exclamation mark.

3.1. Brief overview over the data

There are around 290 occurrences of stylistically unmarked sentences with *welch* (1.12 per million words) in the corpus. 90 per cent of these are nominal *wh*-exclamatives, i.e., they just consist of a *wh*-phrase and do not contain a finite verb. An illustration is given in (13). Some of these occurrences (*n* = 20) contain formulaic expressions like *Welch ein Glück!* ('what luck') that are followed by a complement sentence, see (14).

(13) Welch ein Stress für den Marder!
welch a stress for the marten
'How stressful for the marten!'

(14) Welch ein Glück, dass wir Sternschnuppen nicht fangen können!
welch a luck that we shooting.stars not catch can
'How lucky we are that we can't catch shooting stars!'

An example of a clausal *wh*-exclamative from the corpus is the following:

(15) Context: Speaker points out that handicapped people often do not feel accepted by their parents.
Welch katastrophale Auswirkungen das auf das Selbstbild dieser
welch disastrous effects that on the self-perception these.GEN
Menschen haben muss!
people have must
'What disastrous effects this must have on the self-perception of these people!'
http://www.familienhandbuch.de/cmain/f_Aktuelles/a_Behinderung/s_499.html

Stylistically marked texts yield another 140 occurrences of *welch*. Interestingly, only 60 per cent of these are nominal (as opposed to 90 per cent in stylistically unmarked texts, see above), which seems to suggest that the use of *welch* in contemporary Standard German is receding to the nominal domain. In what follows I will not report on stylistically marked texts anymore.

Of the 29 clausal *wh*-exclamatives, 27 have T-to-C movement. This is quite surprising considering that verb-final exclamatives often are considered more prototypical exclamatives (see previous section). For reasons of space I did not include *wh*-exclamatives with *welch ein* in my investigation. I give some descriptive statistics here but will not have to say more about them in this paper. In 65 per cent of the *welch*-exclamatives, *welch* is followed by the determiner *ein*. The other occurrences are combinations of *welch* with a bare noun (9 per cent), or *welch* with at least one prenominal modifier and a noun (26 per cent). Curiously, none of the *welch ein* occurrences contains a prenominal modifier.[8] For the time being I take *ein* in *welch ein* to be a spurious determiner and leave this issue for future research.

As for *welchE*-exclamatives, the number of occurrences is much lower than for *welch*-exclamatives: 47 vs. 290. 72 per cent of them are nominal. 23 per cent involve prenominal modifiers. These numbers confirm the assumption made above on the basis of intuitions that *welchE* can occur in exclamatives. We also see, however, that *welch* seems to be much more frequent than *welchE*. I suggest that this has two reasons. One is that *welch* makes reference to degrees, which is a hallmark of exclamatives (see above). The other is that *welchE*-phrases are d-linked, which imposes restrictions on the discourse context that will rarely be met. In what follows I argue in detail for both of these assumptions.

3.2. Degrees: *Welch*

All the examples presented in the previous subsection express that some property applies to a high degree. (13) expresses that the situation was very stressful for a contextually salient or a generic marten, (14) expresses that it is very lucky that we cannot catch shooting stars, and (15) expresses that the effects of parental rejection on handicapped people would be very disastrous. The question we need to ask here is whether these degree interpretations are due to the presence of *welch* or whether they are a consequence of these sentences being *wh*-exclamatives, which generally express surprise at a degree.

Observe that at least in (15) above, and probably also in (13) and (14) *welch (ein)* can be replaced by a form of *welchE* without a reduction in acceptability,[9] albeit with a slight change in meaning (which I will discuss below).[10] Importantly, there are cases where *welch* cannot be felicitously substituted by *welchE* at all. In (16) below *welch* occurs in a *nominal* wh-*exclamative* with a modifying adjective. *Welch* seems to have the function of a degree modifier, i.e., the sentence expresses that the mistake was very serious indeed. If *welch* is replaced by *welchE*, as illustrated in (16)B', this meaning is no longer available, and the exclamative is clearly degraded.

(16) From a travel report:
A: Mit gefüllten Vorräten strebten wir nun zum Rimet-Kloster. Uns auf die RV-Autokarte verlassend, wollten wir auf einer Nebenstraße quer durchs Gebirge abkürzen.
'With plenty of provisions we were now aiming for the Rimet Monastery. Relying on the RV road map we decided to take a shortcut on a byroad across the mountains.'

B: Welch	schwerer	Irrtum!	B': ??Welcher	schwere	Irrtum!
welch	serious	mistake	welch.MASC.SING	serious	mistake
'What a serious mistake!'					

---

[8] A quick search for *Was für ein* in clause-initial position (no control of tokens for style, typos etc.), yielded 630 occurrences. 27 per cent of these occurrences were followed by a prenominal modifier. See section 3 for a short comment on *was für ein*.

[9] Recall that this requires an adaptation of the inflection on the adjective.

[10] (15) is different from the other two examples. I will say more about this at the end of this section.

There are many examples like (16)A–B in the corpus, i.e., examples where the original corpus token with *welch* in a nominal *wh*-exclamative cannot be replaced by a version with *welchE* because that would lead to unacceptability. What they all have in common is that the exclamative expresses that the property denoted by the gradable adjective applies to a very high degree. It seems that this meaning cannot be expressed with inflected *welchE*.

Let us assume that nominal *wh*-exclamatives are elliptic copula sentences.[11] So (16)B essentially correspond to (17). There is a salient entity referred to by *das* ('that'/'it'), and that entity is assigned a property. Thus (17) is essentially a predicational copula sentence.

(17) Welch schwerer Irrtum das war!
welch serious mistake that was!
'What a serious mistake this was!'

Let us further assume that *welch* is indeed a degree operator, which combines with gradable properties, and existentially binds their degree variable such that there is a degree that applies to this property which is higher than the standard degree for that property. I assume that *welch* directly combines with the gradable property, and that there is no positive morpheme 'between' the property and *welch*. The meaning contribution of the positive morpheme in the case of gradable properties is usually taken to be that the degree is equal to or exceeds the standard, i.e., it relates the degree argument of the gradable property to an appropriate standard of comparison (cf. Cresswell 1977, Stechow 1984, Bierwisch 1989, Kennedy 1999). I suggest that this meaning contribution is part of the meaning of *welch* with the difference that the degree cannot be equal to but must exceed the standard by a significant amount, see (18).

(18) $[\![welch]\!] = \lambda g_{\langle d,t\rangle} \exists d[g(d) \wedge d > s_w]$

The denotation of (17) is derived in (19). Simplifying somewhat, I assume that *Irrtum* ('mistake') is a gradable noun that allows a degree reading.[12] For mistakes we can assume that it

---

[11] They could also be fragments, if we take these to be instances of semantic ellipsis (cf. Stainton 2006, and especially Merchant 2010). As far as I can see nothing hinges on this choice.

[12] *Schwerer Irrtum* ('serious mistake', lit. *grave error*) patterns in some respects with gradable nouns that are modified by a size adjective. For instance, the latter can receive a non-size degree reading with the adjective in attributive position but not in predicative position, see (i) (Morzycki 2009). *Schwerer Irrtum* is only possible with an attributive adjective, see (ii):

(i) a. that big idiot (= the degree of idiocy in that person is high)
b. that idiot is big (≠ the degree of idiocy in that person is high)

(ii) a. dieser schwere Irrtum
this grave error
b. *dieser Irrtum ist schwer
this error is grave

On the other hand, *schwerer Irrtum* is not restricted to 'large' measures the way size degree readings are:

(iii) %that small idiot (≠ the degree of idiocy in that person is low)

(iv) dieser leichte Irrtum
this light error

is the seriousness e.g., in terms of consequences, that is the scale at issue. Therefore I assume that the adjective *schwer* ('serious') in this example modifies the degree of the noun rather than contributing its own scale. I assume that *serious* in the present context is similar to *very*, it increases the degree of seriousness of the mistake by a certain amount *m*. The contribution of *welch* is that the degree of seriousness of the mistake is required to be above the standard degree for seriousness of mistakes (plus the additional measure *m* contributed by the modifying adjective in the phrase). I am assuming here that the *welch*-DP, which occurs in the specifier of CP in overt syntax is partially reconstructed at Logical Form: the restrictor of *welch* is interpreted in situ. *Welch* itself leaves a trace of type *d*. The trace is lambda-bound via lambda-abstraction just below moved *welch*. The denotation of the copula captures the idea that we are dealing with a predicational copula sentence here.

(19) Welch schwerer Irrtum das war!
welch serious mistake that was
'What a serious mistake!'

$[\![\text{mistake}]\!] = \lambda d\lambda x[\text{mistake}_{w'}(d)(x)]$

$[\![\text{serious}]\!] = \lambda g_{\langle d,\langle e,t\rangle\rangle}\lambda d\lambda x[g(d+m)(x)]$, where *m* is a measure unit on the scale for *g* that is substantially greater than 0

$[\![\text{serious mistake}]\!] = \lambda d\lambda x[\text{mistake}_{w'}(d+m)(x)]$

$[\![\text{t1}_d \text{ serious mistake}]\!]$
$= \lambda x[\text{mistake}_{w'}(d_1+m)(x)]$

$[\![\text{is}]\!] = \lambda P\lambda x[P_{w'}(x)]$

$[\![\text{t1}_d \text{ serious mistake is}]\!]$
$= \lambda x[\text{mistake}_{w'}(d_1+m)(x)]$

$[\![\text{that t1}_d \text{ serious mistake is}]\!]$
$= [\text{mistake}_{w'}(d_1+m)(\iota x.\mathrm{S_{ali}E_{nt}}(x))]$

$[\![\text{Q that t1}_d \text{ serious mistake is}]\!]$
$= [p(w) \wedge p = \lambda w'[\text{mistake}_{w'}(d_1+m)(\iota x.\mathrm{S_{ali}E_{nt}}(x))]]$[13]

$[\![\text{1 Q that t1}_d \text{ serious mistake is}]\!]$
$= \lambda d_1[p(w) \wedge p = \lambda w'[\text{mistake}_{w'}(d_1+m)(\iota x.\mathrm{S_{ali}E_{nt}}(x))]]$

$[\![\text{welch 1 Q that t1}_d \text{ serious mistake is}]\!]$
$= \lambda p\exists d[p(w)$
$\wedge\, p = \lambda w'[\text{mistake}_{w'}(d_1+m)(\iota x.\mathrm{S_{ali}E_{nt}}(x))] \wedge d > s_w]$

It should be noted that not all nouns in *welch*-exclamatives are gradable. Here is an example with a non-gradable noun and a gradable adjective:

Morzycki discusses cases with size adjectives which also show a mixed pattern as 'significance' readings. Since these are not well-understood I will just assume a degree reading here. Nothing hinges on this choice.

13 I am following Beck's (1996) abbreviated notation with lambda-abstraction at the CP level here so that $[\![Q]\!] = \lambda q[p(w) \wedge p = q]$, rather than $\lambda q\lambda p[p(w) \wedge p = q]$. This saves us type adjustment of the *wh*-phrase.

(20) Welch kindische Polemik!
welch childish polemic
'What childish polemic!'

In (20) the degree argument that *welch* binds is delivered by the adjective. Yet there need not be any gradable expression at all. Here is an example from the corpus:

(21) So stapfen wir fast nackt unter unseren Regenumhängen in das Café. Das Gefühl von eiskaltem feuchtem Nylonstoff auf nackter Haut werde ich nicht so schnell vergessen, einfach nur pervers. Zum Glück habe ich als einzige ein paar Schilling eingesteckt, es dürfte für 4 Getränke reichen.
'Half-naked under our rain capes we trudge into the café. I won't forget the feel of ice-cold moist nylon on my naked skin. Wicked. Luckily, I've got some shillings on me. I'm the only one. It should be enough for four drinks.'

Welch Auftritt im Café!
welch entrance in.the café
'What an entrance we had in the café!'

Wir lassen notgedrungen unsere Umhänge an, unten schauen nasse haarige Beine in Badeschlappen oder Gummistiefeln raus, oben sind es die nassen verwuschelten Köpfe ...
'We're forced to leave our capes on, at the bottom wet hairy legs with feet in shower sandals or wellingtons are showing, at the top wet tousled heads ...'

From the *Explorer Magazin*
http://www.explorermagazin.de/landck98/landeck.htm

I suggest that in cases like this there is a silent adjective that introduces a degree variable which later can be bound by *welch* (cf. Castroviejo Miró 2006 for a similar suggestion for exclamatives in Catalan, also cf. Rett 2011).[14] The scale that is relevant here is one of unusualness or remarkableness.

There is a piece of evidence in favour of the degree analysis of *welch* which relates to a close relative of *welch*: *was für* (lit. 'what for', corresponding to 'what' or 'what kind of' in prenominal position). In the introduction I mentioned that *welch (ein)* often is thought to be synonymous with *was für*, see e.g., Gallmann (1997), Leu (2008). And indeed, if one replaces *welch (ein)* by *was für (ein)* the result usually is felicitous. I verified this for many of the corpus data, (22) illustrates:

(22) Was für ein schwerer Irrtum!
what for a serious mistake
'What a serious mistake!'

14 With respect to an analysis of English *what a*, Sæbø (2010) argues against the presence of a silent adjective. He suggests that the covert adjective would have to be uniquely determined by the noun and thus would not add information so it is more parsimonious to assume that nouns in general are measure functions that combine with a positive to yield an individual property. I am not sure, however, that the degree and the scale associated with the degree are indeed determined by the noun. The choice of scale can be rather flexible, depending on the context. For an entrance in a café, for instance, the scale can be one of degrees of glamour, or e.g., ridicule.

Nevertheless, there are some interesting differences that suggest that *welch* has a different semantics from *was für*. (23) illustrates that *was für* can combine with numerals whereas *welch* cannot.

(23) a. Welch (*zwei) (ungeheure) Missverständnisse!
welch two tremendous misunderstandings
b. Was für (zwei) (ungeheure) Missverständnisse!
'What (tremendous) misunderstandings (these two cases were)!'

With the analysis of *welch* that I suggested it is expected that (23)a is not felicitous. *Welch* needs to combine with a degree property whose argument it binds. In (23)a, that argument is already bound by the positive morpheme that we must assume is present: the numeral cannot combine with a degree property but only with an individual property. Hence, the positive morpheme binds the degree variable of *enormous misunderstandings* and delivers an individual property. This is the right input for *was für* later in the derivation but not for *welch*. I take this to be further evidence for the analysis of *welch* as a degree operator. The above data also suggest that *was für* is different from *welch*. I assume that it asks for properties (Beck 1999, Leu 2008) or kinds (Beck 1999).

To sum up so far, with the above semantics of *welch* we may assume that in *welch*-exclamatives the degree at which the speaker expresses surprise is a degree located above the standard degree on a scale for a particular property that a particular entity has. Let us now turn to inflected *welchE*.

3.3. D-linking: *welchE*

I assume that *welchE* is a determiner that does not combine with degree properties. *WelchE* is a generalized quantifier that combines with individual properties. Furthermore I assume with much previous literature that *welchE*-phrases are d-linked. I propose that this is independent of whether a *welchE*-phrase occurs in an interrogative or in an exclamative. *Welch*-phrases, in contrast, I take to be not d-linked. D-linking is a concept that was first introduced by Kuroda (1968), and that was elaborated on under the term *d-linking* by Pesetsky (1987). For questions with d-linked phrases it is assumed that the answer to the question is 'supposed to be drawn from a set of individuals previously introduced into the discourse, or ... part of the "common ground" shared by speaker and hearer' (Pesetsky 2000:16). Comorosvki (1996) suggests that *which* is like an inherently partitive determiner, where the common noun CN that follows it denotes a given subset of Ns in the model. *Which*-phrases can be used felicitously if the interlocutors partition the set that *which* takes as an argument in the same way. We shall see further below that in exclamatives there actually seems to be a difference between ordinary *welchE*-phrases and overtly partitive *welchE*-phrases (see the discussion around example (33)).

If we take exclamatives to share the syntax and semantics of interrogatives, and if we assume that the *wh*-words in both constructions are the same we expect d-linking to play a role in exclamatives. (24) is the clausal variant of the nominal *wh*-exclamative in (16)B'. The translation for (24) reflects the interpretation of the *welchE* phrase as d-linked.

(24) ??Welcher schwere Irrtum das war!
which.MASC.SING serious mistake that was
lit.: 'Which serious mistake that was!'

Now, if we consider what is intuitively wrong with (24) we find that – if anything at all – it seems to express that out of a set of serious mistakes the speaker is surprised at a particular serious mistake. So in the case of *welchE*, the scale that the speaker makes reference to here is not one of degrees of seriousness of a mistake but a scale of different serious mistakes, which might be ordered according to a totally different criterion, and thus on a different scale, such as a scale of frequency of occurrence. There might be contexts where such a scale is contextually supported, and we shall see below that one can accommodate such contexts for other sentence structures than copula sentences to some extent. In the current example, however, the context does not support such a scale.

Note that due to *welchE* singling out (an) individual(s) the copula sentence is a specificational rather than a predicative sentence, as it was in the case of *welch*. It picks out one referent among a set of scalar alternatives and expresses the speaker's surprise at the fact that this referent is the one that is identical to the salient referent. If we look at other specificational copula sentences that prima facie should be felicitous as exclamatives we find that they are just as infelicitous as *welchE*-sentences. This is illustrated in (25) and (26). Non-copula *wh*-exclamatives with a form of *who* are fine in German, see (25)b, whereas (specificational) copula *wh*-exclamatives with *who* are not, see (26)b. (25)a and (26)a show that the corresponding questions are felicitous.

(25) a. Wer ist heute gekommen?
who is today come
'Who came today?'

b. Wer heute gekommen ist!
who today come is
'The person/people that came today!'

(26) a. Wer ist der Sportlehrer?
who is the sports.teacher
'Who is the sports teacher?'

b. *Wer der Sportlehrer ist!
who the sports.teacher is
'The person that is the sports teacher!'

On the basis of these observations I suggest that *welche* has the generalized quantifier denotation in (27) and that the denotation of the specificational copula sentence in (24) is derived as in (28). Note that there is a silent morpheme [pos] here that binds the degree argument of the gradable adjective. Further note that in contrast to the *welch*-phrase the *welchE*-phrase is not predicated of the salient individual. Rather, the copula marks that the two entities are identical. Another difference with the *welch*-case is that there is no reconstruction here.

(27) $[\![welchE]\!] = \lambda P \lambda Q \exists x [P_w(x) \wedge Q_w(x)]$

(28) ??Welcher schwere Irrtum das war!
which.MASC.SING serious mistake that was
lit.: 'Which serious mistake that was!'

$[\![$ serious mistake $]\!]$ $= \lambda d\lambda x[\text{mistake}_w(d+m)(x)]$
$[\![$ *pos* $]\!]$ $= \lambda g_{\langle d,\langle e,t\rangle\rangle}\lambda x\exists d[g(d)(x) \wedge d \geq s_w]$
$[\![$ *pos* serious mistake $]\!]$ $= \lambda x\exists d[\text{mistake}_w(d+m)(x) \wedge d \geq s_w]$
$[\![$ *welchE pos* serious mistake $]\!]$
$= \lambda Q\exists x.\exists d[\text{mistake}_w(d+m)(x) \wedge d \geq s_w] \wedge Q_w(x)$
$[\![$ t1$_e$ $]\!]$ $= x_1$
$[\![$ is$_{spec}$ $]\!]$ $= \lambda x\lambda y[y = x]$
$[\![$ t1$_e$is$_{spec}$ $]\!]$ $= \lambda y[y = x_1]$
$[\![$ that t1$_e$ is $]\!]$ $= [\iota x.\text{S}_{\text{ali}}\text{E}_{\text{nt}}(x) = x_1]$
$[\![$ Q that t1$_e$ is $]\!]$ $= [p(w) \wedge p = \lambda w'[\iota x.\text{S}_{\text{ali}}\text{E}_{\text{nt}}(x) = x_1]]$
$[\![$ 1 that t1$_e$ is $]\!]$ $= \lambda x_1[p(w) \wedge p = \lambda w'[\iota x.\text{S}_{\text{ali}}\text{E}_{\text{nt}}(x) = x_1]]$
$[\![$ *welcheE pos* serious mistake 1 Q that t1$_e$ is $]\!]$
$= \lambda p[\exists x.[\exists d[\text{mistake}_w(d+m)(x) \wedge d \geq s_w$
$\wedge\, p(w) \wedge p = \lambda w'[\iota x'.\text{S}_{\text{ali}}\text{E}_{\text{nt}}(x') = x]]]$

Thus, whereas *welch* ranges over degrees *welchE* ranges over individuals. This has different consequences for the use of the set of propositions denoted by the respective sentence as exclamative. If we assume that exclamatives make use of scalar alternatives (see above), we may assume that the alternatives introduced by the *wh*-phrase seem to be first-choice candidates for scalar alternatives.[15] Since uninflected *welch* is a degree function that combines with gradable properties the scalar alternatives are provided as part of the semantics of the exclamative. In exclamatives with *welchE*, in contrast, a scale has to be accommodated: individuals are not normally ordered along a scale. The success of accommodation is context-dependent. In the example we discussed above, there was no scale that suggested itself for the ordering of the set of individuals provided by the restrictor of the *welchE*-phrase.

That it is indeed the restriction on the set of individuals that plays a role in the accommodation process is supported by a variant of the above example. (29) illustrates that it is felicitous both with *welch* and with *welchE* if there is no modifying adjective.

(29) a. Welch Irrtum!
welch mistake
'What a mistake!'

b. Welcher Irrtum!
welch.MASC.SING mistake
'What a mistake!'

There is a subtle semantic difference between (29)a and (29)b. I suggest that this difference is due to the quantification over degrees vs. individuals. Now, as I said, (29)b is much better than (28). I suggest that this is because it is easier to accommodate a scale on which mistakes can be ordered than it is to accommodate a scale on which serious mistakes can be ordered. As a matter of fact, the scale on which we order mistakes can be one of seriousness, but it is hard to come up with a plausible context where a particular serious mistake would stand out from other serious mistakes. Without the restriction to seriousness the choice of scale is wider. Example (21) from above (*What an entrance we had in the café!*) also supports the role of the restriction. In (21) there is a post-nominal modifier (*in the café*).

[15] I am abstracting away from focus here but see example (32) for a case where there are also focus-induced alternatives.

Welch cannot be replaced by *welchE* in this example. Leaving out the modifier, however, results in an acceptable *welchE*-exclamative.

So far the data seem to pattern according to the proposed analysis. However, there are some data that prima facie are problematic. On the basis of example (4) in the introduction, which is repeated below as (30), Wiltschko (1999) claims that inflected *welchE* cannot occur in exclamatives. We already know that this is false. Still, the judgement in (30) seems sound. So why is (30) not acceptable whereas (29)b, which seems completely parallel, is fine? We should note here that the variant with uninflected *welch* is quite good (although the variant with *was für* might be preferred): when uttering *Welch Mann!* the speaker expresses his/her surprise at, say, the degree of manliness in a person, or some other easy-to-accommodate scale, depending on the context.

(30) *Welcher Mann!
which man
Intended: 'What a man!'

Now, (30) is not a single odd-ball. Other expressions that are used to refer to humans in a non-expressive way do not seem to be able to combine with *welchE* either: **Welcher Junge!* ('boy'), **Welcher Bürgermeister!* ('mayor'), **Welcher Polizist!* ('policeman') etc. In the corpus there are no instances of *welchE* with human referents, except with expressive pejorative descriptions like *Lumpenpack* ('riffraff'). This reminds us of the *who*-data in (25) and (26) above, were we found that *wh*-exclamatives in the form of specificational copula sentences are impossible if the *wh*-word is *who*. Upon closer scrutiny it turns out that it is not just human referents with a non-expressive description that are problematic. Of the 47 *welchE*-exclamatives in the corpus none has a *welchE*-restrictor that is a set of concrete entities, in the sense of 'tangible objects in the real world'. And indeed exclamatives with inanimate concrete entities such as **Welches Buch!* ('book') or **Welcher Tisch!* ('table') are distinctly odd, too.

Interestingly, if we place *welchE*-phrases with the above type of restrictor in a clausal *wh*-exclamative the result seems to be quite acceptable:

(31) Welches Buch der gelesen hat!
which book he.DEM read has
'The book he read!'

This suggests that the acceptability judgements really depend on the availability of an easy-to-accommodate context. In (31) it is quite easy to accommodate a context where one out of a set of books was unexpected to be read by the referent of *der* ('he') – say, because it is the kind of book the speaker him- or herself would never read. This is different from expressing surprise at the identity of entities in a nominal/specificational copula-*wh*-exclamative. As a matter of fact, even for the *welchE*- phrase in example (30) above, which was particularly bad, we find that it can be felicitous in a clausal exclamative. In (32) we have a juxtaposition of two men and their respective roles in relation to a woman. The speaker is surprised at the allocation of roles.

(32) Welchen Mann sie am Ende geHEIratet hat
which man she at.the end married has
und welchen Mann sie als LIEBhaber genommen hat!
and which man she as lover taken has
Roughly: 'That she married THAT man, and took THAT man as lover!'

Note that this example also shows that exclamatives are not information-structurally inert as is sometimes assumed (cf. Altmann 1993). The accents here indicate the focus in each of the two sentences, and they are the respective main accents, i.e., the so-called *exclamative accents*. The exclamative accents could not be anywhere else in this example.

Another data point I would like to discuss in this section on *welchE* are partitive *wh*-phrases. I mentioned above that d-linking sometimes is seen as a function of partitivity (Comorovski 1996). For d-linked phrases speaker and hearer are able to partition the set of individuals into the same parts. Now, we observed above that *welchE*-phrases in exclamatives usually deteriorate when they are modified by an adjective or a post-nominal modifier. I suggested that this is due to the additional restriction of the set of individuals, which tends to lead to the difficulty that no scale can be established for the individuals in the set. Example (33) below illustrates that a clausal *wh*-exclamative with a partitive *wh*-phrase can be acceptable even if an exclamative with an equivalent non-partitive *wh*-phrase is not.

(33) a. Welchen Hausmeister der eingestellt hat!
b. ??Welchen faulen Hausmeister der eingestellt hat!
c. Welchen von den faulen Hausmeistern der eingestellt hat!
which of the lazy janitor(s) he.DEM hired has
a.: 'Of all the janitors, he hired that one!'
b. lit.: 'Which janitor he hired!'
c.. 'Of all the lazy janitors, he hired THAT one!'

These data suggest that the overt marking of partitivity has an effect beyond d-linking. Intuitively, the difference between (33)b and (33)c is that (c) refers to a particular set of lazy janitors, whereas (b) refers to lazy janitors in general. The contextual restriction is made explicit in the partitive so it easier to locate the use of the exclamative in a real situation (i.e., to accommodate the context).

Let us finally turn to a class of *wh*-exclamatives that do not fit the described generalization. One such case is example (15) from the very beginning of this section, which I repeat below as (34) for convenience:

(34) Welch katastrophale Auswirkungen das auf das Selbstbild dieser
welch disastrous effects that on the self-perception these.GEN
Menschen haben muss!
people have must
'What disastrous effects this must have on the self-perception of these people!'

When I introduced this example I said that *welch* can be replaced by *welchE* here. Observe that (34) contains a prenominal modifier in its restrictor so we should expect it to be quite degraded. On the other hand, we are not dealing with a nominal *wh*-exclamative here. Also note, however, that there is one further characteristic of (34) which might produce the greater acceptability: the *wh*-phrase is a plural phrase. It might well be the case that this saves this particular example. However, whether this is a semantic effect or a formal effect is not so clear. Let me explain what I mean by this.

I conducted a corpus search for inflected *welchE* in exclamatives followed by an adjective, i.e., cases like (16)B' (??*Welcher schwere Irrtum!* 'Which serious error!'). There is a small number of such cases in the corpus ($n = 6$), and they do not all involve plural. According to elicited judgements, they are acceptable and not some performance errors. Here is an example:

(35) In diesem Moment erwachte in ihm der Wunsch, so erklärt es Freud, die dreibeinige Gangart zu überspringen und in die einbeinige Gangart des Ruhmes zu wechseln. Statt der sexuellen Neugierde nachzugeben, die wissenschaftliche Neugierde auf das Rätsel der Sexualität zu richten. Welche Verstrickung!
'Freud says that at that moment the wish arose in him to skip the three-legged way of walking and to move on to the one-legged gait of fame. Instead of giving in to sexual curiosity, directing scientific curiosity towards the mystery of sexuality. What a tangle!'

Welche rätselhafte Verklammerung von Kindlichkeit und reifer Wissenschaft!
which mysterious entanglement of childlikeness and mature science!
'What a mysterious entanglement of childlikeness and mature science!'

Und doch muss es für den Knaben ein schwerer Entschluss gewesen sein ...
'And yet, it must have been a hard decision for the boy...'

From *Berliner Blätter für Psychoanalyse und Psychotherapie* (Berlin Gazette for Psychoanalysis and Psychotherapy).

An investigation of the semantic and pragmatic characteristics of these corpus examples did not yield a straightforward generalization. However, there is a morphological feature they share: all of these cases involve singular feminine nouns or plural nouns. The suffix on *welchE* in all these cases is the one that phonetically is the least salient: [ə] vs. [ɐ]/[ən]/[əm]/[əs]. Considering that *welch* is receding we might speculate that *welchE* is taking on the semantics of *welch* and that this transition starts with the form that phonetically is least different from *welch*. So this semantically arbitrary (at least for the singular) but formally probably motivated difference might be a consequence of the *welch-welchE* paradigms being in flux. This needs closer scrutiny.

4. *Welch* in questions

In this section I will show that uninflected *welch* can occur in other speech acts than exclamations. Thus, *welch* is not exclamative-specific. We shall see that the degree analysis that I developed in the previous sections can be fruitfully applied to non-exclamative uses of *welch*. One instance of this are 'positive' rhetorical questions. Apart from that, *welch* also occurs in 'negative' rhetorical question. The analysis of these might be less straightforward but I will sketch a possible solution. The last type of speech act where *welch* occurs is a subgroup of ordinary questions. These questions involve a register shift, and I call them 'mystery' questions here for reasons that will become clear below.

To investigate in what speech acts other than exclamations uninflected *welch* can occur I extracted sentences with *welch* from the corpus that end in a question mark. Question marks do not usually mark an exclamation. Ideally, the investigation should also have included embedded clauses with *welch*. There are many of them in the corpus, and clauses with *welch* do seem to get embedded under question predicates. However, a detailed investigation of embedded *welch* has to await another occasion, especially since it is highly controversial whether or not exclamatives can be embedded, see footnote 5. As for matrix sentences ending in a question mark, there are 20 such sentences in stylistically unmarked texts. 15 of them are rhetorical questions, the remainder are mystery questions.

4.1. Rhetorical questions

When a speaker asks a rhetorical question s/he does not expect an answer. Rather s/he gives the answer him/herself. For instance, by posing the question in (36)a, the speaker really expresses (36)b. The presence of the negation in cases like (36)b has led to the assumption that rhetorical questions have the illocutionary force of negative assertions. In the case of a *wh*-question this means that the set of true answers is empty:

(36) a. Who lifted a finger when Pete was in trouble?
b. Nobody lifted a finger when Pete was in trouble.

Rhetorical questions often come with negative polarity items like *lift a finger* in (36), or *ever* (cf. Krifka 1995, Han 2002). This has motivated analyses according to which rhetorical questions are also *semantically* equivalent to negative statements, which would explain how the NPIs get licensed (Sadock 1971, Progovac 1993, Han 2002). More recently, however, Caponigro and Sprouse (2007) have highlighted the fact that the conception of rhetorical questions as *negative* assertions is too limited. This is illustrated in (37) from Caponigro and Sprouse (2007):

(37) You should stop saying that Luca didn't like the party last night. After all, who was the only one that was still dancing at 3am?
= Luca was the only one that was still dancing at 3 am.

So the idea that rhetorical questions semantically are negative statements is problematic. Caponigro and Sprouse (2007) suggest that a rhetorical question is a question whose answer is mutual shared knowledge of speaker and hearer, i.e., both speaker and hearer know the answer and they know that the other knows the answer as well.[16] This is similar to exclamatives whose truth is often taken to be presupposed (see section 2). In what follows I will refer to rhetorical questions like (36), which express a negative assertion, as *negative-answer RQs*, and to questions like (37), which express a positive assertion, as *positive-answer RQs*.

Since we are looking at a potential restriction of the occurrence of *welch* to specific speech act types in a corpus we need to make sure that we correctly identify the speech type

[16] But see Gutierrez-Rechach (1998) for an argument that mutual knowledge might not be required.

of the corpus tokens. This means that on the one hand we need to distinguish rhetorical questions from ordinary questions, and on the other hand, we also need to distinguish rhetorical questions from exclamatives, because we cannot rely on the authors of the texts to have always used the 'correct' punctuation.[17]

As for the distinction between rhetorical questions and exclamatives, it turns out that rhetorical questions often are expressive in the sense that the speaker wishes to highlight a proposition in the common ground, which to him or her seems 'obvious' but has not been sufficiently appreciated. Therefore rhetorical questions can sound triumphant or reflect other such emotions on the side of the speaker. In contrast to exclamatives, however, they do not express surprise at a high degree. Still, since we are looking at *welch* here, which, according to our hypothesis, expresses that a particular degree was rather high, or at least above the standard, it is not always easy – at least in the case of positive-answer RQs – to tell them apart from exclamatives. Nevertheless, there is a criterion that is quite reliable for the distinction: answerability. We said above that rhetorical questions do not expect an answer. This does not mean, however, that they cannot be answered (Caponigro and Sprouse 2007). The answer can be given by the speaker him/herself or by the hearer. For instance, (37) above, repeated below as (38)A can be followed by a reaction like (38)B:

(38) A: You should stop saying that Luca didn't like the party last night. After all, who was the only one that was still dancing at 3am?
B: Yes, you're right. It was Luca.

Exclamatives, which always 'give an answer' – if we follow D'Avis (2001, 2002) in his analysis of exclamatives as self-answering questions (see section 2) – cannot be answered (Eliot 1974). This is illustrated in (39):

(39) A: How very tall this man is!
B: # 2.10 metres. / # Very. / # Extremely!

In the case of positive-answer RQs with *welch* we expect that they can be answered by something like *very*, or *a very high x*. We shall see below that this expectation is born out.

Are there any reliable means to distinguish rhetorical questions from ordinary questions? For English, Sadock (1971) suggests that discourse markers like *after all*, as in (38), or *yet* are reliable indicators. In German, rhetorical questions often come with particular modal particles (Meibauer 1985, Thurmair 1989)[18] and with verbs in the subjunctive mood, including modal verbs (*sollte* 'should', *würde* 'would'; Meibauer 1986). There has also been some debate around the combined contribution of the subjunctive mood and negation which has been identified as not being propositional (cf. Meibauer 1986). Therefore, modal particles,

[17] In the corpus data where an exclamation mark was used as the search criterion there also were some rhetorical questions. Everything I say below about the question-mark tokens applies to them as well.

[18] Meibauer (1986) identifies *schon* ('admittedly'), *auch* ('too') and *vielleicht* ('perhaps'). He says that the first two only serve to mark the question as a rhetorical question and have no meaning of their own. See Thurmair (1989) for an analysis where the basic semantics of these particles is fruitfully exploited to produce rhetorical readings.

modal verbs, the subjunctive mood and the negative marker *nicht* should be good indicators for rhetoricity.[19]

With this much in hand let us turn to the *welch*-occurences in the corpus that I have suggested are occurrences in rhetorical questions. Let us first look at positive-answer RQs and consider (40). (40) does not contain clear indicators for rhetoricity (the subjunctive of the copula verb in the embedded clause is a consequence of reported speech). Out of context, the sentence could easily be interpreted as an exclamative. Yet the subsequent context consists of two questions that are not easily interpreted as exclamatives. For instance, the first sentence with *why* does certainly not express surprise at the reason why children do not have a lobby comparable to that of animal-rights activists. If we assume that this passage employs the rhetorical means of parallelism the target sentence must be a question. Let us also apply the criterion of answerability. It seems that the target sentence can be answered by something like *Sehr krank* ('very sick').[20]

(40) Da hat sich ein Homöopath wieder geoutet: Mit Hokuspokusmedizin lässt sich im gesättigten Gesundheitsmarkt München bei esoterisch angehauchten Müttern besser punkten als mit der Nüchternheit der wissenschaftlichen Medizin. Tatsache ist, dass Infektionskrankheiten wie die Masern nur durch Impfung ausgerottet werden können, wie es ja bei Pocken und Polio bald geschehen wird.
'Once again, a homeopath has come out of the closet. On the Munich health care market hocus-pocus medicine is easier to sell to mothers with esoteric leanings than is the rationality of scientific medicine. It is a fact that contagious diseases like the measles can only be eradicated through vaccination, just as smallpox and polio soon will be.'

Welch	krankem	Gehirn	entstammt	der	Gedanke,	dass	für	Kinder
welch	sick	brain.DAT	stem.from	the	thought	that	for	children

mehrere	Tage	hohes	Fieber	eine	"positive	Selbsterfahrung"	seien?
several	days	high	fever	a	positive	self-experience	are.SUBJ

'From what sick mind does the thought emanate that a few days of high fever could be a 'positive self-experience' for children?'

Warum haben Kinder nicht die Lobby der Tierschützer? Wo bleibt der Aufstand unserer Universitätsgelehrten? Unsere Demokratie kann "Masernpartys" nicht verhindern, unser soziales Netz muss aber die Folgen, wie Krankenhauskosten etc., bezahlen.
'Why do children not have the lobby of animal-rights activists? Where is the outcry of our university teachers? Our democracy cannot prohibit 'measles parties' but our social network must pay for the consequences such as hospital expenses.'

A letter to the editor by a doctor.

Now, do we know whether the *wh*-clause in (40) is a rhetorical question or an ordinary question? I suggest that we do. (40) expresses that it is a very sick mind that the thought at

---

[19] But note that recent analyses of the negation in questions suggest that it is not confined to rhetorical questions, cf. Romero and Han (2004), Repp (2009, to appear), Krifka (2012).

[20] The judgement is not so clear here. A nominal answer such as *einem sehr kranken* ('from a very sick one') also is somewhat odd but this would be expected because the question is not about an individual.

issue emanated from. It does not ask for the degree of sickness of that mind. However, neither does it ask for a particular mind, i.e., person, as the same sentence with *welchE* would: *welch* can be replaced *welchE* in this context, resulting in a subtle meaning change. With *welchE* the sentence would express that the thought emanated from a person with a sick mind. The assumption that (40) is a rhetorical question is corroborated by an easily available rhetorical interpretation of the two follow-up questions. The first one can be interpreted as expressing that there is no reason that children do not have a comparable lobby to animal-rights activists, and the second one as expressing that there isn't anywhere an outcry of university teachers.

(41) is another example where two rhetorical questions appear in sequence (again there are no clear indicators for rhetoricity). (41) is from a text that falls in the category of stylistically dated texts but since the style is not particularly 'archaic' I will discuss the example here. (41) is interesting because it illustrates how thin the line between rhetorical questions and exclamatives is. Or, to be more precise, that rhetorical questions can be just as expressive as exclamatives. Note that in the original English translation the translator, a British Marxist scholar, chose to use an exclamation mark rather than a question mark. Of course, this does not mean that we are dealing with an exclamative in the German version here but it shows that there is a high degree of expressivity. One indicator for the rhetorical question status of the original German version is again the discourse structure. Again, I suggest that the critical *wh*-clause and the one following it are intended to be discourse-parallel. Considering that the second *wh*-clause can only be interpreted as a negative-answer RQ and not as an exclamative – there is no expression of surprise at a high degree – it is plausible to assume that the *welch*-sentence also is a rhetorical question. Another indicator is the occurrence of *überhaupt* ('anyway') in the clause. This adverb is odd in clause-internal position in verb-final exclamatives, i.e., in exclamatives for which there is no alternative interpretation as question available, see (42).[21] Finally, (41) can probably be answered by *sehr töricht* ('very silly').

[21] Note that the *if*-clause does not indicate that we cannot be dealing with an exclamative. The verb-final variant of (41) is fine (if we leave out *überhaupt*). Furthermore, there are corpus occurrences of exclamatives with *if*-clauses, e.g.,

(i)

Welch	ein	Glück,	wenn	wir	doch	noch	rechtzeitig	stolpern
welch	a	luck	if	we	PART	enough	in.time	stumble
und	auf	die	Nase	fallen!				
and	on	the	nose	fall				

'How lucky we are if we stumble in good time and fall on our noses!'

Peter Kafka: *Zeit zum Aufstehen. Anmerkungen zur Überwindung der globalen Beschleunigungskrise* (*Time to get up. Notes on how to overcome the global acceleration crisis*).

(41)

Welch	eine	törichte,	unpraktische	Illusion	ist	überhaupt	ein	parteiloser
welch	a	silly	impractical	illusion	is	anyway	a	impartial

Richter,	wenn	der Gesetzgeber	parteiisch	ist?
judge	if	the legislator	partial	is?

'How altogether foolish and impractical an illusion is an impartial judge when the legislator is not impartial!'

Was soll ein uneigennütziges Urteil, wenn das Gesetz eigennützig ist?
'What is the use of a disinterested sentence when the law favours self-interest!'

Karl Marx (1842): *Debatten über das Holzdiebstahlsgesetz.*
(Debates on the law on thefts of wood). Translation by Clemens Dutt (1893-1974).

(42) a.

??Wen	der	überhaupt	eingeladen	hat!
who.ACC	he.DEM	anyway	invited	has

b. Überhaupt! Wen der eingeladen hat!
'The people that he invited!'

These two examples should suffice to illustrate that *welch* can occur in positive-answer RQs.

I suggest that *welch* is suitable in positive-answer RQs because it encodes that the degree it asks for is above the standard. In this characteristic it contrasts with *wie* ('how'), which just asks for a degree. The difference can be seen in the following two examples. (43)a means that Peter's height is above or equal to the standard of tallness (say, of men). It is usually assumed that this meaning component is contributed by a silent positive morpheme, and which I assume to be present in a slightly different form in the denotation of *welch* (see section 3.2). The question in (43)b does not ask for the degree that Peter is above the standard degree of tallness. It asks for his height, e.g., in terms of some precise measurement (5ft or 6ft2), or in terms of a vague description (*very tall, not so tall, short*). Peter does not have to be tall for that question to be felicitous. Indeed, he can be very short.

(43) a. Peter is tall.
b. How tall is Peter?

Thus there is no positive morpheme in (43)b and *how* has a different semantics from *welch*.

Since rhetorical questions – similarly to exclamatives – are essentially self-answering questions the felicity of *welch* in these questions does not come as a surprise – at least for positive-answer RQs. A positive-answer RQ always expresses that the degree to which the property in the restrictor of *welch* holds is a high degree, or more precisely, one above the standard for that property. So when in (41) the speaker 'asks' what a silly impractical illusion an impartial judge is if the legislator is partial, what s/he asserts is that an impartial judge is a very silly impractical illusion.

Let us next turn to negative-answer RQs. Recall that negative-answer RQs usually denote the empty set. (44) is a negative-answer RQ with *welch*. It is possibly a little more complex than need be but the meaning is intuitively clear, and such more intricate examples are in no way rare or exceptional. (44) occurs in a text passage that is highly sarcastic. Since sarcasm, as a form of irony, says the opposite of what is meant – which is quite similar to what rhetorical questions do –, we need to be careful when disentangling the precise meaning here.

The text passage as a whole says that it is very obvious that the times for football matches are scheduled in a way that the media would gain maximum profit from broadcasting the matches (presumably through advertising revenue). The negative assertion that the rhetorical question here expresses is that nobody would draw the ludicrous conclusion that the media would have anything to do with the scheduling of match times. This is supported by the next sentence essentially giving the answer (*Nein* ... ('no')). Since the whole passage is ironic the speaker eventually means the opposite but the rhetorical question works in the way that negative-answer RQs are expected to work.

(44) Bravo, Herr Meier. Da sitzen also die wahren Schuldigen. Wir, die Deutschen, spielen jetzt rein zufällig ein Top-Spiel am Samstag Abend aus. Aber nicht weil das Fernsehen es so möchte.
'Well done, Mr Meier. That's where the real culprits are. It is pure coincidence that we, the Germans, are playing a top game on Saturday night. It is not that television wants it like that.'

Welch	normal	denkender	Mensch	mit	Schulabschluss	würde	zu	so
welch	normal	thinking	person	with	school.leaving.certificate	would	to	such

einer	irrsinnigen	Schlussfolgerung	kommen?
a	ludicrous	conclusion	come

'What rational person with some school education would arrive at such a ludicrous conclusion?'

Nein, Premiere wurde von der Bundesliga geradezu gezwungen ein Samstagabendspiel zu übertragen.
'No, Premiere [a pay TV station] was virtually forced by the Bundesliga to broadcast a Saturday night game.'

From www.blutgraetsche.de, a webpage with football comments.
http://www.blutgraetsche.de/he/24/02405620010403.php

In this example the restrictor of *welch* in (44) is not a gradable predicate: it denotes the set of people that have a 'normal' view on life and that had a school education. I suggested in section 3 that in such cases there is a silent gradable predicate whose degree argument *welch* binds. Now, the only way to rephrase (44) in a 'degree-relevant' way seems to ask to what rather high degree a sane, normal person must be unusual (in other domains than views on life) to actually arrive at such a conclusion. So the question is one about what an individual would have to be like to arrive at this conclusion, and the assertion the rhetorical question contributes is that there is no degree of unusualness that would make the proposition true, and one can deduce from this that there is no person that would fit that description. Note that this is slightly different from a minimal variant with *welchE*, which would be felicitous in this context as well. This variant would ask for a person and the assertion that the rhetorical question contributes would be that no-one with a normal view on life and with a school education would come to such a conclusion. So the answer *no-one* should be more appropriate for the *welchE* variant than for the *welch* variant, which seems to be correct. However, the judgement is very subtle and possibly not reliable.

The example in (44) is representative of the eight negative-answer RQs in the corpus. When compared to a *welchE* variant, most[22] of them express that the speaker 'wonders' about the high degree of unusualness, which s/he considers so unlikely that the answer is a negative one. How exactly this negative answer is to be derived is not so clear at present. I do not have the space to work this out in detail here. A conclusive account would have to take into consideration data like those in footnote 22, and it would have to account for embedded *welch*-clauses as well. I am leaving this for another occasion.

We saw above that rhetorical questions often come with negative polarity items. It has been suggested that the rhetorical force in these questions is actually *induced* by (strong) negative polarity items (e.g., Progovac 1994, Giannakidou 1998, Den Dikken and Giannakidou 2002). Negative polarity items have been argued to be elements on a scale (Krifka 1995). This is similar to *welch*, which also relates to a scale. There is an important difference, though: strong negative polarity items denote elements at the bottom of the contextually associated scale. This is not the case for *welch*, which denotes a high degree. Let us nevertheless ask the question of whether or not *welch* induces the question it occurs in to be interpreted as a rhetorical question, see Zifonun, Hoffmann and Strecker (1997) for the remark that *welch*-questions (in stylistically dated texts) often seem to have the effect of a rhetorical questions. The answer seems to be: *welch* does induce a question to be rhetorical. Otherwise its presence causes a register shift. We will see evidence for this in the next section.

4.2. Register shift: 'mystery' questions

In the corpus there are five matrix questions that we could call 'mystery' questions: they express that something is particularly mysterious or wonderful-impressive like in a fairy tale. Here are two examples:

---

[22] There are two examples that do not fit this description. One is the following from a webpage for Bavarian dentists, where it is implausible to speak of degrees of unusualness. I have no explanation for the felicity of *welch* in this example. If there is a difference with the *welchE* variant, which would be possible here as well, it is the d-linking characteristic of *welchE*.

(i) Der floatende Punktwert bedeutet, dass der Arzt oder Zahnarzt immer erst im Nachhinein weiß, was er für seine Leistungen bekommt. Zudem führt er zu dem bekannten Hamsterrad-Effekt.
'Due to the floating credit point calculation the doctor or dentist only knows after the treatment how much he can charge. Another consequence is the well-known rat race effect.'

Welch anderer Freiberufler muss unter diesen Rahmenbedingungen tätig werden?
welch other freelancer must under these conditions busy become
'What other freelancer has to work under such conditions?'

(45) From a book review of a thriller: Im Februar 1968 wurde ein junger Leutnant kaltblütig erschossen - vermutlich von seinem Vorgesetzten. Warum hat die Army plötzlich Interesse an diesem Fall??
'In February 1968 a young lieutenant is shot in cold blood – presumably by a superior. Why, all of a sudden, is the army interested in this case??'

Welch	lang	gehütetes	Geheimnis	verbirgt	sich	hinter	der	Geschichte?
welch	long	guarded	secret	hides	REFL	behind	this	story

'What well-kept secret is there behind this story?'

(46) Und das ist die geheimnisvolle Büchse! Das Etikett ist schon seit vielen Jahren verschwunden.
'And that's the mysterious tin! The label went missing years ago.'

Welch	fremdartige	Wunder	sind	darin	verborgen?
welch	foreign	wonders	are	in.it	hidden

'What foreign wonders are hidden within?'

Ein Schatz? Hundefutter?
'Treasure? Dog food?'

(From *The Simpsons*, Cartoon, German version.)

Such 'mystery' questions are the only matrix questions in the corpus where *welch* occurs. I suggest that what we find here is a temporary register shift – temporary with respect to the concrete discourse – to an older stage of the grammar, which has the rhetoric effect of enhancing the mysteriousness / wondrousness of what the speaker utters. I propose that the use of *welch* in questions in modern German does not reflect the grammar of contemporary German. Rather, in a neutral register, *welch* in (45) would be replaced by *welchE*, and in (46) it would be replaced by *was für*.

5. Conclusion

I have argued in this paper that the two *which*-phrases that German has have a different semantics and therefore have a different distribution in different types of speech acts. Uninflected *welch* ranges over degrees (cf. Gallmann 1997, D'Avis 2001, 2002). Inflected *welchE* ranges over individuals such that the sets of individuals in its restrictor must be contextually given, i.e., *welchE*-phrases are d-linked. This imposes conditions on the context which are rarely met so that *welchE*-phrases in exclamatives are not very frequent. They do occur, though, and are clearly part of the grammar of modern Standard German.

I have shown that *welch* is not restricted to formal styles or archaic text types as has been claimed in previous literature. *Welch* reliably occurs in discourses that do not belong to the formal register or to texts predating 1945. My analysis has also shown, however, that *welch* predominantly occurs in nominal *wh*-exclamatives, which does not seem to be the case in older discourses. I have suggested that nominal *wh*-exclamatives are elliptical copula sentences. In the case of *welch* they are predicational copula sentences, and in the case of *welchE* they are specificational copula sentences. I assumed a simple semantics for the copulas in these two types of sentences without going into the specific characteristics of copula sentences in general. The main goal was to account for differences between *welch* and *welchE* in nominal *wh*-exclamatives which I argued can be explained in an intuitive way via predication vs. identification.

Furthermore, I have shown that *welch* is not restricted to exclamatives but also occurs in rhetorical questions. I have argued that this is a natural extension because both exclamatives and rhetorical questions can be viewed as giving the answer to the question they formally encode. We might take this as indirect evidence for the question analysis of exclamatives, which I have adopted here, yet a conclusive analysis can only be provided once occurrences of embedded *welch* have been taken into account.

Overall the analysis has shown that the data in the domain of exclamatives with *welch*, *welch ein*, *welchE* and expressions like *was für* are fairly complex and that the phenomenon needs more research. We have seen that the pragmatics in terms of contextual restrictions must be well-controlled to understand the way the data pattern. We have also seen that a detailed investigation of individual *wh*-phrases is able to shed light on *wh*-clauses in their various uses as ordinary questions, rhetorical questions and exclamatives. This will lead to a better understanding of exclamatives as a sentence type, which – and that is an option which has not been taken serious enough in the literature so far – might well differ from language to language.

Bibliography

Abels, K. (2005): Remarks on Grimshaw's clausal typology. In: E. Maier, C. Bary and J. Huitink (eds.), *Proceedings of Sinn und Bedeutung 9*: 1–15.

Abels, K. (2010): Factivity in exclamatives is a presupposition. *Studia Linguistica 64*: 141–157.

Altmann, H. (1993): Fokus-Hintergrund-Gliederung und Satzmodus. In: M. Reis (ed.), *Information und Satzstruktur*. Tübingen: Niemeyer, 1–39.

Baroni, M, S. Bernardini, A. Ferraresi and E. Zanchetta (2009): The WaCky Wide Web: A collection of very large linguistically processed web-crawled corpora. *Language Resources and Evaluation 43:* 209–226.

Beck, S. (1996): Wh-*constructions and transparent Logical Form*. PhD thesis, University of Tübingen.

Bierwisch, M. (1989): The semantics of gradation. In: M. Bierwisch and E. Lang (eds.), *Dimensional adjectives*. Berlin: Springer, 71–262.

Caponigro, I. and J. Sprouse (2007): Rhetorical questions as questions. *Proceedings of Sinn und Bedeutung 11*: 121–133.

Castroviejo Miró, E. (2006): *Wh-Exclamatives in Catalan*. PhD thesis, University of Barcelona.

Comorovski, I. (1996): *Interrogative phrases and the syntax-semantics interface.* Dordrecht: Kluwer.

Cresswell, M.J. (1977): The semantics of degree. In: B. Partee (ed.), *Montague grammar*. New York: Academic Press, 261–292.

D'Avis, F.-J. (2001): *Über w-Exklamativsätze im Deutschen.* Tübingen: Niemeyer (=Linguistische Arbeiten 429).
D'Avis, F.-J. (2002): On the interpretation of WH-clauses in exclamative environments. *Theoretical Linguistics 28*: 5–31.
Delsing, L.-O. (2010): Exclamatives in Scandinavian. *Studia Linguistica* 64:16–36.
Elliott, D.E. (1974): Toward a grammar of exclamatives. *Foundations of Language* 11: 231–246.
Gallmann, P. (1996): Die Steuerung der Flexion in der DP. *Linguistische Berichte* 164: 283–314.
Gallmann, P. (1997): Zu Morphosyntax und Lexik der w-Wörter. *Arbeitspapiere des Sonderforschungsbereichs 340*, Sprachtheoretische Grundlagen für die Computerlinguistik, Bericht 107.Tübingen: Universität Tübingen.
Grimshaw, J. (1979): Complement selection and the lexicon. *Linguistic Inquiry* 10: 279–326.
Gutierrez-Rexach, J. (1996): The semantics of exclamatives. In: E. Garrett and F. Lee (eds.), *Syntax at Sunset. UCLA Working Papers in Linguistics*. Los Angeles: Dept. of Linguistics, UCLA, 146–162.
Gutierrzes-Rexach, J. (1998). Rhetorical questions, relevance and scales. *Revista Alicantina de Estudios Ingleses* 11: 139–155.
Han, C.-h. (2002): Interpreting interrogatives as rhetorical questions. *Lingua* 112: 201–229.
Huddleston, R. (1993): Remarks on the construction 'You won't believe who Ed has married'. *Lingua* 91: 175–184.
Jónsson, J.G. (2010): Icelandic exclamatives and the structure of the CP Layer. *Studia Linguistica* 64: 37–54.
Kennedy, C. (1999): *Projecting the adjective: The syntax and semantics of gradability and comparison.* New York: Garland.
Krifka, M. (1995): The semantics and pragmatics of polarity items. *Linguistic Analysis* 25: 1–49.
Krifka, M. (2012): Negated polarity questions as denegations of assertions. To appear in F. Kiefer and C. Lee (eds.), *Contrastiveness and scalar implicatures*. Berlin: Springer.
Kuroda, S-Y. (1968): English relativization and certain related problems. *Language* 44: 244–266.
Leu, T. (2008): *The internal syntax of determiners.* PhD thesis, New York University, Dept. of Linguistics.
Lipták, A. (2006): The left periphery of Hungarian exclamatives. In: L. Brugè, G. Giusti, N. Munaro, W. Schweikert and G. Turano (eds), *Contributions to the 30th Incontro di Grammatica Generativa*, Venezie: Cafoscarina, 161–183.
Meibauer, J. (1986): *Rhetorische Fragen.* Tübingen: Niemeyer.
Merchant, J. (2010): Three kinds of ellipsis. In: F. Recanati, I. Stojanovic and N. Villanueva (eds.), *Context-dependence, perspective, and relativity.* Berlin/New York: de Gruyter, 141–192.
Morzycki, M. (2009): Degree modification of gradable nouns: size adjectives and adnominal degree morphemes. *Natural Language Semantics* 17: 175–203.

Müller, G. (2004): Remarks on nominal inflection. In: I. Kaufmann and B. Stiebels (eds.), *More than words: A festschrift for Dieter Wunderlich*. Berlin: Akademie Verlag, 113–145.

Olsen, S. (1989): AGR(eement) in the German noun phrase. In: C. Bhatt, E. Löbel and C. Schmidt (eds.), *Syntactic phrase structure phenomena in noun phrases and sentences*. Amsterdam: Benjamins, 39–49.

Olsen, S.(1991a): AGR(eement) und Flexion in der deutschen Nominalphrase. In: G. Fanselow and S. Felix (eds.), *Strukturen und Merkmale syntaktischer Kategorien*. Tübingen: Narr, 51–70.

Olsen, S. (1991b): Die deutsche Nominalphrase als 'Determinansphrase'. In: S. Olsen and G. Fanselow (eds.), *DET, COMP und INFL. Zur Syntax funktionaler Kategorien und grammatischer Funktionen*. Tübingen: Niemeyer, 35–56.

Ono, H. (2006): *An investigation of exclamatives in English and Japanese: Syntax and sentence processing*. PhD thesis, University of Maryland, College Park.

Pesetsky, D. (1987): *Wh*-in-situ: Movement and unselective binding. In: E.J.Reuland and A. ter Meulen (eds.), *The representation of (in)definiteness*. Cambridge, MA.: MIT Press, 98–129.

Pesetsky, D. (2000): *Phrasal movement and its kin*. Cambridge, MA: MIT Press.

Progovac, L. (1994): *Positive and negative polarity: A binding approach*. Cambridge: Cambridge University Press.

Repp, S. (2009): *Negation in gapping*. Oxford: Oxford University Press.

Repp, S. (to appear): Common ground management: Modal particles, illocutionary negation and VERUM. In: D. Gutzmann and H.-M. Gärtner (eds.), *Expressives and beyond. Explorations of conventional non-truth-conditional meaning*. Oxford: Oxford University Press.

Rett, J. (2008): *Degree Modification in Natural Language*. PhD thesis, The State University of New Jersey.

Rett, J. (2011): Exclamatives, degrees and speech acts. *Linguistics and Philosophy* 34: 411–442.

Roehrs, D. (2009): *Demonstratives and definite articles as nominal auxiliaries*. Amsterdam: John Benjamins.

Roguska, M. (2008): *Exklamation und negation*. Berlin: Logos.

Romero, M. and C.-h. Han (2004): On negative yes/no questions. *Linguistics and Philosophy* 27: 609–658.

Rosengren, I. (1997): Expressive sentence types – a contradiction in term. The case of exclamation. In: T. Swan and O. Jansen Westvik (eds.), *Modality in Germanic languages. Historical and comparative Perspectives*. Berlin/New York: de Gruyter, 151–184.

Sadock, J. (1971): Queclaratives. In: D. Adams, M. A. Campbell, V. Cohen, J. Lovins, E. Maxwell, C. Nygren, and J. Reighard (eds.), *Papers from the 7th Regional Meeting of the CLS*. Chicago: University of Chicago, 223–331.

Sæbø, K. (2010): On the semantics of 'embedded exclamatives'. *Studia Linguistica* 64: 116–140.

Stainton, R. J. (2006): *Words and thoughts: Subsentences, ellipsis, and the philosophy of language*. Oxford: Oxford University Press.

Thurmair, M. (1989): *Modalpartikeln und ihre Kombinationen*. Tübingen: Niemeyer.

von Stechow, A. (1984): Comparing semantic theories of comparison. *Journal of Semantics* 3: 1–77.

Wiltschko, M. (1997): D-linking, scrambling and superiority in German. *Groninger Arbeiten zur germanistischen Linguistik* 41: 107–142.

Zanuttini, R., and Portner, P. (2003): Exclamative clauses: At the syntax–semantics interface. *Language* 79: 39–81.

Zifonun, G., L. Hoffmann, and B. Strecker, B. (eds.) (1997): *Grammatik der deutschen Sprache. 3 Bde.* Berlin/New York: de Gruyter.

Reflexivization and intensification in syntax and lexicon

Karin Pittner

1. Introduction

Reflexivization and intensification are closely related concepts, which are expressed by the same means in a number of languages, e.g. in English. German, on the other hand, uses different expressions for them, as far as syntax is concerned.

(1) a. She corrected herself. (reflexivization)
'Sie korrigierte sich.'
b. The queen herself was there. (intensification)
'Die Queen selbst war da.'

While English and German have developed different means and strategies for reflexivity in syntax, the means for word-internal reflexivization und intensification are strikingly similar. Word-internally, both English and German use the same means to express reflexivity and intensification, namely *self/selbst*.

In this paper, we will first take a look at the different means for reflexivization in section 2 and the types of intensification in section 3, before word-internal reflexivization and intensification are discussed in section 4.

2. Reflexivization in English and German

English and German use different means for reflexivization. German *sich* is a reflexive pronoun which may be used for dative and accusative in the 3rd person singular and plural. For other forms, personal pronouns are used reflexively. After the English equivalent of *sich* had disappeared, English reflexive pronouns were formed by personal pronouns in combination with intensifying *self*.

However, the means for reflexivization in English and German are not as completely disparate as it seems. The means of the other language may be marginally used. German has the possibility to reinforce a reflexive pronoun or personal pronoun in reflexive use with intensifying *selbst*. Indeed, this is nearly obligatory when the pronoun is in genitive case as in the following example:

(2) Lena Meyer-Landrut hat keine große Stimme – eine Entdeckung ist sie trotzdem: als Performerin ihrer selbst.
'Lena Meyer-Landrut has no great voice – she is nevertheless a discovery: as a performer of herself.'
(Süddeutsche Zeitung 28. Mai 2010, p. 11)

In English, on the other hand, a personal pronoun may be used reflexively in colloquial language:

(3) a. I'm gonna get me a gun. (Cat Stevens)
b. I'm gonna brew me a cup of tea. (König and Gast 2009: 158)

Also, if pragmatically no other interpretation is possible, English uses personal pronouns instead of reflexive pronouns as in the following sentences (cf. König and Gast 2009: 153):

(4) a. John did not have any money on him.
b. She has a week full of work before her.

Whereas German has separate expressions for reflexivization and intensification, English uses the same expressions.

Moreover, in German the reflexive pronoun is used with inherently reflexive verbs (such as *sich schämen, sich erholen*) and as a marker of derived intransitivity which may be considered a medium marker (*die Tür öffnete sich – the door opened*). English has only a few inherently reflexive verbs (e.g., *to pride oneself, to absent oneself from, to avail oneself of*) and no medium marker. These differences in the use of reflexive pronouns may be due to their greater grammaticalization in German, where reflexive pronouns have less semantic and phonological substance than English reflexives have (cf. König and Gast 2009: 149).

With regard to the means for intensification and reflexivization, languages fall into three types (König and Gast 2006):

Type I: complete identity of intensifiers and reflexives (e.g., English, Mandarin)
Type II: differentiation of intensifiers and anaphors, which can often be combined (e.g., German *sich/selbst*, Italian *stessi/si*)
Type III: partial identity of intensifier and reflexive marker which share morphological material (e.g., Dutch *zich/zichself,* Scandinavian languages)

Intensifiers in type III languages often are the result of a combination of a pronoun and an intensifier as is the case in English.

3. Intensification in syntax

That intensifiers are identical with reflexive pronouns in a number of languages can be taken as evidence that identification and reflexivization are closely related concepts. The common core of both lies in the expression of "identity" (cf. König and Gast 2006, Gast 2006).

In a number of languages, the intensifier agrees with its noun, e.g., in person, number, and gender, as it does in English:

(5) a. The Queen herself was there.
    b. He did it himself.

Intensifiers can be used either adnominally or adverbially with an inclusive and an exclusive interpretation. German uses *selbst* and its colloquial variant *selber* for this purpose.[1]

Intensification shares some characteristics with focus particles. Siemund (2000: 238) describes intensifiers as "operators which structure sets of entities into a central element (the focus value) and peripheral elements related to it". He holds this description also as applicable for the adverbial uses. While the scope and focus is restricted to an NP in adnominal use, "adverbial intensifiers, by contrast, have scope over the sentence they are contained in". (2000: 238)

The category of German *selbst* has been controversially discussed. Either it is described as a focus particle in all its uses (Primus 1991, König and Siemund 1996, Duden 2009) or there is a differentiation between a use as focus particle and as an adverb (Zifonun et al. 1997, Eckardt 2001, Hole 2002).

In the following, it is argued that intensifiers in their adverbial uses are best categorized as adverbs belonging to different adverbial classes with regard to their scope and distribution. German *selbst* (like Spanish *mismo*, French *même)* has a use as focus particle, which is nearly synonymous to *sogar*. Its nearest English equivalent is *even*.

(6) a. Selbst Bill Gates könnte das nicht bezahlen.
    b. Even Bill Gates could not pay for this.

As a focus particle, *selbst* occurs adjacent to the focussed constituent to its left. It is an additive/inclusive particle which includes at least one of the possible alternatives to the focus value and indicates that the focus value ranges high on a scale of unexpectedness. The focus particle *selbst* will be of no further interest in this article. We will concentrate on intensifiers which can occur either adnominally or adverbially with an inclusive or an exclusive reading (Siemund 2000, König and Gast 2006, 2009: 142).

(7) a. Er selbst/selber konnte ihr nicht helfen. (adnominal centering)
       'He himself could not help her.'
    b. Er ist selbst/selber ein Alkoholiker. (adverbial inclusive)
       'He is an alcoholic himself.'
    c. Sie erledigte alle Aufgaben selbst/selber. (adverbial exclusive)
       'She completed all the tasks herself.'

The intensifier in its adnominal use indicates a central role of the noun phrase. In its inclusive reading, the intensifier indicates that the proposition is valid for an alternative referent

---

[1] *Selber* and *selbst* were inflected forms of the same stem, but today are seen as two separate stems which do not inflect. Originally, *selber* was a strongly inflected nominative form, and *selbst* a genitive form *selb(e)s*, to which *-t* was added (DWB vol. 16, sp. 432 und 485).

(usually of the subject NP), whereas in its exclusive reading alternative referents are excluded.

König and Siemund (1996) argue that the intensifier in these three uses is a focus particle because it relates to alternatives and interacts with the focus-background of the sentence. These intensifiers have some characteristics, however, which are untypical for focus particles. They bear the nuclear accent, while the focussed constituent has no accent. Usually, a focus particle bears no accent, whereas the NP bears a focus accent. Moreover, German *selbst/selber* may stand alone in the prefield (i.e., the position before the finite verb in verb-second clauses), which is not possible for focus particles but for adverbs. It can also occur as the complement of a preposition as, e.g., in *die Tür öffnete sich von selbst* ('the door opened by itself'), which would also be unusual for a focus particle. And last but not least, its meaning contribution changes with its position in the sentence, which is typical for adverbs but not for focus particles. In the following, it will be argued that exclusive and inclusive intensifiers are best described as adverbs belonging to different adverbial classes with different base positions.

The meaning contribution of intensifiers is seen by various authors (Eckardt 2001, Hole 2002, König and Gast 2006) in expressing the identity function (ID(x) = x). Since it is under normal circumstances not informative to state that an element is identical to itself, this can explain the obligatory accent on the intensifier. The meaning component of identity becomes relevant only by the focus accent which signals possible alternatives and gives pragmatic prominence to the referent of the NP in question.

Siemund (2000) assumes that adverbial intensifiers have the sentence in its scope. In accord with the assumption made by several authors (e.g., Frey and Pittner 1998, Frey 2003) that adverbs have different scope and different base positions reflecting that scope, it will be shown that exclusive and inclusive intensifiers belong to different adverbial classes.

3.1. Adverbial exclusive intensification

A sentence with an exclusive intensifier presupposes that from all persons that might carry out an action the one referred to by the focussed constituent is the most affected and involved and therefore the central one.[2] The focussed constituent may be either the responsible or interested party, a beneficiary or maleficiary (cf. Siemund 2000: 260).

For a reading in which intensifiers exclude possible alternatives such alternatives have to be possible. Siemund (2000: 186) sees the "transferability" of a situation as a precondition for exclusive intensifiers, which he defines as follows. "What transferability indicates is whether a situation is inalienably tied to one particular referent or whether it can be passed on to another referent." This often means that an action carried out by the subject referent may be delegated to another person. In these cases, the exclusive intensifier can be paraphrased by "alone" or "without assistance". If a situation is not transferrable, no exclusive interpretation is possible, as in the following example:

2 Cf. the presupposition of exclusive *selbst* as formulated by König and Siemund (1996: 292): „Ein Satz mit exklusivem *selbst* präsupponiert, dass von allen in einer bestimmten Situation zur Debatte stehenden Personen die von der Fokuskonstituente bezeichnete Person von der durch den Satz ausgedrückten Handlung am stärksten betroffen wird und somit zentral ist." (cf. also Siemund 2000)

(8) a. Er schnarcht selbst/selber. (only inclusive)
he snores himself

Transferability need not always take the form of delegation of an action, but can also lie within the range of permitting. It may even consist in an alternative activity of the focus referent as in the following example (cf. Siemund 2000: 238f.):

(9) a. Es geht schneller, wenn du selbst hingehst, aber du kannst dich auch per Post bewerben.
'It is quicker to go there yourself but you can also apply by post.'

According to Siemund (2000: 234) exclusive intensifiers are possible only with animate, agentive referents, not with experiencer subjects, which allow only an inclusive reading:

(10) a. Ich habe Pavarotti selbst gehört. (only inclusive)
'I have heard Pavarotti myself.'

In certain cases, however, an experiencer can occur with an intensifier in exclusive reading.

(11) a. Anna hat Maria beschimpft. Peter hat das selbst gehört.
'Anne has scolded at Mary. Peter did himself hear this.'

Siemund (2000: 255, fn. 1) argues that the experiencer has characteristics of an agent in examples like this. It can be objected that *hören (hear)* in contrast to *zuhören (listen)* implies no active participation. Rather perception verbs exhibit a special kind of transferability: perceptions must not be first hand, but can be reported by others and are in this way transferrable. The second sentence in (11) fits into the sequence, if Peter heard the scolding himself, but not if somebody told him about it.

The meaning contribution of exclusive intensifiers has been controversially discussed. Some authors hold that the intensifier does not make a contribution to the truth-conditional meaning of a sentence (Primus 1991), whereas others hold the opposite view (e.g., Edmondson and Plank 1978). Let us consider the following example:

(12) a. Fast jeder Promi schreibt seine Biografie.
'Nearly every VIP writes his biography.'
b. Fast jeder Promi schreibt seine Biografie selbst.
'Nearly every VIP writes his biography himself.'

There is a clear difference in meaning between the (a) - and the (b) - sentences: the (b) - sentences entail the (a) - sentences, but not the other way round. This hints at a difference in truth-conditional meaning between the two sentences. The following example from a German TV interview (Reinhold Beckmann questioning Peer Steinbrück, 12.4.2010) points in the same direction:

(13) a. Sie schreiben ein Buch. [...] Schreiben Sie das Buch selbst?
'You are writing a book. [...] Are you writing the book yourself?'

The question in (13) would be irrelevant if the proposition it contains were exactly the same as the proposition in the preceding assertive clause.

To sum up, exclusive intensifiers express the direct participation of the subject referent in an event. They stress the identity of the participant with the subject referent giving it thereby pragmatic prominence and excluding possible alternatives.

3.2. Adverbial inclusive intensification

Intensifiers with an inclusive interpretation have often been compared to additive focus particles like German *auch* and English *also* and *too*. An inclusive interpretation is possible if a situation is repeatable. Repeatability occurs in combination with indefinite *aktionsarten*, definite object NPs pattern with exclusive intensifiers, indefinite object NPs with inclusive ones (cf. Siemund 2000: 184f.).

If an action is transferrable but not repeatable, only an exclusive reading is possible, as in (14)a. If a situation is not transferrable and repeatable, an inclusive reading is triggered, as in (14)b. If the situation is transferrable and repeatable, both interpretations are possible in principle, as in (14)c and (14)d, cf. Siemund (2000: 184ff.).

(14) a. Der Bischof taufte das Mädchen selbst. (exclusive)
'The bishop christened the little girl himself.'
b. Das Mädchen musste selbst niesen. (inclusive)
'The girl had to sneeze herself.'
c. Der Präsident hält die Rede selbst (inclusive and exclusive)
'The president holds the speech himself.'
d. Der Präsident hält selbst eine Rede. (inclusive and exclusive)
'The president holds a speech himself.'

The position of exclusive *selbst/selber* corresponds to the base position of manner adverbials (process-oriented adverbials according to Frey and Pittner 1998, Frey 2003), which have a base position adjacent to the verb in final position in German.[3]

(15) a. Er hat selbst einen Film produziert. (inclusive)
he has himself produced a film
b. Er hat einen Film selbst produziert. (exclusive)
'He has produced a film himself.' (exclusive or inclusive)

In German, the different base positions of the intensifiers can be tested with the indefinite pronoun *was*, which may not scramble and therefore can serve as an indicator of the base position of arguments. This test shows that the intensifier has a base position behind the object in an exclusive interpretation, but before the object in an inclusive interpretation.

(16) a. Er hat selbst was repariert. (inclusive)
he has himself something repaired
b. Er hat was selbst repariert. (exclusive)
he has something himself repaired

---

[3] Already König and Siemund (1996: 290) assume a position of exclusive *selbst* after all objects and other adjuncts.

The exclusive intensifier is preceded by other adjuncts:

(17) a. Ich habe ein Auto selbst schon mal repariert (inclusive)
I have a car myself once repaired
b. Ich habe ein Auto schon mal selbst repariert (exclusive)
I have a car once myself repaired

The exclusive intensifier can occur in the scope of negation, whereas the inclusive intensifier has scope over negation (cf. Huddleston et al. 2002: 1498, König and Gast 2009: 145):

(18) a. Er hat das Auto nicht selbst repariert. (exclusive)
'He did not repair the car himself.'
b. Ich mag das Bild selbst nicht. (inclusive)
'I don't like the picture myself.'

Wide focus is possible, if the intensifier and the verb carry an accent, which again corresponds to the behaviour of manner adverbials (cf. Pittner 1999: 162):

(19) a. [er hat das Auto SELBST repaRIERT]$_F$
b. er hat das Auto [SELBST]$_F$ repariert

While exclusive intensifiers exhibit a base position close to the final verb, the base position of inclusive intensifiers is higher in the sentence, namely after the highest ranking argument and before objects. This corresponds to the base position of event-internal adverbials, which are c-commanded by the highest ranking argument they are related to (cf. Frey and Pittner 1998):

(20) a. weil Hans selbst Lehrer ist
because Hans himself teacher is
b. *weil selbst Hans Lehrer ist
because himself Hans teacher is

Inclusive *selbst* must occur on the surface after the argument it is related to and may not be topicalized, which shows the close relation of the intensifier to its argument:[4]

(21) a. Hans ist selbst Lehrer.
b. *Selbst ist Hans Lehrer. (* with an inclusive reading)

In contrast to exclusive *selbst,* the inclusive intensifier may occur higher than other scope bearing elements like negation or focus particles.

(22) a. Hans ist selbst nicht Lehrer/*nicht selbst Lehrer. (*with an inclusive reading)
b. Hans ist selbst nur Lehrer/*nur selbst Lehrer. (*with an inclusive reading)

---

4 Siemund (2000: 181) states that for inclusive intensifiers the same restrictions apply as for adnominal intensifiers. The NP they relate to must be definite, it cannot occur when the NP is indefinite and can neither be interpreted generically nor specifically, cf. **A minister will be surprised himself.*

The function of inclusive *intensifiers* is not to modify an event; rather it lies on a textual level. Its meaning is often considered to be closely related to the meaning of the additive focus particle *auch/also,* but there are clear differences:

(23) a. Er ist auch kein Alkoholiker.
he is also no alcoholic
b. Er ist selbst kein Alkoholiker.
he is himself no alcoholic

In (23)a there must be somebody else who is not an alcoholic (*auch* as an additive focus particle), but not in (23)b. Thus (23)b, but not (23)a, is felicitous in the following context:

(24) a. Er ist zwar ständig beruflich mit Alkoholproblemen konfrontiert, doch er ist selbst/#auch kein Alkoholiker.
he is in his profession continually confronted with alcohol problems, but he is himself/#also no alcoholic

For the interpretation of (23)b intonation is decisive. If the nuclear accent is placed on *selbst,* it has an inclusive meaning corresponding to (23)a. If, however, there is a further accent on *kein,* the meaning is not inclusive. Siemund (2000) explains (23)b as an instance of I-topicalization and considers it as a variant of adnominal *selbst* (cf. the next section).

Inclusive intensifiers often require accommodation. Siemund (2000: 260) states that "inclusive intensifiers typically occur in sentences which give the premise, reason, or explanation for another proposition in the previous or following discourse". Additional context is needed to accommodate inclusive intensifiers, whereby pragmatic inferences are generated. Siemund (2000: 261) suggests that "inclusive intensifiers can be analyzed as operators which identify two referents with respect to a conditional schema of the form, if p, then q". According to him, the "felicity conditions of inclusive intensifiers require that there is such a conditional schema salient in discourse".

(25) Liz wears glasses herself. => Liz cannot drive in the dark.
Conditional schema: If somebody wears glasses s/he cannot drive in the dark.

The raisonnement in connection with inclusive intensifiers is not yet completely understood. As Siemund (2000: 262) notes, future research has to establish ''why adverbial inclusive intensifiers produce precisely those implicatures which can be described as consequences of the situations described by their host sentences."

3.3. Adnominal intensification

Adnominal intensifiers establish a relation to alternatives for the referent of the NP they are adjoined to.

(26) a. Die Queen selbst war da.
'The Queen herself was present.'

The kind of alternatives is determined by the NP, e.g., the alternatives to the queen must be from her surroundings.

Adnominal intensifiers can only modify definite descriptions (cf. Siemund 2000: 259):

(27) a. *Manche Leute selbst waren da.
'*Some people themselves were present.'
b. *Eine Frau selbst erledigte das.
'*A woman herself got that done.'

Indefinite NPs can only be modified by an intensifier, if they allow a specific or generic interpretation. It must be possible to consider the referent of the NP as central in a certain way. König and Siemund (1996: 284), (2000: 46) formulate the following conditions for NPs that are modified by an intensifier:

(28) a. X has a higher position than Y in a hierarchy of the real world
b. X is in a specific situation more important than Y
c. Y is identified in relation to X
d. X is the perspectivized center of the text

The following example illustrates the first two conditions:

(29) [The anti-Greek campaign might become a problem for the elections.]
Dass *auch die Bundeskanzlerin selbst* derlei befürchtet, bewies Angela Merkel am Montag im CDU-Präsidium.
'That the chancellor herself fears this Angela Merkel proved on Monday in the CDU-presidency.'
(Süddeutsche Zeitung 28.4.2010, p. 5)

The chancellor has a higher position than other members of the party in parliament and she is more important in this particular situation. This example also shows that adnominal *selbst* can be combined with a focus particle.

A difference in the semantics of the adnominal intensifier and the homonymous focus particle *selbst* consists in the additive meaning of the focus particle:

(30) a. Die Queen selbst war da, aber sonst niemand.
'The Queen herself was there, but nobody else.'
b. *Selbst die Queen war da, aber sonst niemand.
*'Even the queen was there, but nobody else.'

As already mentioned, Siemund describes instances of adnominal intensifiers, which exhibit the intonation contour typical for I-topicalization (Büring 1997, Jacobs 1997). Edmondson and Plank (1978) speak of "role reversal" because the same referent occurs in different roles.

(31) Lucrezia poisoned Lorenzo, and was herself poisoned by Cesare. (agent → patient)
'Lucrezia vergiftete Lorenzo und wurde selbst von Caesar vergiftet.'

In 31, *herself* in English is disambiguating. Siemund shows that the same effect may occur without *self* (2000: 175), if a topic accent is present (S-topic according to Büring 1997):

(32) Paul insulted Mary. [$_T$HE] was insulted by [$_F$FRED].
Paul beschimpfte Maria. [$_T$Er] wurde von [$_F$FRED] beschimpft.

Siemund's analysis is based on the intonation contour typical for I-topicalization as well as the typical adversative implicature (cf. Siemund 2000: 177f. for details). He sees a center and periphery in these sentences on a more abstract level, with the topic being the center ("what the sentence is about") and the predicate the periphery.

By subsuming cases like these under adnominal intensifiers, he presupposes adnominal intensifiers to be able to appear without an explicit head as well as in distance to the noun phrase they relate to. He argues that these cases can be transformed into sentences with adnominal intensifiers (cf. 2000: 85ff. for further arguments).

(33) Paul insulted Mary. He himself was insulted by Fred.
'Paul beleidigte Maria. Er selbst wurde von Fred beleidigt.'

A distance position as well as topicalization is possible for adnominal *selbst*, if there is a double focus. The cases of I-topicalization exhibit characteristics similar to adnominal intensifiers.

3.4. Conclusions

While intensifiers share some characteristics with focus particles, there are clear differences. Intensifiers always bear sentential stress, whereas focus particles usually remain unstressed. Moreover, the interpretation of intensifiers varies according to their position and scope, which is characteristic for adverbials. Exclusive intensifiers pattern with manner adverbials (process-oriented adverbials) which occupy a base position adjacent to the verb in final position. Inclusive intensifiers have a base position in front of objects and have scope over negation, thus patterning with event-internal adverbials which are closely related to the highest ranking argument and c-commanded by it.

4. Word-internal reflexivization and intensification

As already noted in the introduction, the close relationship between reflexivization and intensification becomes evident also in their word-internal expressions, which are the same both in English and German. Since the means for word-internal reflexivization and syntactic reflexivization are different, reflexivization can be used to delimitate the boundary between syntax and the lexicon. German *selbst* and English *self* occur word-internally as exclusive intensifiers and as markers of reflexivization. German *selbst* also has a centering use similar to the adnominal intensifier. German *selber* may occur word-internally as an exclusive intensifier (cf. Pittner 2010).

4.1. Centering intensifiers

The English reflexive pronouns can be considered combinations of pronouns plus an adnominal intensifier. In German, *selbst* may occur word-internally with a function similar to the adnominal intensifier. The *Rückläufiges deutsches Wörterbuch* by Muthmann (2001: 889) lists the elements *daselbst, hierselbst, hieselbst, woselbst, dortselbst,* which are the combination of an adverb and the intensifier, and *ebendaselbst, ebendortselbst,* which are a combination of a focus particle with an adverb and an intensifier. These formations show that "adnominal" intensifiers can also be combined with elements other than nouns or pronouns.

4.2. Exclusive intensifiers

Exclusive intensifiers stress that an action is carried out by the external argument itself. In order to be relevant information, it is a necessary precondition that the action is usually not carried out by the external argument. König and Vezzosi (2004: 225) note "a general tendency of using intensifiers in nominal compounds only for other-directed situations."

(34) Selbstanzeige, Selbstanklage, Selbstliebe, Selbstverachtung, Selbstverteidigung, Selbstzerstörung etc.
self-accusation, self-contempt, self-love, self-defense, self-destruction, etc.

Exclusive *selber/selbst* operates on an agent or experiencer provided by the second part of the compound. The colloquial variant *selber* may occur in this function word-internally. *Selber-* and *selbst*-compounds may co-occur in some instances (examples from IDS-corpora):

(35) Selberläufer/Selbstläufer, Selberstreicher/Selbststreicher, Selberspieler/Selbstspieler

In present-day German, *selber* occurs word-internally only in an exclusive function. An exception is the use by Jean Paul of *selber* in reflexive function, which may be considered idiosyncratic:

(36) selberdünkel, -genügsamkeit, -hass, -mord, -opferung, -retter, -sucht, -täuschung, -verlag, -zünder
selberballenbinderin, selberbelachung, selberentzweiung, selbergefrieren, selber entzünden, selbergiftmischer, selbersattheit, selberwürdigung
(all according to DWB)

Today, *selber* occurs reflexively only in the formations *Selberlebensbeschreibung* und *Selberlebensbeschreiber*, which can be traced back to Jean Paul. The formations with *selber* in present-day German are mainly ad-hoc formations which have not been lexicalized apart from a few exceptions. The comprehensive dictionary *Deutsches Universalwörterbuch* only lists *Selbermachen*. The IDS-corpora contain around 400 formations, many of which are nominalized infinitives (cf. Pittner 2010).

(37) a. nominalized infinitives:
Selbermachen, Selberdenken, Selberkombinieren, Selber-Färben, Selberlesen, Selberbasteln, Selberkochen, Selberputzen, Selbernähen, …
b. phrasal compounds:
Selber-Schlag-Aktion, Selber-Back-Aktion, Selberbauverfahren, Selbermachgeschichte, Selbermachshow, Selber-Föhn-Konzept, Selber-Pflück-Angebote, Selber-Schuld-These,…
c. adjectival and nominalized participles:
selberdesignte, selberkreierte, Selbergekochtes, Selbergebackenes, Selbergenähtes, Selbergestricktes,...
d. compounds:
Selberbastler, Selbermacher, Selberzahler, Selber-Studierer, Selberhelfer,…
Selberbastler-Möbel, Selberspieler-Habitus

Most of these word formations have a very low frequency. Around 260 of the 400 lexical items occur only once, another 60 only twice, and 30 only three times. A frequency of over 100 tokens is found only with *Selbermachen* (929 tokens), *Selberpflücken* (110 tokens), *Selberlesen* (107 tokens) und *Selberbasteln* (101 tokens). These numbers hint at a low degree of lexicalization of the formations with *selber*, which are often ad-hoc formations with a colloquial flavor.

4.3. Reflexivization

First of all, the question is whether there is word-internal reflexivization at all. Edmondson and Plank (1978: 394) formulate the question "why it is not the pronoun that shows up in complex words but invariably the intensive or emphatic element alone". Their answer is that "intensification proper rather than reflexivization is the concept that is crucially relevant there".

Pronouns usually do not occur within lexemes, and reflexivization is usually expressed by pronouns. Fleischer (1993) considers formations with *selbst* as an exception to the rule that pronouns do not occur word-internally. We, on the contrary, see word-internal *selbst* as an indicator of its non-pronominal nature.

Starting from a general definition of reflexivization, that a predicate is reflexive whenever two of its arguments have the same referent, i.e., whenever there is co-reference between two arguments, it seems reasonable to assume word-internal reflexivization when the argument structure of nouns is taken into consideration. It is well known that deverbal nouns may inherit the arguments of the verb. And *selbst*/*self* can be used in a compound to indicate co-reference between two arguments of the second part of the compound.

We posit the following hypothesis:

(38) If a language has different expressions for reflexivization and intensification, intensification is used for word-internal reflexivization.

This holds not only for German, but also, e.g., for Dutch, Russian, and Polish. Some languages, especially those which do not use composition intensively appear to avoid these formations and use phrases instead, like French and Spanish (*self-consciousness – conscience de soi*, *seguridad en sì mismo*. *self-contempt – mépris de soi-même*, *deprecio de sí mismo*) and Romanian (*self-praise – lauda de sine*). Alternatively, a formation with the prefix *auto-* may be used.

In type I languages, where intensification and reflexivization are expressed by the same means, a shortened form is often used word-internally, like in English and Mandarin:

(39) English: self-love, self-portrait, self-reliance, self-consciousness, etc.
Mandarin: *zìliàn/zì'ài* 'self-love', *zìhuàxiàng* 'self-portrait' *zìshā* 'self-murder/suicide', *zìxìn* 'self-confidence'
But: *zìwǒzhǔzhāng* 'self-assertion' *zìwǒyìshi* 'self-esteem' *zìwǒqīngshì* 'self-contempt', *zìwǒbiǎoyáng* 'self-praise'[5]

English uses the non-pronominal part of the reflexive/intensifier. It may be assumed that this is a cross-linguistic tendency. In Mandarin, the reflexive pronoun/intensifier is combined from *zì* und *ji* which could both be used separately as reflexive pronouns in earlier stages. *Zi* was always co-referent with the subject and locally bound; *ji* was long-distance bound or could be free (cf. Yu 2000:103). The reflexive marker *ziwo* which can occur word-internally is always locally bound if it occurs in syntactic structures. It is possibly a cross-linguistic tendency that word-internally reflexive pronouns, which are locally bound if they occur in syntactic structures, are used.

Selbst/*self*-word-internally expresses reflexivization, which in syntax is expressed by reflexive pronouns. Thus, the means employed for reflexivization can provide insights into the syntax-morphology border. In German, nominalized infinitives of inherently reflexive verbs are not formed with *selbst* but with the reflexive pronoun *sich: Sich-Entrüsten, Sich-Einfügen, Sich-in-Szene-Setzen* (examples from Fleischer 1995: 542). Occasionally, *sich* can be omitted in nominalized infinitives of inherently reflexive verbs if there is no non-reflexive variant of the verb it could be mixed up with, e.g. *Räuspern* and *Sehnen.* The fact that not *selbst* but *sich* occurs in nominalized infinitives shows that nominalized infinitives are conversions from verbal phrases.

Sich may also occur in certain derivations, hinting at a phrasal base. *Insichnahme* and *Ansichnahme,*[6] for instance, are derivations by means of the nominal suffix *-e,* the basis of these derivations being the verb phrases *an sich nehm-* and *in sich nehm-.*

In English, *self* may occur within verbs as a reflexive marker:

(40) The rocket self-destroys. (cf. König and Gast 2009: 155)

This is due to back-formation of the verb from the noun *self-destruction.*

To sum up, *selbst*/*self* may occur word-internally as a marker of reflexivity and as a centering or exclusive intensifier. Intensifiers and intensifying parts of reflexive pronouns are used word-internally to express reflexivity, pronouns do not occur word-internally on account of their anaphoric functions. Also, inclusive intensifiers do not occur word-internally due to their textual functions.

---

[5] My thanks goes to Mi Liu for the examples from Mandarin.

[6] Both words occur in a quote from a lecture given by Heribert Prantl: "Die Insichnahme ist die intensivste Form der Ansichnahme." (quoted from Süddeutsche Zeitung 30.4./1./2.5.2010, S. VI/1)

5. Summary

Reflexivization and intensification are related concepts which are expressed by the same means in a number of languages. English is a case in point, whereas German uses different means for the expression of reflexivization (the reflexive pronoun *sich* and personal pronouns) and intensification (*selbst* and its colloquial variant *selber*).

Intensifiers are best described as adverbial expressions belonging to different adverbial classes with regard to their scope and base position. Exclusive intensifiers pattern with manner adverbials (process-oriented adverbials) which take a base position adjacent to the verb in final position, whereas inclusive intensifiers pattern with event-internal adverbs which are c-commanded by the highest ranking argument.

Word-internally, both English and German use the same means for the expression of reflexivization and intensification, namely *self/selbst,* which may occur as a centering or an exclusive intensifier. Due to their textual functions, inclusive intensifiers do no occur word-internally.

In a number of languages, reflexivization within lexemes is expressed by intensifiers or intensifying parts of reflexive pronouns. The cross-linguistic validity of some observations concerning word-internal reflexivization made in the last section of the paper remains to be proved by future research.

Bibliography

Büring, D. (1997): *The Meaning of Topic and Focus. The 59th Street Bridge Accent.* London/New York: Routledge.

Dimroth, C. (2004): *Fokuspartikeln und Informationsgliederung im Deutschen.* Tübingen: Stauffenburg.

Duden (2007): *Deutsches Universalwörterbuch.* 6., überarbeitete und erweiterte Auflage. Mannheim: Dudenverlag.

Duden (2009): *Grammatik der deutschen Sprache.* 8., überarbeitete Auflage. Mannheim: Dudenverlag.

DWB (2004): *Deutsches Wörterbuch.* Elektronische Ausgabe der Erstbearbeitung von Jacob Grimm und Wilhelm Grimm. Frankfurt/M.

Eckardt, R. (2001): Reanalysing *selbst. Natural Language Semantics* 9: 371–412.

Edmondson, J. A. and F. Plank (1978): Great Expectations: An intensive self-analysis. *Linguistics & Philosophy* 2: 373–413.

Eisenberg, P. (2006): *Grundriss der deutschen Grammatik. Bd. 2: Der Satz.* Stuttgart: Metzler.

Fleischer, W. (1993): Zur Wortbildungsaktivität des Lexems »selbst«. In: G. Jäger, K. Gommlich and G. M. Shreve (eds.), *Text and Meaning.* Institute for Applied Linguistics, Kent State University, Kent (Ohio), 35–40 (= Kent Forum on translation studies, 1).

Fleischer, W. (1995): Zur Wortbildungsaktivität reflexiver Verben. In: H. Popp (ed.), *Deutsch als Fremdsprache. An den Quellen eines Faches. Festschrift für Gerhard Helbig zum 65. Geburtstag.* München: iudicium, 533–544.

Frey, W. (2003): Syntactic conditions on adjunct classes. In: E. Lang, C. Maienborn and C. Fabricius-Hansen (eds.), *Modifying Adjuncts*. Berlin/New York: de Gruyter, 163–209.

Frey, W. and K. Pittner (1998): Zur Positionierung von Adverbialen im deutschen Mittelfeld. *Linguistische Berichte* 176: 489–534.

Frey, W. and K. Pittner (1999): Adverbialpositionen im deutsch-englischen Vergleich. In: M. Doherty (ed.), *Sprachspezifische Aspekte der Informationsverteilung*. Berlin: Akademie-Verlag, 14–41. (studia grammatica)

Gast, V. (2006): *The Grammar of Identity. Intensifiers and Reflexives in Germanic Languages*. London: Routledge

Hole, D. (2002): Agentive *selbst* in German. In: G. Katz, S. Reinhard and P. Reuter (eds.), *Sinn & Bedeutung*. VI. Proceedings of the Sixth Annual Meeting of the Gesellschaft für Semantik, University of Osnabrück, 133–150.

Huddleston, R. and G. Pullum (2002): *The Cambridge Grammar of the English Language*. Cambridge: Cambridge University Press.

Jacobs, J. (1997): I-Topikalisierung. *Linguistische Berichte* 168: 91–133.

Kemmer, S. (1993): *The Middle Voice*. Amsterdam: Benjamins.

König, E. and V. Gast (2006): Focussed assertion of identity: A typology of intensifiers. *Linguistic Typology* 10: 223–276.

König, E. and V. Gast (2009): *Understanding English-German Contrasts*. Berlin: Schmidt.

König, E. and P. Siemund (1996): *Selbst*-Reflektionen. In: G. Harras and M. Bierwisch (eds.), *Wenn die Semantik arbeitet. Festschrift für Klaus Baumgärtner*. Tübingen: Niemeyer, 277–302.

König, E. and P. Siemund (1999): Intensifiers and reflexives: A typological perspective. In: Z. Frajzyngier and T. S. Curl (eds.), *Reflexives. Form and Functions*. Amsterdam/Philadelphia: Benjamins, 41–74.

König, E. and L. Vezzosi (2004): The role of predicate meaning in the development of reflexivity. In: W. Bisang, N. Himmelmann and B. Wiemer (eds.), *What Makes Grammaticalization? – A Look from its Fringes and its Components*. Berlin/New York: de Gruyter, 214–244.

Leys, O. (1973): Das Reflexivpronomen: Eine Variante des Personalpronomens. In: H. Sitta and K. Brinker (eds.), *Studien zur Texttheorie und zur deutschen Grammatik. Festgabe für Hans Glinz zum 60. Geburtstag*. Düsseldorf: Schwann, 223–242.

Muthmann, G. (2001): *Rückläufiges deutsches Wörterbuch. Handbuch der Wortausgänge im Deutschen mit Beachtung der Wort- und Lautstruktur*. Tübingen: Niemeyer.

Mutz, K. (2004): Zur Argumentstruktur der deverbalen Ableitungen von *auto-*. In: R. Kailuweit and M. Hummel (eds.), *Semantische Rollen*. Tübingen: Narr, 355–374.

Pittner, K. (1999): *Adverbiale im Deutschen. Untersuchungen zu ihrer Stellung und Interpretation*. Tübingen: Stauffenburg.

Pittner, K. (2010): *Selber* und *selbst* als Wortbestandteile. *Muttersprache* 1: 1–9.

Pittner, K. (2012): *Selbst*-Analysen: Wortarten und wortinterne Funktionen. In: B. Rothstein (ed.), *Nicht-flektierende Wortarten*. Berlin/New York: de Gruyter, 148–169.

Plank, F. (1979): Zur Affinität von *selbst* und *auch.* In: H. Weydt (ed.), *Die Partikeln der deutschen Sprache.* Berlin/New York: de Gruyter, 269–284.

Primus, B. (1991): *Selbst* – Variants of a Scalar Adverb in German. In: J. Jacobs (ed.), Informationsstruktur und Grammatik. *Linguistische Berichte. Sonderheft 4*, Opladen: Westdeutscher Verlag, 54–88.

Siemund, P. (2000): *Intensifiers in English and German. A comparison.* London: Routledge.

Stanescu, S. (2006): Von *Fremd* und *Selbst.* Zur Reflexivität im Deutschen und Rumänischen. In: E. Breindl, L. Gunkel and B. Strecker (eds.), *Grammatische Untersuchungen, Analysen und Reflexionen. Festschrift für Gisela Zifonun.* Tübingen: Narr, 241–257.

Wilss, W. (1997): Zusammensetzungen mit *selbst* in der deutschen Gegenwartssprache. *Muttersprache* 107: 330–338.

Yu, W. X.-F. (2000): *Chinese Reflexives.* Leuven et al.: Peeters.

Zifonun, G., L. Hoffmann and B. Strecker et al. (1997): *Grammatik der deutschen Sprache.* 3 Volumes. Berlin/New York: de Gruyter

IDS-corpora, Archive of written language, provided by the Institut für Deutsche Sprache in Mannheim.

Don't mince your words: In defense of lexical integrity*

Markus Egg

1. Introduction

Semantics considerably influences syntactic theory-building in that the (non-)ability to account for specific semantic intuitions is often adduced as an argument for or against specific syntactic theories. Syntactic theories that include *morphemes* (and other parts of words) among the atomic units (and thus assume that surface-level words can be the result of syntactic processes like incorporation) seem to have an advantage over surface-oriented syntactic theories that do not: The resulting flexibility for the first kind of theory in arranging parts of words can mediate between syntactic and semantic structure, thereby facilitating the mapping from (morpho-)syntax to semantics even in challenging cases of semantic construction.

As examples, consider the time-honoured cases of ambiguity in nominal modification (Larson 1998, Egg 2008) like in (1):

(1) beautiful dancer

(1) has the readings 'someone who dances and is beautiful' and 'someone who dances beautifully'. If one assumes that the affix means something like 'someone who *V*-s', for a given stem *V*, the two readings can be derived straightforwardly by giving the affix scope over its stem only or over the stem and the modifier (which then pertains to the stem exclusively):

(2) a. -er(beautiful(dance))
b. beautiful(-er(dance))

The first scope constellation seems to suggest a position of the affix above the modifier *beautiful*. I.e., there is a *mismatch* between the surface arrangement of morphemes into words and the interpretation of the phrase.[1]

The success in accounting for such phenomena is often taken as an argument in favour of an approach to syntax that dispenses with *lexical integrity* (Anderson 1992, Booij 2009). Such an approach assumes that the syntax can manipulate and/or access the internal structure of words, consequently, allows basic syntactic units below the word level.

* Thanks to Holden Härtl for valuable comments on an earlier version of this paper.

1 Larson (1998) resolves the mismatch differently; he assumes a low position for the modifier (sister of the noun), whose content then emerges as the scope of the generic quantification introduced by the noun.

Therefore, advocates of surface-oriented syntactic approaches such as HPSG (Pollard and Sag 1994) or LFG (Dalrymple 2001) must show that they can also derive the desired semantic interpretations for these phenomena on the basis of the postulated syntactic structures. This is a challenge because of the *semantic opacity* of words, i.e., semantic construction can only handle the semantic contribution of a word as a whole, which seems to suggest that it cannot access proper parts of this contribution which correspond to the interpretation of individual morphemes within the word.

But in recent years, surface-oriented analyses have caught up in this respect, which is due to a general trend towards underspecified approaches to ambiguity: The very powerful interfaces needed to build up meta-level semantic representations of ambiguous expressions lend themselves to tricky cases of semantic construction that do not necessarily involve ambiguity. The price (developing complex syntax-semantics interfaces) has already been paid to make underspecified representations of ambiguity possible. This advance in linguistic theory-building can be fruitfully applied to cases in which there seem to be syntactically relevant units below the level of words, irrespective of whether there is ambiguity or not.

But if it is possible to re-use the powerful interfaces that have been developed for underspecified accounts of ambiguity in order to treat these cases on the basis of a surface-oriented syntactic analysis that respects lexical integrity, then these cases are no longer an argument in favour of analyses that dispense with lexical integrity.

I will discuss some challenging cases for semantic construction and show how they can be handled on the basis of a surface-oriented syntactic analysis that respects lexical integrity. The core of this account is a very flexible syntax-semantics interface that can express scope relations for individual morphemes.

2. The data

This section presents the data that seem to provide arguments against lexical integrity. All the data resembles (1) in that morphemes within a word have scope over other words in the same phrase.

The first example is the Turkish (3), in which the adjective *yağız* ('dark brown') can be in the scope of the affix *-lı* ('[provided] with'), which yields the interpretation 'someone with a dark brown horse'. In addition, there is the straightforward interpretation 'dark brown rider'. Since *yağız* is used predominantly for horses, the first interpretation is preferred out of the blue.[2]

(3)	yağız	at	-lı
	dark.brown	horse	provided.with

In example (4), an instance of the Turkish '*-ip*-construction', two VPs are coordinated, and the verbal ending of the first conjunct is replaced by the suffix *-ip* (Kornflit 1997, Göksel

2 In motivated contexts, the other interpretation is possible, too, e.g., (3) refers to the Black Knight in the Turkish translation of Walter Scott's Ivanhoe (Gözde Böcü, p.c.).

and Kerslake 2011). But the first conjunct in (4) is interpreted as 'I will eat', due to the first person future ending in the second conjunct.[3]

This suggests giving the verb ending *-eceğim* wide scope over both verb stems:

(4)	yi	-yip	iç	-eceğ	-im
	eat	IP	drink	FUT	1sg
	'I will eat and drink.'				

Similarly, in Island (as opposed to Mainland) Scandinavian languages, enclitic determiners that are attached to a noun still can have scope over modifiers of the noun, e.g., the Icelandic (5):

(5)	rauða	hús	-ið
	red	house	the
	'the red house'		

I will offer an account of (3)–(5) that captures the intuition that their readings are due to the scope of morphemes beyond their word.

3. Semantic underspecification

The analysis is based on previous work on scope ambiguity as illustrated by the quantifier scope ambiguity in (6). The functional nature of semantic interpretation is preserved for such expressions by setting up a 1–1 correspondence between a single syntactic structure and one underspecified semantic representation that encompasses all the readings of the expression (rather than a one-to-many correspondence between syntactic and semantic structures).

(6) Every man loves a woman.

The resulting semantic representation would roughly state that the semantic contribution of the verb is outscoped by the meanings of both DPs, but deliberately leave open the relative scope of the DP meanings.

In previous work, I applied this strategy fruitfully to model ambiguities that involve only parts of words, in particular, to cases like (1) or the 'repetitive'/'restitutive' readings of *again*-sentences such as (7) (von Stechow 1996, Egg 2008). The readings presuppose that there was a previous opening and that the door had been open before, respectively (see section 6.3 for further discussion of this example):

(7) The door opened again.

But once the syntax-semantics interface for these cases of ambiguity is established, it turns out that it can also be felicitously applied to other difficult cases of semantic construction where there is no ambiguity. Consider e.g., Abney's (1987) account of the modification of

---

[3] 'FUT' glosses future tense and '1sg' first person singular. After stems ending in a vowel, *-ip* takes the form *-yip*.

indefinite pronouns like in (8). Here, the challenge is to derive a semantic representation (a set of properties) from the representations of the pronoun (also a set of properties) and of the modifier (a property or a function from properties to properties). Giving the 'every' part of *everyone* wide scope over the modifier would immediately solve this question.

(8) everyone in this room

In a number of papers (Egg 2004, 2008) I have used underspecification formalisms to model the presented semantic intuitions about cases like (8) on the basis of surface-oriented syntactic structures. I have used the expressive power of the syntax-semantics interfaces for the construction of underspecified representations of scopally ambiguous expressions, which allow one to manipulate *parts* of semantic representations of constituents without having to move corresponding morphemes in the syntax – if they exist at all, which might be straightforward for (8) but much less so for (7).

E.g., in the semantic construction of (8), the semantic representation of *everyone* distinguishes the restriction of the quantification (the property of being a person) in a (secondary) fragment of its own. The interface rule for adjunction then states that a modifier (here, *in this room*) takes scope over the secondary fragment of the modified expression only (here, over the semantics of the stem). This deliberately leaves open the scope relation of modifier and main fragment of the modified expression, which in the case of (8) means that the adjective can be inside the restriction of the universal quantification.

In fact, it must end up as part of this restriction; otherwise, the resulting representation would not be well-formed (due to the attempt to apply a function from properties of individuals to properties of individuals to a set of such properties). This blocking of potential ambiguity is mandatory, since (8) is not ambiguous. This example thus illustrates clearly that one can only use this strategy for challenging examples of the morphology-semantics interface, if the resulting ambiguity is strictly controlled.

The interface strategy sketched in this section uses a so-called *underspecification formalism*. These formalisms preserve the 1-1 relation between syntactic and semantic structure by capturing the set of readings of a given syntactic structure in terms of a meta-level representation that defines exactly the set of readings (by describing their common ground) without enumerating them disjunctively.

The following sections will introduce an underspecification formalism in detail and apply it to the difficult cases of semantic construction (3)–(5).The last section then discusses related work that also tackles such cases.

4. The formalism

This section introduces the proposed underspecified approach to semantic construction by sketching how it is used to handle the semantic construction of (8) in Egg (2004). As opposed to movement analyses as in, e.g., Kishimoto (2000) und Abney (1987), this analysis assumes a simple syntactic structure for (8), viz., adjunction of the PP to the pronoun (after projection to $\bar{D}$) which then projects to DP. The mismatch between syntactic and semantic structure is handled in the syntax-semantics interface. The challenge is the derivation of (9), the semantics of (8), from the pronoun meaning (10) and the modifier meaning (11). Note that applying (11) to the underlined part of (10) would yield (9), here the semantics of *this room* is abbreviated as 'R':

(9) $\lambda P \forall x.\text{person}'(x) \wedge \text{in}'(x, \text{R}) \rightarrow P(x)$

(10) $\lambda P \forall x.\underline{\text{person}'(x)} \rightarrow P(x)$

(11) $\lambda P \lambda x.P(x) \wedge \text{in}'(x, \text{R})$

4.1. The representation format

The analysis is based on the underspecification formalism Constraint Language for Lambda Structures (CLLS; Egg et al. 2001). With such a formalism, one can define very flexible syntax-semantics interfaces. Its expressions are so-called *constraints* that describe a set of semantic representations, one for each reading of a structurally ambiguous expression. For the purpose of this paper, an abbreviated form of CLLS suffices, whose constraints describe λ-terms. Semantic representations are called *solutions* of a constraint when they are compatible with it. For the present paper, we can restrict ourselves to a subset of solutions, viz., those that comprise only material explicitly mentioned in the constraint. Under this restriction, constraints can be regarded as a *partial order* on a set of fragments of semantic representations.

For instance, the CLLS constraint for the meaning of (8) is given in (12). Please ignore for the time being any labels like '⟦C⟧ ', I will explain them in subsection 4.2. (12) illustrates the ingredients of simplified CLLS expressions:

- *fragments* of λ-terms
- not yet known parts of these fragments, indicated by 'holes'
- *dominance relations* (depicted by dotted lines) that relate fragments to holes

Dominance relations between a fragment and a hole indicate that the fragment is an (im-) proper part of what the hole stands for. These dominance relations model scope and are therefore also used to model quantifier scope ambiguities.

(12)

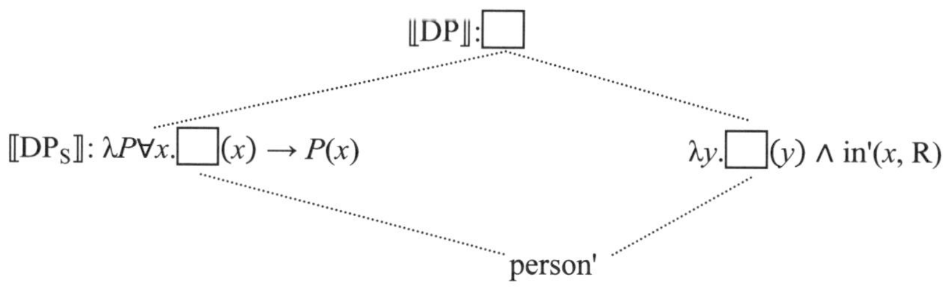

The semantic contribution of the PP constitutes the right hand fragment. The meaning of the pronoun is expressed in the left and the bottom fragment, which together make up (10). The underlined part of (10), viz., the restriction of the quantification, emerges as a fragment of its own in (12).

The fact that there is only a hole on top in (12) indicates that the λ-term described by the constraint cannot yet be specified. However, due to the dominance relations between this hole and the fragments on the right and the left we know that these fragments are the immediate parts of this λ-term. The restriction of the quantification of the pronoun constitutes the bottom fragment, which is dominated by holes in the right and left fragments, thus, ends up in the scope of both quantification and modifier. Structures like (12) are called *dominance diamonds*.

To resolve ambiguity in constraints, information is added monotonically, in particular, by strengthening dominance relations between holes and fragments to *identity*. For (12), there is only one choice, viz., identifying the bottom fragment with the hole in the modifier fragment, and the modifier fragment, with the hole in the right fragment. This returns (9); here the PP pertains only to the restriction of the quantification introduced by the pronoun and is thus outscoped by the 'every' part of the pronoun. The other option is blocked due to the types of the involved fragments. I.e., (12) is an adequate representation of the semantics of (8) and does not overgenerate, because unwanted ambiguity is blocked by the types of the involved fragments. While in this example the potential ambiguity of the constraint is resolved immediately, the ambiguity is crucial for an analogous analysis of (1), which has two readings. See Egg (2004) for such an analysis in terms of a similar constraint, whose ambiguity encompasses the two readings of (1).

Note that the interface strategy does not depend on a specific underspecification formalism. Much of my analyses, which are cast in the Constraint Language for Lambda Structures (Egg et al. 2001), could be rephrased directly in other formalisms such as Underspecified DRT (Reyle 1993), Minimal Recursion Semantics (Copestake et al. 2005), Glue Language Semantics (Dalrymple et al. 1997), or Lexical Tree-Adjoining Grammar (Joshi et al. 2007).

4.2. The interface rules

This subsection describes the syntax-semantics interface that allows the derivation of constraints like (12) on the basis of a surface-oriented syntactic analysis. The interface presumes that the semantic contribution of every syntactic constituent distinguishes a *main* and an embedded *secondary* fragment. In CLLS constraints like (12), '⟦C⟧' indicates the main fragment of a constituent C and '⟦C_S⟧', the secondary fragment of C. '⟦C⟧:F' expresses that the main fragment of C is defined as fragment F. Consider, e.g., the lexical entry for the semantics of *everyone*, in which the restriction of the quantification is singled out as the secondary fragment, while the rest of the semantic representation shows up in the main fragment:

(13) $$[\![D]\!] : \lambda P \forall x. \square(x) \rightarrow P(x)$$
$$[\![D_S]\!] : \text{person}'$$

Interface rules specify for a constituent C how the constraints Con_1 and Con_2 of its immediate constituents C_1 and C_2, inherited by C, are combined into a new constraint for C. The rules combine Con_1 and Con_2 by addressing their main and secondary fragments and determine these features for *C*. E.g., the rule that non-branching $\overline{X}$ constituents inherit their fragments from their heads is written as (14):

(14) $[_{\overline{X}}X] \overset{(SSI)}{\Longrightarrow} [\![\overline{X}]\!] : [\![X]\!]; \quad [\![\overline{X}_S]\!] : [\![X_S]\!]$

The semantic representation of modification (adjunction) structures like in (8) is constructed by the interface rule (15). The main fragment $[\![\overline{X}_1]\!]$ of the whole constituent is $[\![\overline{X}_2]\!]$, the one from the modified expression. In contrast, its secondary fragment $[\![\overline{X}_{1S}]\!]$ is not inherited from this expression, instead, it consists of an application of the modifier fragment $[\![Mod]\!]$ to a hole that dominates the secondary fragment $[\![\overline{X}_{2S}]\!]$ of the modified expression. In this way, we can construct the bottom half of a dominance diamond in which $[\![Mod]\!]$ and $[\![\overline{X}_1]\!]$ are scopally ambiguous in that they both dominate $[\![\overline{X}_2]\!]$. Dominance between $[\![\overline{X}_1]\!]$ and $[\![\overline{X}_{2S}]\!]$is specified in the semantic representation of $\overline{X}_2$ (recall that $[\![\overline{X}_1]\!]$ is equated with $[\![\overline{X}_2]\!]$), e.g., it can eventually follow from lexical entries as (13). The equation of the modifier fragments ($[\![Mod]\!]$:$[\![Mod_S]\!]$) is introduced to facilitate reading.

(15)

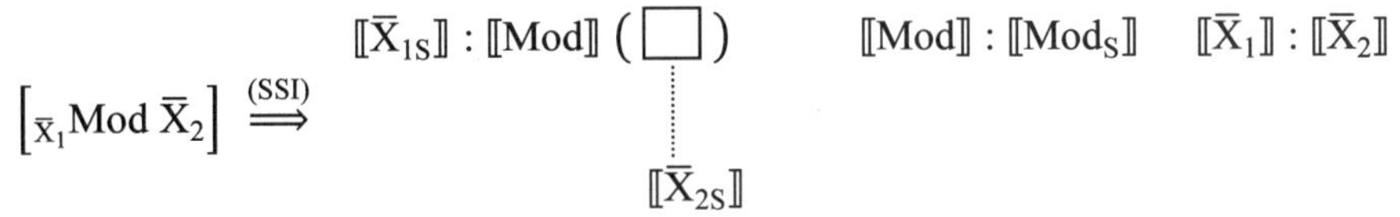

The rule that constructs the upper half of the dominance diamond corresponds to the syntax rule XP → $\overline{X}$. The main fragment of the XP is a hole that dominates both fragments of the $\overline{X}$ constituent:

(16)

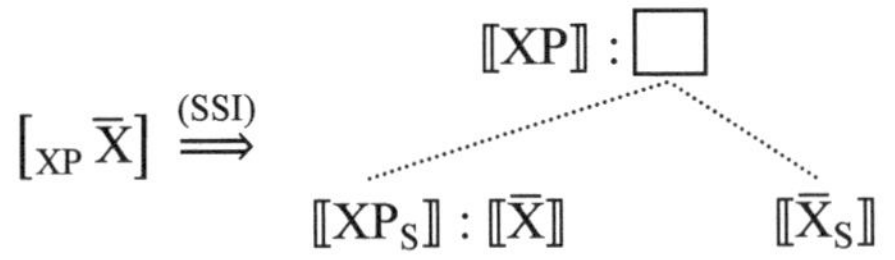

Semantic construction for *everyone in this room* is based on an analysis that regards *everyone* as an intransitive determiner (i.e., it does not subcategorize for an NP complement) that is modified by a PP before projecting to the phrasal level:

(17)

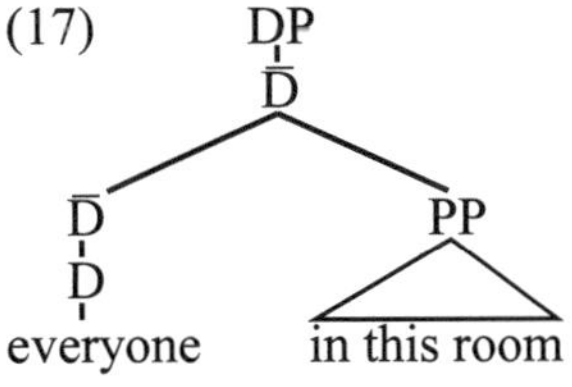

The derivation of its interpretation starts with the semantic representations (13) and (18) of pronoun and PP (whose derivation I cannot go into any further in this paper). Rule (14) states that (13) is the semantics of the $\overline{D}$ *everyone* too.

(18) $[\![PP]\!], [\![PP_S]\!]: \lambda P \lambda x.P(x) \wedge \text{in}'(x, \text{R})$

By rule (15) the constraints of $\overline{D}$ and the PP are combined into (19), the lower half of a dominance diamond as a consequence of adjoining the PP to the $\overline{D}$ *everyone*. Finally, this lower half serves as the input to rule (16), which then yields the dominance diamond (12). Rule (16) applies because the $\bar{\mathrm{D}}$ *everyone in this room* projects to DP.

(19) $[\![\bar{\mathrm{D}}]\!] : \lambda P \forall x.\square(x) \rightarrow P(x)$ $\qquad$ $[\![\bar{\mathrm{D}}_{\mathrm{S}}]\!] : \lambda x.\square(x) \wedge \mathrm{in}'(x, \mathrm{R})$

person'

5. The analysis

In this section I will show how the challenging examples (3)–(5) can be handled on the basis of simple syntactic analyses. First, the underlying syntactic analyses for the examples will be discussed, then the derivation of their semantic representations will be expounded in detail.

5.1. Syntax

For the Icelandic data, a generative analysis would regard the determiner suffix as the head of a DP, whose NP complement involves adjunction. After Merge, the N head moves to D and combines with the (strong) affix:

(20)

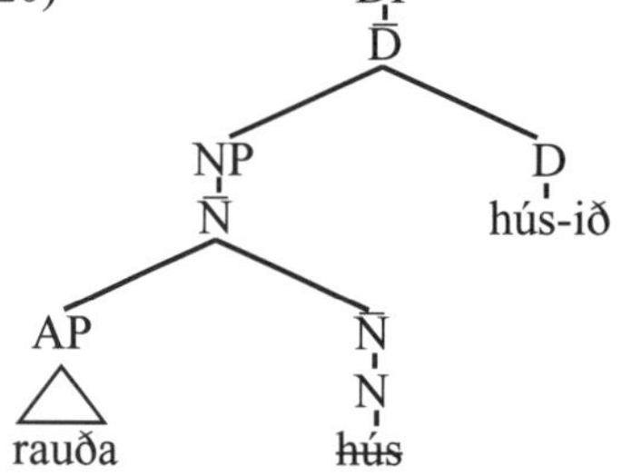

In this analysis, the interpretation would be straightforward, in particular, scope of the affix over the AP, if we assume that syntactic c-command[4] immediately entails semantic scope: The AP modifies the noun *hús* first, and the meaning (21)a of the resulting NP is then the argument of the semantic contribution of the determiner suffix, which returns the desired semantic representation (21)b, the set of properties that the unique red house has.[5]

(21) a. $\lambda P \lambda x.P(x) \wedge \mathrm{red}'(x)[\mathrm{house}'] \equiv \lambda x.\mathrm{house}'(x) \wedge \mathrm{red}'(x)$

b. $\lambda P \exists! x.[\mathrm{house}'(x) \wedge \mathrm{red}'(x)] \wedge \mathrm{P}(x)$

However, as soon as one does not want to regard elements below the word level as independent syntactic units, a different analysis is called for. I assume that the suffix *-ið* attaches

4 The most common definition is that node A c-commands node B in a tree if A is the daughter of a node that also dominates B, and A does not dominate B, and vice versa.

5 The determiner semantics is simplified; here $\exists! x.[P(x)] \wedge Q(x)$ means that there is a unique x with the property P, and that this x also has the property Q.

to nouns and returns an intransitive determiner (of the same syntactic class as *everyone*), which can then be modified by APs before projecting to the phrase level. This analysis maximises the common ground between (5) and (8) by assigning them the same syntactic structure. The only difference is that *húsið* is the output of a productive morphological process while *everyone* is not:

(22)

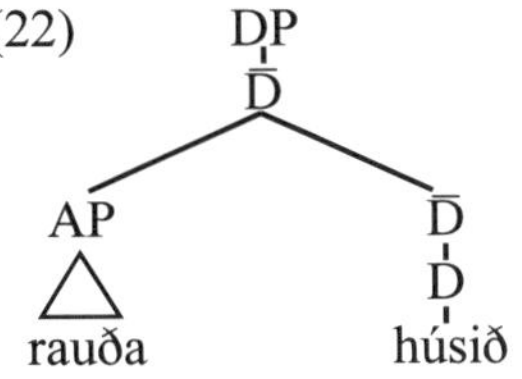

For (3), a similar story can be told. In a generative-style analysis (23)a, the modifier *yağız* pertains to the stem *at* exclusively, which returns an NP whose expression fits in nicely with the semantics of the affix *-lı*. We assume that the NP serves as complement of an N head *-lı*; its head *at* moves to this N after Merge.

But regarding *atlı* as aminimal syntactic unit means that we have to assume a modification structure in which *yağız* pertains to the morphologically complex noun *atlı* as a whole (23)b:

(23)

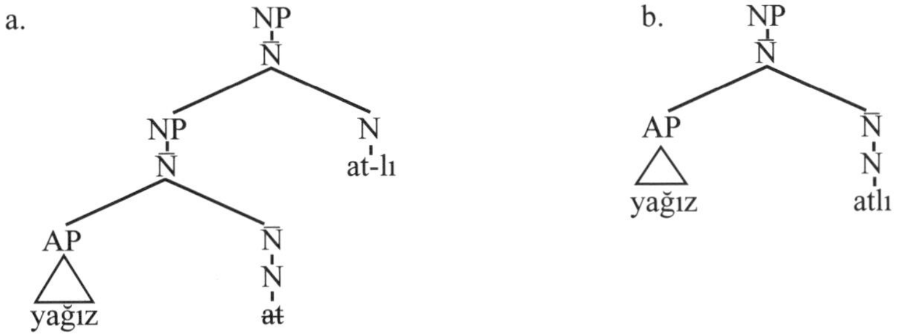

Semantic construction for (23)a would once again be straightforward; applying the affix meaning (24)a, a function from properties P to the property of being provided with an entity that has P, to the NP meaning (24)b, which is the result of modifying *at* by *yağız*, returns the NP semantics (24)c, the set of entities provided with a dark brown horse:

(24) a. $\lambda P \lambda x \exists y.P(y) \wedge$ provided-with'(x,y)
b. $\lambda x.$horse'$(x) \wedge$ dark-brown'(x)
c. $\lambda x \exists y.$horse'$(y) \wedge$ dark-brown'$(y) \wedge$ provided-with'(x,y)

Finally, there is the question of how to analyse the *-ip*-construction syntactically. In a generative framework, one can model wide scope of the verb ending in cases like (4) straightforwardly if one regards it as head T of a Tense Phrase whose complement is a VP *yiyip iç-*.

The VP itself then breaks down into the specifier (the base position of the subject) and a $\overline{V}$, in which the two verb stems are coordinated. In this way, one can model the intuition that the subject of the two verbs must be the same. In our example, the subject is the unexpressed first person singular pronoun, which is modelled by the 'little *pro*', since Turkish is a so-called 'pro-drop language', in which pronominal subjects are optional.

Then $\overline{V}$ itself is a coordination structure, following Moltmann (1992), coordination is analysed in terms of adjunction, here, of a 'Boolean Phrase' or '&P' (whose head is *-ip*) to an appropriate $\overline{X}$ constituent[6], here, *iç-* 'drink'. Since complementation precedes adjunction, this brings out the fact that only maximal $\overline{V}$ constituents (i.e., with only the subject lacking but any complements already in place) may show up in the *-ip*-construction (Kornflit 1997: 110, Göksel and Kerslake 2011: 131). The &P, finally, consists of the head *-ip* and its $\overline{V}$ complement *ye-* 'eat' (the form *yi-* is due to the following glide). Integration of the suffixes with their bases is then another case of head movement, attracting the closest suitable heads to the (strong) affixes:

(25)

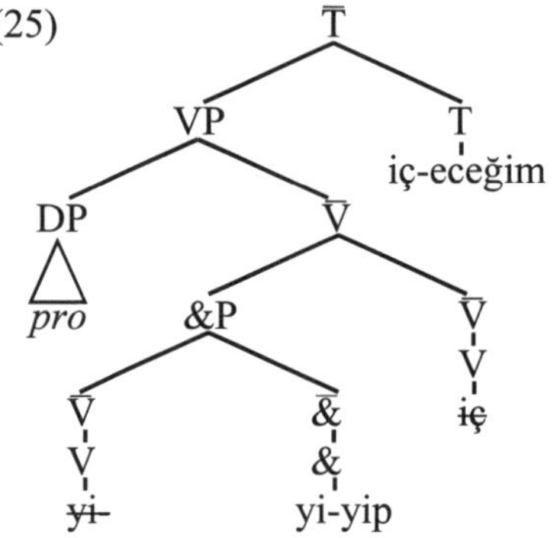

Semantic construction for (4) is then once again a matter of functional application, based on appropriate representations of the basic syntactic units. For the future affix, it is necessary to model the semantic contribution of tense (albeit in a very simple form). I assume a Davidsonian semantics, i.e., every verb includes in its semantic representation an *eventuality* argument. (Eventualities are states of affairs of every kind.) The semantics of the verb ending in (4) is then glossed as a function from properties P of eventualities to the property of eventualities e such that e is in the extension of P and follows the utterance eventuality e_0:

(26) $\lambda P \lambda e. e_0 < e \wedge P(e)$

The DP semantics maps relations P between individuals and eventualities onto properties of eventualities. For the interpretation of the little *pro*, one can assume that the relevant ϕ-features (for number and person) are first copied (via syntactic agreement) from T to DP, and then determine the first argument of P:

(27) $\lambda P \lambda e. P(\text{speaker'})(e)$

The semantics of *-ip* introduces a conjunction of two relations between individuals and eventualities, then the semantic representations of the highest $\overline{V}$, VP, and $\overline{T}$ emerge as (28)a-c, respectively.

[6] The exact syntactic analysis of coordination still is a matter of considerable debate; see Zhang (2010) for a thorough discussion.

(28) a. $\lambda x \lambda e$.drink'(x)(e) ∧ eat'(x)(e)
b. λe.drink'(speaker')(e) ∧ eat'(speaker')(e)
c. $\lambda e.e_0 < e$ ∧ drink'(speaker')(e) ∧ eat'(speaker')(e)

(28)c is the meaning of (4), the set of events following the utterance eventuality e_0 which are simultaneously a drinking and an eating of the speaker.

In a surface-oriented structure, however, suffixes cannot appear as heads of &P and TP, respectively. They are firmly attached to their stems; *-ip* returns an expression of category & (which then projects to &P). But we can adopt the analysis of the coordination as adjunction, here, of *içeceğim* as a whole, by a &P:

(29)
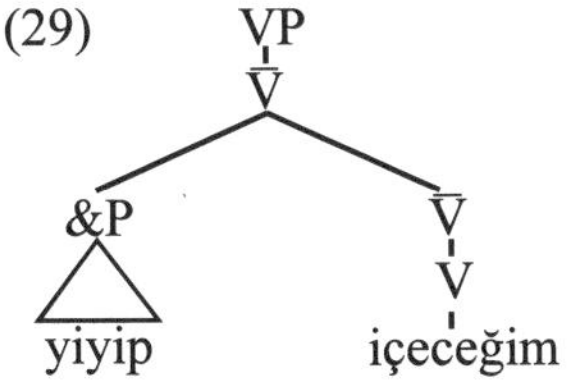

In sum, the common ground between the examples (3)–(5) is that they all involve affixed constituents that are modified. This can lead to ambiguity, as in the case of (3), or not, as in (4) or (5), which depends on the semantic contributions of both modifier and modified expression.

5.2. Semantics

To handle the semantic impact of affixation, we need a general rule that describes the way in which the interpretation of the resulting expression is derived from the semantic contributions of stem and affix. This rule has already been introduced in Egg (2004) for the semantics of English agentive nouns like *dancer* in (1) and can be reused here directly (in a slightly simplified form, since binding the arguments of the base is not an issue here; see Egg 2008):

(30)
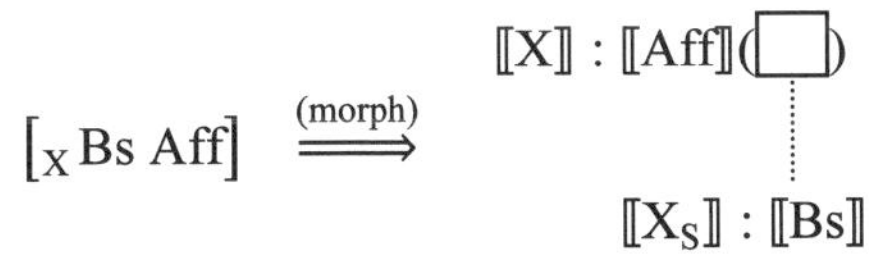

In prose: The affix semantics contributes the main fragment of the new constituent X. It applies to a hole that dominates the semantic contribution of the stem, which becomes the secondary fragment.

I will now show in detail how this rule—together with the interface rules sketched in section 4.2.—allows the derivation of the desired semantic representations for (3)–(5), starting with semantic construction for (4).

The semantics of the 1st person singular future ending in (4) is modelled—in a slightly different way from (26) above—as a function from relations P between individuals and eventualities to properties of eventualities e iff e follows the utterance eventuality e_0, and P relates the speaker and e:

(31) $[\![\text{Aff}]\!], [\![\text{Aff}_S]\!]: \lambda P\lambda e.e_0 < e \wedge P(\text{speaker}')(e)$

Following (30), the semantic representation for the second conjunct in (4), *içeceğim* ('I will drink'), is thus (32). Inflected verbs—like any kind of affixed entities—have a structured semantic representation, in which the stem contributes the secondary and the inflection, the primary fragment.

(32) $[\![\text{V}]\!]: \lambda e.e_0 < e \wedge \square(\text{speaker}')(e)$

$[\![\text{V}_S]\!]: \text{drink}'$

Regarding the semantic contribution of *-ip* once again as a conjunction of relations between individuals and eventualities returns (33)a as the semantic representation for *yiyip*. (33)b is the semantics of *yiyip* as a $\overline{\&}$ constituent, too, for *yiyip* as &P, we get (33)c:

(33) a. $[\![\text{Aff}]\!], [\![\text{Aff}_S]\!]: \lambda Q\lambda P\lambda x\lambda e.P(x)(e) \wedge Q(x)(e)$

b. $[\![\text{V}]\!]: \lambda P\lambda x\lambda e.P(x)(e) \wedge \square(x)(e)$

$[\![\text{V}_S]\!]: \text{eat}'$

c. $[\![\&\text{P}]\!]: \square$

$[\![\&\text{P}_S]\!]: \lambda P\lambda x\lambda e.P(x)(e) \wedge \square(x)(e)$

eat'

Modification of *içeceğim* by *yiyip* then returns (34)a projecting the resulting $\overline{\text{V}}$ expression to VP, (34)b:

(34) a. $[\![\overline{\text{V}}]\!]: \lambda e.e_0 < e \wedge \square(\text{speaker}')(e) \quad [\![\overline{\text{V}}_S]\!]: \lambda x\lambda e.\square(x)(e) \wedge \square(x)(e)$

$\text{drink}' \qquad \text{eat}'$

b. $[\![\text{VP}]\!]: \square$

$[\![\text{VP}_S]\!]: \lambda e.e_0 < e \wedge \square(\text{speaker}')(e) \quad \lambda x\lambda e.\square(x)(e) \wedge \square(x)(e)$

$\text{drink}' \qquad \text{eat}'$

The sole solution (35) [= (28)c] of (34)b denotes the set of eventualities e in the future at which the speaker eats and drinks:

(35) $\lambda e.e_0 < e \wedge \text{drink}'(\text{speaker}')(e) \wedge \text{eat}'(\text{speaker}')(e)$

In sum, the desired semantic representation for (4) can be derived on the basis of the surface-oriented semantic representation (29) as well, using only rules that handle the syntax-semantics interface for modification structures in general.

The other examples can now be treated in the same fashion. Since (5) and (8) have the same syntactic structure, the derivation of (21)b, the semantic representation of (5), follows the pattern expounded for (8) in section 3.

The only difference is that the structured semantic representation for *everyone* is introduced in the lexicon, whereas it is derived by rule (15) in the case of *húsið*. Assuming the semantics of the definite article for the suffix like in (21), we get (36) as the semantics of *húsið*:

(36) $[\![\mathrm{D}]\!]: \lambda P \exists! x.[\square(\mathrm{x})] \wedge P(x)$

$[\![\mathrm{D_S}]\!]$: house'

(36) is the desired input for the interface rule for modification. Here the restriction of the quantifier introduced by the NP constituent constitutes the embedded fragment of this constituent, which can then be addressed by the modification interface rule (15). The rest of the derivation of the semantics of (5) follows the pattern laid out for (8), by rules (15) and (16) we obtain the structures (37)a and (37)b, and the sole solution of the latter is (37)c [= (21)b].

(37) a. $[\![\bar{\mathrm{D}}]\!]: \lambda P \exists! x.\square(x) \wedge P(x)$ $[\![\bar{\mathrm{D}}_\mathrm{S}]\!]: \lambda y.\square(y) \wedge \mathrm{red'}(y)$

house'

b. $[\![\mathrm{DP}]\!]: \square$

$[\![\mathrm{DP_S}]\!]: \lambda P \exists! x.\square(x) \wedge P(x)$ $\lambda y.\square(y) \wedge \mathrm{red'}(y)$

house'

c. $\lambda P \exists! x.[\mathrm{house'}(x) \wedge \mathrm{red'}(x)] \wedge P(x)$

For (3), we reuse the interpretation (24)a of the affix in (38)a, which returns (38)b as the semantics of *atlı* 'someone provided with a horse'. After modification, the interpretation of *yağız atlı* as an $\bar{\mathrm{N}}$ constituent is (38)c, its interpretation as an NP is (38)d with the preferred solution (38)e [= (24)c]:

(38) a. $[\![\mathrm{Aff}]\!], [\![\mathrm{Aff_S}]\!]: \lambda P \lambda x \exists y.P(y) \wedge \mathrm{provided\text{-}with'}(x,y)$

b. $[\![\mathrm{X}]\!]: \lambda x \exists y.\square(y) \wedge \mathrm{provided\text{-}with'}(x,y)$

$[\![\mathrm{X_S}]\!]$: horse'

c. $[\![\bar{\mathrm{N}}]\!]: \lambda x.\square(x) \wedge \mathrm{dark\text{-}brown'}(x)$ $[\![\bar{\mathrm{N}}_\mathrm{S}]\!]: \lambda x \exists y.\square(y) \wedge \mathrm{provided\text{-}with'}(x,y)$

horse'

d.

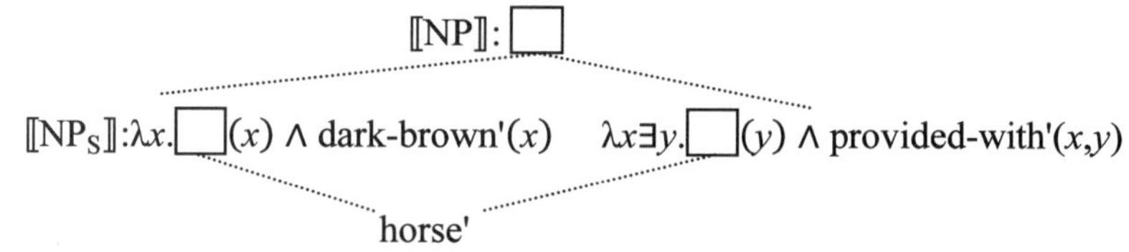

e. $\lambda x \exists y.\text{horse'}(y) \wedge \text{dark-brown'}(y) \wedge \text{provided-with'}(x,y)$

However, this time, there is a second solution, which differs only in attributing the property of being dark brown to the rider instead of the horse:

(39) $\lambda x \exists y.\text{horse'}(y) \wedge \text{provided-with'}(x,y) \wedge \text{dark-brown'}(x)$

To sum up, it has been shown in this section that semantic construction is possible for examples (3)–(5) on the basis of surface-oriented syntactic analyses using an interface for an underspecification formalism. The analyses show that even if both lexical integrity and semantic opacity of words are respected (in that words are minimal syntactic units, whose semantic contribution is processed as a unified whole in semantic construction), it is possible to derive the readings for these examples in which one morpheme within a word has scope over other words in the same phrase. In the next section, I will discuss related work.

6. Related work

6.1. HPSG

Fokkens et al. (2009) suggest an analysis of the *-ip*-construction on the basis of a surface-oriented syntactic analysis. For cases like (4), scope of the tense affix over both VPs coordinated by *-ip* can be handled straightforwardly by coindexing their INDEX values (which correspond to eventuality arguments in my approach), which carry information about tense, aspect, and mood.

However, this simple approach does not work for more involved cases with scope-bearing modal affixes, e.g., *-ebil* in (40), which expresses possibility:[7]

(40)	Çocuk	-lar	film	izle	-yip	pizza	yi	-yebil	-ir	-ler.
	child	PL	movie	watch	IP	pizza	eat	can	AOR	PL

'The children can watch a movie and eat pizza.'

For these examples, Fokkens et al. (2009) offer a solution similar to the one proposed in this paper, in that these suffixes outscope their stem, but leave room for intervening operators. At the same time, the stem semantics remains visible for semantic construction, and can be coordinated in terms of the *-ip*-construction. Consequently, the whole coordination ends up in the scope of the suffix. However, their implementation of this intuition requires a unary

---

[7] In the gloss for this and the next example, PL stands for plural, AOR for aorist, LOC for locative case, and KI is the 'relative suffix' described in section 6.2 that is used for genitive or locative DPs that modify nouns.

syntactic rule which introduces the semantic contribution of the affix (it is thus not directly contributed by verbs with the affix, only licensed by them in terms of a special feature).

The problem I see for this analysis is that it does not capture the common ground between (4) and (40): In both cases, there is scope of the affix of the second coordinated constituent over the whole construction, but this is modeled in two radically different ways.

6.2. Turkish LFG

In the Turkish LFG that is being developed as part of the ParGram project (Çetinoğlu and Oflazer 2006), challenges for semantic construction like (3) and (4) have received ample attention. As an example, consider (41), where a modifier, here the adjective *eski* ('old'), does not pertain to a morphologically complex modified expression completely, but only to a part of it, which excludes some affixes, here, *-ki* ('that which'). This gives the affix scope over the modifier:

(41)	eski	kitap	-lar	-ım	-da	-ki	hikaye	-ler
	old	book	PL	my	LOC	KI	story	PL

'the stories in my old books'

Such cases have been tackled in a way that resembles the generative strategies sketched in section 5.1: Çetinoğlu and Oflazer (2006) assume that specific stems (called *inflectional groups*) and their affixes show up as nodes in the constituent structure. Consequently, the stems are accessible for processes such as adjunction already in the syntax. The syntactic analysis for (41) is (42):

(42)

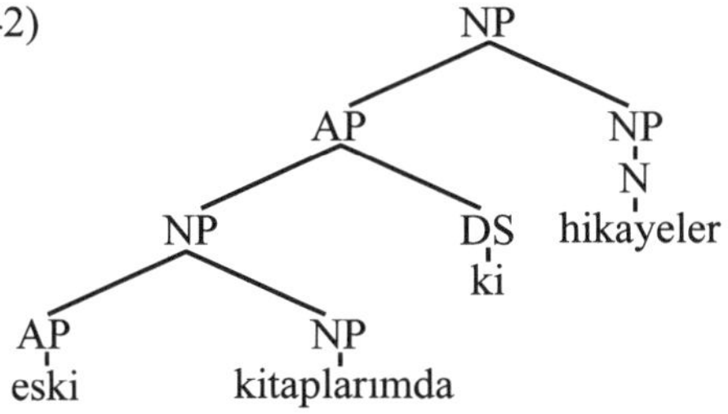

Here the element *-ki* ('related to') is singled out in a constituent 'DS' (derivational suffix) of its own, and *eski* ('old') ends up in its scope, as desired. One could argue in favour of this analysis by pointing out that *-ki* is indeed not a standard derivational suffix as it (mostly) does not undergo vowel harmony (which characteristically applies at word level) and comes after inflectional suffixes. This has led, e.g., Kornflit (1997) to analyze it as a particle, which would be in line with the analysis in (42).

From a semantic point of view, this does not completely solve the problem, however, since, semantically, *eski* ('old') pertains to the root *kitap* ('book') exclusively, and not to *kitaplarımda* ('located in my books') as a whole: otherwise, the meaning of (42) would be predicted to be 'old item(s) located in my books' instead of 'items located in my old books'.

The point here is that the locative has a semantic interpretation of its own, which maps the meaning of *eski kitaplarım* ('my old books') (an individual or a set of properties) onto the property of being located in my books. I.e., this is an instance of *semantic case* (as opposed to structural case), which determines syntactic and semantic properties of the whole DP in which it shows up (Butt and King 2005). So, from a semantic point of view, one would have to postulate (at least) another DS node for the locative suffix *-da*, which would be much less straightforward than the analysis in (42) for the affix *-ki*.

Çetinoğlu and Oflazer (2006) furthermore propose treating *-lı* in a similar fashion, which would solve the problem with semantic construction in (3), but does not mesh with the fact that the arguments in favor of the particle status of *-ki* do not carry over to *-lı*, which does undergo vowel harmony and does not come after inflectional suffixes. I.e., they would have to give up lexical integrity at this point.

In sum, their solution to the discussed challenges for the syntax-semantics interface for Turkish goes some way in representing the fact that modifiers sometimes relate semantically only to a part of the constituent which they modify but cannot fully account for these cases nor preserve lexical integrity.

6.3. Lexical Tree-Adjoining Grammar

In the introduction to this paper I pointed out that the presented analyses could be cast in terms of other underspecification formalisms as well. However, one of these formalisms lends itself particularly well to this goal, viz., Lexical Tree-Adjoining Grammar (L-TAG): The mechanism presented in Joshi et al. (2007) for scope underspecification lends itself directly for a representation of cases such as (5).

The reason for this is the philosophy behind (L-)TAG-based approaches: If heads themselves introduce the whole subtree for their own projection (including nodes to be substituted by subtrees for the complements), they must at the same time introduce the semantics for this whole projection. E.g., the tree fragment for *sometimes* (43)b would be inserted at the VP node of the tree (43)a introduced by *laughs*, yielding (43)c (NP substitution is ignored in the following):

(43)
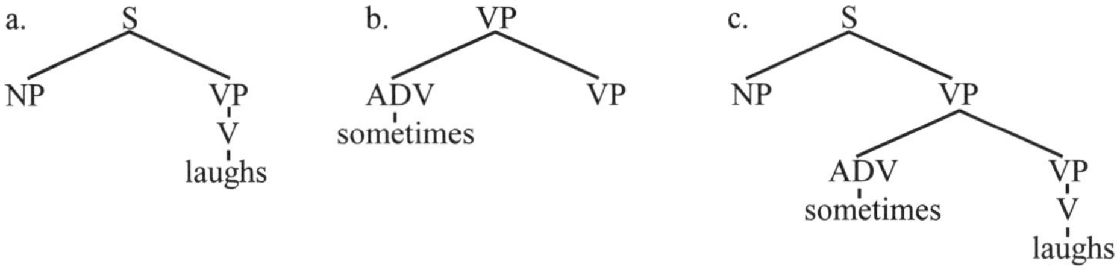

But then the following problem emerges: Adjunction in TAG is modelled by replacing an internal node by a tree fragment, i.e., the original tree is split in two parts, and then the tree fragment is inserted between these two parts. But, if relations between syntactic nodes define semantic scope in the usual way (i.e., by c-command), then the adjoined modifier should get intermediate scope with respect to the tree it is adjoined to, i.e., only over the tree part below the node in the original tree that has been replaced during adjunction (in (43)a, VP).

While this intermediate scope is motivated syntactically, it must be specified in the semantic representation of the tree that can undergo adjunction: This representation determines the scope of a potential modifier. This is exactly parallel to the anticipation of intermediate modifier scope in my approach, where the choice of the secondary fragment determines a possible intermediate scope of a potential modifier.

Joshi et al. (2007) and Kallmeyer and Romero (2008) present such a formalism in detail. At its core are semantic feature structures like (44) that accompany semantic representations like l_1: *laugh*($\boxed{1}$, $\boxed{2}$), where $\boxed{2}$ is a situation (corresponding to the eventuality argument in my approach), and $\boxed{1}$, an individual. The feature structure anticipates the semantic effect of adjunction of a VP modifier tree fragment by distinguishing for the VP a top and a bottom feature:

(44)
$$\begin{bmatrix} \text{NP} & \begin{bmatrix} \text{TOP} \mid \text{INDEX} & \boxed{1} \end{bmatrix} \\ \text{VP} & \begin{bmatrix} \text{TOP} & \begin{bmatrix} \text{PROPOSITION} & \boxed{4} \\ \text{SITUATION} & \boxed{3} \end{bmatrix} \\ \text{BOTTOM} & \begin{bmatrix} \text{PROPOSITION} & l_1 \\ \text{SITUATION} & \boxed{2} \end{bmatrix} \end{bmatrix} \end{bmatrix}$$

This can be paraphrased as follows. We do not yet know what the top proposition and situation of the VP (and, hence, also of the sentence) are. On the one hand, if there is no adjunction, and only then, TOP and BOTTOM features of the VP are identified, in that case, top proposition and situation of the VP are identical to l_1 and $\boxed{2}$, respectively. On the other hand, if there is modification by a scope-bearing VP modifier such as *sometimes*, the modifier introduces a top proposition and a situation of its own. In the case of VP modification, the proposition l_1 is in the scope of the modifier, along with its situation argument $\boxed{2}$.

This strategy could immediately be extended to cases like (3) or (5). E.g., a semantic representation for *húsið* that models the very same intuition as the CLLS constraint (36) could be sketched in the following way. The semantics (simplifying issues of scope) would be l_1:*def*($\boxed{3}$, $\boxed{4}$, $\boxed{5}$), i.e., we have a definite determiner with index $\boxed{3}$, restriction $\boxed{4}$, and scope $\boxed{5}$. The semantic feature structure is (45):

(45)
$$\begin{bmatrix} \text{D} & \begin{bmatrix}\text{TOP} & \begin{bmatrix}\text{PROPOSITION} & l_1 \\ \text{INDEX} & \boxed{3}\end{bmatrix}\end{bmatrix} \\ \text{NP} & \begin{bmatrix} \text{TOP} & \begin{bmatrix}\text{PROPOSITION} & \boxed{4} \\ \text{INDEX} & \boxed{3}\end{bmatrix} \\ \text{BOTTOM} & \begin{bmatrix}\text{PROPOSITION} & \boxed{1} \\ \text{INDEX} & \boxed{2}\end{bmatrix}\end{bmatrix}\end{bmatrix}$$

In prose: Restriction and index of the DP are determined by *hús* (as $\boxed{1}$ and $\boxed{2}$, respectively) only if the noun is not modified. Otherwise, the modifier can introduce index and restriction of its own. The division between top and bottom serves precisely the same end as the dominance relation between main and secondary fragment in the CLLS analysis, viz., to indicate the position for the semantic contribution of a modifier in the semantics of the whole adjunction structure.

However, there is a difference between the two approaches: Since in LTAG such intermediate scope effects are ultimately based on syntactic adjunction structures, LTAG approaches are forced to assume syntactic decomposition even in cases like (7)–(8), but such decompositions are not always independently motivated: While one might argue for a decomposition of *everyone* in a determiner *every* and an N(P) *one*, no such syntactic decomposition seems to be readily available for change-of-state verbs like *open*, even though their poststate is a possible target of modification, e.g., in (46) [= (7)]:

(46) The door opened again.

The restitutive reading of (46) only presupposes that the door had been open before the opening took place (no previous opening required). The presupposition is introduced by *again*, whose semantics (roughly) is an identity mapping of its argument *P* (a property of eventualities), with the presupposition that there was a previous eventuality in the extension of *P*.

This reading of (46) can be modelled by first decomposing the meaning of *open* into 'BECOME(open'(d))', where d is the semantic contribution of the DP, and BECOME(ϕ) expresses a change from $\neg\phi$ to ϕ, and then giving *again* narrow scope over the argument of the operator BECOME only (Dowty 1979, von Stechow 1996, Egg 2008). But there is no morphological correlate to the argument of BECOME, which suggests that it is preferable to avoid syntactic decomposition and handle not only cases like (46) but also cases like (3)–(5) in the way proposed in this paper.

In sum, the competing approaches all share the intuition of this paper that the semantics of modified expressions must predetermine potential positions for the integration of the semantic contribution of a modifier. However, they all are forced to some extent to handle these cases in the syntax, which causes problems that the proposed approach does not suffer from.

7. Conclusion and outlook

In this paper, I showed that underspecified approaches to semantics, which emerged as attempts to handle ambiguity in natural language, lend themselves for the derivation of difficult cases of semantic construction on the basis of surface-oriented syntactic analyses. It was not necessary to dispense with lexical integrity in order to derive the scope relations in these examples, which can hold between parts of words. The very powerful syntax-semantics interfaces in these approaches provide the necessary machinery to handle these cases of semantic construction. I have reviewed a number of such cases and outlined their semantic construction, comparing the proposed analysis to other competing approaches.

The increasing (re-)use of underspecified approaches to ambiguity for semantic construction is highly relevant for the question of what syntax is necessary from a semantic point of view, because powerful and flexible syntax-semantics interfaces can do a lot of the work of semantic construction themselves, and are less dependent on specific preprocessing of syntactic structures than, e.g., those offered in the Logical Form of Generative Grammar.

From a more general perspective, the data and the analysis presented in this paper can also contribute to the ongoing discussion of whether the notion of word is tenable at all (Haspelmath 2011; Jacobs 2011): Semantic opacity can be added to Haspelmath's list of potential criteria of a word, and the examples discussed in this paper suggest counterexamples to this criterion, which can be explained away with the help of syntax-semantics interfaces based on underspecification formalisms.

Bibliography

Abney, S. (1987): *The English noun phrase in its sentential aspect*. Unpublished Diss., MIT, Cambridge (MA).

Anderson, S. (1992): *A-morphous morphology*. Cambridge: Cambridge University Press.

Booij, G. (2009): Lexical integrity as a formal universal. A constructionist view. In: S. Scalise, E. Magni, and A. Bisetto (eds.), *Universals of language today*. Berlin: Springer Science+Business Media, 83–100.

Butt, M. and T. H. King (2005). The status of case. In: V. Dayal and A. Mahajan (eds.), *Clause Structure in South Asian Languages*. Dordrecht: Kluwer, 153–198.

Çetinoğlu, Ö. and K. Oflazer (2006). Morphology-syntax interface for Turkish LFG. In: *Proceedings of the 21st International Conference on Computational Linguistics and the 44th annual meeting of the ACL*. Association for Computational Linguistics, 153–160.

Copestake, A., D. Flickinger, C. Pollard, and I. Sag (2005). Minimal Recursion Semantics. An introduction. *Research on Language and Computation* 3: 281–332.

Dalrymple, M. (2001): *Lexical Functional Grammar* (= Number 34 in Syntax and Semantics). New York: Academic Press.

Dalrymple, M., J. Lamping, F. Pereira, and V. Saraswat (1997): Quantifiers, anaphora, and intensionality. *Journal of Logic, Language, and Information* 6: 219–273.

Dowty, D. (1979): *Word meaning and Montague grammar*. Dordrecht: Reidel.

Egg, M. (2004): Mismatches at the syntax-semantics interface. In: S. Müller (ed.), *Proceedings of the 11th International Conference on Head-Driven Phrase Structure Grammar*. Stanford: CSLI Publications, 119–139.

Egg, M. (2008): Reference to embedded eventualities. In: J. Dölling, T. Heyde-Zybatow, and M. Schäfer (eds.), *Event structures in linguistic form and interpretation*. Berlin: de Gruyter, 149–172.

Egg, M., A. Koller, and J. Niehren (2001): The constraint language for lambda-structures. *Journal of Logic, Language, and Information* 10: 457–485.

Fokkens, A., L. Poulson, and E. Bender (2009): Inflectional morphology in Turkish VP coordination. In: S. Müller (ed.), *Proceedings of the HPSG 09 Conference*. Stanford: CSLI Publications, 110–130.

Göksel, A. and C. Kerslake (eds.) (2011): *Turkish. An essential grammar*. Routledge Essential Grammars. London: Routledge.

Haspelmath, M. (2011): The indeterminacy of word segmentation and the nature of morphology and syntax. *Folia Linguistica* 45: 31–80.

Jacobs, J. (2011): Grammatik ohne Wörter? In: S. Engelberg, A. Holler, and K. Proost (eds.), *Sprachliches Wissen zwischen Lexikon und Grammatik*. Institut für Deutsche Sprache. Jahrbuch 2010. Berlin: de Gruyter, 345–372.

Joshi, A., L. Kallmeyer, and M. Romero (2007): Flexible composition in LTAG: Quantifier scope and inverse linking. In: H. Bunt and R. Muskens (eds.), *Computing Meaning*, Volume 3. Amsterdam: Springer, 233–256.

Kallmeyer, L. and M. Romero (2008): Scope and situation binding in LTAG using semantic unification. *Research on language and computation* 6: 3–52.

Kishimoto, H. (2000): Indefinite pronouns and overt N-raising. *Linguistic Inquiry* 31: 557–566.

Kornflit, J. (1997): *Turkish*. Descriptive Grammars. London: Routledge.

Larson, R. (1998): Events and modification in nominals. In: D. Strolovitch and A. Lawson (eds.), *Proceedings from SALT VIII*. Ithaca: CLC Publications, 145–168.

Moltmann, F. (1992): *Coordination and comparatives*. Unpublished Diss., MIT, Cambridge (MA).

Pollard, C. and I. Sag (eds.) (1994): *Head-driven phrase structure grammar*. Chicago: University of Chicago Press.

Reyle, U. (1993): Dealing with ambiguities by underspecification: Construction, representation, and deduction. *Journal of Semantics* 10: 123–179.

von Stechow, A. (1996): The different readings of 'wieder': A structural account. *Journal of Semantics* 13: 87–138.

Zhang, N. (2010): *Coordination in syntax*. Cambridge: Cambridge University Press.

Expertengeprüft und *vom Experten geprüft*: Zur Semantik von Nomen-Partizip II-Komposita und ihrer präpositionalen Partner*

Claudia Maienborn und Sascha Geldermann

1. Einleitung

Zuweilen scheint sich die Sprache Luxus- und Redundanznischen zu erlauben, die bei näherem Hinsehen dann doch viel von ihrer Opulenz verlieren und in ihrer filigranen Differenzierung Grundsätzliches über das Zusammenwirken sprachlicher Strukturebenen verraten können. Einem solchen Redundanzphänomen im Grenzbereich zwischen Wortbildung und Syntagma widmet sich dieser Beitrag und knüpft damit an Susan Olsens Arbeiten zur Wortbildung in Abgrenzung zur Syntax und zur Interpretation von Komposita an. Es geht uns hier um die Verbindung des Partizips II mit Nomen wie in (1) bzw. mit PPn wie in (2).

(1) a. Die Violine ist *expertengeprüft.*
  b. Die Internet-Seite ist *passwortgeschützt.*
  c. Der Likör ist *fassgelagert.*

(2) a. Die Violine ist *vom Experten geprüft.*
  b. Die Internet-Seite ist *mit einem Passwort geschützt.*
  c. Der Likör ist *im Fass gelagert.*

In einem intuitiven Sinne leisten die kursivierten Ausdrücke in (1) und (2) jeweils weitgehend identische Bedeutungsbeiträge. Worin also bestehen ihre Gemeinsamkeiten, und was unterscheidet die Paarungen in (1) und (2)? Dies ist der Gegenstand des vorliegenden Artikels. Er behandelt die Bildungsbedingungen und die kompositionale Semantik für Nomen-Partizip II-Verbindungen in Abgrenzung zu Kombinationen des prädikativ gebrauchten Partizips II mit PP-Modifikatoren. Letztere haben in jüngerer Zeit einige Aufmerksamkeit im Zusammenhang mit der Theoriebildung zur Semantik des sog. Zustandspassivs erhalten (s. Kratzer 1994, 2000, Rapp 1996, 1997, Schlücker 2005, Maienborn 2007, 2009, 2011, Gehrke 2011, 2012, Gese 2011, 2012, in Arb.). Zu den Nomen-Partizip II-Verbindungen hingegen finden sich bislang kaum, zumal formalsemantisch ausbuchstabierte, Überle-

* Diese Arbeit ist im Rahmen des Projekts A1 (Maienborn) „Kombinatorische Bedeutungsvariation an der Semantik-Pragmatik-Schnittstelle“ innerhalb des SFB 833 *Bedeutungskonstitution*, Tübingen, entstanden. Wir danken den Projektmitarbeiterinnen, Frauke Buscher, Helga Gese und Johanna Herdtfelder, für ihre Unterstützung und die gemeinsamen Besprechungen. Herzlichen Dank auch an Sebastian Bücking, Holden Härtl und Ewald Lang für ihre Kommentare zu einer Vorversion des Artikels und sehr anregende Diskussionen.

gungen.[1] Beide Strukturkonfigurationen sind im Deutschen äußerst produktiv. Wir haben es also, speziell bei (1), nicht lediglich mit Lexikalisierung zu tun, sondern die Nomen-Partizip II-Verbindungen sind regulär bildbar. Vorweg sei gesagt, dass der vorliegende Beitrag allein Konstellationen betrachtet, in denen PP bzw. Nomen Modifikatoren des Partizips sind, ihr jeweiliger semantischer Beitrag also nicht schon qua Verbbedeutung lexikalisch fixiert sein kann, sondern konfigurationell festgelegt wird.

In Abschnitt 2 werden wir zunächst den Stand der Forschung zur Zustandspassiv-Konstellation in (2) zusammenfassen und dabei den Vorschlag von Maienborn zur Semantik adjektivierter Partizipien II darstellen. In Abschnitt 3 stellen wir zunächst einige Überlegungen zum morphologischen Status von Nomen-Partizip II-Verbindungen aus (1) an und präsentieren anschließend die Ergebnisse einer Korpusstudie, welche die empirische Grundlage für unseren semantischen Analysevorschlag bildet. Im Zentrum stehen dabei die Fragen nach einer adäquaten strukturellen Analyse und nach der semantischen Rolle des Nomens. In Abschnitt 4 schließlich entwickeln wir unseren Vorschlag für die kompositionale Semantik von Wortbildungen vom Typ (1) in Abgrenzung zu syntaktischen Strukturen vom Typ (2).

2. Ereignisbezogene Modifikatoren beim Zustandspassiv

2.1. Kompositionale Semantik des Adjektivierungsaffixes

Für das sogenannte Zustandspassiv hat sich in der heutigen Forschungsliteratur die Adjektivierungshypothese durchgesetzt. Danach ist das Zustandspassiv – entgegen seinem ins Verbalparadigma verweisenden Namen – die Spezialform einer adjektivischen Kopula-Konstruktion: Es handelt sich um eine Verbindung der Kopula *sein* mit einem adjektivierten Partizip II als Prädikativ. Auf eine Wiederholung der Argumente und ein neuerliches Durchspielen der einschlägigen Adjektiv-Diagnostiken (z.B. *un*-Affigierung, Komparation, Koordination mit genuinen Adjektiven, adjektivische Wortbildung) wollen wir hier verzichten und verweisen stattdessen auf die Übersichten in Rapp (1996) und Maienborn (2007). Experimentelle Evidenz für die Adjektivierungshypothese bieten Stolterfoht et al. (2010).[2]

Mit Hinweis auf Liebers (1980) Feststellung einer vollständigen Formübereinstimmung adjektivischer und verbaler Partizipien schlägt Kratzer (1994, 2000) die systematische Ableitung adjektivierter Partizipien von ihren verbalen Pendants über ein adjektivisches Null-

---

1 Etwas besser ist die Literaturlage bei Nomen-Partizip I-Verbindungen wie *chromglänzend* oder *arbeitssuchend*; s. Rapp (2002: 275ff), Fuhrhop (2006: Kap. 8.2), Lübbe (2012). Aber auch hier sind semantische Analysen rar und konzentrieren sich zumeist auf die Frage der Argumentvererbung der jeweils involvierten Verben; s. hierzu Härtl (2012a).

2 Vor diesem Hintergrund ist die Redeweise vom „Zustandspassiv" unglücklich gewählt, denn es handelt sich gerade *nicht* um eine passive Verbform als sozusagen „kleine Schwester" des Vorgangspassivs; s. hierzu auch die Studie von Gese et al. (2011) zum prädikativen Gebrauch adjektivierter Partizipien bei unakkusativen Verben. Da sich dieser Terminus zur Bezeichnung des in Rede stehenden Phänomens inzwischen aber in der deutschsprachigen Literatur etabliert hat, werden wir ihn beibehalten.

affix vor; s. (3). Diese Analyse bietet sich für eine kompositionale Bedeutungsbestimmung des Zustandspassivs an und wird deshalb hier übernommen.[3]

(3) Der Kuchen ist gekauft.
COP $[_{AP}\ [_{A}\ [_{VPART}\ \text{gekauft}]\ _{A}^{aff}\ \text{ø}\ ]]$

Der in Maienborn (2007, 2009) entwickelte Vorschlag zur Semantik des Zustandspassivs orientiert sich an dessen grammatischer Einordnung als Spezialfall einer Kopula-Konstruktion. Entsprechend dem allgemeinen Kopula-Muster besteht sein semantischer Beitrag damit in der Zuschreibung einer Eigenschaft an den Subjektreferenten; s. Maienborn (2003a, 2005). Die besonderen Interpretationsbedingungen des Zustandspassivs sind demnach zurückzuführen auf die semantische Umsetzung des mit der Adjektivierung des verbalen Partizips einhergehenden grammatischen Kategorienwechsels und dessen pragmatischer Deutung.

Maienborns These zur Semantik des Zustandspassivs ist, dass die Adjektivierung des Partizips zur Bildung einer semantisch unterbestimmten *Ad hoc-Eigenschaft* dient, welche aus dem vom Basisverb bezeichneten Ereignis resultiert. Während Standard-Kopulasätze mit adjektivischem Prädikativ dem Subjektreferenten eine lexikalisch kodierte Eigenschaft zuschreiben, die einen fest vorgegebenen Platz im Eigenschaftsraum des Subjektreferenten einnimmt, ist das Zustandspassiv ein grammatisches Ausdrucksmittel, um potenziell neue, ereignisbasierte Eigenschaften zu bilden, deren genaue Kontur und Platzierung im Eigenschaftsraum durch Kontext und Weltwissen mitbestimmt wird. Betrachten wir zur Veranschaulichung Beispielsatz (4):

(4) Der Kuchen ist gekauft.

Dieser drückt mehr aus als einen bloßen Resultatszustand des Gekauftseins (vgl. Kratzer 2000). Vielmehr ziehen wir – je nach kontextuell verfügbarem Weltwissen – weitere Schlussfolgerungen: Ein Kuchen, der gekauft ist, wird möglicherweise als weniger lecker eingeschätzt als ein selbstgebackener Kuchen – es sei denn, wir wissen, dass unser Gastgeber kein begnadeter Bäcker ist. In diesem Fall können wir aus (4) darauf schließen, dass der Kuchen immerhin den üblichen Qualitätsstandards von Bäckereien entspricht. Schlussfolgerungen wie diese, die über das Gesagte hinausgehen, ziehen wir sicherlich ständig. Ein ähnliches Räsonnement könnten wir beispielsweise bei der Vorgangspassiv-Variante (4') anstellen.

(4') Der Kuchen ist gekauft worden.

[3] Olsen (1986) bezeichnet Kategorienwechsel unter Einschluss von Flexion wie hier im Fall der Adjektivierung verbaler Partizipien als *Transpositionen* und unterscheidet diese von genuiner Konversion morphologischer Stämme. Transpositionen werden in der Literatur häufig als semantisch leere Operationen aufgefasst; s. die Diskussion und Kritik in Lieber (2012). Unser Artikel versteht sich als ein Beitrag zur weiteren Klärung der durchaus beträchtlichen semantischen Konsequenzen des systematisch möglichen Wortartenwechsels von verbalen zu adjektivischen Partizipien. Die Annahme des Nullaffixes dient lediglich dazu, den kompositional-semantischen Gehalt strukturell sichtbar zu machen.

Der wesentliche Punkt bei Maienborns Analyse ist, dass wir in (4), anders als in (4'), eine weitergehende Eigenschaft erschließen *müssen*. Die Semantik des Zustandspassivs zwingt uns dazu. Kurz: das Zustandspassiv dient zur Kategorisierung des Subjektreferenten auf der Basis des vom Verb bezeichneten Ereignistyps im Hinblick auf kontextuell relevante Ziele und unter Ausnutzung von verfügbarem Weltwissen.

Unter (5) – (7) fassen wir die in Maienborn (2009, 2011) entwickelte formalsemantische Modellierung der vorgestellten Analyse zusammen. Als Orientierungspunkt dient die Semantik von Kopulasätzen. Gemäß der semantischen Repräsentation in (5)b bezeichnet der Kopulasatz (5)a einen Zustand *s*, in dem die Eigenschaft, lecker zu sein auf den Kuchen zutrifft.[4] Parallel dazu schlägt Maienborn für das Zustandspassiv in (6)a die semantische Repräsentation (6)b vor. Danach bezeichnet das Zustandspassiv einen Zustand *s*, in dem auf den Kuchen eine semantisch unterbestimmte Eigenschaft *Q* zutrifft, wobei *s* als Resultat eines Kaufereignisses des Kuchens ausgewiesen ist. Der Subjektreferent beim Zustandspassiv nimmt also immer die Rolle des Themas in dem vom Basisverb bezeichneten Ereignis ein. (7) gibt den korrespondierenden Beitrag des adjektivischen Nullaffixes an.[5]

(5) a. Der Kuchen ist lecker.
b. $\exists s$ [LECKER (s, DEF-KUCHEN)]

(6) a. Der Kuchen ist gekauft.
b. $\exists s, e$ [Q (s, DEF-KUCHEN) $\wedge$ RESULT (e, s) $\wedge$ KAUF (e, DEF-KUCHEN)]

(7) A^{aff}: $\lambda P\, \lambda x\, \lambda s\, \exists e\, [Q(s, x) \wedge$ RESULT $(e, s) \wedge P(e, x)]$

Der Vergleich der beiden semantischen Repräsentationen in (5) und (6) zeigt, dass die Semantik des Zustandspassivs dem Muster regulärer Kopulastrukturen folgt. Der Unterschied gegenüber adjektivischen Basisprädikaten besteht lediglich darin, dass das Zustandspassiv dem Subjektreferenten eine intern komplexe und semantisch unterbestimmte Eigenschaft zuweist. Um interpretierbar zu sein, muss die freie Variable *Q* innerhalb des gegebenen Kontexts einen geeigneten Wert erhalten. Dies kann z.B. über ein abduktives Schlussverfahren à la Hobbs et al. (1993) modelliert werden oder im Rahmen von Ashers (2011) Ansatz einer typengesteuerten, kontextsensitiven lexikalischen Semantik. Die ökonomischste/beste Spezifizierung der freien Variable *Q* ist diejenige, die mit den wenigsten kontextuell nicht lizensierten Zusatzannahmen auskommt; s. hierzu Langs (1985: 106) „unspecified argument rule". Wenn, wie im Falle resultativer Verben, eine entsprechende Eigenschaft bereits lexikalisch eingeführt ist, so ist diese ein bevorzugter Belegungskandidat für *Q*. In einem neutralen Kontext ist damit die präferierte Belegung für *geöffnet* in (8)a die resultierende Eigenschaft des Offenseins; s. (8)b. Unter dem in (9)a gegebenen Kontext

4 Zur Semantik der Kopula s. Maienborn (2003a, 2005). Für die Zwecke des vorliegenden Beitrags belassen wir es bei einer vereinfachten Zustandsanalyse und gehen nicht auf Einzelheiten zum ontologischen Typ des Zustandsarguments ein. Als Lexikoneintrag für die Kopula *sein* sei damit angenommen: $\lambda P \lambda x \lambda s\ [P(s, x)]$

5 Wir verwenden im Weiteren die folgende Notationskonvention: Variablen über Eventualitäten werden mit *e* gekennzeichnet, Zustandsvariablen mit *s*. Bei einer im Zuge der Komposition erfolgenden engeren Festlegung einer Eventualitätsvariable auf einen Zustand ändert sich entsprechend deren Bezeichnung von *e* zu *s*.

käme es damit aber zu einem Konflikt: Die Filmschachtel kann nicht zugleich offen und zu sein. Zur Widerspruchsvermeidung wird deshalb eine andere, kontextuell plausible Belegung für *Q* erschlossen. Im Falle von (9) kann dies z.B. die Eigenschaft sein, nicht im Originalverpackungszustand (ansonsten aber neuwertig) zu sein; s. Maienborn (2011). Für Primäradjektive besteht diese Option nicht; der Widerspruch in (9')a ist nicht auflösbar. Selbst bei resultativen Verben besteht also pragmatischer Spielraum bei der Bestimmung der resultierenden Eigenschaft *Q*. Dies unterstreicht die Kontextsensitivität des Zustandspassivs.

(8) a. Die Filmschachtel ist geöffnet.
  b. $\exists s, e\ [Q\ (s, \text{DEF-FS}) \wedge \text{RESULT}\ (e, s) \wedge \text{ÖFFN}\ (e, \text{DEF-FS})]$
  mit $Q = \text{OFFEN}$

(9) a. Die Filmschachtel ist geöffnet aber wieder zugeklebt.
  b. $\exists s\ \exists e\ [Q\ (s, \text{DEF-FS}) \wedge \text{RESULT}\ (e, s) \wedge \text{ÖFFN}\ (e, \text{DEF-FS})]$
  mit $Q = \text{OHNE-ORIGINALVERPACKUNG}$

(9') a. *Die Filmschachtel ist offen aber wieder zugeklebt.

Während also der erforderliche pragmatische Aufwand zur Belegung der freien Variable *Q* erheblich variieren kann – von weitgehender Vorhersagbarkeit der zu erschließenden Eigenschaft aus dem lexikalischen Gehalt des Basisverbs bis zu massiver Einbeziehung von Kontext und Weltwissen –, so ist doch der grundlegende Interpretationsmechanismus derselbe. Wir werden auf die Details eines solchen pragmatischen Schlussverfahrens hier nicht näher eingehen, sondern setzen eine im jeweiligen Kontext plausible Instanziierung von *Q* im Weiteren voraus.

Soweit die Skizze einer formalen Umsetzung der hier zugrundegelegten Zustandspassiv-Analyse: Die Adjektivierung des Partizips bietet ein produktives Ausdrucksmittel für die Konzeptualisierung einer prinzipiell beliebig komplexen, ereignisbasierten Ad hoc-Eigenschaft zur kontextuell induzierten Kategorisierung des Subjektreferenten.

2.2. Integration ereignisbezogener Modifikatoren

Der semantische Beitrag ereignisbezogener Modifikatoren im oben skizzierten Zustandspassiv-Setting besteht nun darin, eine weitergehende Spezifizierung und Differenzierung von Ad hoc-Eigenschaften zu ermöglichen. In (10)a etwa, können wir auf der Basis der Temporalangabe *in einer Nacht* darauf schließen, dass das Manuskript z.B. besonders genial und aus einem Guss ist – oder aber ausgesprochen schlampig. Entsprechend erfolgt die pragmatische Spezifizierung der semantisch unterbestimmten Eigenschaft *Q*. In (10)b erlaubt die Agensangabe *vom Experten* die Schlussfolgerung darauf, dass die Violine hohen Qualitätsanforderungen genügt; die Lokalangabe *im Fass* in (10)c unterstützt die Schlussfolgerung, dass der Likör aufgrund seiner Lagerung ein besonderes Aroma hat usw.

(10) a. Das Manuskript ist in einer Nacht geschrieben.
  b. Die Violine ist vom Experten geprüft.
  c. Der Likör ist im Fass gelagert.

Bemerkenswert ist hier, dass etwa (10)b, anders als seine Vorgangspassiv-Variante, die Implikatur hat, dass die Prüfung erfolgreich war. So besagt die Interpretation des Vorgangspassivs lediglich, dass die Violine Gegenstand einer von einem Experten durchgeführten Prüfung war. Dies ist mit der Annahme kompatibel, dass diese Prüfung negativ ausfiel; s. (11)a. Zustandspassiv und Kompositum erlauben diese Deutung kaum: (11)b & c sind hochgradig markiert. Es bedürfte hier massiver kontextueller Stützung, um die Erfolgs-Implikatur aufzuheben; s. hierzu Maienborn (2011). Die Daten in (11) sind mit Maienborns These, dass die Adjektivierung des Partizips nicht bloß einen Resultatszustand ausdrückt, sondern eine kontextuell zu erschließende Eigenschaft damit verbindet, gut erklärbar: Eine relevante Eigenschaft lässt sich aus dem Unterziehen einer Prüfung (ohne zusätzliche kontextuelle Klimmzüge) nur dann ziehen, wenn die Prüfung bestanden wurde.

(11) a. Die Violine ist vom Experten geprüft worden. Leider war die Prüfung negativ.
b. Die Violine ist vom Experten geprüft. ??Leider war die Prüfung negativ.
c. Die Violine ist expertengeprüft. ??Leider war die Prüfung negativ.

Kurz: die betreffenden Modifikatoren erweitern das Spektrum potenzieller ereignisbasierter Ad hoc-Eigenschaften. Im Prinzip ist jeder ereignisbezogene Modifikator dafür geeignet – solange er die Vorhersage weiterer, über das sprachlich Ausgedrückte hinausgehender Merkmale des Subjektreferenten unterstützt. Aus diesem Grunde liefert die Agensangabe *von Chomsky* in (12)a eine gute Ad hoc-Eigenschaft, die Variante *von Sandberger* in (12)b hingegen nicht. Aufgrund unseres Weltwissens können wir aus dem Umstand, dass ein Manuskript von Chomsky zitiert wurde, auf weitere Eigenschaften dieses Manuskripts schließen: dass es syntaktisch besonders innovativ ist, dass es auf große Resonanz innerhalb der linguistischen Community stoßen wird, o.ä. Damit gelingt die pragmatische Spezifizierung der freien Variable *Q*. Im Falle eines unbekannten Individuums namens Sandberger in (12)b ist dies ohne weitere Kontextannahmen nicht möglich. Entsprechend pragmatisch abweichend ist der betreffende Satz; s. die Diskussion in Maienborn (2011).

(12) a. Das Manuskript ist von Chomsky zitiert.
b. ?Das Manuskript ist von Sandberger zitiert.

Soweit zum semantischen Beitrag der hier interessierenden Agens-, Instrumental-, Lokal- und Temporalangaben usw. Aus den obigen Ausführungen wird deutlich, dass die betreffenden PPn unmittelbar an das vom Basisverb eingeführte Ereignisargument anknüpfen. Dies setzt voraus, dass sie strukturell unterhalb der Position des Adjektivierungsaffixes angesiedelt sind, denn nach der Adjektivierung steht das verbale Ereignisargument kompositional nicht mehr zur Verfügung; s. die Diskussion der verschiedenen Lösungsvorschläge in Maienborn (2007, 2011).

Maienborn argumentiert, dass die betreffenden PPn in der Tat keine beliebigen VP-Modifikatoren sind, sondern, dass sie im Sinne von Jacobs (1993, 1999) verbnah *integriert* sind.[6] Maienborn (2011) diskutiert prosodische, syntaktische und semantische Daten, die zeigen, dass die betreffenden Modifikatoren beim Zustandspassiv eine andere, enger am Verb verortete strukturelle Position haben als ihre Entsprechungen beim Vorgangspassiv.[7] Maienborn et al. (2012) präsentieren weitere experimentelle Evidenz für diese strukturelle Differenz. Adverbiale Modifikatoren in dieser verbnahen strukturellen Konfiguration liefern nicht bloß ergänzende Zusatzinformationen zu einem vom Verb unabhängig eingeführten *Ereignisreferenten* – dies ist der Beitrag regulärer VP-Modifikatoren im Falle des Vorgangspassivs – sondern sie tragen zur Konturierung des bereitgestellten komplexen *Ereignistyps* bei.

Als ein Beispiel für den unterschiedlichen grammatischen Status sei der Verlust anaphorischer Zugänglichkeit genannt. Während das interne Argument der PP beim Vorgangspassiv eine eigenständige, referenziell unabhängige Informationseinheit bildet, die im Anschluss anaphorisch wiederaufgenommen werden kann (13)a, trifft dies auf das Zustandspassiv nicht zu; s. (13)b. Dieses verhält sich vielmehr eher wie sein Kompositum-Pendant. Dessen nominales Erstglied ist anaphorisch nicht zugänglich; s. (13)c.[8]

(13) a. Die Violine ist von Experten geprüft worden. Sie schicken ihren Bericht morgen.
b. Die Violine ist von Experten geprüft. ??Sie schicken ihren Bericht morgen.
c. Die Violine ist expertengeprüft. *Sie schicken ihren Bericht morgen.

---

6 Jacobs führt *Integration* als eine spezielle syntaktische Relation zwischen einem Kopf und seiner Schwesterkonstituente ein, die in verschiedener Hinsicht grammatisch relevant ist (z.B. Akzentplatzierung, Merkmalsperkolation, Bewegung, Extraktionsverhalten). Die definierende Eigenschaft von Integration ist, dass Kopf und integrierte Konstituente eine kompakte informationelle Einheit bilden, die holistisch, "in einem Zug" semantisch verarbeitet wird. Prosodisch wird Integration durch primären Satzakzent auf dem integrierten Element angezeigt. Während Jacobs Integration für das Verhältnis zwischen Köpfen und ihren Argumenten reserviert, argumentiert Maienborn (2001, 2003b, 2011), dass Jacobs' Integrationskriterien auch auf eine Subklasse von Modifikatoren zutreffen.

7 Für die Zwecke der vorliegenden Arbeit mag der Hinweis genügen, dass die Integration des Modifikators prosodisch markiert wird, indem unter neutralen Satzakzentbedingungen der Hauptakzent auf den verbadjazenten Modifikator fällt (i), während im Falle regulärer VP-Modifikatoren das Verb den Hauptakzent trägt (iii). Eine Umkehrung der Akzentverhältnisse, wie in (ii) vs. (iv) ist nur mit kontrastivem Fokus auf dem Verb (ii) bzw. Modifikator (iv) vereinbar. Siehe die ausführliche Diskussion der prosodischen Effekte von Integration in Maienborn (2001, 2003b, 2011):

(i) Maria sah, dass der Brief mit WACHS versiegelt war.
(ii) ?Maria sah, dass der Brief mit Wachs VERSIEGELT war (und nicht VERSCHMIERT).
(iii) Maria sah, dass der Brief mit Wachs VERSIEGELT wurde.
(iv) Maria sah, dass der Brief mit WACHS versiegelt wurde (und nicht mit SIEGELLACK).

8 Die genauen PP-internen referenziellen Verhältnisse bedürfen der weiteren Klärung. Es fällt auf, dass beim Zustandspassiv häufig Amalgamierungen von Präposition und Artikel (*vom Experten*) auftreten, deren Deutung als Funktionalbegriffe (Löbner 1985, 2011) sich für die weitere Ereignistypspezifikation besonders eignet. Darauf können wir hier nicht näher eingehen.

Die enge Anbindung des Modifikators an das Verb beim Zustandspassiv zeigt sich auch daran, dass diese Konfiguration nicht durch weiteres, nicht integriertes sprachliches Material getrennt werden kann, während dies im Falle des Vorgangspassivs (unter den geeigneten informationsstrukturellen Voraussetzungen) möglich ist. Scrambling der PP über ein Satz- oder Negationsadverbial hinweg ist beim Vorganspassiv prinzipiell zulässig, beim Zustandspassiv nicht; s. (14)a und b vs. (14)c und d.

(14) a. Die Violine ist von Experten wahrscheinlich geprüft worden.
b. Die Violine ist von Experten nicht geprüft worden.
c. *Die Violine ist von Experten wahrscheinlich geprüft.
d. *Die Violine ist von Experten nicht geprüft.

Die Daten in (13) und (14) unterstreichen den via Integration erreichten, in gewisser Hinsicht wort-ähnlichen Status der Verbindung aus PP und Partizip. Für bestimmte grammatische Operationen ist die PP nicht mehr vollständig zugänglich.

Für die Zwecke der vorliegenden Arbeit sei angenommen, dass V' die strukturell besonders ausgewiesene Integrationsdomäne des Verbs sei, die den Grenzbereich abnehmender lexikalischer Integrität zwischen Wort und Syntagma bildet. Innerhalb dieser V'-Zone wird der komplexe Ereignistyp bestimmt. Die Modifikatoren vom Typ (10) können damit als V'-Adjunkte analysiert werden, während ihre Vorgangspassiv-Pendants an VP adjungiert werden. Wenn wir davon ausgehen, dass das in (7) aufgeführte Adjektivierungsaffix genau auf diese mit V' gegebene, kompakte informationelle Einheit appliziert, so ergibt sich für unsere Zustandspassiv-Sätze vom Typ (2) und (10) die strukturelle Analyse in (15).

(15)

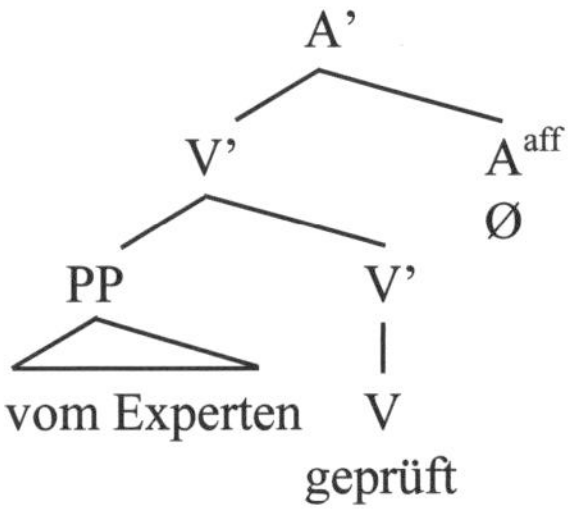

Die Analyse in (15) vermag zu erfassen, dass bei *un*-Affigierung des Partizips keine PP-Modifikatoren mehr zulässig sind; s. (16). Da *un*-Affigierung die vorherige Adjektivierung des verbalen Partizips auf lexikalischer Ebene voraussetzt – d.h. das Negationsaffix *un*-selegiert nur A^0-Einheiten (s. Kratzer 1994, 2000) –, steht die V'-Domäne für die ereignisbezogenen Modifikatoren nicht mehr zur Verfügung.

(16) a. Die Anlage ist (*vom TÜV) ungeprüft.
b. Die Internet-Seite ist (*mit einem Passwort) ungeschützt.
c. Der Besucher war (*in Parfum) ungebadet.

Als Fazit zur Semantik ereignisbezogener Modifikatoren beim Zustandspassiv halten wir fest: Die PPn bilden zusammen mit dem verbalen Partizip eine strukturelle Einheit im Übergangsbereich zwischen Wort und Syntagma und tragen darüber zur Konturierung des Ereignistyps bei, über den die für das Zustandspassiv charakteristische, semantisch unterbestimmte Ad hoc-Eigenschaft bestimmt wird. Dies bildet den Orientierungspunkt für die folgenden Überlegungen zu den Verbindungen aus Nomen und Partizip II.

3. Nomen-Partizip II-Komposita

3.1. Überlegungen zum morphologischen Status

Was lässt sich vor dem oben skizzierten Hintergrund zum morphologischen Status und der Bedeutungskonstitution der Komposita-Bildungen in (1) sagen? Wie eng ist die Parallele zu den PP-Modifikatoren?

(1) a. Die Violine ist expertengeprüft.
b. Die Internet-Seite ist passwortgeschützt.
c. Der Likör ist fassgelagert.

Die bei der Gegenüberstellung der Ausdrücke in (1) und (2) ins Auge springenden Gemeinsamkeiten laden dazu ein, den semantischen Bezug des nominalen Erstglieds mit dem der entsprechenden PPn gleichzusetzen, sprich: auch die Nomen auf das verbale Ereignisargument zu beziehen. Der/die Experten[9] in (1)a könnte/n somit als Agens des Prüfens ausgewiesen werden, das Passwort in (1)b als Instrument des Schützens, das Fass in (1)c als Ort des Lagerns. Dies setzt allerdings – wie wir bereits oben festgestellt haben – voraus, dass die betreffenden Nomen sich an das *verbale* Partizip anschließen, denn nur dieses stellt das Ereignisargument als kompositionalen Anknüpfungspunkt bereit. Nach Adjektivierung des Partizips ist das Ereignisargument existenziell gebunden und als referenzielles Argument steht nurmehr das Zustandsargument *s* für die resultierende Ad hoc-Eigenschaft zur Verfügung; s. die in (7) angeführte Semantik des Adjektivierungsaffixes.

Das heißt, nach diesem Räsonnement wäre als Wortbildungsmuster für die Ausdrücke in (1) die morphologische Struktur in (17)a anzusetzen, in der Nomen und verbales Partizip zunächst ein komplexes Verb bilden und dieses im Anschluss adjektiviert wird. (17)a wäre in der Tat das direkteste morphologische Pendant zu unserer für die ereignisbezogenen PPn angenommenen syntaktischen Struktur (13). Die Frage, über welchen morphologischen Prozess – Inkorporierung, Stripping, Univerbierung, ... ? – (17)a möglicherweise aus (13) abgeleitet werden könnte, lassen wir hier dahingestellt; s. hierzu Fuhrhop (2006).

(17) a.

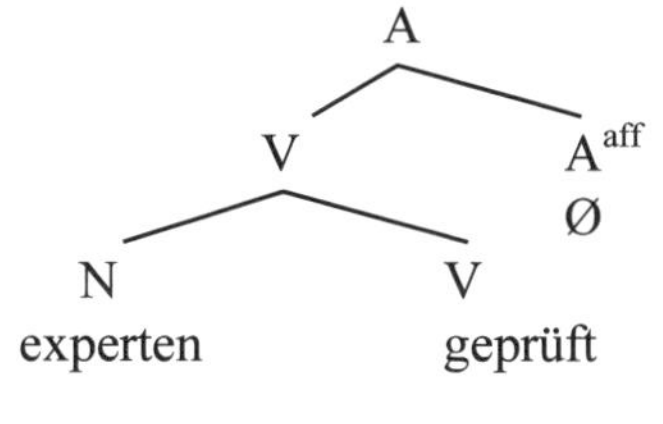

b.

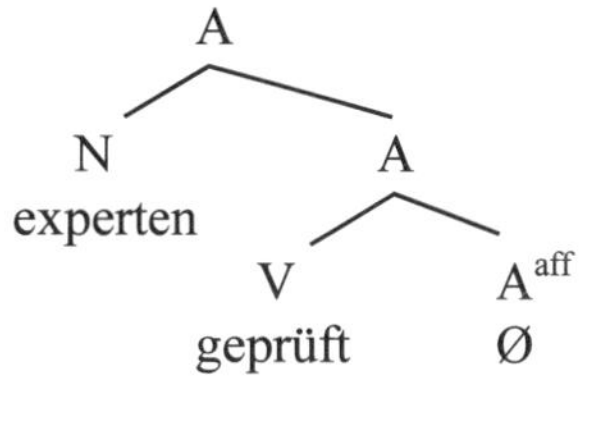

[9] Die nominalen Erstglieder sind in der Regel Numerus-neutral und ohne partikulare Referenz. Zu zwei Deutungsvarianten der hier gegebenen referenziellen Verhältnisse s. Bücking (2009a, b) und Härtl (2012b). Wir kommen auf diesen Punkt in Abschnitt 5 zurück.

Gegen (17)a spricht, dass das Deutsche keine regulären N-V-Komposita bildet; s. z.B. Wunderlich (1986, 1987), Pittner (1998), Fuhrhop (2006, 2007). Die mit (17)a postulierten Verben vom Typ *expertenprüfen, passwortschützen, fasslagern* existieren nicht, auch nicht in der bloß partizipialen Variante; s. (18). Dies ist als schwerwiegender Einwand gegen die Strukturannahme (17)a zu werten.

(18) a. *Die Akademie hat die Violine expertengeprüft.
b. *Sue hat die Internet-Seite passwortgeschützt.[10]
c. *Dieter hat den Likör fassgelagert.

Die mit den im Deutschen regulär auftretenden Wortbildungsmustern kompatible Strukturvariante ist in (17)b angegeben. Danach handelt es sich bei den betreffenden Ausdrücken um Komposita aus nominalem Erstglied und einem adjektivierten Partizip als Kopf. Dies entspricht einem für Adjektive typischen Bildungsprinzip; vgl. z.B. *himmelblau, erntefrisch, menschenleer, Numerus-neutral, fußnotenfleißig*[11]. Die Strukturvariante (17)b ist also dem Muster (17)a in jedem Fall vorzuziehen. Allerdings wirft (17)b für die Semantik der Ausdrücke überraschende Probleme auf und zwingt zu einem deutlichen Abrücken vom Vorbild der PP-Modifikatoren. Hierbei ist zu bedenken, dass gemäß (17)b nicht lediglich der relationale Bezug des nominalen Referenten zum verbalen Ereignis gelockert wird. Dies entspräche der vertrauten interpretativen Freiheit bei der Deutung des Erstgliedbezugs von Komposita, eindrücklich veranschaulicht durch die legendäre *Fischfrau*; s. z.B. Fanselow (1981), Olsen (1986) und Bücking (2009a, b). Vielmehr steht bei Zugrundelegung der oben vorgeschlagenen Adjektivierungssemantik das verbale Ereignis gar nicht erst als kompositionaler Bezugspunkt für das nominale Erstglied zur Verfügung. Damit entfällt folglich eine Verankerung über die typischen Ereignisrollen wie Agens, Instrumental, Lokal usw., auf die wir uns bei unserer bisherigen Charakterisierung der Nomen-Partizip II-Komposita gestützt haben. Einer solchen am Vorbild der PPn orientierten, ereignisbezogenen Deutung des nominalen Erstglieds ist somit der Boden entzogen. (Zumindest gibt es dafür keine geradlinige kompositionale Umsetzung.) Dies ist ein einigermaßen überraschender Befund, denn das vom Basisverb bezeichnete Ereignis bietet sich zweifellos für die kompositionale Verankerung des nominalen Erstglieds an. Hingegen erscheint der Bezug zu einem die resultierende Ad hoc-Eigenschaft exemplifizierenden Zustand weit weniger klar. Dennoch wollen wir die morphologischen und semantischen Strukturvorgaben soweit es geht ernstnehmen und auf ihre interpretativen Implikationen hin überprüfen.

Unabhängige Evidenz für die Strukturanalyse in (17)b und gegen (17)a liefert die Verbindung von Nomen-Partizip-Komposita mit *un*-Affigierung. Wenn auch selten, so lassen sich doch Vorkommen wie z.B. *messe-ungeübt, passwortungeschützt* oder *TÜV-ungeprüft* nachweisen; s. (19). Das Negationsaffix verbindet sich hier zunächst mit dem Partizip (das folglich bereits adjektiviert sein muss), bevor das nominale Erstglied hinzutritt. Hingegen finden sich keine Belege für das nach (17)a erwartbare Muster, **unmessegeübt, *unpasswortgeschützt, *un-TÜV-geprüft.*

[10] Satz (18)b mag marginal akzeptabel sein. In diesem Fall liegt aber eine irreguläre Reanalyse des adjektivischen Partizips vor. Wie werden auf derartige Rückbildungen in 3.2 zurückkommen.

[11] COSMAS-Beleg entnommen aus Donalies (2002: 80)

(19) a. Den zu einem grossen Teil *Messe-ungeübten* Rorschacher Detaillisten und Unternehmern kommen die Ferien gerade recht, um sich auf die Regionalmasse, die vom 22. bis 30. August dauert, vorzubereiten.
COSMAS-Beleg A98/JUL.49008
b. Die ganzen Röntgengeräte bei den Ärzten halte ich schon *TÜV-ungeprüft* für ein Risiko, die ganze Sicherheitschose können wir natürlich auch diskutieren.
http://www.wer-weiss-was.de/theme50/article6558799.html (Abruf: 19.08.2012)
c. Wenn dieser Server nun vollkommen offen und *Passwortungeschützt* ist, so kann jeder welche Inhalte auch immer darauf hochladen [...].
http://www.gutefrage.net/nutzer/Blueman3636/antworten/beliebte/1 (Abruf: 19.08.2012)

Bemerkenswert ist hierbei, dass die präpositionalen Pendants zu (19) ungrammatisch sind; s. die Diskussion zu (16). Dies unterstreicht die abweichende, nämlich adjektivische, strukturelle Integration des nominalen Erstglieds gegenüber der verbalen Integration der PPn; s. (15). Wir gehen deshalb im Weiteren davon aus, dass es sich bei den uns interessierenden Wortbildungen vom Typ (1) um adjektivische Determinativkomposita handelt, bestehend aus einem adjektivierten Partizip II in Verbindung mit einem nominalen Erstglied; s. (17)b. Gegen eine Univerbierungsanalyse spricht, dass die hier betrachteten Partizipialverbindungen im Deutschen sehr produktiv und reihenbildend sind. Dies trifft auf Univerbierungen nicht zu; s. Jacobs (2005: 107), Fuhrhop (2006: 19). Ferner zeigt auch die (im Übrigen recht häufige) Präsenz von Fugenelementen wie in (20) die fortgeschrittene Morphologisierung der hier beteiligten Strukturen als Komposita; s. Fuhrhop (2000).

(20) a. familiengeführt
b. ordnungsverliebt
c. wüstenerprobt
d. männerdominiert
e. bundesgeschützt

Wenn die Strukturen in (1) also adjektivische Determinativkomposita sind, so wirft dies die Frage nach der strukturellen Parallele zu den PP-Modifikatoren auf und nach der Deutung des Erstgliedbezugs über thematische Rollen. Um hier zu einer empirisch grundierten Datenbeurteilung zu gelangen, haben wir eine Korpusrecherche zu Nomen-Partizip II-Verbindungen durchgeführt, deren zentrale Ergebnisse wir im folgenden Abschnitt vorstellen.

3.2. Korpusanalyse

Ziel der Korpusrecherche war die Schaffung einer hinreichend breiten empirischen Grundlage für die angestrebte semantische Analyse von Nomen-Partizip II-Verbindungen in Abgrenzung zur PP-Konstellation beim Zustandspassiv.[12] Für die Suche nutzten wir das Archiv morphosyntaktisch annotierter Korpora des Instituts für Deutsche Sprache in Mannheim. Über das Recherchewerkzeug COSMAS II wurde nach Adjektiven mit den typischen Präfixen von Partizipien II wie *ge-*, *an-*, *be-*, *zer-* gesucht, die auf *-n* oder *-t* enden, und denen

[12] Die hier vorgestellte Korpusanalyse ist Teil von Sascha Geldermanns 2012 am Deutschen Seminar der Universität Tübingen verfassten Masterarbeit zu Mechanismen und Restriktionen der Bildung von Nomen-Partizip II-Komposita.

mindestens noch vier Zeichen vorangehen. Gefordert war außerdem das Vorkommen einer Form von *sein* im selben Satz. Manuell wurde im Anschluss sichergestellt, dass es sich dabei um ein prädikativ gebrauchtes Partizip in Verbindung mit der Kopula *sein* handelte. Ferner wurden – wiederum manuell – Treffer ausgeschlossen, bei denen das nominale Erstglied als Argument des adjektivierten Partizips aufgefasst werden kann. Dies trifft z.B. auf die präpositionalen Begleiter und ihre nominalen Entsprechungen von adjektivierten psychischen Wirkungsverben wie *beeindruckt, begeistert* zu. Gleiches gilt für die Adjektivierungen von Zustandsverben mit Lokatum vom Typ *bewohnt, umgeben, bedeckt*; s. Rapp (1997: 203ff). Wenn der präpositionale bzw. nominale Begleiter seinen Argumentstatus im Zuge der Adjektivierung beibehält, so kann der Bezug auf das vom Basisverb bezeichnete Ereignis lexikalisch vererbt werden. Diese Konstellation ist für unsere Fragestellung hier nicht von Interesse. Die entsprechenden adjektivischen Rektionskomposita werden deshalb aussortiert.[13] Rapp (1996, 1997) nennt mit Blick auf PPn beim Zustandspassiv zwei Eigenschaften, die Argumente von Adjektiven typischerweise aufweisen und die zur Abgrenzung gegenüber Modifikatoren herangezogen werden können: die Argumente von Adjektiven können rechts und links vom adjektivischen Kopf auftreten; s. (21) und (22). Und sie werden nicht notwendigerweise durch *un*-Affigierung blockiert; s. (23).

(21) a. weil er von der Musik beeindruckt ist
(Rapp 1996: 247)
b. weil er auf seinen Vater stolz ist
c. weil sie von Schuld frei ist

(22) a. weil er beeindruckt von der Musik ist
(Rapp 1996: 247)
b. weil er stolz auf seinen Vater ist
c. weil sie frei von Schuld ist

(23) a. weil er von der Musik unbeeindruckt ist
(Rapp 1996: 248)
b. weil sie (un)glücklich über die Antwort ist
c. weil sie mit dem Zeugnis (un)zufrieden ist

Dieses Verhalten unterscheidet die Argumente von Adjektiven von den hier interessierenden adverbialen Modifikatoren. Letztere können nicht rechts vom Partizip auftreten; s. (24) und (25). Und sie werden durch *un*-Affigierung blockiert; s. die Diskussion zu (16).

(24) a. Der Brief ist mit roter Tinte geschrieben und gut lesbar.
b. *Der Brief ist geschrieben mit roter Tinte und gut lesbar.

(25) a. Die Suppe ist von Maja gewürzt und besonders bekömmlich.
b. *Die Suppe ist gewürzt von Maja und besonders bekömmlich.

[13] Die Frage, ob die Argumente des Verbs bei Adjektivierung oder Nominalisierung tatsächlich vererbt werden, wird in der Literatur kontrovers diskutiert; s. z.B. Olsen (1986, 1992), Fanselow (1988, 1991), Bücking (2012a). Wir wollen hierzu keine Position beziehen. Mit der Aussortierung potenzieller Argumentfälle stellen wir lediglich sicher, dass die zu findende kompositional-semantische Lösung nicht argumentstrukturell vorgebahnt ist.

Im Ergebnis erhielten wir eine Datenbasis von 470 Nomen-Partizip II-Verbindungen (ohne Dopplungen). Diese wurde im Anschluss nach zwei Kriterien annotiert: (a) PP-Parallele und (b) thematische Rolle. Bei (a) geht es um die Frage, ob es zu der Nomen-Partizip II-Verbindung eine (oder mehrere) PP-Varianten gibt, die analog zu den Paarungen (1) – (2) im jeweiligen Satzkontext als äquivalent angesehen werden können. Dies war bei der überwiegenden Mehrzahl gegeben: In über 95 Prozent der Fälle ließen sich den Nomen-Partizip-Verbindungen weitgehend äquivalente Zustandspassiv-Entsprechungen mit PP-Modifikator zuordnen.[14] Verschiedentlich kamen dabei mehrere Präpositionen in Frage, wie etwa bei den Belegen in (26).

(26) a. Das Fleisch ist zart, die Panade knusprig und gar nicht *fettgetränkt.*
HAZ09/NOV.02360

b. Er ist *Viererkette-geschult*, kann aber auch offensiver spielen [...]
NON09/JUL.03139

c. Deshalb erhebe ich den Aufruf an alle Politiker, Verwaltungsmandatsträger und Vorstandsmitglieder: Lasst die Touristiker wieder arbeiten statt zu planen, fordert keine unmöglichen Zahlen, nur weil ihr besonders „tough" und *wirtschaftserprobt* seid.
SOZ09/APR.03847

In (26)a kommen gleichermaßen *in* und *mit Fett getränkt* als präpositionale Entsprechungen in Frage; *viererkette-geschult* in (26)b kann prinzipiell mit *für die Viererkette* oder *in der Viererkette geschult* korrespondieren; mögliche Entsprechungen für *wirtschaftserprobt* in (26)c sind *von der Wirtschaft erprobt*, *in der Wirtschaft erprobt* und *in Bezug auf die/im Umgang mit der Wirtschaft erprobt*. Solche Freiheitsgrade bei der PP-Zuordnung liefern ein erstes wichtiges Indiz für die kompositionale Semantik der Komposita. Wir werden darauf in Abschnitt 4 zurückkommen.

Bei der überwiegenden Mehrzahl der Fälle liegen also nach unseren bisherigen Ausführungen Determinativkomposita vor, bei denen das Nomen einen semantischen Beitrag leistet, der dem eines PP-Modifikators gleich kommt. Dies ist das produktive Muster, dessen kompositionale Semantik wir hier beschreiben wollen. Bei den verbleibenden Fällen handelt es sich um Rückbildungen. Dazu gehören Wortbildungen wie die folgenden:

(27) a. frauenbewegt
b. sommerbereift
c. denkmalgeschützt
d. umweltzertifiziert
e. zimmertemperiert

(28) a. Frauenbewegung
b. Sommerreifen/Sommerbereifung
c. Denkmalschutz
d. Umweltzertifikat
e. Zimmertemperatur

Die Bildungen in (27) lassen sich so auf die Nomen-Nomen-Komposita in (28) zurückführen. Das adjektivische Kompositum *frauenbewegt* beispielsweise leitet sich demnach von dem nominalen Kompositum *Frauenbewegung* ab, mit dem deverbalen Nomen *Bewe-*

[14] Weil im Rahmen der Masterarbeit von Sascha Geldermann keine Überprüfung der Annotationen über unabhängige Annotatoren vorgenommen werden konnte, werden wir im Folgenden keine weitergehenden quantitativen Analysen vornehmen, sondern belassen es bei einer groben quantitativen Orientierung und nutzen das Korpus primär als empirische Grundlage für qualitative Aussagen.

gung als Kopf. Dieses nominale Kompositum wird reanalysiert zu einem komplexen Verbstamm *frauenbeweg-*, der dann als Basis für die Partizipbildung dient.[15]

Fuhrhop (2006: 21) nennt als Bedingungen für Rückbildung das Fehlen eines korrespondierenden regulären Syntagmas und das Vorhandensein einer alternativen Wortbildung, die eine transparente Ableitung zulässt. Aufgrund der Herleitungsverhältnisse ist ferner eine niedrigere Frequenz der Rückbildung gegenüber der Ableitungsbasis zu erwarten. Sämtliche Bedingungen sind für die hier diskutierten Fälle erfüllt.[16] Die Frequenzen wurden mit dem Recherchewerkzeug COSMAS II anhand aller öffentlichen Korpora des Archivs W des IDS ermittelt. Die Frequenzen sind in (29) und (30) angegeben. Hierbei wurden neben den prädikativen auch attributive Vorkommen der Partizipien berücksichtigt.

Frequenzverhältnisse bei Rückbildung:

(29)	a. frauenbewegt	22	(30)	a. Frauenbewegung	7.168
	b. sommerbereift	7		b. Sommerreifen	3.742
				Sommerbereifung	64
	c. denkmalgeschützt	525		c. Denkmalschutz	17.790
	d. umweltzertifiziert	11		d. Umweltzertifikat	114
	e. zimmertemperiert	2		e. Zimmertemperatur	946

In (31) und (32) sind zum Vergleich die Frequenzverhältnisse bei einigen Stichproben der regulären Determinativkomposita aufgeführt. Da hier die Adjektivierung des Partizips und die Nominalisierung unabhängig auf der verbalen Basis operieren, sind hier – jenseits möglicher Frequenzunterschiede zwischen Adjektivierungen und Nominalisierungen – keine vergleichbaren Asymmetrien zu Lasten der Adjektive zu erwarten. Die Befunde in (31) und (32) bestätigen diese Hypothese.

Frequenzverhältnisse bei Determinativ-Komposita:

(31)	a. TÜV-geprüft	129	(32)	a. TÜV-Prüfung	182
	b. passwortgeschützt	36		b. Passwortschutz	37
	c. fassgelagert	9		c. Fasslagerung	16
	d. handgepflückt	11		d. Handpflückung	1
	e. bühnenerprobt	25		e. Bühnenerprobung	0

15 Die betreffenden reanalysierten komplexen Verben zeichnen sich durch defektive Flexionsparadigmen aus; vgl. z.B. (i) – (iii). Siehe z.B. Eschenlohr (1999: 146ff), Fuhrhop (2006: 20ff).
(i) *Die 68er-Generation hat die Republik frauenbewegt.
(ii) *weil Peter gerade seinen Wagen sommerbereift
(iii) ?Peter hat den Wein zimmertemperiert.

16 Im Falle von *sommerbereift* mag eine PP-Entsprechung wie *im/für den Sommer bereift* in den Sinn kommen. Allerdings erweist sich diese Annahme bei genauerem Hinsehen als nicht haltbar: Ein Auto, das sommerbereift ist, muss weder im Sommer bereift worden sein, noch ist es lediglich für den Sommer bereift. Die Bereifung erfolgt vielmehr für alle Monate des Jahres, in denen keine winterlichen Straßenverhältnisse herrschen, also für die Zeit von Frühling bis Herbst.

Damit ist die Rückbildungsanalyse für die Belege in (27) hinreichend abgesichert. Bei den weiteren Überlegungen zur kompositionalen Semantik werden wir Rückbildungen aufgrund ihrer irregulären Bauform ausklammern.

Eine Annotation der adjektivischen Determinativkomposita nach der vom nominalen Erstglied eingenommenen thematischen Rolle ergab die in (33) wiedergegebene Verteilung:[17]

(33) Prozentuale Verteilung der vom nominalen Erstglied eingenommen thematischen Rollen:

Force	25,5
Instrument	19,7
Goal	19,7
Frame	17,9
Ort	5,8
Lokatum	4,4
Agens	4,0
Manner	1,6
Time	1,4

Im Folgenden sind für jede der thematischen Rollen kurz die Annotationskriterien und einige Beispiele sowie ggf. Kommentare aufgeführt. Hierzu sei vorab angemerkt, dass uns bewusst ist, dass diese, wie jede andere Bestimmung und Einteilung von thematischen Rollen mit einer Vielzahl von Problemen konfrontiert ist. Wir nutzen die hier vorgenommene Zuordnung lediglich zu einer groben Orientierung innerhalb des Interpretationsspektrums. Das Orientierungsraster erlaubt einige interessante Beobachtungen und wird uns zu Problemfällen führen, die für die formale Analyse besonders aufschlussreich sind.

(34) *Agens:* intentional handlungsfähiger Kontrolleur der vom Basisverb bezeichneten Situation

a. Dieser Kurs ist *Krankenkassen-anerkannt*, und das Erlernte wird nochmals überprüft.

A09/JAN.07676

b. Die Unternehmensgruppe Bellersheim ist seit 125 Jahren *familiengeführt* und beschäftigt derzeit mehr als 350 Mitarbeiter.

RHZ09/DEZ.01672

c. Selbstverständlich ist der Hänger *TÜV-geprüft* [...]

BRZ09/AUG.06193

[17] Bei dieser Aufstellung sind Mehrfachzuordnungen wie die in (26) angegebenen Fälle entsprechend berücksichtigt.

(35) *Force:* nicht intentional handelnder Träger der vom Basisverb bezeichneten Situation[18]

a. 70 Prozent des Gemeindegebietes *sind baumbeschattet*

BRZ06/MAI.02001

b. Die Anordnung der Bilder auf dem Bildschirm war *zufallsgesteuert*

SPK/J98.00607

c. Dabei bin ich überhaupt nicht *karrierevergiftet*

A99/JAN.01430

In der Literatur finden sich zuweilen Hinweise, dass eine Agens-Interpretation des Erstglieds von Nomen-Partizip II-Verbindungen grundsätzlich ausgeschlossen sei; s. z.B. Rapp (2002: 277).[19] Dies ist selbst bei einer engen Festlegung von Agens auf intentional handlungsfähige Kontrolleure nicht zutreffend. Das Erstglied kann potenziell die Agens-Rolle einnehmen, wiewohl die Verteilung in (33) zeigt, dass dies selten geschieht. Umso auffälliger ist, dass auf die eng mit dem Agens verwandte Rolle Force immerhin ein Viertel der Erstgliedbezüge entfallen.

(36) *Instrument:* von einem Agens in der vom Basisverb bezeichneten Situation eingesetztes Hilfsmittel

a. Der Thurgauer scheint mehrheitlich nicht auf den Schalthebel verzichten zu wollen: 5831 Autos waren *handgeschaltet* [...]

A00/MAR.20332

b. Allerdings tut ein Aufkleber an der Tür kund, dass die Kassenbestände gering gehalten würden und der Tresor *zeitschlossgesichert* sei.

RHZ08/JUL.04922

c. Die Rinder sollen zu *hormonbehandelt* gewesen sein.

RHZ07/JUL.1181

(37) *Goal:* Ziel, auf das die vom Basisverb bezeichnete Situation ausgerichtet ist

a. Ist er ein radikaler Sanierer im Globalisierungswettstreit oder einfach *machtverliebt* [...]

VDI06/JUL.00336

b. Ich bin auch nicht *grippegeimpft* [...]

NON09/SEP.05950

[18] Die Bezeichnung *Force* findet sich z.B. bei Cruse (2000: 283). Alternativ wird diese thematische Rolle in der Literatur häufig auch als *Causer* bezeichnet; s. z.B. Solstad (2006), Härtl (2008), Schäfer (2012).

[19] Noch genereller wird diese These von der Unzulässigkeit einer wortinternen Realisierung externer Argumente in der Komposition von Selkirk (1982) und Grimshaw (1990) vertreten. Siehe aber die Einwände z.B. von Di Sciullo (1992) und Härtl (2012a).

(38) *Ort:* Räumliche Lokalisierung der vom Basisverb ausgedrückten Situation

a. Was im Sortiment der Brände und Liköre aber auf keinen Fall fehlen darf, ist der „Golden Delicious Apfelbrand *fassgelagert*“.

BVZ08/APR.02016

b. „Wir haben das Ticket noch nicht in der Tasche“, warnte Portugals Trainer Carlos Queiroz, der trotz kühler Temperaturen nach der spannenden Partie *schweißgebadet* war.

BRZ09/NOV.07086

c. Und *oktoberfest-erprobt* ist die Methode auch.

V99/APR.1678

Bei einer engen Auslegung der thematischen Rolle Ort auf räumliche Lokalisierung der Gesamtsituation finden sich in unserem Korpus vergleichsweise wenig Belege für diese Erstgliedinterpretation. Davon abzugrenzen ist die in (39) erläuterte Frame-Variante, die mit knapp 18 Prozent zu den vier Rollen gehört, auf die ca. 82 Prozent der Erstgliedinterpretationen entfallen. Präpositionale Entsprechungen für Frames werden häufig über lokale Präpositionen realisiert (vgl. etwa *an den Kanten gerundet* in (39)b) sind aber in ihrem semantischen Beitrag systematisch von reiner Situationslokalisierung zu unterscheiden; s. Maienborn (2001).

(39) *Frame:* Geltungsbereich für die vom Basisverb ausgedrückte Prädikation

a. Die Mannschaften wurden erst am Wettkampftag gebildet und waren *altersgemischt* [...]

RHZ09/JUL.10029

b. Die Gesteinsstücke der Grundmoräne sind intensiver *kantengerundet* als die aus anderen Moränen [...]

RHZ08/JUL.04922

c. Er gibt überdies zu bedenken, dass die Konjunkturzahlen «nicht *verkaufsflächenbereinigt* sind»

A98/NOV.69869

Am Beispiel von (38)c sei nochmals darauf hingewiesen, dass sich häufig mehrere Rollenzuordnungen anbieten; s. die Diskussion zu (26). In (38)c kann das Nomen *Oktoberfest* die Rolle Ort einnehmen (d.h. die Erprobung der Methode fand auf dem Oktoberfest statt, vgl. *Die Methode ist auf dem Oktoberfest erprobt.*) oder Frame (vgl. *Die Methode ist in Bezug auf das Oktoberfest erprobt.*). Wir werden auf den besonderen Status von Frames in 3.3 zurückkommen.

(40) *Lokatum:* lokalisiertes Objekt in einer räumlichen Lokalisierungsrelation[20]

a. Diese wurde über einen Projektor zusätzlich in das Erdgeschoss übertragen, das wie der Keller *menschengefüllt* war.

NON09/MAI.16651

b. Jacob sah an seiner Uniform herab, die nach dem Einstieg durch das zerborstene Fenster zerrissen und *blutbefleckt* war, [...]

HAZ09/OKT.01885

c. Die Fässer waren *restentleert* und verschlossen, aber nicht vorschriftsmäßig gereinigt.[21]

BRZ06/MAR.06894

Bei den verbleibenden beiden Rollen handelt es sich um Einzelfälle: Unter 'Manner' haben wir vorläufig die Komposita mit *Zwang* als Erstglied eingeordnet: z.B. *zwangsversteigert, zwangsverwaltet, zwangsverheiratet*. Die Rolle 'Time' ist vergeben an Komposita mit *Dauer* als Erstglied: *dauerbeflaggt, dauerbelegt, dauerverstrubbelt* usw.

3.3. Lockerung des Ereignisbezugs des Nomens

Die in 3.1 begründete strukturelle Analyse der Nomen-Partizip II-Komposita impliziert, dass die Nomen – anders als ihre PP-Pendants – keinen unmittelbaren Ereignisbezug haben können; s. (17)b vs. (17)a. Zumindest kompositional steht das Ereignisargument des Basisverbs nach der Adjektivierung des Partizips nicht mehr zur Verfügung. Als kompositionale Anschlussstelle dient vielmehr das für die resultierende Ad hoc-Eigenschaft eingeführte Zustandsargument; s. (7). Andererseits legt die in 3.2 vorgenommene Grobsortierung der Nomen-Interpretation über thematische Rollen just einen solchen Ereignisbezug nahe. Wie sind diese beiden Perspektiven miteinander vereinbar? Wir werden in diesem Abschnitt auf einige im Zuge der Korpusanalyse aufgedeckte Problemfälle eingehen, die den unmittelbaren Ereignisbezug des Nomens weiter in Frage stellen und die wichtige Hinweise für den Entwurf der kompositionalen Analyse liefern.

Die erste Bemerkung gilt der oben eingeführten Rolle Frame. Diese gehört nicht zum Standardrepertoire thematischer Rollen, und sie unterscheidet sich von allen übrigen Rollen darin, dass sie gerade keinen Ereignisbezug herstellt, sondern – in semantisch unterbestimmter Weise – den Geltungsbereich der Prädikation beschränkt; s. z.B. Maienborn (2001). Betrachten wir hierzu nochmal die unter (39) angeführten Frame-Beispiele:

---

[20] Während das Lokatum-Argument von Zustandsverben wie *umgeben, bewohnen* bei der Adjektivierung vererbt wird (s. die Diskussion in 3.2), zeigt Rapp (1997: 208ff), dass dies für die kausativen Lokatum-Verben nicht gilt. Entsprechende Belege sind deshalb in unserem Korpus verblieben.

[21] In (40)c ist das Nomen *Rest* Lokatum in einer negierten Lokalisierungsrelation: Der Resultatszustand ist dadurch gekennzeichnet, dass keine Reste mehr in den Fässern lokalisiert sind.

(39) *Frame:* Geltungsbereich für die vom Basisverb ausgedrückte Prädikation

a. Die Mannschaften wurden erst am Wettkampftag gebildet und waren *altersgemischt* [...]

RHZ09/JUL.10029

b. Die Gesteinsstücke der Grundmoräne sind intensiver *kantengerundet* als die aus anderen Moränen [...]

RHZ08/JUL.04922

c. Er gibt überdies zu bedenken, dass die Konjunkturzahlen «nicht *verkaufsflächenbereinigt sind»*

A98/NOV.69869

Im Falle von (39)a und (39)c bezeichnen die Nomen *Alter* und *Verkaufsfläche* offensichtlich keine Ereignispartizipanten, Ereignisdimensionen o.ä. im üblichen Sinne. Am ehesten mag dies noch für (39)b in Betracht kommen. Danach bezeichnen die Kanten den Teil der Gesteinsstücke, der von der Rundung betroffen ist. Allerdings ist gerade hier fraglich, ob überhaupt ein Ereignis gegeben ist. Ein Objekt kann kantengerundet sein, ohne einen Prozess der Rundung durchlaufen zu müssen. Insgesamt lässt sich zu den Frame-Belegen in unserem Korpus sagen, dass sie eine semantisch sehr lockere und variable Beschränkung der vom Partizip ausgedrückten Prädikation in Bezug auf das Erstglied ausdrücken. Dieser dehnbare Bezug geht bei den präpositionalen Pendants zum Teil verloren, oder er kann nur über eine sperrige Formulierung wie *in Bezug auf* hergestellt werden. Ein instruktives Beispiel liefert die okkasionelle Bildung *festplattenunterwandert* in (41).[22]

(41) Wolfgang Schäuble jedenfalls hat längst Lunte gerochen und die Sicherheitslawine bereits ins Rollen gebracht – die gesamte Republik nebst ihren Repräsentanten ist flächendeckend verwanzt, videoüberwacht und *festplattenunterwandert*: Prinzipiell sind alle verdächtig.

RHZ09/APR.04719

Welches Verhältnis ist in (41) zwischen *Festplatte* und *unterwandert* anzusetzen, und wie ließe es sich präpositional ausdrücken? Einige Versuche sind in (42) angegeben.

(42) a. $^{?}$Die gesamte Republik ist auf/in den/ihren Festplatten unterwandert.
b. Die gesamte Republik ist über die/ihre Festplatten unterwandert.
c. Die gesamte Republik ist in Bezug auf die/ihre Festplatten unterwandert.

Die räumliche Variante (42)a ist als nicht wohlgeformt auszuschließen. Die Festplatten sind nicht der Ort, an dem die Unterwanderung stattfindet – jedenfalls lässt sich dies nicht über eine räumliche Relation ausdrücken. Satz (42)b ist wohlgeformt, transportiert aber nicht die gleiche Bedeutung wie das Kompositum in (41). Satz (42)b hat vielmehr die weitergehende Interpretation, dass die gesamte Republik unterwandert und somit bar jeder Geheimnisse

[22] Da bei okkasionellen Bildungen noch keine mit Usualisierung und Lexikalisierung möglicherweise einhergehenden Interpretationsidiosynkrasien einsetzen können, sind sie besonders geeignet, die allein auf die jeweilige Strukturkonfiguration entfallenden kompositionalen Bedeutungsaspekte offenzulegen; s. hierzu auch die Überlegungen von Bücking (2009a, b) im Zusammenhang mit nominalen Komposita.

und Privatsphäre ist, und zwar wurde dieser Zustand umfassender Bespitzelung über die Nutzung von Festplatten als Einfallstor erreicht. Dies ist nicht die primäre Interpretation von *festplattenunterwandert* in (41) – wiewohl das Kompositum diese Interpretation auch zulässt. In der präferierten Interpretation aber wird die Aussage, die Republik sei unterwandert vielmehr eingeschränkt auf den Bereich der Festplatten. Diese sind der Gegenstand der Bespitzelung. Präpositional ließe sich das am ehesten wie in (42)c ausdrücken. Das Präpositionalgefüge *in Bezug auf* dient gerade dazu, jegliche lexikalisch-semantische Vorgaben an die hergestellte Relation, wie sie Präpositionen üblicherweise mitbringen, zu neutralisieren. Dies entspricht den Verhältnissen der Nomen-Partizip II-Komposita.

Die präpositionalen Partner von Nomen-Partizip II-Komposita bringen also über die lexikalische Semantik der Präposition immer semantische Vorgaben über die Ausgestaltung der Relation zwischen Nomen und Partizip mit; die Komposita unterliegen hingegen keinen solchen Auflagen und nutzen ihren semantischen Freiraum entsprechend. Dies zeigen auch Bildungen wie *wutgeöffnet* in (43), für das sich kein geeignetes PP-Pendant angeben lässt. Die Unzulässigkeit von *in Bezug auf* in (43')e zeigt, dass selbst diese präpositionale „Nullform" immer noch semantische Vorgaben an die Ausgestaltung der Relation macht, die im Falle von *wutgeöffnet* nicht erfüllt werden. Bei den lexikalisch aufgeladenen Varianten (43')a–d fällt auf, dass sich hier die Wut immer auf den Vorgang des Augenöffnens bezieht. Genau dies sagt unsere Semantik für präpositionale Modifikatoren beim Zustandspassiv voraus, da diese Modifikatoren an das verbale Partizip anknüpfen. Für das Kompositum *wutgeöffnet* gilt dies aber gerade nicht. Die Wut bezieht sich nicht auf den Vorgang des Öffnens, sondern sie charakterisiert allein den resultierenden Zustand: Die Augen sind auf eine besondere, von Wut geprägte Art und Weise offen bzw. offener als sonst.

(43) Seine Augen waren wutgeöffnet.

nach: Gabriel García Marquéz: Hundert Jahre Einsamkeit

(43') a. Seine Augen waren vor Wut geöffnet.
b. Seine Augen waren von Wut geöffnet.
c. Seine Augen waren mit Wut geöffnet.
d. Seine Augen waren unter Wut geöffnet.
e. *Seine Augen waren in Bezug auf Wut geöffnet.

Einen weiteren Hinweis auf ein Abrücken vom Ereignisbezug liefern die (sehr produktiven) Komposita mit *erprobt* als Partizip II-Kopf. Interessant ist hierbei das Verhältnis zwischen Subjektreferent und Partizip. Beim Zustandspassiv ist der Subjektreferent als Thema des Basisverbs ausgewiesen; s. die Ausführungen zu (7) in Abschnitt 2.1. Dies führt bei den Komposita zu Problemen. Betrachten wir hierzu die Auswahl in (44).

(44) a. Alle vier sind sie *rennerprobt.*

A99/JUL.50959

b. Der Thurgauer ist *tropenerprobt*: «Im Amazonas habe ich schon ganz andere Sachen gemacht.»

A99/SEP.60092

c. Die Gäste sind zwar *rasenplatzerprobt,* wollen aber dennoch auf Asche ihre positive Auswärtsbilanz bestätigen.

RHZ09/DEZ.05363

d. Der neue Pächter Andreas Gratz [...] ist „*alpenvereinserprobt*“: Die Familie führte eine große Alpenvereinshütte am Untersberg bei Salzburg.

NON08/AUG.11775

e. Einige Nickerchen brauche ich ganz bestimmt, aber ich bin langjährig *party-erprobt.*

BRZ06/AUG.11553

f. Die Laubacher selbst sind mittlerweile *Baustellen-erprobt.*

RHZ09/MAR.06185

g. Wiktoria Pelzer, eine der Veranstalterinnen, ist bereits als Mitarbeiterin des »Stuttgarter Filmwinters« *kurzfilm-erprobt:* »Wir haben uns bemüht, viel Experimentelles zu zeigen, was man anderswo kaum zu sehen bekommt.«

NUN06/JAN.03260

Thema und somit Gegenstand der Erprobung ist allenfalls der Subjektreferent – es handelt sich um Schlittenhunde – in (44a).[23] In den übrigen Fällen unter (44) führt die Annahme, der Subjektreferent sei allein passiver Gegenstand einer Erprobung gewesen, zu keiner plausiblen Interpretation. Mit (44)e beispielsweise, will der Sprecher sicherlich nicht ausdrücken, dass er einer langjährigen Erprobung auf Partys oder auch nur in Bezug auf Partys unterzogen wurde. Damit korrespondiert, dass nur für (44)a eine präpositionale Übersetzung mit lexikalisch gehaltvoller Präposition in Frage kommt; s. (45a). Bei den übrigen Fällen lassen die Varianten (45)b–g allein die wenig plausible Interpretation zu, dass der Subjektreferent in der Tat Gegenstand einer Erprobung war. Dies offenbart einen deutlichen Unterschied zwischen Nomen-Partizip II-Komposita und ihren präpositionalen Partnern.

(45) a. Die Schlittenhunde sind in Rennen erprobt.
b. ?Der Thurgauer ist in den Tropen erprobt.
c. ?Die Gäste sind auf dem Rasenplatz erprobt.
d. ?Der neue Pächter ist im Alpenverein erprobt.
e. ?Ich bin langjährig auf Partys erprobt.
f. ?Die Laubacher sind auf Baustellen erprobt.
g. ?Wiktoria Pelzer ist mit Kurzfilmen erprobt.

Für eine angemessene präpositionale Entsprechung für (44) bleibt wiederum nur die für Frames typische präpositionale Nullform *in Bezug auf* oder die hier besonders geeignete Formulierung *im Umgang mit*, die dem Subjektreferenten zusätzlich zu seiner Rolle als Thema eine aktive, kontrollierende Funktion bei der Erprobung zuschreibt.

---

[23] Analoges gilt für die oktoberfest-erprobte Methode in (38c).

(46) a.	Die Methode ist	in Bezug auf / ?im Umgang mit	Rennen	erprobt
b.	Der Thurgauer ist	in Bezug auf / im Umgang mit	Tropen	erprobt
c.	Die Gäste sind	in Bezug auf / im Umgang mit	Rasenplätzen	erprobt
d.	Der neue Pächter ist	in Bezug auf / im Umgang mit	Alpenvereinen	erprobt
e.	Ich bin langjährig	in Bezug auf / im Umgang mit	Partys	erprobt
f.	Die Laubacher sind	in Bezug auf / im Umgang mit	Baustellen	erprobt
g.	Wiktoria Pelzer ist	in Bezug auf / im Umgang mit	Kurzfilmen	erprobt

Festgehalten sei an dieser Stelle, dass die Komposita-Interpretation keine derartigen Einschränkungen aufweist. Bei den Belegen in (44) bedarf es keiner expliziten sprachlichen Maßnahmen, um gegen eine alleinige Thema-Deutung des Subjektreferenten anzugehen. Auch hierin zeigt sich die Lockerung des Ereignisbezugs.

Zum Abschluss unserer Revue aufschlussreicher Problemfälle wollen wir auf die okkasionelle Bildung *waldkindergeprüft* in (47) eingehen.

(47) Alle Texte und Lieder haben also ihren Elchtest bereits bestanden und sind *waldkindergeprüft.*

SOZ07/APR.04479

Auf den ersten Blick mag eine Agens-Interpretation des Nomens *Waldkinder* naheliegen. Diese erweist sich aber in dem konkreten Kontext als wenig plausibel. Es sind nicht die Waldkinder (= Kinder eines Waldkindergartens), die die Texte und Lieder einer Prüfung unterzogen haben, sondern höchstwahrscheinlich ihr Betreuer und Text- und Lieddichter. Die Interpretation von (47) stimmt demzufolge nicht mit der Agens-Interpretation in (48)a überein. Auch müssen die Kinder keine Begleiter eines Prüfers, wie in (48)b ausgedrückt, sein. Und sie sind auch weder bloße „Versuchskaninchen" (vgl. (48)c) noch unbeteiligte Zielpersonen (vgl. (48)d).

(48) a. Alle Lieder sind von Waldkindern geprüft.
b. Alle Lieder sind mit Waldkindern geprüft.
c. Alle Lieder sind an Waldkindern geprüft.
d. Alle Lieder sind für Waldkinder geprüft.
e. Alle Lieder sind in Bezug auf Waldkinder geprüft.

Wieder gibt es also keinen tatsächlich äquivalenten präpositionalen Partner für (47). Die Versuche in (48) zeigen, dass PP-Modifikatoren immer eine Spezifizierung der Rolle des nominalen Referenten innerhalb des zugrundeliegenden Ereignisses vornehmen müssen. Dies gilt selbst für unseren präpositionalen Dummy (48)e. Bei den Komposita ist dies nicht der Fall. Sie erlauben deshalb weit losere Verbindungen zwischen Nomen und Partizip. In (47) z.B. sind die Waldkinder nicht unmittelbare und bewusste Prüfungsbeteiligte, sondern sie sind zunächst einmal die Zuhörer und Sänger. An ihre dabei gezeigte Reaktion wird offenbar dann das Prüfungsabschneiden der Texte und Lieder gebunden.

Die in diesem Abschnitt näher beleuchteten Problemfälle weisen damit auf einen subtilen Unterschied zwischen Nomen-Partizip II-Komposita und den PP-Konstellationen hin, die den ursprünglichen Eindruck weitgehender semantischer Äquivalenz in Zweifel ziehen: Ja, es gibt sie, die annähernd bedeutungsgleichen Fälle vom Typ (1) vs. (2). Aber es gibt auch die Abweichungen, die allesamt auf eine weitergehende Lockerung der Ereignisanbindung des nominalen Erstglieds bei den Komposita hinweisen, die im präpositionalen Rahmen entweder nur über die Formulierungskrücke *in Bezug auf* nachgespielt werden kann oder ganz über die präpositionalen Möglichkeiten hinausgeht. Beiden Befunden – der annähernden Gleichheit und der subtilen Interpretationsunterschiede – gilt es, kompositional Rechnung zu tragen.

4. Kompositionale Semantik

4.1. Ereignisbezogene Modifikatoren beim Zustandspassiv

Beginnen wir mit dem PP-Fall. Die Vorgaben hierfür sind die in (15) vorgeschlagene syntaktische Struktur und die Semantik des Adjektivierungsaffixes in (7), hier wiederholt als (49) und (50).

(49)

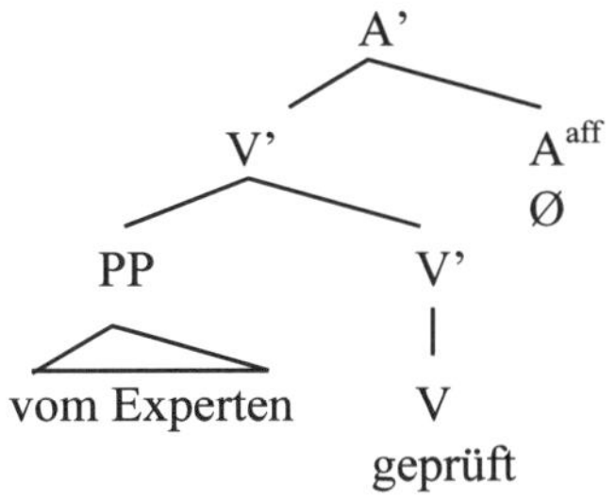

(50) A^{aff}: $\lambda P\ \lambda x\ \lambda s\ \exists e\ [Q(s, x) \wedge \text{RESULT}(e, s) \wedge P(e, x)]$

In Abschnitt 2.2 haben wir festgehalten, dass die beim Zustandspassiv zulässigen ereignisbezogenen Modifikatoren eine verbnahe strukturelle Position einnehmen, bei der sie in den Verbalkomplex integriert sind, und darüber zur Konturierung des Ereignistyps beitragen, über den die für das Zustandspassiv charakteristische, semantisch unterbestimmte Ad hoc-Eigenschaft bestimmt wird. Um dies formal zu explizieren, greifen wir Vorschläge von Landman und Morzyzky (2003) und Gehrke und McNally (2011) auf, die für eine konsequente ontologische Unterscheidung von Ereignisarten (*kinds*) und deren partikuläre Realisierungen analog zu der seit Carlson (1977) gängigen Unterscheidung im Objektbereich eintreten.[24] Wie Gehrke und McNally (2011) werden wir bei der *kind*-Variante weiterhin von Ereignistypen sprechen und deren partikuläre Realisierungen als Ereignistoken bezeich-

[24] Landman und Morzyzky (2003) entwickeln ihren Vorschlag mit Blick auf Manner-Modifikatoren. Diese analysieren sie als Ereignistyp-Modifikatoren; s. die Diskussion zu (53). Gehrke und McNally (2011) behandeln Frequenzadjektive. (Siehe hierzu die Auseinandersetzung in Bücking 2012b.) Die Überlegungen zu Ereignistypen sind also durch unabhängige Fragestellungen ausgelöst. Für das Zustandspassiv argumentieren Gehrke (2011, 2012) und Gese (2011, 2012, in Arb.) für einen „event kind"-Bezug des resultierenden Zustands anstelle einer Verankerung relativ zu einem partikulären Ereignis. Der hier entwickelte Vorschlag greift diese Grundeinsicht auf, wählt aber eine andere Umsetzung.

nen.[25] Zur Kennzeichnung von Ereignis- und Objekttypen verwenden wir den Index k; der Index α rangiert über Typen und Token. Zur Illustration gibt (51) Gehrke und McNallys semantische Repräsentation für ein Verb wie *strolled by* wieder.[26]

(51) *strolled by*: $\lambda x_\alpha\ \lambda e_\alpha$ [STROLLED_BY (e_α, x_α)], where α ranges over both kinds and tokens.

Gehrke und McNally (2011: 192)

Gehrke und McNallys Axiom in (52) legt das Verhältnis zwischen Ereignistypen und ihren Realisierungen fest: Wenn es zu einem Welt-Zeit-Index i einen Ereignistyp e_k gibt, auf den das Prädikat P zutrifft, dann folgt daraus die Existenz von zumindest einem Ereignistokene- zu i, das den Ereignistyp realisiert (R).

(52) $\forall e_k, x_k, P, i\ [P(e_k, x_k)$ at $i \leftrightarrow \exists e, x\ [R\ (e, e_k) \wedge R\ (x, x_k) \wedge P\ (e, x)$ at $i]]$

Gehrke und McNally (2011: 193)

Wie kommen die Ereignistypen in unserem Fall nun ins Spiel? Wir wollen hier die Überlegungen von Landman und Morzyzky (2003) aufgreifen, die vorschlagen, Manner-Modifikatoren als Prädikate über Ereignistypen aufzufassen. Auch wenn wir hier nicht auf die Argumente im Einzelnen eingehen können, sei zumindest eine zentrale Beobachtung genannt, dass nämlich Manner-Modifikatoren von der Ereignistyp-Proform *so* miterfasst werden, während dies z.B. für übliche lokale oder temporale VP-Modifikatoren nicht gilt; s. (53).

(53) a. Maria hat laut getrommelt, und Paul hat auch so getrommelt.
b. Maria hat schnell getrommelt, und Paul hat auch so getrommelt.
c. *Maria hat im Wohnzimmer getrommelt, und Paul hat auch so getrommelt.
d. *Maria hat heute Morgen getrommelt, und Paul hat auch so getrommelt.

Von Manner-Modifikatoren ist bekannt, dass sie eine syntaktische Basisposition unmittelbar beim Verb haben; s. Frey und Pittner (1998), Frey (2003). Das heißt, sie sind gleich unseren PP-Modifikatoren beim Zustandspassiv in den Verbalkomplex integriert. Wir wollen deshalb den Vorschlag von Landman und Morzyzky (2003) verallgemeinern und annehmen, dass der Ereignistypbezug für die Wortdomäne[27] gilt und sich darüber hinaus auf alle innerhalb der Integrationsdomäne V' angesiedelten Argumente und Modifikatoren erstreckt,

---

[25] Ob der Rekurs auf *kinds* tatsächlich der richtige Weg ist, um die hier intendierte Unterscheidung von Ereignistypen und Ereignisinstanzen formal umzusetzen, lassen wir dahingestellt. Aus kompositionaler Perspektive erfordert es Variablen über Ereignistypen vom logischen Typ e, über die die PP-Modifikatoren als einstellige Prädikate ebenso prädizieren können wie über Ereignisinstanzen. Vorläufig modellieren wir dies in dem von Landman und Morzyzky (2003) und Gehrke und McNally (2011) angebotenen Rahmen.

[26] Wie (51) zeigt, nehmen Gehrke und McNally an, dass weder Verben noch ihre Argumente zunächst auf eine Typ-Token-Spezifizierung festgelegt sind.

[27] Zu den referenziellen Bedingungen auf Wortebene s. aktuell die Analysen von A-N- und V-N-Komposita von Bücking (2009a, b) sowie Härtl (2012b). Während Härtl von einem unmittelbaren *kind*-Bezug ausgeht, hebt Bücking den konzeptbildenden Charakter von A-N-Komposita hervor, der eine *kind*-Akkommodation erleichtert.

während strukturell höher platzierte VP-Modifikatoren sich auf Ereignistoken beziehen.[28] V' liefert also die Beschreibung eines komplexen Ereignistyps. Damit können wir erfassen, dass der Ereignistypbezug nicht nur für Manner-Adverbiale gilt, sondern auch für andere Modifikatoren, sofern sie – erkennbar an ihrer prosodischen Markierung – in den Verbalkomplex integriert sind. Dies gilt z.B. für Instrumentale, Komitative, aber auch für prosodisch integrierte Lokative und Temporalangaben; s. (54).

(54) a. Maria hat mit KOCHLÖFFELN getrommelt, und Paul hat auch so getrommelt.
b. Maria ist mit FREUNDEN verreist, und Paul ist auch so verreist.
c. Maria hat auf HAWAII geheiratet, und Paul hat auch so geheiratet.
d. Maria hat die Erdbeeren bei VOLLMOND gepflanzt, und Paul hat die Tomaten auch so gepflanzt.

In (54)c beispielsweise wird *auf Hawaii geheiratet* als Bezeichnung für einen komplexen Ereignistyp verstanden, der zu unterschiedlichen Zeiten und mit unterschiedlichen Beteiligten realisiert werden kann. Bei der prosodischen Variante (54')c handelt der erste Teilsatz hingegen von einem partikulären, auf Hawaii lokalisierten Ereignis vom Typ *heiraten* und bietet folglich keinen darüberhinausgehenden Anknüpfungspunkt für die Ereignistyp-Anapher *so* im zweiten Teilsatz.

(54') c. *Maria hat auf Hawaii GEHEIRATET, und Paul hat auch so geheiratet.

In (55) ist das innerhalb der Integrationsdomäne V' zum Einsatz kommende Modifikationstemplate MOD_k für Ereignistyp-Modifikation angeführt. Es handelt sich dabei um eine für Ereignistypen adaptierte Version des in Maienborn (2001, 2003b) für verbnahe Modifikatoren vorgeschlagenen Templates. Der wesentliche Punkt bei MOD_k ist, dass die betreffenden Modifikatoren nicht unmittelbar das Ereignis als Ganzes spezifizieren, sondern einen internen Aspekt des Ereignistyps näher bestimmen:[29] Das vom Modifikator beigesteuerte Prädikat Q wird auf eine freie Variable v_k angewandt, welche über die Relationenvariable R_{INT} als integraler Bestandteil von e_k ausgewiesen ist. Die konzeptuelle Spezifizierung von v_k und R_{INT} erfolgt unter Einbeziehung von Kontext und Weltwissen.[30]

(55) MOD_k: $\lambda Q\ \lambda P\ \lambda e_k\ [P(e_k) \wedge R_{INT}(e_k, v_k) \wedge Q(v_k)]$

---

28 Siehe hierzu auch die Analyse von Bücking (2009c) zu Modifikatoren von *-ung*-Nominalisierungen, in der er ebenfalls für ein Aufsplitten möglicher Ankerargumente von Lokativen eintritt: Interne Lokative werden als Modifikatoren über sogenannte Ereigniskonzepte behandelt, externe Lokative als Modifikatoren über Ereignisinstanzen.

29 Maienborn bezeichnet die betreffenden Modifikatoren deshalb in früheren Arbeiten als *ereignisinterne* Modifikatoren. Haider (2000, 2002) und Frey (2003) nennen sie *prozessbezogen*. Unter der hier entwickelten Perspektive wäre die Redeweise von *Ereignistyp-Modifikatoren* treffender.

30 Siehe Maienborn (2003b) zu den Details der konzeptuellen Variablenbelegung. Um die Dinge nicht unnötig zu erschweren, ist das Schema in (55) auf den uns hier allein interessierenden Fall der verbalen Integrationsdomäne zugeschnitten; s. aber Bücking (2009a, b) für eine Übertragung in die nominale Domäne zur kompositionalen Analyse von A-N- und V-N-Komposita. Olsen (2012a, b) setzt das Modifikationsschema als grundlegendes Muster für die Kompositabildung an und zeigt generelle kognitive Beschränkungen für die konzeptuelle Spezifizierung auf.

Mit diesen Ingredienzien können wir nun am Beispiel von (56) die kompositionale Bedeutung von ereignisbezogenen Modifikatoren beim Zustandspassiv berechnen.

(56) Die Violine ist vom Experten geprüft.

In (57)a und b sind die semantischen Repräsentationen für das Verb und die PP angegeben.[31] Wir gehen anders als Gehrke und McNally (2011) davon aus, dass die lexikalische Repräsentation von Verben zunächst immer einen Ereignistyp einführt. Die Integration verbnaher Modifikatoren über MOD_k führt zu einer weiteren Spezifikation des Ereignistyps; s. (57)c–e. Im Falle von unserem Beispielsatz (56) ergibt sich die einfachste/ökonomischste Belegung der freien Variablen bei konzeptueller Spezifizierung der Relationenvariable R_{INT} als Identitätsrelation und damit einhergehender Identifikation von v_k als e_k; s. (57)f.

(57) a. *geprüft*$_V$: $\lambda x_\alpha \lambda e_k\, [\text{PRÜF}\,(e_k) \wedge \text{THEMA}\,(e_k, x_\alpha)]$
b. *vom Experten*: $\lambda e_\alpha\, [\text{AGENS}\,(e_\alpha, \text{DEF}\, y_k\, [\text{EXPERTE}\,(y_k)])]$[32]
c. [$_{V'}$ *vom Experten geprüft*]: $\lambda Q\, \lambda P\, \lambda e_k\, [\text{P}\,(e_k) \wedge R_{INT}(e_k, v_k) \wedge Q\,(v_k)]$
$(\lambda e_\alpha\, [\text{AGENS}\,(e_\alpha, \text{DEF}\, y_k\, [\text{EXPERTE}\,(y_k)])])(\lambda x_\alpha \lambda e_k\, [\text{PRÜF}\,(e_k) \wedge \text{THEMA}\,(e_k, x_\alpha)])$
d. $\equiv \lambda P\, \lambda e_k\, [P\,(e_k) \wedge R_{INT}(e_k, v_k) \wedge \text{AGENS}\,(v_k, \text{DEF}\, y_k\, [\text{EXPERTE}\,(y_k)])]$
$(\lambda x_\alpha \lambda e_k\, [\text{PRÜF}\,(e_k) \wedge \text{THEMA}\,(e_k, x_\alpha)])$
nach λ-Konversion
e. $\equiv \lambda x_\alpha \lambda e_k\, [\text{PRÜF}\,(e_k) \wedge \text{THEMA}\,(e_k, x_\alpha) \wedge R_{INT}(e_k, v_k)$
$\wedge\, \text{AGENS}\,(v_k, \text{DEF}\, y_k\, [\text{EXPERTE}\,(y_k)])]$
nach λ-Konversion
f. $\lambda x_\alpha \lambda e_k\, [\text{PRÜF}\,(e_k) \wedge \text{THEMA}\,(e_k, x_\alpha) \wedge \text{AGENS}\,(e_k, \text{DEF}\, y_k\, [\text{EXPERTE}\,(y_k)])]$
bei konzeptueller Spezifizierung von R_{INT} als Identität

Die für Ereignis- und Zustandstypen adaptierte Version unseres Adjektivierungsaffixes ist in (58)a angegeben.[33] Seine Kombination mit der für V' berechneten semantischen Struktur (57)f führt zu (58)b/c.

---

[31] In (57)b ist das interne Argument der PP als Objekttyp ausgewiesen. Dies trägt der Einordnung der PP als Funktionalbegriff Rechnung; s. die Diskussion zu (13) sowie Anmerkung 8. Wenn Eigennamen als interne Argumente von Ereignistypmodifikatoren figurieren, wie bei *von Chomsky zitiert sein* oder *vom TÜV geprüft sein*, so müssen diese gleichsam „Markenlabel“ sein; s. die Diskussion zu *Chomsky* vs. *Sandberger* in (12).

[32] Die Festlegung des lexikalischen Beitrags von *von* auf die AGENS-Rolle ist eine Vereinfachung. Genau genommen wäre die lexikalisch vorgegebene Relation zunächst unterbestimmt zu belassen. Eine AGENS-Spezifikation erfolgt erst auf konzeptueller Ebene; s. hierzu Maienborn (2003b). Auf die uns hier interessierende kompositionale Kombinatorik hat dies allerdings keine wesentlichen Auswirkungen und sei deshalb zur besseren Lesbarkeit abgekürzt.

[33] Gese (2011, in Arb.) schlägt im Zuge ihres Plädoyers für einen Ereignistypenbezug des Adjektivierungsaffixes anstelle von RESULT eine alternative Supervenienzrelation vor. Wir können auf die Details dieses Vorschlags hier nicht näher eingehen und belassen es daher bei RESULT.

(58) a. A^{aff}: $\lambda P\,\lambda x_\alpha\,\lambda s_\alpha\,\exists e_k\,[Q\,(s_\alpha, x_\alpha) \wedge \text{RESULT}\,(e_k, s_\alpha) \wedge P\,(e_k, x_\alpha)]$

b. $\lambda P\,\lambda x_\alpha\,\lambda s_\alpha\,\exists e_k\,[Q\,(s_\alpha, x_\alpha) \wedge \text{RESULT}\,(e_k, s_\alpha) \wedge P\,(e_k, x_\alpha)]$
$(\lambda x_\alpha\,\lambda e_k\,[\text{PRÜF}\,(e_k) \wedge \text{THEMA}\,(e_k, x_\alpha) \wedge \text{AGENS}\,(e_k, \text{DEF}\,y_k\,[\text{EXPERTE}\,(y_k)])])$

c. $\equiv \lambda x_\alpha\,\lambda s_\alpha\,\exists e_k\,[Q\,(s_\alpha, x_\alpha) \wedge \text{RESULT}\,(e_k, s_\alpha) \wedge \text{PRÜF}\,(e_k) \wedge \text{THEMA}\,(e_k, x_\alpha)$
$\wedge\ \text{AGENS}\,(e_k, \text{DEF}\,y_k\,[\text{EXPERTE}\,(y_k)])]$

nach λ-Konversion

Für unsere Zwecke soll es weiter genügen, anzunehmen, dass die Kopula keine Festlegungen hinsichtlich einer Typ/Token-Unterscheidung trifft. Der korrespondierende Lexikoneintrag ist in (59)a angegeben; s. Anmerkung 4.

(59) a. Kopula *sein*: $\lambda P\,\lambda x_\alpha\,\lambda s_\alpha\,[P\,(s_\alpha, x_\alpha)]$

b. *vom Experten geprüft sei-*: $\lambda P\,\lambda x_\alpha\,\lambda s_\alpha\,[P\,(s_\alpha, x_\alpha)]\,(\lambda x_\alpha\,\lambda s_\alpha\,\exists e_k\,[Q\,(s_\alpha, x_\alpha)$
$\wedge\ \text{RESULT}\,(e_k, s_\alpha) \wedge \text{PRÜF}\,(e_k) \wedge \text{THEMA}\,(e_k, x_\alpha)$
$\wedge\ \text{AGENS}\,(e_k, \text{DEF}\,y_k\,[\text{EXPERTE}\,(y_k)])])$

c. $\equiv \lambda x_\alpha\,\lambda s_\alpha\,\exists e_k\,[Q\,(s_\alpha, x_\alpha) \wedge \text{RESULT}\,(e_k, s_\alpha) \wedge \text{PRÜF}\,(e_k) \wedge \text{THEMA}\,(e_k, x_\alpha)$
$\wedge\ \text{AGENS}\,(e_k, \text{DEF}\,y_k\,[\text{EXPERTE}\,(y_k)])]$

nach λ-Konversion

Wir verzichten auf die Ausbuchstabierung der weiteren funktionalen Etagen, AspP, TP usw., oberhalb von VP, weil damit keine Besonderheiten für unsere Fragestellung verknüpft sind. Als Bedeutungsrepräsentation für Satz (56) sei damit abkürzend (60)a angenommen. Abschließend gilt es, eine im jeweiligen Kontext plausible Belegung der semantisch unterbestimmten Variablen Q zu finden. Dies kann uns z.B. zu der Schlussfolgerung führen, dass die Violine eine strikte Qualitätsüberprüfung erfolgreich bestanden hat und somit hohen Ansprüchen als Musikinstrument, Ausstellungsstück o.ä. genügt. Wir führen hierfür abkürzend das Prädikat SUITABLE ein, mit einem zusätzlichen kontextuellen Parameter e'_k für den Ereignistyp, auf den sich die Eignung bezieht. Damit kann Satz (56) z.B. die konzeptuell angereicherte Interpretation in (60)b erhalten.

(60) *Die Violine ist vom Experten geprüft:*

a. $\exists s_\alpha\,\exists e_k\,[Q\,(s_\alpha, \text{DEF}\,o\,[\text{VIOLINE}\,(o)]) \wedge \text{RESULT}\,(e_k, s_\alpha) \wedge \text{PRÜF}\,(e_k)$
$\wedge\ \text{THEMA}\,(e_k, \text{DEF}\,o\,[\text{VIOLINE}\,(o)]) \wedge \text{AGENS}\,(e_k, \text{DEF}\,y_k\,[\text{EXPERTE}\,(y_k)])]$

b. $\exists s_\alpha\,\exists e_k\,[\text{SUITABLE}\,(s_\alpha, \text{DEF}\,o\,[\text{VIOLINE}\,(o)], e'_k) \wedge \text{SPIEL}\,(e'_k) \wedge \text{RESULT}\,(e_k, s_\alpha)$
$\wedge\ \text{PRÜF}\,(e_k) \wedge \text{THEMA}\,(e_k, \text{DEF}\,o\,[\text{VIOLINE}\,(o)]) \wedge \text{AGENS}\,(e_k, \text{DEF}\,y_k\,[\text{EXPERTE}\,(y_k)])]$

Über das Axiom in (52) ist sichergestellt, dass mit (60)b nicht nur die Existenz des Ereignistyps e_k assertiert wird, sondern dass dieser auch durch ein partikuläres Ereignis realisiert wird. Die referenzielle Spezifikation des Zustandsarguments erfolgt im Zuge der aspektuellen Bestimmung der Kopula durch AspP.

Bevor wir auf die Unzulässigkeit von VP-Modifikatoren eingehen, sei mit den Sätzen unter (61) noch der pragmatische Spielraum bei der Belegung der freien Variablen v_k im Modifikationstemplate MOD_k in (55) illustriert. Im Falle von (56) verlangte die Integration der Agens-Information keine weitergehende Aktivierung der konzeptuellen Binnenstruktur des Ereignistyps; v_k konnte als e_k identifiziert werden. Dies ist die ökonomischste Lösung. Für die Fälle in (61) trifft dies nicht zu.

(61) a. Die Kartoffeln sind in der SCHALE gekocht.
b. Der Vertrag ist auf der RÜCKSEITE unterschrieben.

In (61)a wird durch die lokale PP nicht die gesamte Situation des Kartoffel-Kochens im Innenraum von Schalen lokalisiert (vgl. *Die Kartoffeln sind in einer FRITTENBUDE gekocht.*). Auch die Kartoffeln als Ganze werden nicht lokalisiert, sondern lokalisiert wird ein integraler Bestandteil der Kochsituation, nämlich die Kartoffeln abzüglich ihrer Schale. Ganz analog kann in (61)b die Unterschrift als dasjenige Objekt identifiziert werden, das auf der Rückseite des Vertrags lokalisiert ist. In diesen Fällen muss konzeptuelles Wissen herangezogen werden, um die adäquate Belegung für v_k zu bestimmen; s. dazu Maienborn (2003b) und Olsen (2012a).

Die in MOD_k erfassten kompositionalen Interpretationsauflagen an ereignisinterne bzw. Ereignistyp-Modifikatoren haben zunächst einmal nichts mit dem Phänomen des Zustandspassivs zu tun. Sie gelten für beliebige verbnah integrierte Modifikatoren. Unsere Diskussion hier zeigt, dass die unabhängig motivierte Annahme von MOD_k sich leicht auf die Modifikationsverhältnisse beim Zustandspassiv übertragen lässt und dass die in MOD_k über die freie Variable erfasste Flexibilisierung des Modifikationsbezugs ein verbreitetes Phänomen ist.

Bleibt die Frage nach dem Ausschluss von VP-Modifikatoren. Hierzu nehmen wir an, dass das Standard-Template für intersektive Modifikation auf partikuläre Individuen, also hier: Ereignistoken, festgelegt ist; s. (62). Die Kombination mit einem Ereignistypprädikat erzwingt dessen vorausgehende Partikularisierung.[34] Damit kommt es zu einem Kompatibilitätskonflikt; s. (58a): A^{aff} verlangt ein Ereignistypenprädikat, jenseits von V' modifizierte Verbalprojektionen stellen dies nicht mehr zur Verfügung.

(62) MOD: $\lambda Q\, \lambda P\, \lambda e\, [P(e) \wedge Q(e)]$

Das Bild, das sich ergibt, ist das einer Zweiteilung der VP in einen unmittelbaren Verbalkomplex, innerhalb dessen der Ereignistyp festgelegt wird, und in einen darauf aufbauenden VP-Teil innerhalb dessen die partikuläre Ereignisrealisierung spezifiziert wird. Mit den beiden Templates MOD_k und MOD stehen jeweils kompositionale Operationen für die Modifikation von Ereignistypen und Ereignistoken zur Verfügung. Die Ereignistypen-Modifikation zeichnet sich dabei durch eine flexiblere, konzeptuell gesteuerte Verankerung des kompositionalen Beitrags des Modifikators aus. All dies gilt unabhängig vom Zustandspassiv. Alle Besonderheiten ereignisbezogener Modifikatoren beim Zustandspassiv in Bezug auf Syntax, Distribution und Interpretation folgen allein aus den Selektionsanforderungen des Adjektivierungsaffixes nach einem Ereignistyp-Prädikat.

---

34 Zur Illustration seien hier die beiden möglichen VP-Repräsentation für *auf Hawaii heiraten* angegeben; s. die Diskussion zu (54c): (i) zeigt den MOD_k-Anschluss innerhalb von V' und (ii) den MOD-Anschluss in VP.

(i) M. hat $[_{\text{VP}}\ [_{\text{V'}}$ auf HAWAII $[_{\text{V'}}$ geheiratet]]]: $\lambda x_\alpha \lambda e_k\, [\text{HEIRAT}\ (e_k, x_\alpha) \wedge \text{LOC}\ (e_k, \text{AUF (H)})]$

(ii) M. hat $[_{\text{VP}}$ auf Hawaii $[_{\text{VP}}$ GEHEIRATET]]: $\lambda x_\alpha \lambda e\, \exists e_k\, [\text{HEIRAT}(e_k, x_\alpha) \wedge R(e, e_k) \wedge \text{LOC}(e, \text{AUF (H)})]$

4.2. Nomen-Partizip II-Komposita

Wie stellt sich nun die Semantik der Nomen-Partizip II-Komposita dar? Betrachten wir dazu das nominale Pendant (63) zu dem bislang betrachteten PP-Fall. Aus den im vorigen Abschnitt entwickelten Annahmen ergibt sich zunächst für das adjektivierte Partizip *geprüft* die semantische Repräsentation in (64)d.

(63) Die Violine ist expertengeprüft.

(64) a. *geprüft*$_V$: $\lambda x_\alpha \lambda e_k$ [PRÜF $(e_k) \wedge$ THEMA (e_k, x_α)]
b. A^{aff}: $\lambda P \lambda x_\alpha \lambda s_\alpha \exists e_k [Q(s_\alpha, x_\alpha) \wedge$ RESULT $(e_k, s_\alpha) \wedge P(e_k, x_\alpha)]$
c. *geprüft*$_A$: $\lambda P \lambda x_\alpha \lambda s_\alpha \exists e_k [Q(s_\alpha, x_\alpha) \wedge$ RESULT $(e_k, s_\alpha) \wedge P(e_k, x_\alpha)]$
($\lambda x_\alpha \lambda e_k$ [PRÜF $(e_k) \wedge$ THEMA (e_k, x_α)])
d. $\equiv \lambda x_\alpha \lambda s_\alpha \exists e_k [Q(s_\alpha, x_\alpha) \wedge$ RESULT $(e_k, s_\alpha) \wedge$ PRÜF $(e_k) \wedge$ THEMA (e_k, x_α)]

Die Ereignistypen-Variablee_k ist in (64)d existenziell abgebunden, kompositional somit nicht mehr zugänglich. Wenn wir für das Nomen eine einfache Prädikatanalyse annehmen (65)a und für die N-A-Kompositon wiederum das Modifikationstemplate MOD$_k$ einsetzen (s. Olsen 2012a, b), so ergibt sich als semantische Repräsentation für das Nomen-Partizip II-Kompositum die Struktur in (65)e. Die Individuenvariable des Nomens wird dabei kompositional auf die Typenlesart festgelegt.

(65) a. *Experte*: λy_α [EXPERTE (y_α)]
b. MOD$_k$: $\lambda Q \lambda P \lambda e_k [P(e_k) \wedge R_{INT}(e_k, v_k) \wedge Q(v_k)]$
c. *expertengeprüft*$_A$: $\lambda Q \lambda P \lambda e_k [P(e_k) \wedge R_{INT}(e_k, v_k) \wedge Q(v_k)]$ (λy_α [EXPERTE (y_α)]) ($\lambda x_\alpha \lambda s_\alpha \exists e_k [Q(s_\alpha, x_\alpha) \wedge$ RESULT $(e_k, s_\alpha) \wedge$ PRÜF $(e_k) \wedge$ THEMA (e_k, x_α)])
d. $\equiv \lambda P \lambda e_k [P(e_k) \wedge R_{INT}(e_k, v_k) \wedge$ EXPERTE (v_k)]
($\lambda x_\alpha \lambda s_\alpha \exists e_k [Q(s_\alpha, x_\alpha) \wedge$ RESULT $(e_k, s_\alpha) \wedge$ PRÜF $(e_k) \wedge$ THEMA (e_k, x_α)])
e. $\equiv \lambda x_\alpha \lambda s_\alpha \exists e_k [Q(s_\alpha, x_\alpha) \wedge$ RESULT $(e_k, s_\alpha) \wedge$ PRÜF $(e_k) \wedge$ THEMA (e_k, x_α)
$\wedge R_{INT}(s_\alpha, v_k) \wedge$ EXPERTE (v_k)]

Der weitere kompositionale Aufbau erfolgt analog zum PP-Fall. Dies führt für Satz (63) zur semantischen Repräsentation in (66)a. Die freie Individuenvariable v_k vom Typ 'Experte' ist hier als integraler Bestandteil des Resultatszustands s_α ausgewiesen. Die anschließende konzeptuelle Spezifikation der semantischen Struktur muss also kontextuell plausible Belegungen für die Variablen Q, R_{INT} und v_k finden. Aufgrund unserer Erfahrung, dass Experten häufig in der Rolle von Handelnden – zumal in Prüfsituationen – auftreten, ist eine konzeptuelle Spezifikation als Agens vone_k analog zum PP-Fall naheliegend; s. (66)b.

(66) *Die Violine ist expertengeprüft:*
a. $\exists s_\alpha \exists e_k [Q(s_\alpha$, DEF o [VIOLINE (o)]) $\wedge$ RESULT $(e_k, s_\alpha) \wedge$ PRÜF (e_k)
$\wedge$ THEMA $(e_k$, DEF o [VIOLINE (o)]) $\wedge R_{INT}(s_\alpha, v_k) \wedge$ EXPERTE (v_k)]
b. $\exists s_\alpha \exists e_k \exists v_k$ [SUITABLE $(s_\alpha$, DEF o [VIOLINE (o)], $e'_k) \wedge$ SPIEL $(e'_k) \wedge$ RESULT (e_k, s_α)
$\wedge$ PRÜF $(e_k) \wedge$ THEMA $(e_k$, DEF o [VIOLINE (o)]) $\wedge$ AGENS $(e_k, v_k) \wedge$ EXPERTE (v_k)]

Dies entspricht unserer Eingangsbeobachtung einer weitgehenden Interpretationsgleichheit von ereignisbezogenen Modifikatoren beim Zustandspassiv und Nomen-Partizip II-Komposita. Zum Vergleich sind in (67) nochmals semantische Struktur und konzeptuelle Spezifikation des PP-Falls gegenübergestellt.

(67) *Die Violine ist vom Experten geprüft:*
a. $\exists s_\alpha \exists e_k$ [Q (s_α, DEF o [VIOLINE (o)]) $\wedge$ RESULT (e_k, s_α) $\wedge$ PRÜF (e_k)
$\wedge$ THEMA (e_k, DEF o [VIOLINE (o)]) $\wedge$ R_{INT} (e_k, v_k)
$\wedge$ AGENS (v_k, DEF y_k [EXPERTE (y_k)])]
b. $\exists s_\alpha \exists e_k$ [SUITABLE (s_α, DEF o [VIOLINE (o)], e'_k) $\wedge$ SPIEL (e'_k) $\wedge$ RESULT (e_k, s_α)
$\wedge$ PRÜF (e_k) $\wedge$ THEMA (e_k, DEF o [VIOLINE (o)])
$\wedge$ AGENS (e_k, DEF y_k [EXPERTE (y_k)])]

Während im PP-Fall die durch den lexikalischen Beitrag der Präposition konturierte Verankerung von v_k relativ zum verbalen Ereignisreferenten kompositional vorgegeben ist, erfolgt diese Festlegung im Nominal-Fall aufgrund konzeptueller Plausibilitätserwägungen. Folglich sind hier auch andere Spezifikationen möglich. Im Falle des in Abschnitt 3.3 diskutierten Beispielsatzes (47) etwa bieten sich neben der – wenig plausiblen – Deutung der Kinder als Agens des Prüfens (68)b auch andere Lösungen an, z.B., dass das Lied im Hinblick auf seine Eignung zum Singen oder Unterhalten von Kindern geprüft wurde (68)c; oder, dass die Prüfung erfolgte, indem das Lied von Kindern gesungen wurde (68)d.

(68) *Das Lied ist kindergeprüft:*
a. $\exists s_\alpha \exists e_k$ [Q (s_α, DEF o [LIED (o)]) $\wedge$ RESULT (e_k, s_α) $\wedge$ PRÜF (e_k)
$\wedge$ THEMA (e_k, DEF o [LIED (o)]) $\wedge$ R_{INT} (s_α, v_k) $\wedge$ KIND (v_k)]
b. $\exists s_\alpha \exists e_k \exists v_k$ [SUITABLE (s_k, DEF o [LIED (o)], e'_k) $\wedge$ RESULT (e_k, s_α) $\wedge$ PRÜF (e_k)
$\wedge$ THEMA (e_k, DEF o [LIED (o)]) $\wedge$ AGENS (e_k, v_k) $\wedge$ KIND (v_k)]
c. $\exists s_\alpha \exists e_k \exists v_k$ [SUITABLE (s_α, DEF o [LIED (o)], e'_k) $\wedge$ SING (e'_k) $\wedge$ RESULT (e_k, s_α)
$\wedge$ PRÜF (e_k) $\wedge$ THEMA (e_k, DEF o [LIED (o)]) $\wedge$ AGENS (e'_k, v_k) $\wedge$ KIND (v_k)]
d. $\exists s_\alpha \exists e_k \exists e''_k \exists v_k$ [SUITABLE (s_k, DEF o [LIED (o)], e'_k) $\wedge$ RESULT (e_k, s_α)
$\wedge$ PRÜF (e_k) $\wedge$ THEMA (e_k, DEF o [LIED (o)]) $\wedge$ BY-MEANS-OF (e_k, e''_k) $\wedge$ SING (e''_k)
$\wedge$ AGENS (e''_k, v_k) $\wedge$ KIND (v_k) $\wedge$ THEMA (e''_k, DEF o [LIED (o)])]

Die in 3.3 diskutierten Komposita vom Typ *alpenvereinserprobt, partyerprobt* usw. lassen sich ganz analog analysieren; s. die Diskussion zu (44)–(46). Auch hier ist die aus der Erprobung erschlossene Eigenschaft die, dass der Subjektreferent eine besondere Eignung für einen kontextuell gegebenen Ereignistyp aufweist. Relativ zu diesem kann die Verankerung der freien Variable v_k erfolgen.

Die semantischen Formen der Kompositums-Variante (66)a und der Zustandspassiv-Variante (67)a unterscheiden sich neben Zustands- vs. Ereignisbezug und fehlenden bzw. vorhandenen Präpositionalvorgaben in einem dritten Punkt. Beim Kompositum ist es das nominale Erstglied, das durch die freie Variable v_k vertreten wird und dessen Bindung allein im Zuge der konzeptuellen Spezifikation erfolgt. Beim Zustandspassiv ist das interne Argument der PP hingegen schon auf der semantischen Ebene gebunden, v_k vertritt hier seinen relationalen Partner. Diese Differenz vermag die in Abschnitt 2.1 erwähnte Abstufung im Hinblick auf anaphorische Zugänglichkeit zu erklären; s. die Diskussion zu (13) und (13'). Ein allein konzeptuell bereitgestellter Referent bietet einen noch schlechteren Anker für anaphorische Wiederaufnahme als ein zwar in das komplexe Ereignistypprädikat integriertes aber immerhin eigenständig konstituiertes internes PP-Argument.

Betrachten wir abschließend den Fall *wutgeöffnet* aus (43). Die semantischen und konzeptuellen Strukturvorschläge sind in (69) angegeben. Für unsere Zwecke hier sei angenommen, dass das Nomen *Wut* relational sei und neben einem Träger der Eigenschaft ein Zustandsargument einführt. Dieses Zustandsargument kann dann mit dem vom Partizip eingebrachten Resultatszustand s_α identifiziert werden. Satz (69) bezeichnet danach einen Zustand vom Typ Offen-sein von Ottos Augen als Resultat eines Öffnens, der zugleich einen Zustandstyp des Wut-Habens (oder -Zeigens) mit Otto als Träger realisiert.

(69) *Ottos Augen waren wutgeöffnet:*
a. $\exists s_\alpha \exists e_k\, [Q\,(s_\alpha, \text{DEF}\ o\ [\text{AUGE}\ (o, \text{OTTO})]) \wedge \text{RESULT}\ (e_k, s_\alpha) \wedge \text{ÖFFN}\ (e_k)$
$\wedge\ \text{THEMA}\ (e_k, \text{DEF}\ o\ [\text{AUGE}\ (o, \text{OTTO})]) \wedge R_{\text{INT}}\,(s_\alpha, v_k) \wedge \text{WUT}\ (s'_\alpha, v_k)]$
b. $\exists s\ \exists s'_k \exists e_k\, [\text{OFFEN}\ (s_\alpha, \text{DEF}\ o\ [\text{AUGE}\ (o, \text{OTTO})]) \wedge \text{RESULT}\ (e_k, s_\alpha) \wedge \text{ÖFFN}\ (e_k)$
$\wedge\ \text{THEMA}\ (e_k, \text{DEF}\ o\ [\text{AUGE}\ (o, \text{OTTO})]) \wedge R\,(s, s'_k) \wedge \text{WUT}\ (s'_k, \text{OTTO})]$

Die genauen Verhältnisse bei (69) und den übrigen in diesem Abschnitt angenommenen konzeptuellen Ausbuchstabierungen sind sicherlich komplexer. Für unsere Zwecke mögen diese vereinfachten Annäherungen an eine reichhaltigere konzeptuelle Struktur jedoch genügen. Die Beispielanalysen in (66)–(69) zeigen erstens, dass bei Nomen-Partizip II-Komposita das nominale Erstglied sich nicht notwendigerweise auf das vom Partizip eingeführte Ereignis beziehen muss. Sie unterstreichen zweitens die mit der s_α-Anbindung einhergehende größere interpretative Freiheit gegenüber den PP-Modifikatoren, deren Ereignisbezug durch die lexikalische Semantik der Präposition eingeschränkt ist. Und sie führen drittens Unterschiede in der anaphorischen Zugänglichkeit auf grammatische vs. konzeptuelle Bindung zurück. Dies erklärt die subtilen Interpretationsdifferenzen zwischen Nomen-Partizip II-Komposita und ihren PP-Partnern.

Der hier eingeschlagene Weg, Jacobs' Integrationsgedanken mit der Typ/Token-Unterscheidung in Verbindung zu bringen und strukturell über die Annahme eines typaffinen Modifikationstemplates MOD_k zu unterfüttern, weist über das hier betrachtete Phänomen der wortinternen bzw. -externen Kombinatorik adjektivierter Partizipien hinaus und bietet sich zur weiteren Untersuchung des unmittelbaren Verbalkomplexes bzw. allgemeiner der Ränder und Übergangszonen lexikalischer Integrität an. Unsere Überlegungen zur konzeptuellen Spezifikation freier semantischer Variablen an der Semantik/Pragmatik-Schnittstelle lenken den Blick ferner auf die Notwendigkeit und den Nutzen einer stärkeren Einbeziehung begrifflichen Wissens für die Bedeutungskonstitution. Erst wenn der pragmatische Interpretationsspielraum und die dabei genutzten Wissensquellen hinreichend berücksichtigt sind, tritt der eigentliche kompositionale Beitrag in Erscheinung.

Bibliographie

Asher, N. (2011): *Lexical Meaning in Context. A Web of Words*. Cambridge: Cambridge University Press.

Bücking, S. (2009a): How do phrasal and lexical modification differ? - Contrasting adjective-noun combinations in German. *Word Structure* 2: 184–204.

Bücking, S. (2009b): German nominal compounds as underspecified names for kinds. In S. Olsen (ed.), *New Impulses in Word-Formation (Linguistische Berichte Sonderheft 17)*. Hamburg: Buske, 253–281.

Bücking, S. (2009c): Modifying Event Nominals: Syntactic Surface Meets Semantic Transparency. In A. Riester und T. Solstad (eds.), *Proceedings of Sinn und Bedeutung 13*. Stuttgart:OPUS, 93-107.

Bücking, S. (2012a): *Kompositional flexibel. Partizipanten und Modifikatoren in der Nominaldomäne*. Tübingen: Stauffenburg.

Bücking, S. (2012b): The semantics of frequency adjectives. Erscheint in: *Proceedings of the 48th Annual Meeting of the Chicago Linguistic Society*, Chicago.

Carlson, G. N. (1977): *Reference to Kinds in English.* Ph.D.Diss., University of California, Irvine.

Cruse, D. A. (2000): *Meaning in Language. An Introduction to Semantics and Pragmatics.* Oxford: Oxford University Press.

Di Sciullo, A. M. (1992): Deverbal compounds and the external argument. In: I. M. Roca (ed.), *Thematic Structure. Its Role in Grammar*. Dordrecht: Foris, 65–78.

Donalies, E. (2002): *Die Wortbildung des Deutschen. Ein Überblick.* Tübingen: Narr.

Eschenlohr, S. (1999): *Vom Nomen zum Verb: Konversion, Präfigierung und Rückbildung im Deutschen*. Hildesheim: Olms.

Fanselow, G. (1981): Neues von der Kompositafront oder zu den drei Paradigmata in der Kompositagrammatik. *Studium Linguistik* 11: 43–57.

Fanselow, G. (1988): 'Word syntax' and semantic principles. *Yearbook of Morphology* 1988: 95–122.

Fanselow, G. (1991): Ein modulares Konzept der Lexikonerweiterung. *Theorie des Lexikons. Arbeiten des Sonderforschungsbereichs 282*, Nr. 6, 1–32.

Frey, W. (2003): Syntactic conditions on adjunct classes. In: E. Lang, C. Maienborn und C. Fabricius-Hansen (eds.), *Modifying Adjuncts*. Berlin: de Gruyter, 163–210.

Frey, W. und K. Pittner (1998): Zur Positionierung der Adverbiale im deutschen Mittelfeld. *Linguistische Berichte* 176: 489–534.

Fuhrhop, N. (2000): Zeigen Fugenelemente die Morphologisierung von Komposita? In: R. Thieroff et al. (eds.), *Deutsche Grammatik in Theorie und Praxis*. Tübingen: Niemeyer, 201–213.

Fuhrhop, N. (2006): *Zwischen Wort und Syntagma: Zur grammatischen Fundierung der Getrennt- und Zusammenschreibung*. Tübingen: Niemeyer.

Fuhrhop, N. (2007): Verbale Komposition: Sind *brustschwimmen* und *radfahren* Komposita? In: R. Métrich und M. Kauffer (eds.), *Verbale Wortbildung im Deutschen*. Tübingen: Stauffenburg, 49–58.

Gehrke, B. (2011): Stative passives and event kinds. In: I. Reich, E. Horch und D. Pauly (eds.), *Sinn und Bedeutung 15: Proceedings of the 2010 Annual Conference of the Gesellschaft für Semantik*. Saarbrücken: Universaar - Saarland University Press, 241–257.

Gehrke, B. (2012): Passive states. In: V. Demonte und L. McNally (eds.), *Telicity, Change, and State: A Cross-Categorial View of Event Structure*. Oxford: Oxford University Press.

Gehrke, B. und L. McNally (2011): Frequency adjectives and assertions about event types. In: E. Cormany, S. Ito und D. Lutz (eds.), *Proceedings of SALT XIX*: Ohio State University, 180–197.

Gese, H. (2011): Events in Adjectival Passives. In: I. Reich, E. Horch und D. Pauly (eds.), *Sinn und Bedeutung 15: Proceedings of the 2010 Annual Conference of the Gesellschaft für Semantik*. Saarbrücken: Universaar - Saarland University Press, 259–273.

Gese, H. (2012): Pragmatic enrichment in adjectival passives: The case of the post state reading. In: F. Liedtke und C. Schulze (eds.), *Beyond the Words. Content, context and inference*. Berlin: de Gruyter, 229–250.

Gese, H. (in Arb.): *Empirische Untersuchungen zum Zustandspassiv*. Dissertation, Deutsches Seminar, Universität Tübingen.
Gese, H, C. Maienborn und B. Stolterfoht (2011): Adjectival conversion of unaccusatives in German. *Journal of Germanic Linguistics* 23: 101–140.
Grimshaw, J. (1990): *Argument Structure*. Cambridge, MA: MIT Press.
Haider, H. (2000): Adverb Placement - Convergence of Structure and Licensing. *Theoretical Linguistics* 26: 95–134.
Haider, H. (2002): Adverbials at the syntax-semantics interface. In: H. Kamp und U. Reyle (eds.), *How We Say WHEN It Happens*. Tübingen: Niemeyer, 53–70.
Härtl, H. (2008): *Implizite Informationen: Sprachliche Ökonomie und interpretative Komplexität bei Verben*. Berlin: Akademie-Verlag.
Härtl, H. (2012a): Argument structural restrictions on word-formation patterns. To appear in: P. Müller et al. (eds.), *HSK Word Formation: An International Handbook of the Languages of Europe*. Berlin/New York: de Gruyter.
Härtl, H. (2012b): Situationsargumente von Nicht-Köpfen: Verb-Nomen-Komposita im Zusammenspiel von Morphologie, Syntax und Pragmatik. To appear in: C. Fortmann, W. Geuder, A. Lübbe und I. Rapp (eds.), *Situationsargumente im Nominalbereich*. Berlin/New York: de Gruyter.
Hobbs, J. et al. (1993): Interpretation as Abduction. *Artificial Intelligence* 63: 69–142.
Jacobs, J. (1993): Integration. In: M. Reis (ed.), *Wortstellung und Informationsstruktur*. Tübingen: Niemeyer, 63–116.
Jacobs, J. (1999): Informational Autonomy. In: P. Bosch und R. v. d. Sandt (eds.), *Focus: Linguistic, Cognitive, and Computational Perspectives*. Cambridge: Cambridge University Press, 56–81.
Jacobs, J. (2005): *Spatien. Zum System der Getrennt- und Zusammenschreibung im heutigen Deutsch*. Berlin/New York: de Gruyter.
Kratzer, A. (1994). *The Event Argument and the Semantics of Voice*. Ms. University of Amherst.
Kratzer, A. (2000): Building Statives. In: L. Conathan et al. (eds.), *Proceedings of the 26th Annual Meeting of the Berkeley Linguistics Society*. Berkeley: University of California, Berkeley Linguistics Society, 385–399.
Landman, M. und M. Morzycki (2003): Event-kinds and manner modification. In: N. M. Antrim et al. (eds.), *Proceedings of the Western Conference in Linguistics (WECOL) 2002*. California State University, Fresno.
Lang, E. (1985). Symmetrische Prädikate: Lexikoneintrag und Interpretationsspielraum. Eine Fallstudie zur Semantik der Personenstandslexik. *Linguistische Studien* 127: 75–112. Berlin: Akademie Verlag.
Lieber, R. (1980): *On the organization of the lexicon*. Cambridge, MA: MIT Press.
Lieber R. (2012): Semantics of derivational morphology. In: C. Maienborn, K. von Heusinger und P. Portner (eds.), *Semantics. An international handbook of natural language meaning; Volume 3*. (HSK 33.3), Berlin/New York: de Gruyter, 2098–2119.
Löbner, S. (1985): Definites. *Journal of Semantics* 4: 279–326.
Löbner, S. (2011): Concept types and determination. *Journal of Semantics* 28: 279–333.
Lübbe, A. (2012): Das regulär prädikative Partizip I. To appear in: C. Fortmann, W. Geuder, A. Lübbe und I. Rapp (eds.), *Situationsargumente im Nominalbereich*. Berlin/New York: de Gruyter.
Maienborn, C. (2001): On the Position and Interpretation of Locative Modifiers. *Natural Language Semantics* 9: 191–240.
Maienborn, C. (2003a): *Die logische Form von Kopula-Sätzen*. Berlin: Akademie-Verlag.

Maienborn, C. (2003b): Event-internal modifiers: Semantic underspecification and conceptual interpretation. In: E. Lang, C. Maienborn und C. Fabricius-Hansen (eds.), *Modifying Adjuncts*. Berlin/New York: de Gruyter, 475–509.

Maienborn, C. (2005): On the Limits of the Davidsonian Approach: The Case of Copula Sentences. *Theoretical Linguistics* 31: 275–316.

Maienborn, C. (2007): Das Zustandspassiv: Grammatische Einordnung – Bildungsbeschränkungen – Interpretationsspielraum. *Zeitschrift für germanistische Linguistik* 35: 83–15.

Maienborn, C. (2009): Building event-based *ad hoc* properties: On the interpretation of adjectival passives. In: A. Riester und T. Solstad (eds.), *Proceedings of Sinn und Bedeutung 13*. Stuttgart: OPUS, 35–49.

Maienborn, C. (2011): Strukturausbau am Rande der Wörter: Adverbiale Modifikatoren beim Zustandspassiv. In: S. Engelberg, A. Holler und K. Proost (eds.), *Sprachliches Wissen zwischen Lexikon und Grammatik. Institut für Deutsche Sprache, Jahrbuch 2010.* Berlin/New York: de Gruyter, 317–343.

Maienborn, C., H. Gese und B. Stolterfoht (2012). *Adverbial Modifiers in Adjectival Passives*. Ms. Universität Tübingen.

Olsen, S. (1986): *Wortbildung im Deutschen. Eine Einführung in die Theorie der Wortstruktur*. Stuttgart: Kröner.

Olsen, S. (1992): Zur Grammatik des Wortes – Argumente zur Argumentvererbung. *Linguistische Berichte* 137: 3–32.

Olsen, S. (2004): Coordination in morphology and syntax. In: A. ter Meulen und W. Abraham (eds.), *The composition of meaning: from lexeme to discourse*. Amsterdam: John Benjamins, 17–37.

Olsen, S. (2012a): Der Einfluss des mentalen Lexikons auf die Interpretation von Komposita. In: L. Gaeta und B. Schlücker (eds.), *Das Deutsche als kompositionsfreudige Sprache*. Berlin/New York: de Gruyter, 135–170.

Olsen, S. (2012b): Semantics of compounds. To appear in: C. Maienborn, K. von Heusinger und P. Portner (eds.), *Semantics. An international handbook of natural language meaning; Volume 3.* (HSK 33.3), Berlin/New York: de Gruyter, 2120–2150.

Pittner, K. (1998): *Radfahren – mit dem Rad fahren*: Trennbare Verben und parallele syntaktische Strukturen. In: I. Barz und G. Öhlschläger (eds.), *Zwischen Grammatik und Lexikon*. Tübingen: Niemeyer, 103–112.

Rapp, I. (1996): Zustand? Passiv? - Überlegungen zum sogenannten "Zustandspassiv". *Zeitschrift für Sprachwissenschaft* 15: 231–265.

Rapp, I. (1997): *Partizipien und semantische Struktur. Zu passivischen Konstruktionen mit dem 3. Status*. Tübingen: Stauffenburg.

Rapp, I. (2002): Argumentstruktur und Erstgliedinterpretation bei deverbalen Derivaten - ein semantikbasierter Ansatz. *Folia Linguistica* 35: 243–283.

Schäfer, F. (2012): Two types of external argument licensing – the case of causers. *Studia Linguistica* 66: 128–180.

Schlücker, B. (2005): Event-related modifiers in German adjectival passives. In: E. Maier, C. Bary und J. Huitink (eds.), *Proceedings of SuB9*. Nijmegen: NCS [http://www.ru.nl/ncs/sub9], 417–430.

Selkirk, E. O. (1982): *The Syntax of Words*. Cambridge, MA: MIT Press.

Solstad, T. (2006): *Mehrdeutigkeit und Kontexteinfluss: Die Spezifikation kausaler Relationen am Beispiel von durch.* Dissertation, Universität Oslo.

Stolterfoht, B., H. Gese und C. Maienborn (2010): Word category conversion causes processing costs: Evidence from adjectival passives. *Psychonomic Bulletin & Review* 17: 651–656.

Wunderlich, D. (1986): Probleme der Wortstruktur. *Zeitschrift für Sprachwissenschaft* 5: 209–252.

Wunderlich, D. (1987): Schriftstellern ist mutmaßen, ist hochstapeln, ist Regeln mißachten – Über komplexe Verben im Deutschen. In: B. Asbach-Schnitker und J. Roggenhofer (eds.), *Neuere Forschungen zur Wortbildung und Historiographie der Linguistik. Festgabe für Herbert E. Brekle zum 50.Geburtstag*. Tübingen: Narr, 91–107.

Arguments of non-heads*

Holden Härtl

1. Introduction

It is over twenty years ago that Susan Olsen and Gisbert Fanselow took opposite perspectives as to whether the formation and interpretation of complex words is based on regularities of core grammar or not, see Fanselow (1989), (1991) and Olsen (1991), (1992).[1] But note how relevant the subject matter still is today: While Gisbert Fanselow argued against an exclusive word structure component of the language faculty and attributed the interpretation of compounds to general conceptual-semantic principles, Susan Olsen maintained the view that word-formation operations such as argument inheritance are structurally regular and thus part of UG.

Clearly, both views have their merits. On the one hand, a conceptual perspective towards word-formation, like Fanselow's, allows a uniform treatment of argument-structural dependencies occurring in compounds and, thus, certain semantic parallels between different types of compounds involving thematic relations are predicted. For example, synthetic compounds like *Kastanienesser* (*chestnut eater*) as well as verb-noun compounds like *Esskastanie* ('eat_chestnut', *chestnut*) both involve a nominal representing a theme, i.e., *chestnut*, of the verbal predicate *ess-*, and this nominal could be argued to be conceptually associated with the verb's corresponding argument slot in both cases. On the other hand, there are characteristic regularities, like the well-known (and much debated) *Right Hand Head Rule*, see Williams (1981: 248), which suggest a more restricted rule system may be at work here and thus the existence of a separate, word-formation-specific grammatical domain. In this context, for example, the (also often-discussed) ban on external arguments to appear within a complex nominal, cf. **child-sleeper*, **girl-writing* (see Grimshaw 1990 among others), could be considered an expression of a particular morphological restriction holding exclusively in word-formation patterns.

Large parts of the discussion in the literature on the above issue center around aspects of argument inheritance in deverbal nouns and if this is a syntactically rooted operation or not.

* I wish to thank Sven Kotowski, Andrew McIntyre and the audiences of the annual workshops "Event Semantics" in Tübingen (2010) as well as Flensburg (2011) for useful comments and discussion.

[1] About sixteen years ago, the aforementioned papers were my first encounters with system-theoretical aspects of word-formation and morphology, in general. I therefore dedicate this paper to Susan Olsen, to whom I owe so much.

A standard assumption maintains that deverbal *er*-nominals, in some way, inherit the object arguments of the verbal base of the head noun, cf. *baker of bread, giver of presents to children*, see, among others, Lieber (2004: 61f.). Less attention, though, has been paid to arguments of non-heads and the question if a thematic relation between a predicate in a non-head position and an expression "outside" the compound is based on structural argument inheritance processes or not. Consider the following examples:

(1) a. Fahrgemeinschaft nach Italien
ride_community to Italy
'ride sharing to Italy'
b. Ausreiseverbot in die BRD
departure_ban into the FRG
'ban on traveling to West Germany'
c. Anschlagsversuch auf Ackermann
attack_attempt on Ackerman
'attempted attack on Ackerman'
d. Umsteigepunkt zu den documenta-Stätten
change_point to the documenta_locations
'interchange point to the …'

The examples all contain a predicate, e.g., *fahr-* in (1)a, located in the non-head position of a compound, which is accompanied by a phrase (i.e., *nach Italien*) apparently serving as the argument of the non-head predicate. The pattern is linguistically marked[2] to a considerable extent but exhibits a significant degree of productivity so that we cannot simply move these expressions into the realm of performance-based slips. From a prescriptive viewpoint, attachments to non-heads of this kind have occasionally been described as "incorrect" (cf., for example, DUDEN *Richtiges und gutes Deutsch*: 507f.)—which, however, does not match descriptive reality as, intuitively, certain structural factors seem to play a role in the formation of the construction. For example, we can plausibly argue aspects of linguistic economy to be involved in (1) if we consider the complexity and clumsiness of (per se regular) morphologically formed correspondents like, e.g., *documenta-Stätten-Umsteigepunkt* for (1)d. Besides, certain instances of thematic relations between non-head and post-nominal phrase are considerably less marked, as in, for example, *Designanalyse des Geschirrs* ('design_analysis of the dinnerware'), where *des Geschirrs* can be argued too to saturate the argument slot of the (relational) non-head noun, i.e. *Design.* Note, however, that in this case the post-nominal DP functions as an argument of the head noun *Analyse* also; a circumstance which could provide an anchor point to explain the unconditioned acceptability of this type of construction.

The current paper investigates these cases from a lexicalist perspective. In particular, I will discuss whether realizations of arguments of non-heads of the above types are based on a regular grammatical[3] process or not. I will argue that this is the case indeed with constructions of the type *Designanalyse des Geschirrs*, where the post-nominal element figures as

[2] Here, *markedness* relates to the notion of grammatical / linguistic acceptability. The more acceptable an expression is, the less marked it is considered.

[3] *Grammatical* does not mean *syntactic*.

argument of both the head as well as the non-head. In contrast, (prepositional) external argument realizations of the type in (1)—i.e. constructions in which the post-nominal element satisfies an argument slot of the non-head predicate alone—will be approached from a non-grammatical, pragmatically oriented perspective.

In the second part of the paper, I will take a closer look upon verb-noun compounds like *Fahrgemeinschaft* in (1)a, *Sägewerk* (*sawmill*) etc. I will claim that the argument variables of the verbal non-heads are nevertheless lexically still active after the word-formation process, that is, in some way "inherited" to the compound. At this point it is vital to note that my assumptions do not necessarily imply a syntactic feature percolation operation (as proposed by, e.g., Harley 2008). Rather, I will assume a (lexical-semantic) operation of function composition to be at work in constructions like *Designanalyse des Geschirrs*. Furthermore, based on insights from PRO-configurations as well as sentential complements, I will implement a lexical-structural projection below the word level, under the assumption of two separate grammatical domains, i.e., syntax and morphology, which share a common generative structure building apparatus.

2. Some problems for conditions on argument inheritance

Argument-structural restrictions on word-formation patterns have been associated with a broad array of principles and conditions, which we cannot even come close to describe in their entirety in this paper; see Baeskow (2011) and Härtl (2011) for overviews. A classic example is the above-mentioned sanction against external arguments in complex deverbal nominals, a restriction also formulated in Selkirk's (1982) *Subject Condition*. Note, however, that the condition is watered down by examples in which subjects are nevertheless realized within compounds. For instance, compounds based on intransitive verbs like *Hundeheulen* ('dog_ howling') and *Möwengeschrei* ('seagull_yelling') and also complex adjectival participles like *experten-getestet* ('expert_tested') or *fachmann-geprüft* ('specialist_inspected') all contain what could conceivably be grammatically represented as an external argument of the verbal predicate in the non-head position; see Di Sciullo (1992) and her critical discussion of the *Subject Condition*. A potential way out could be to exclude intransitive verbal bases from the condition, cf. *Hundeheulen* vs. ??*Hundefressen*[4] ('dog_eating'), which, however, entails a special treatment of the participles as the above examples contain transitive bases. Consider, on the other hand, that complex participles containing an agent argument are probably not based on a regular inheritance process, because novel expressions of this type are often marked, cf. ??*großmutter-gestrickt* ('grandmother_knitted'), ??*professoren-gelehrt* ('professor_taught'). Further, *experten-getestet* does not have a verbal pendant, cf. **experten-testen* (see, among others, Fuhrhop 2007 for details), which suggests that the "agent" nominal is attached *after* the adjectivization of the verbal base has taken place; see Maienborn and Gelderman (this volume) for such an analysis. Instead, what seems to play a key role in the licensing of this pattern is the conceptual salience of the

4 The latter example is odd with the—here intended—agent reading of the non-head.

property expressed with the adjective, which determines its interpretability and which makes its analysis as "synthetic" composite in the narrow sense redundant (see ibid.)

Rule-based accounts of argument inheritance are also challenged by apparent violations of the theta criterion. A standard analysis of complex nominalizations like *Personenbeschreibung* ('person_description') implies that the non-head element *person-* satisfies the internal argument slot of the predicate *beschreib-*; cf. Grimshaw (1990), Lieber (2004). This assumption, however, is less unproblematic in light of the option to add a genitive DP realizing a thematic function quite identical to the one of the non-head: *Personenbeschreibung des Täters* ('person_description of the culprit'); see Solstad (2010) for discussion. Expressions like these seemingly violate the restriction, formulated by Di Sciullo (2005), that as soon as an argument position is satisfied within a compound, this position is no longer accessible to any compound-external DP as *meat-eating* (**a steak*) illustrates; cf. Di Sciullo (2005: 27) and also Baker (1998: 190). A potential explanation could be that phrases like *Personenbeschreibung des Täters* contain actually a (deverbal) root compound as syntactic head and that the genitive DP alone satisfies the internal argument slot of the deverbal element. This, however, has the unattractive implication of two distinct analyses to be applied to one and the same compound: (i) as root compound when accompanied by a genitive DP of the above type and (ii) when it occurs in isolation, as compound containing a non-head which saturates the predicate's internal argument.[5] To get a clearer picture, let us inspect some other examples exhibiting instances of apparent double argument saturation:[6]

(2) a. Designanalyse des Geschirrs
design_analysis of the dinnerware
b. Namensanalyse des Flusses
name_analysis of the river
c. Stabilitätsprüfung der Dachkonstruktion
stability_check of the roof_construction
d. Belastbarkeitstest des Fahrzeuges
capacity_test of the vehicle

Noticeably, the non-heads of the compounds in these examples are all relational in a broader sense: nouns like *design*, *name*, etc. have relational meanings and, thus, contain an additional argument variable: λyλx.NAME(x,y). Upon closer inspection, it appears that this argument slot is consistently "saturated"[7] by the genitive DP in the examples in (2), which is also indicated by the corresponding paraphrases: *Design des Geschirrs*, *Name des Flusses*, etc. This configuration gives us reason to believe that the apparent double argument saturation should rather be seen as external argument realization, i.e., an instance of the saturation of an argument of a non-head and, thus, similar to the constructions in (1) above.

---

5 This is expected under the *Argument Linking Principle*; see Lieber (1983: 258). It dictates that if a verbal head appears as sister to a (potential) internal argument that can figure as logical object this argument slot will be linked, i.e., saturated.

6 The examples in (2) are all extracted from Google results or adaptations thereof.

7 I am not implying a *syntactic* argument percolation (cf. Selkirk 1982) to be at work here. Below, I will assume a lexical-semantic anchoring of the mechanism in the lexically oriented style of Lieber (1983).

Note that this insight is bolstered by the ungrammaticality of examples like **Bonitatsprüfung der Liquidität* ('reliability_assessment of the solvency'), where the genitive DP *der Liquidität* cannot saturate the theme role of *Bonität.* Thus, it seems that for constructions like those in (2) to be felicitous a thematic relation between non-head and genitive DP needs to be construable. From a structural viewpoint, a dependency like this, however, violates several grammatical principles, among them the *Head Principle* formulated in Selkirk (1982), which holds that only arguments of heads can be satisfied whereas arguments of non-heads are blocked from linking, cf. *baker of bread* vs. **baking man of bread.* Hence, the question is raised if constructions like the ones in (1) and (2) are indeed grammatically licensed or if they should rather be explained on a pragmatic-conceptual basis—which, in turn, connects to the original question about the locus of word-formation in the language system. Note that two separate analyses for (1) and (2) may be also conceivable in light of the fact that only the latter have pendants which are acceptable with simplex head nouns, cf. *Analyse des Geschirrs* ('analysis of the dinnnerware') vs. **Gemeinschaft nach Italien* in (1)a above. In the following section I will address this issue. First, I will review some previous analyses of arguments of non-heads and consider the implications for an analysis of outside argumental genitive DPs. In the second part, I will concentrate on verb-noun compounds like *Fahrgemeinschaft*, *Tauchanzug* ('dive_suit', *diving suit*), etc. and their grammatical behavior in this respect.

3. Inheritance of arguments of non-heads

Note that attachments of a phrasal element to the non-head of the type in (1), i.e., constructions like *Fahrgemeinschaft nach Italien*, are restricted to arguments, while adjuncts seem to be generally excluded in this configuration, cf. ??*Fahrgemeinschaft mit dem Volkswagen.* Should we therefore analyze felicitous constructions of this type as the result of a structural mechanism of argument inheritance—wherever in the grammatical system we wish to locate it?

3.1. Some previous analyses and their implications

From a lexicalist viewpoint, Höhle (1982) argued that cases like *Wartezeit auf den Arzt* ('wait_time for the doctor') are indeed instances of grammatical argument inheritance, which are, however, significantly restricted in their productivity by idiosyncratic properties of the head nouns. While the author remains silent about the exact nature of these properties, Fabricius-Hansen (1993) identifies a restriction to be at work here, which limits external argument realizations to constructions in which head noun and argument phrase together constitute a syntactically and semantically possible noun phrase (ibid.: 230). This criterion would explain why a construction like *Designanalyse des Geschirrs* (see (2)a above) is considerably more acceptable than, e.g., ??*Nachfolgefrage des Bürgermeisters*[8] ('suc-

---

8 Observe that grammaticality judgments are notoriously difficult in this domain. For example, Fabricius-Hansen (1993: 229) considers *Nachfolgefrage Brandts* ('succession_question Brandt's')

cession_question of the mayor') because in the former, but not in the latter case, the head noun and the genitive DP form a semantically coherent constituent. Besides, Wunderlich (1986) discusses aspects of lexicalization to be relevant in the formation of constructions of this type. He maintains that lexicalized complex nouns are available to external argument realization to a lesser extent in comparison to novel formations, which would explain the contrast between **Sprechzimmer mit dem Direktor* ('speak_room to the director') and ?*Verhandlungszimmer mit dem Direktor* ('negotiation_room with the director'); see ibid.: 224 and also Fabricius-Hansen (1993: 231).

We can conclude that extra-grammatical factors are at work to a significant extent here, which control the creation of the constructions in question. Regarding productivity and linguistic acceptability as the decisive criteria, we have reason to believe that constructions with an argumental genitive DP of the type in (3), i.e., a DP satisfying an argument *exclusively* of the non-head, should be analyzed based on pragmatic grounds:[9]

(3) Pattern I: [[NON-HEAD$_{I}$ HEAD] DP-GEN$_{ARG-I}$]
  a. Abrissgenehmigung des schnellen Brüters
     demolition_permit of the fast breeder reactor
     (from Wunderlich 1986: 224)
  b. Absturzursache des Flugzeugs
     crash_cause of the airplane
     (from Fabricius-Hansen 1993: 197)
  c. Impfpflicht des Truthahngeflügels
     vaccinate_obligation of the turkey_poultry
     (based on an example I heard)[10]

I am not claiming that occurrences of this type should generally be considered performance-based slips of the tongue. However, due to their limited productivity and, in particular, because of their noticeable departure from the usual acceptability standards, constructions like those in (3) can be surmised to be occasional formations which are licensed through pragmatic intervention. This may be based on the well-known conversational maxims (see Grice 1975), which, among other things, regulate a linguistic expression to be communicatively economical, to the extent that the expression remains interpretable. For example, due to its length, the grammatically regular pendant for (3)c, i.e., *Truthahngeflügelimppflicht*, appears

to be better than *Reisemöglichkeit nach Bonn* ('travel_opportunity to Bonn'), which, however, is against my own intuition. Likewise, the judgments for constructions of the type *Verhandlungszimmer mit dem Direktor* (see below) vary considerably; compare Fabricius-Hansen (1993: 195) and Wunderlich (1986: 224), see also Toman (1987: 61). See also McIntyre (2012) for a discussion of idiolectal aspects relevant in this context.

9 A pragmatic analysis is compatible with an observation made in McIntyre (2012), who points out that the argumental genitive DPs like in (3) are systematically optional. Therefore, McIntyre proposes a semantic-conceptual approach in which—according to McIntyre—the genitive DPs are licensed by the fact that the (complex) head nouns are inherently relational.

10 Note that the kind reading for the genitive DP is intended in this example; see, among others, Krifka et al. (1995) for details. We cannot go into the details of the complex interplay between the name giving function of compounds and kind interpretations of nominals but see, among others, Bücking (2010), Kotowski et al. (2012) for more.

rather odd from a functional-communicative point of view. Consequently, a less "heavy" genitive DP argument should lead to a higher degree of markedness when realized externally, which indeed seems to be the case, cf. ??*Impfpflicht des Wildes* ('vaccinate_ obligation of the wild_animal'), with the possible explanation that the grammatically regular and thus more conventional expression *Wildimpfflicht* would do the job pertfectly.

Note that an alternative reading is conceivable for (3)c, in which the genitive DP is also linked to the nominal argument of the relational noun *Pflicht* ('obligation'), producing the somewhat peculiar interpretation for the terriers themselves to be under the expressed obligation. This interpretation corresponds to the configuration displayed in (2) above, where *both* the head and the non-head stand in a thematic relation to the genitive DP. Some additional examples are given in (4):

(4) Pattern II: [[NON-HEAD$_I$ HEAD$_J$] DP-GEN$_{ARG-I/J}$]
  a. Oberflächenzerteilung des Knochens
   surface_dispersion of the bone
  b. Unterbodenreinigung des Fahrzeuges
   undercarriage_cleaning of the vehicle
  c. Persönlichkeitscheck des Bewerbers
   personality_check of the applicant

Constructions of this type, displaying instances of apparent double argument linking, exhibit certain resemblances to the expressions in (3). For example, their paraphrases are structurally identical:

(5) a. Oberflächenzerteilung des Knochens → Zerteilung der Oberfläche des Knochens
  b. Absturzursache des Flugzeugs → Ursache des Absturzes des Flugzeugs

In contrast to that in (3), however, the pattern displayed in (4) and (2) is fully regular and linguistically unmarked and, crucially, with the latter the internal argument variable of the deverbal head is compatible with the ontological-semantic type of the genitive DP. In accordance with the argumentation in Fabricius-Hansen (1993), see above, I will argue that that this a vital licensing condition for the construction, explaining its unmarkedness. Pursuing this view, we can assume the construction to be based on a regular grammatical pattern—be it "morphological" or "syntactic". The structure can be argued to have its formal, lexical-semantic reflexes in an operation of functional composition $\alpha/\beta\ \beta/\gamma \rightarrow \alpha/\gamma$, in which two functions are combined and unsaturated arguments are inherited to the function resulting from the composition.[11] Informally speaking, for example, in (4)a, the relational nominal *Oberfläche*, representing a function itself, is applied to the deverbal *Zerteilung*[12] to satisfy its internal argument. In this operation, the relational argument of *Oberfläche* is inherited to the resulting expression (i.e., *Oberflächenzerteilung*), which will then be saturated by the genitive DP.

---

[11] See Bierwisch (1989) and Gamerschlag (2005) and, in particular, also the discussion in Fanselow (1991: 16f.), who argues against an approach making use of functional composition to derive the interpretation of compounds containing a predicate non-head.

[12] Aspects of the derivation of the *ung*-nominalization are ignored here; see Bierwisch (1989), (2009), and Ehrich and Rapp (2000) for a discussion of the relevant aspects.

So far I have argued for two distinct analyses of external argument realization. The first analysis applies to constructions of the type *Absturzursache des Flugzeugs*, as in (3), where I have opted for a pragmatic approach on grounds of the conversational maxims. The second analysis concerns constructions of the type in (2) and (4), which I consider to be based on grammatical principles and to have its reflexes in functional composition, i.e., a lexical-semantic operation. Assuming two separate analyses for external argument realization leaves us unsure about which of the two analyses should be applied to externally realized arguments of non-heads in verb-noun compounds, that is, constructions of the type in (1). On the one hand, an expression like *Fahrgemeinschaft nach Italien* is—at least to my mind—significantly more acceptable than *Absturzursache des Flugzeugs*, which moves the former closer to the domain of grammatical regularity. On the other hand, as is pointed out in Härtl (2012), external argument realizations of the type in (1) cannot easily be argued to be productive—something we would expect from a regular grammatical option—as many prepositional objects are in fact blocked from being "inherited" in the above sense, cf. $^{??}$*Auswanderphantasie nach Neuseeland* ('emigrate_fantasy to New Zealand') or $^{??}$*Steiganleitung auf Kirchdächer* ('climb_instruction on church_roofs').

3.2. The case of verb-noun compounds

Note that a grammatically anchored approach towards external argument realizations in verb-noun compounds (VNC) would imply a violation of the *Principle of lexical integrity* (see, among others, Anderson 1992, Booij 2009, Egg (this volume)), which blocks external access to word-internal elements. The structure in (6) illustrates the problem on a pre-theoretical level:[13]

(6) *Fahrgemeinschaft nach Italien*

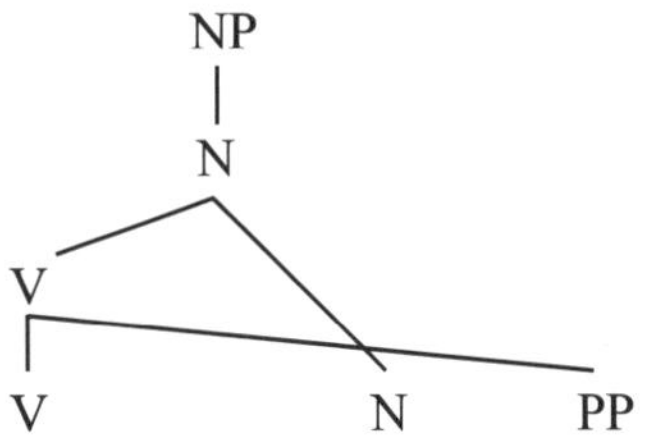

Fahr- *gemeinschaft* *nach Italien*

Let us have a brief look at some lexical-semantic characteristics of VNCs in German. To begin with, the word-formation pattern is fully productive and can involve all possible thematic relations between dependent and head: for instance, an agentive role as in *Tanzbär* (*dancing bear*), a theme role (*Lesebuch* (*reading book*)), or a locative role (*Esszimmer* (*din-*

[13] We have to leave it for future research to ask to what extent an analysis for (6) should be on a par with the one covering the well-known bracketing paradox, as displayed in [[*functional grammar*] *-ian*]; cf., e.g., Booij 2009. Observe that in the latter case, too, a modifier (i.e., *functional*) relates to a non-head element (*grammar*). I wish to thank André Meinunger for the discussion about this point.

ing room)); cf. Donalis (2005). The majority of VNCs are endocentric in German although a couple of exocentric ones also exist, such as, for example, *Schreihals* ('scream_throat', *screaming child*) or Plappermaul (*chatterbox*). In contrast to German, in English the fully productive counterpart is provided by the pattern VERB-ing NOUN, cf. *swimming cap, drawing board*. Another difference between German and English is that English has exocentric "imperative" VNCs (corresponding to the productive pattern in Romance languages), in which the head noun functions as the internal argument of the verbal predicate, as in *pickpocket* or *killjoy*; cf., among others, Gast (2008), Sauer (2004) for details. Lastly, in a number of VNCs, e.g., *Stinkedecke* ('stink_blanket') or *Riechesocken* ('smelling_socks'),[14] the event variable of the verbal predicate can be argued to refer non-generically but specifically, which is reflected in the fact that their interpretation does not involve a kind in the sense that a subset of the head noun's extension is referred to; cf. Härtl (2012).

What evidence could be used to promote a pragmatic approach to the structural configuration displayed in (6)? First of all, as already mentioned above, this type of breakup of a word-internal structure is not generally available since adjuncts are blocked in this configuration, cf. *Fahrgemeinschaft *mit dem Volkswagen/*mit hoher Geschwindigkeit* ('at high speed'). Note that this does not necessarily provide evidence for a grammatical argument inheritance view towards external argument realizations of the type in (6): We may just as well declare conceptual-informational salience of the goal role to be responsible for the licensing of the construction. Note, furthermore, that argumental genitive DPs are considerably less regular in this configuration than prepositional argumental constituents: **Fahrerlaubnis des Motorrads* ('drive_license of the motorbike'), **Lesevergnügen des Bestsellers* ('read_enjoyment of the bestseller'). A possible explanation for this effect could again aim at the heaviness of prepositional phrases: A canonical realization of the goal argument within the compound, i.e., something like *Italienfahrgmeinschaft*, 'Italy_ride_community', removes the prepositional element and appears just as odd for functional-communicative reasons as the respective syntactic paraphrase *Gemeinschaft zur Fahrt nach Italien* ('community for a ride to Italy'). Furthermore, compound-internal realizations of goals and locations, respectively, are generally not fully regular in German (cf. ??*Seespringer* ('lake_jumper'), ??*Deckenbaumeln* ('ceiling_dangling'), ??*Briefkasteneinwerfer* ('mailbox_thrower-inner)), which is another factor promoting a compound-external realization of prepositional arguments.[15]

That the heaviness of argumental PPs correlates with the option to realize them externally explains the contrast between **Aufnahmeverbot in die Mannschaft* ('admission_ban to the team') versus ?*Aufnahmeverbot sowohl in die Nationalmannschaft als auch die Bundesligamannschaft* ('admission_ban to the national_team as well as the Bundesliga_team'),[16] which, in turn, supports a pragmatic analysis of the construction. Additional support for a

14 Note that these forms often involve a linking element *-e-*, in contrast to the generic non-head predicates in clearly lexicalized VNCs of this kind, cf. *Stinktier* ('stink_animal', *skunk*), *Riechfläschchen* ('smell_bottle', *vinaigrette*). In how far the pattern can be regarded as productive must be left to future considerations.

15 I wish to thank Andrew McIntyre for this insight.

16 I wish to thank Andrew McIntyre for these examples.

pragmatic analysis for external argument realization in VNCs comes also from sentential arguments of the verbal non-head. Consider the following examples:

(7) a. das Denkverbot, dass die Erde rund ist
the think_ban that the earth is round
b. das Mitteilbedürfnis, dass man verliebt ist
the tell_need that one is in love
'the need to tell that you are in love'
c. die Ignorier-Anweisung, dass der Wert überschritten wurde
the ignore_command that the value has been exceeded

Evidently, sentential arguments, too, can be considered heavy elements and can thus, as such, be realized compound-externally, as the examples in (7) illustrate. This option is again accounted for by the functional oddity of the grammatically regular correspondent, which, in this case, is provided by a phrasal compound, cf. *Dass-die-Erde-rund-ist-Denkverbot*.[17] We can conclude that the same pragmatically based analysis applied to Pattern I (e.g., *Absturzursache des Flugzeugs*) is also appropriate for external argument realizations in VNCs.

External argument realizations like those in (7) as well as in (1) and (3) demonstrate that the arguments of the non-heads involved have not been discarded in the corresponding word-formation process. That the argument variables are indeed still active can, for example, be deduced also from the fact that the slots can be saturated compound-internally in a canonical way, see the examples in (8):

(8) Schuhputzzeug (shoe_clean_kit, 'shoe cleaning kit')
Apfelschälmaschine (apple_peel_machine, 'apple peeling machine')
Eisensägewerk (iron_saw_mill, 'iron sawmill')
Schneekehrmaschine (snow_sweep_machine, 'snow-sweeping machine')

In these examples, the left-hand nominal element can be surmised to saturate the internal argument of the verbal non-head,[18] which—just like the instances of external argument realizations examined above—challenges the traditional view that only arguments of (syntactic) heads can be saturated; cf. Selkirk (1982). Of course, as an alternative explanation, one may also maintain that in the underlying word-formation process root elements are combined that have abdicated any argument-structural potential; which would be well-suited to the fact that basically any type of modifier is acceptable in non-head positions of compounds.[19] According to the latter view, the left-hand element in the examples in (8) wouldn't represent an argument in the narrow sense of the verbal non-head after all; see

[17] See Meibauer (2007) for a discussion on the expressivity (i.e., the linguistic markedness) of phrasal compounds.

[18] For a more sophisticated discussion on the assignment of thematic roles stemming from non-heads, see, e.g., Boase-Beier and Toman (1986).

[19] For example, agent arguments are, at least marginally, also acceptable in the respective position: *Männerputzkurs* ('men_clean_seminar', *men cleaning seminar*), as well as locative or temporal modifiers of the type *Frühjahrsputzplan* ('spring_clean_schedule', *spring cleaning schedule*). It should be obvious that these patterns are not limited to occur exclusively in verb-noun compounds but can be found with other types of compounds as well, cf. section 2 above.

Fanselow (1991) for such a view. However, the activeness of the argument slots of the verbal non-head can also be inferred from the fact that sentential arguments of VNCs, see (7) above, are licensed through the presence of the predicate in the non-head and, hence, corresponding simplex nouns render semantically deviant readings of the corresponding sentential complementations:

(9) a. #das Verbot, dass die Erde rund ist
'the ban that the earth is round'
b. #das Bedürfnis, dass man verliebt ist
'the need that one is in love'
c. #die Anweisung, dass der Wert überschritten wurde
'the command that the value has been exceeded'

Indications that the verb's argument positions in VNCs are grammatically present also come from syntactic constructions involving control configurations. In a number of VNCs including control verbs, the implicit argument can be argued to control a PRO-element contained in a non-finite clause. Consider the following examples:[20]

(10) a. der *Bitt*brief [PRO Geld zu spenden]
the ask_letter ('petition') [PRO to spend money]
a'. ??der Brief [PRO Geld zu spenden]
b. das *Empfehl*schreiben [PRO das Urteil anzuerkennen]
the recommend_letter ('recommendation letter') [PRO to accept the sentence]
b'. ??das Schreiben [PRO das Urteil anzuerkennen]
c. die *Schwör*rede [PRO sich für die Bürger einzusetzen]
the swear_speech ('swearing-in speech') [PRO to speak for the citizens]
c'. ??die Rede [PRO sich für die Bürger einzusetzen]

In the acceptable examples, see (10)a–c, the PRO-element can be argued to be controlled by an implicit argument of the verbal predicate in the VNCs. This is indicated, first, by the unacceptability of the examples in (10)a'–c', containing simplex nouns, where no verbal argument structure is present and, second, by the varying PRO-reference, which is determined by the corresponding thematic argument: PRO is controlled by the verb's indirect object in (10)a and (10)b, i.e., the one who is asked and the one who receives the recommendation, respectively, whereas in (10)c PRO is controlled by the subject, i.e., the one who swears.

In conclusion, we have good reason to assume that argument positions of the verbal dependent are grammatically still present in VNCs after the word-formation process has taken place. A question that is still open is how we can account for this insight from a grammatical point of view. From a lexicalist morphological perspective—and this is the one I would like to defend here—a syntactic analysis which relies on a formal argument inheritance operation is not plausible (cf., e.g., Lieber (1992, 2004) for a discussion). What I would like to propose instead is a structural projection below the word level: Argument saturation, phenomena like PRO-control and external sentential complements, as well as

[20] The compounds in (10) are all attested but archaic. The reason for this is that the pattern is no longer productive with the control verbs in question and has generally been replaced by the noun-noun pattern, cf., e.g., *Empfehlungsbeschluss* ('recommendation_decision').

adverbial modifications of the verbal non-head as in *Schnellkochtopf* ('fast_cook_pot', *pressure cooker*) suggest the presence of a (non-functional) lexical-structural projection in the VNCs' representation, as is illustrated in (11), see Härtl (2012) for details:

(11)

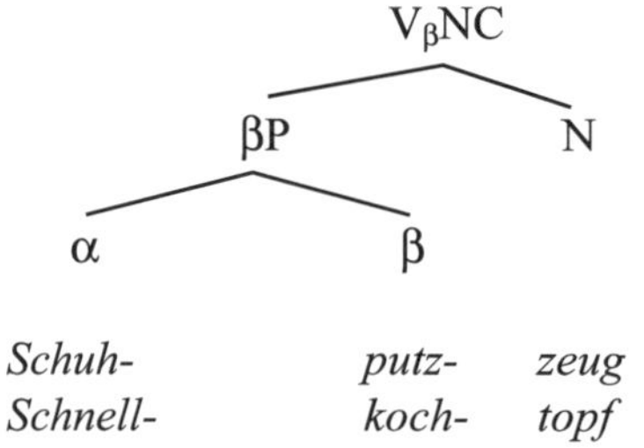

In this (tentative) representation, *β* is used to represent the verbal root, while *α* signifies the satellite of *β*, i.e., a modifier or an argument. It is vital to note that the proposed analysis does not imply the giving up of the boundary between morphology and syntax. Rather, the analysis is compatible with the assumption, from Ackema and Neeleman (2004, 2010), that morphology and syntax—standing in competitive relation to each other—are two separate domains of grammar that, however, share a common generative structure building apparatus. According to this view, canonical, unmarked structure building is rooted in syntax, which explains the unacceptability of expressions like **to truck-drive* as it is blocked by the syntactically produced alternative, i.e., *to drive a truck*. Besides, the notion of competition (possibly in the optimality-theoretic sense) relates suitably to the idea discussed above that pragmatic factors influence the choice of structure building route selected for a complex nominal. In such a framework, a theoretically solid basis can be given to the insight that the functional markedness of a morphological product such as *Dass-die-Erde-rund-ist-Denkverbot* (cf. (7)a) can pave the way for external argument realization as in *Denkverbot, dass die Erde rund ist*.

4. Conclusion

We have investigated arguments of non-heads against the background of the question as to whether thematic relations expressed in compounds are based on a grammatically anchored operation of argument inheritance or not. On closer inspection, (at least) two different interpretations of this question can be identified in the literature. On the one hand, we can ask if argument inheritance in compounds is a mechanism that is rooted in the grammatical system *at all* and, thus, a function of universal grammar. On the other hand, if we accept that argument inheritance exists, we can ask about its location *within* the grammatical system, where some scholars have argued argument inheritance to be a syntactic operation, while others have maintained it to be rooted in a separate, lexical-morphological system. Predominantly, these questions have been investigated with a particular focus on the argument-structural properties of deverbal heads, as in *dog owner* or *owner of a dog*.

The current paper has examined the argument-structural potential of the non-head of a compound and the conditions on external argument realizations (i) with an argumental genitive DP as in *Absturzursache des Flugzeugs* ('crash_cause of the airplane') as well as *Designanalyse des Geschirrs* ('design_analysis of the dinnerware') and (ii) with argumental PPs of the type *Fahrgemeinschaft nach Italien* ('ride_community to Italy'), with a special focus on verb-noun compounds. For argumental genitive DPs as in *Absturzursache des Flugzeugs*, in which the genitive DP stands in a thematic relation only to the non-head, I have argued for a pragmatically-anchored analysis, based on conversational maxims à la Grice. For the second type, i.e., argumental genitive DPs which relate to both the head and the non-head as in *Designanalyse des Geschirrs*, I have proposed a grammatical analysis, which relies on a lexical-semantic operation of functional composition of the head noun predicate (*Analyse*) and the relational noun (*Design*). The argument "inherited" to the resulting expression is saturated by the genitive DP.

Note that the latter analysis does not necessarily imply a softening of the *Principal of lexical integrity*. However, the situation is different with VNCs, because here, just as with the argumental genitive DPs of pattern type I, the PP saturates the argument slot of the non-head alone. Thus, the pragmatic analysis I put forward above is less costly, considering lexical integrity as a grammatical directive; cf. Egg (this volume). Evidence on behalf of a pragmatic approach comes again from the "heaviness" of PPs as well as external argument realizations involving sentential arguments as in *Denkverbot, dass die Erde rund ist* ('think_ban that the earth is round').

The analyzed data indicate that the argument variables in question have not been discarded in the word-formation process involved. In fact, we have good reason to assume that they are active in the lexical representation underlying the expressions. Evidence comes from internal argument saturation as in *Schuhputzzeug* ('shoe_clean_kit') as well as the fact that externally realized sentential arguments are deviant if no verbal non-head is present, cf. #*Verbot, dass die Erde rund ist*. Finally, we have looked at configurations involving PRO, as in *Bittbrief, Geld zu spenden* ('ask_letter to spend money'), and concluded that the binding of PRO can be argued to be dependent on an implicit argument of the verbal non-head.

The above results lead is to the conclusion that there is a lexical-structural projection below the word level, see (11) above. I have argued such an analysis to be compatible with a lexicalist perspective, under the assumption of a model in which, competing with each other, syntax and morphology represent two distinct domains, which, however, rely on a common generative structure building apparatus.

Bibliography

Ackema, P. and A. Neeleman (eds.) (2004): *Beyond morphology: Interface conditions on word formation*. Oxford: Oxford University Press.

Ackema, P. and A. Neeleman (eds.) (2010): The role of syntax and morphology in Compounding. In: S. Scalise and I. Vogel (eds.), *Cross-disciplinary issues in compounding.* Amsterdam/Philadelphia: John Benjamins, 21–36.

Anderson, S. R. (1992): *A-morphous morphology*. Cambridge, MA: Cambridge University Press.

Baeskow, H. (2011): Rules, Patterns and Schemata in Word-Formation. To appear in: P. O. Müller, I. Ohnheiser, S. Olsen and F. Rainer (eds.), *An international handbook of the languages of Europe. HSK Word-Formation*. Berlin/New York: de Gruyter.

Baker, M. (1998): Comments on the paper by Sadock. In: S. G. Lapointe, D. K. Brentari and P. M. Farrell (eds.), *Morphology and its relation to phonology and syntax*. Stanford, CA: CSLI Publications, 188–212.

Bierwisch, M. (1989): Event nominalizations: proposals and problems. In: *Linguistische Studien 194*. Berlin: ZISW, Akademie der Wissenschaften, 1–73.

Bierwisch, M. (2009): Nominalization – lexical and syntactic aspects. In: A. Giannakidou and M. Rathert (eds.), *Quantification, definiteness, and nominalization* (Oxford Studies in Theoretical Linguistics 24). Oxford: Oxford University Press, 281–320.

Boase-Beier, J. and Jindřich T. (1986): On θ-Role assignment in German compounds. *Folia Linguistica* 20: 319–340.

Booij, G. (2009): Lexical integrity as a formal universal. A constructionist view. In: S. Scalise, E. Magni and A. Bisetto (eds.), *Universals of language today*. Berlin: Springer Science and Business Media, 83–100.

Bücking, S. (2010): German nominal compounds as underspecified names for kinds. In: S. Olsen (ed.), *New impulses in word-formation* (=Sonderheft *Linguistische Berichte* 17). Hamburg: Buske, 253–281.

Di Sciullo, A. M. (1992): Deverbal compounds and the external argument. In: I. M. Roca (ed.), *Thematic structure. Its role in grammar*. Dordrecht: Foris, 65–78.

Di Sciullo, A. M. (2005): Decomposing compounds. *Skase Journal of Theoretical Linguistics* 2 (3): 14–33.

Donalies, E. (2005): *Die Wortbildung des Deutschen. Ein Überblick* (2. Auflage). Tübingen: Narr.

Ehrich, V. and I. Rapp (2000): Sortale Bedeutung und Argumentstruktur. *ung*-Nominalisierungen im Deutschen. *Zeitschrift für Sprachwissenschaft* 19 (2): 245–303.

Fabricius-Hansen, C. (1993): Nominalphrasen mit Kompositum als Kern. *Beiträge zur Geschichte der deutschen Sprache und Literatur* 115: 193–243.

Fanselow, G. (1988): Word formation and the human conceptual system. *Linguistische Studien* (= Arbeitsberichte der Akademie der Wissenschaften der DDR) 179: 31–52.

Fanselow, G. (1991): Ein modulares Konzept der Lexikonerweiterung. In: J. Lenerz, S. Siebert and D. Büring (eds.), *Theorie des Lexikons* (=Arbeiten des Sonderforschungsbereichs 282. Nr. 6). Universität Düsseldorf, 1–32.

Fuhrhop, N. (2007): Verbale Komposition: Sind *brustschwimmen* und *radfahren* Komposita? In: R. Métrich and M. Kauffer (eds.), *Verbale Wortbildung im Deutschen*. Tübingen: Stauffenburg, 49–58.

Gamerschlag, T. (2005): *Komposition und Argumentstruktur komplexer Verben: Eine lexikalische Analyse von Verb-Verb-Komposita und Serialverbkonstruktionen* (=Studia grammatica, Band 61). Berlin: Akademie Verlag.

Gast, V. (2008): V-N Compounds in English and German. *Zeitschrift für Anglistik und Amerikanistik* 56 (3): 269–282.

Grice, H. P. (1975): Logic and conversation. In: P. Cole and J. L. Morgan (eds.), *Syntax and semantics: Vol. 3. Speech Acts*. New York: Academic Press, 41–58.

Grimshaw, J. (1990): *Argument structure*. Cambridge, MA: MIT Press.

Harley, H. (2008): Compounding in Distributed Morphology. In: R. Lieber and P. Štekauer (eds.), *The Oxford handbook of compounding.* Oxford: Oxford University Press, 129–144.

Härtl, H. (2011): Argument structural restrictions on word-formation patterns. To appear in: P. Müller, I. Ohnheiser, S. Olsen and F. Rainer (eds.), *HSK word-formation: An international handbook of the languages of Europe*. Berlin/New York: de Gruyter.

Härtl, H. (2012): *Situationsargumente von Nicht-Köpfen: Verb-Nomen-Komposita im Zusammenspiel von Morphologie, Syntax und Pragmatik.* To appear in: Fortmann, C., W. Geuder, A. Lübbe and I. Rapp (eds.), *Situationsargumente im Nominalbereich.* Berlin/New York: de Gruyter.

Höhle, T. (1982): Über Komposition und Derivation: zur Konstituentenstruktur von Wortbildungsprodukten im Deutschen. *Zeitschrift für Sprachwissenschaft* 1: 76–112.

Kotowski, S., K. Böer and H. Härtl (2012): Compounds vs. phrases: The cognitive status of morphological products, accepted for publication in the volume *Morphology and meaning.* (=*Current Issues in Linguistic Theory*). Amsterdam: John Benjamins.

Krifka, M. et al. (1995): Genericity. An introduction. In: G. N. Carlson and F. J. Pelletier (eds.), *The generic book.* Chicago/London: University of Chicago Press, 1–124.

Lieber, R. (1983): Argument linking and compounds in English. *Linguistic Inquiry* 14 (2): 251–285.

Lieber, R. (1992): *Deconstructing morphology. Word formation in syntactic theory.* Chicago: University of Chicago Press.

Lieber, R. (2004): *Morphology and lexical semantics.* Cambridge, NY: Cambridge University Press.

McIntyre, A. (2012): Constraining argument structure in nominalizations: The case of English *-er*. Submitted to a special volume of *Lingua.*

Meibauer, J. (2007): How marginal are phrasal compounds? Generalized insertion, expressivity, and I/Q-interaction. *Morphology* 17: 233–259.

Olsen, S. (1991): Zur Grammatik des Wortes: Argumente zur Argumentvererbung. In: J. Lenerz, S. Siebert and D. Büring (eds.), *Theorie des Lexikons.* (=Arbeiten des Sonderforschungsbereichs 282. Nr. 6). Universität Düsseldorf, 33–56.

Olsen, S. (1992): Zur Grammatik des Wortes: Argumente zur Argumentvererbung. *Linguistische Berichte* 137: 3–32.

Sauer, H. (2004): Lexicalization and demotivation. In: G. Booij, C. Lehmann, J. Mugdan and S. Skopeteas (eds.), *Morphology / Morphologie: Ein Internationales Handbuch zur Flexion und Wortbildung / An international handbook on inflection and word-formation*, Vol. 2 / 2. Halbband. Berlin/New York: de Gruyter, 1625–1636.

Selkirk, E. O. (1982): *The syntax of words.* Cambridge, MA: MIT Press.

Solstad, T. (2010): Postnominal genitives and prepositional phrases in German. A Uniform Analysis. In: A. Alexiadou and M. Rathert (eds.), *The syntax of nominalizations across languages and frameworks.* Berlin: de Gruyter, 219–252.

Toman, J. (1987): *Wortsyntax* (2. erw. Aufl.). (=*Linguistische Arbeiten* 137), Tübingen: Niemeyer.

Williams, E. S. (1981): On the notions 'lexically related' and 'head of a word'. *Linguistic Inquiry* 12: 245–274.

Wunderlich, D. (1986): Probleme der Wortstruktur. *Zeitschrift für Sprachwissenschaft* 5: 209–252.

Aspekte des Absentivs: *Wir sind Sue gratulieren* – Zum Problem der Lokalisierung im Absentiv*

Angelika Wöllstein

1. Einleitung

In einer Reihe von Arbeiten ist vorgeschlagen worden, Formen wie *Wir sind Sue gratulieren* (also momentan abwesend) als Instantiierung einer universellen grammatischen Kategorie anzusehen, die, anknüpfend an deren Interpretation, als *Absentiv* bezeichnet wird. De Groot (1995, 2000), Ebert (1996, 2000), Krause (2002), Vogel (2007) u.a. gehen davon aus, dass der Absentiv als grammatischer Ausdruck von Abwesenheit in nicht weniger als 26 europäischen Sprachen (in Voll- oder Teilkategorie) nachgewiesen werden kann.

Unter dem Gesichtspunkt der Schnittstellenproblematik ist die Betrachtung des sog. Absentivs lohnend, weil Wechselbeziehungen unterschiedlicher grammatischer und nichtsprachlicher Aspekte in der Literatur thematisiert wurden und sich die dargelegten Argumente für dessen Etablierung als grammatische Kategorie im Speziellen problematisieren lassen. Vor diesem Hintergrund stellt sich dann auch die Frage, warum Absenz ein sprachliches Primitivum sein sollte, das als sprachübergreifende Kategorie zur Verfügung steht.

2. Worum geht's

Der sog. Absentiv in (1) wird als eigenständige grammatische Kategorie zum Ausdruck der Abwesenheit des Subjektreferenten aufgefasst – ausgehend von de Groot (2000). Als Rechtfertigung dafür wird vorgebracht, dass der Form „NP$_{NOM}$ + *sein* + Infinitiv" (im Deutschen) jeglicher lexikalischer Index für Absenz fehlt – entgegen einem Muster wie *meine Frau ist weg einkaufen*.

* Der Beitrag stellt einen Teil der gemeinsamen Forschung und Diskussion dar, die in Kooperation mit Christian Fortmann und Irene Rapp innerhalb des SFB 833 im Projekt „Bedeutungskonstitution bei infiniten Verbalformen" angesiedelt ist. Für die inhaltliche Diskussionen, Anregungen und Hinweise und sonstige Unterstützung danke ich Eric Fuß, Monica Fürbacher, Freya Opfermann, Anna Volodina, Bernd Wiese und Gisela Zifonun.

(1) a. Ich zaubere an der Pfanne – meine Frau ist einkaufen – wie ein Künstler in seinen seligen Momenten.
(HAZ08/JUN.05782 Hannoversche Allgemeine, 30.06.2008, S. 11)
b. Immer war das Wetter ja nicht schlecht, und wenn es möglich ist, bin ich mit Freunden baden. Und auch wenn das Wetter einmal nicht passt, vertreibe ich mir die Zeit mit meinen Freunden im Jugendzentrum.
(NON09/JUL.07039 NÖN, 14.07.2009, S. 3)
c. Eine Mattersburgerin war vergangene Woche in Mattersburg beim Eurospar einkaufen. Als sie die Einkaufswaren in ihr Auto räumte, hörte sie plötzlich lautes Babygeschrei aus dem daneben geparkten Auto. Das Baby war bei eisigen Temperaturen alleine in dem Auto zurückgelassen worden. Die Mutter aus dem Bezirk Neunkirchen war in der Zwischenzeit einkaufen.
(NON09/JAN.10270 Niederösterreichische Nachrichten, 26.01.2009, S. 4)

Dass es sich beim sog. Absentiv um ein Phänomen handelt, das sich selbst einer Exploration an den Schnittstellen Morphologie/Syntax und Syntax/Semantik verschließt, wird u.a. bei Abraham (2008) dadurch begründet, dass die Konstruktion eine „poor syntax“ aufweist. Charakteristisch bei allen Analysen zum sog. Absentiv ist daher, dass eine kompositionale Erklärung der Absenz und ihrer interpretatorischen Eigenschaften – wenigstens implizit – zurückgewiesen wird (ausgenommen Haslinger (2007) und Fortmann und Wöllstein (2012)). In der Folge sind die Analysen entweder morphologischen oder konstruktionellen Ansätzen verpflichtet und bedürfen eines (je nach theoretischer Perspektive unterschiedlichen) Lexikoneintrags.

Wegen des Fehlens einer Abgrenzung zwischen *Bedeutung* einerseits und *Interpretation* andererseits, die bei allen Analysen zum sog. Absentiv zu beobachten ist, ist aber keineswegs entschieden, was an grammatischen Mitteln (syntaktisch und/oder morphologisch) vorliegt bzw. aus ihnen semantisch abgeleitet werden kann und muss und was schließlich pragmatisch implikatiert ist und auf welcher Basis dies dann eigentlich geschehen muss. Die vorliegenden Analysen der Konstruktionen vom Typus „NP_{NOM} + *sein* + Infinitiv“ weisen in die folgend skizzierten Richtungen:

In ihrem morphologisch-konstruktionellen Ansatz argumentieren Ebert (1996) und De Groot (2000, 2001) für eine periphrastische grammatische Kategorie bestehend aus der Kopula *sein* + Infinitiv. Vogel (2007, 2009) vertritt einen lexikalischen Ansatz, in welchem sie eine konzeptionelle Verknüpfung von (*weg*)*gehen* und *sein* annimmt und [*sein* + Infinitiv] aus diachron [*gehen* + Infinitiv] ableitet.

Abraham (2008) argumentiert für eine elliptische Konstruktion. Dabei wird die Absentivbedeutung aus der Tilgung eines Bewegungsverbs im Partizipperfekt innerhalb der Struktur *sein* + (*gegangen*) + Infinitiv rekonstruiert. Abraham (2008) diskutiert wie auch Ebert (1996), Vogel (2007), Wöllstein (2005, 2009) und Rapp und Wöllstein (2007) Parallelen zwischen dem sog. Absentiv und der Form *sein* + *am* + Infinitiv. Schwerpunkte bilden dabei diachrone, aspektuelle und verbsemantische Überlegungen sowie auch die Etablierung einer weiteren Kategorie *Adsentiv* (=Anwesenheit) neben dem Absentiv (Abraham 2008: 369).

König (2009) verfolgt einen lexikalistisch-paradigmatischen Ansatz; dabei bildet Absentiv-*sein* ein Paradigma mit *sein* im Zentrum der Reihe *kommen* (*kommt essen*) – *sein* (*ist essen*) – *gehen* (*geht essen*). Wöllstein (2005, 2009) und Rapp und Wöllstein (2007) argumentieren für einen (teilweise) kompositionalen, paradigmatischen Ansatz, wobei die Kennzeichnung von An- vs. Abwesenheit des Subjektreferenten an einem sog. *Topikort* verknüpft wird mit dem Auftreten und Fehlen von *am* (Topikort wird hier i.S. der lokalen Rahmensetzung in Topik-Kommentar-Strukturen bei Jacobs 2001: 655 aufgefasst):

(2) a. sein + Ø + Infinitiv[1]
    b. sein + am + Infinitiv

Die fusionierte Form *am* erfüllt die Sättigung der Ortsrolle intrinsisch[2] und sorgt für den Zusammenfall von Topikort und Ereignisort – das Fehlen von *am* (im sog. Absentiv) bewirkt die Trennung der Lokalisierungen und verortet den Subjektreferenten am Ereignisort. Ungeklärt bleibt das Faktum, dass der sog. Absentiv eine Beschränkung auf intentionale Verben und intentionale Subjekte aufweist – entgegen der *am*-Form.

(3) a. *Alex ist einschlafen. / Alex ist am einschlafen.
    b. *Der Wein ist gären. / Der Wein ist am gären.

Aber nicht nur unter dem Aspekt der Bezugnahme auf den *am*-Progressiv ist das Faktum in (3) problematisch; es wird in keiner der Analysen zum sog. Absentiv bislang abgeleitet, sondern bleibt dessen idiosynkratische Eigenschaft.

Haslingers (2007) bindungstheoretischer syntaktischer Ansatz diagnostiziert als einziger eine komplexe Struktur mit Absentiv-*sein* als einem Verb, das eine Kontrollstruktur selegiert; dabei wird dem PRO-Subjekt im Komplement ein vom Kontrollsubjekt zu unterscheidender lokaler Index zugewiesen. Aus der unterschiedlichen Indizierung und damit auch der unterschiedlichen Verortung des Kontrollsubjekts einerseits und des PRO-Subjekts andererseits soll die Absenzbedeutung hervorgehen; vgl. Haslinger (2007: 34f.).

Fazit ist, dass die spezifische Bedeutung der Absenz in allen Ansätzen Eigenart der Konstruktion(sbestandteile) bleibt bzw. dieser/diesen zugeschrieben wird; Abgrenzungen zwischen Form, Funktion, Bedeutung, Interpretation und ggf. Gebrauch fehlen. Eine ernsthafte Prüfung, ob sich denn die resp. Phänomene kompositional klären ließen, wird gar nicht unternommen, sondern der Status einer *grammatischen Kategorie* wird vor dem Hintergrund des Mangels eben solchen Bemühens geschlossen und mehr oder minder explizit die Möglichkeit einer kompositionalen Erklärung unter Rückführung auf allgemeine Prinzipien als unangemessen mit dem Ansinnen einer Widerlegung beurteilt. Damit bleibt die Struktur und die beteiligten grammatischen Mittel des sog. Absentivs bislang rätselhaft und sein Status als grammatische Kategorie fragwürdig.

Nichtsdestotrotz scheint entschieden, dass es sich beim sog. Absentiv um eine sprachliche Kategorie handelt, die im Zuge dessen auch grammatikographisch erfasst ist: Bezugnehmend auf Krause (2002) finden sich sowohl im DUDEN (2009: §594) Hinweise auf den

---

1 Die lokale Präposition *an* verfügt über semantische und kategoriale Selektionseigenschaften (=S- und C-Selektion). Angenommen wird a) ein Wandel der C-Selektion bei *am; am* C-selegiert neben N/NP nun auch V, parallel zum Statusmarker *zu* und b) erfolgt eine Abstraktion über die S-Selektion: DAT (als semantische Rolle „Ort“) wird inkorporiert und *am* S-selegiert den Topik-Ort.

2 Der implizite Topik-Ort erfüllt die Funktion, die in Prädikativkonstruktionen *ohne* Infinitive und in nicht-Prädikativkonstruktionen <u>ausschließlich</u> rahmensetzende (lokale) Modifikatoren (d.h. spezifizierte Topiks) leisten; vgl. Maienborn (2001).

absentive mit Bildung eines Verbalkomplexes von *sein* + Infinitiv (bei Tätigkeitsverben) als auch im Handbuch *Deutsche Morphologie* (Hentschel und Vogel 2009). Hier wird *Absentiv* durch Vogel (2009) als ein morphologischer Terminus etabliert.

Neben der vermeintlichen Bedeutung des sog. Absentivs als „Absenzkennzeichnung des Subjektreferenten“ von einem sog. deiktischen Zentrum (bei de Groot 2000) oder Ausgangsort (bei Vogel 2009) werden eine Reihe (interpretatorischer) Eigenschaften als konstitutiv erachtet:

(a) Der Subjektreferent ist (lokal) nicht präsent;
(b) Der Subjektreferent ist in eine durch den Infinitiv bezeichnete Aktivität verwickelt;
(c) Auf der Basis pragmatischen Wissens sind Dauer oder Annahme über die Dauer der Abwesenheit prognostizierbar;
(d) Der Subjektreferent wird zurückkehren.

Um im Gegenzug das Postulat einer grammatischen Kategorie zu rechtfertigen, sollten sich erstens Konstruktionen des Typs (a) einer kompositionalen Analyse gänzlich entziehen – dem wird in diesem Beitrag ausdrücklich widersprochen – und zweitens sollten die genannten spezifischen Eigenschaften in (a) – (d), *Rückkehrpostulat*, *Abwesenheitsdauer-Prognose*, *Verwickelung in die Aktivität* und *lokale Nicht-Präsenz*, nur bei Konstruktionen wie (1) zu finden sein. In Fortmann und Wöllstein (2012) wird gezeigt, dass diese Eigenschaften keineswegs konstitutiv sind; die Beispiele in (4) illustrieren das:

(4) a. Die Leute hier draußen auf der Straße sind alle frische Luft schnappen.
(Subjektreferent kann (lokal) präsent sein)
b. David ist seine Haare schneiden.
(keine Verwickeltheit des Subjekts in die Infinitivaktivität)
c. Theo ist Holz hacken, aber ich weiß nicht wie lange.
(Abwesenheitsdauer nicht prognostizierbar)
d. Theo ist Hornhechte angeln und wird leider nie wieder zurückkehren.
(keine Notwendigkeit der Rückkehr)

Ausgehend von Fortmann und Wöllstein (2012) behandelt dieser Beitrag zum Einen die zentrale Problematik des angeblichen Fehlens jeglichen lexikalischen Indexes für eine Lokalisierung und legt zum Anderen Evidenz für eine „reichere Syntax“ vor; der sog. Absentiv wird folglich weder als eine elliptische Form (entgegen Abraham 2008) aufgefasst, noch hat er die Konstruktionsbedeutung *Absenz*. Dies geschieht mit Blick darauf, dass nach den Untersuchungen in Fortmann und Wöllstein (2012) a) der einschlägige Index ein Lokationsausdruck sein muss und b) mit einem Gesamtensemble zu rechnen ist, bei dem die enthaltenen (lexikalischen) Einheiten nicht bedeutungslos bleiben und insbesondere der Infinitiv als ein adjungiertes Final-Adverbial fungiert.

Diskutiert wird im Folgenden die vermeintlich fehlende Lokalisierung im sog. Absentiv, die Morphologie und Semantik des Infinitivs im 1. Status unter diachronen (Curme 1922, Haspelmath 1989) und synchronen Gesichtspunkten (Rapp und Wöllstein 2009, 2012) sowie die wechselseitigen lexikalischen bzw. semantischen Beschränkungen beim Verb und der Subjekt-NP. Das erfolgt in drei Schritten:

In Abschnitt 2 wird gezeigt, dass die Lokalisierung in der einschlägigen Konstruktion grammatisch kodiert ist, nämlich entweder durch passende Ausdrücke oder Leer-Elemente.

Abschnitt 3 diskutiert die syntaktische Komplexität; ausgehend von den Fakten, dass Kopula-*sein* weder Verben subkategorisiert (Rapp 1996, Maienborn 2003) noch Auxiliar-*sein* den reinen Infinitiv statusregiert (Bech 1955/57), liegt die Überlegung nahe, dass der Infinitiv nicht als Komplement fungiert. Die Indizien (prädikatives Komplement mit lokaler Ausprägung und der reine Infinitiv als Adjunkt) deuten dann auf Zweigliedrigkeit der Struktur hin. In Abschnitt 4 wird für die Grammatik des sog. Absentivs vorgeschlagen, dass das infinite Adjunkt eine finale Semantik aufweist, die *grammatisch* ausgedrückt wird und nicht wie bei *um-zu* lexikalischen Ausdruck hat.

3. Lexikalischer Index für eine Lokalisierung

Konstruktionen mit overtem Lokationsausdruck überhaupt als *Absentive* in Betracht zu ziehen wird insbesondere von de Groot (2000) zurückgewiesen; dies geschieht ohne eine nähere triftige Begründung und sorgt mehr oder weniger hintergründig dafür, dass eine womöglich parallele kompositionale Analyse von vornherein ausgeschlossen wird, obwohl man doch prinzipiell jede explizite Konstruktion in eine implizite umwandeln kann und vice versa. Im Fall von (5) führt das nur zu einer spezifischen Aussage bzgl. der Lokation; in keiner Weise ist die Grammatikalität beeinträchtigt:

(5) a. Theo ist in Mannheim arbeiten.
b. Theo ist arbeiten.

Drei Thesen werden für die Annahme eines Element vom semantischen Typ eines Lokationsausdrucks diskutiert: 1. Eine *wo*-Frage lizenziert nicht den *Absentiv* als passende Antwort. Seit de Groot (2000) wird gerade das Gegenteil vertreten und behauptet, dass der sog. Absentiv ein Lokationsausdruck ist und auch das alleinige (durch diesen Test verifizierte) *explicans* zur Begründung der universellen Kategorie – der fehlende Lokalisierungsindex fungiert dann nur mehr ex negativo: und wenn kein lexikalischer Ausdruck für die Lokalisierung vorzufinden ist, muss es in der Konstruktion liegen. Ergo ist die Konstruktion selbst Ausdruck von Lokalisierung. 2. Im sog. Absentiv sind Lokalisierungsausdrücke overt realisiert und 3. zeigen Daten zum Intonationsmuster des sog. Absentivs, dass die Struktur zweigliedrig ist und über einen – wenn nicht overten dann doch coverten – Lokalisierungsausdruck verfügt.

Kommen wir zu Punkt 1: Als *explicans* zur Begründung einer (universellen) Kategorie *Absentiv* gilt neben dem fehlenden Lokalisierungsindex, dass dieser die Antwort auf einen Fragekontext nach der Lokalisierung des Subjektreferenten gibt:

(6) A: Wo ist Theo?
B: Theo ist arbeiten!

Damit herrscht die implizite Annahme vor, dass die *wo*-Frage (6)A die grammatische Kategorie *Absentiv* quasi lizensiert. Betrachtet man allerdings die suggestive Kraft von Frage-Antwort-Paaren wie (6), so fungieren diese bestenfalls als *explicandum* eines (grammatischen) Sachverhalts – so in Fortmann und Wöllstein (2012) –, denn neben (6)B ist weder eine Antwort wie (7)B unangemessen, noch liefert (8)A eine unpassende Frage für die Antworten (6)B und (7)B – wiederholt als (8)B.

(7) A: Wo ist Theo?
B: Theo arbeitet.

(8) A: Was macht Theo eigentlich?[3]
B: Theo ist arbeiten/arbeitet!

Betrachtet man Korpusbelege, so finden sich ohne weiteres Beispiele mit einem lexikalischen Index zur Lokalisierung des Subjektreferenten. Absenz findet hier auch keinen lexikalischen Ausdruck bspw. durch *weg*, wäre jedoch pragmatisch aus (9) wie auch aus (1) zu folgern:

(9) a. Wenn er mal nicht aus dem Flugzeug springt oder operiert, geht Thiele gern auf die Jagd oder betreibt „Freizeitsport, wie Fitness, Schwimmen oder Rad fahren". Die Höhe scheint Thiele jedenfalls zu mögen: Erst vor Kurzem war er in den Alpen wandern.
RHP09/SEP.01405 Rheinpfalz, 11.09.2009, S. 16
b. Eisenstadt hat Glück mit dem Schlosspark, ein tolles Erholungsgebiet. Doch Hundebesitzer verleiden manchem Spaziergänger den Spaß. Verärgert erzählt ein Eisenstädter: „Samstag waren wir *im Schlosspark* spazieren. Schon von weitem sahen wir zwei Riesendoggen frei laufen."
BVZ09/DEZ.00807 NÖN, 02.12.2009, S. 6
c. Piet hat einen Fotoapparat, aber er arbeitet. Tja Piet! Hast Du das Foto weggegeben? Ich möchte sehen, wie ich Dich umarmt habe auf dem Foto. Ich erinnere mich gerade an alles, als ob es gestern gewesen wäre. Hör zu, liebst Du noch oder denkst Du daran, zu vergessen? Ich habe Angst davor. Oj, oj, was für ein Lärm! Unsere Mädchen waren *im Wald* spazieren. Zwei Mädchen, das habe ich Dir schon geschrieben, sind zurückgefahren in die KDF.
BRZ09/NOV.08397 Braunschw. Z., 18.11.2009
d. Neulich war ich *in der Stadt* essen. Die Menschen um mich herum waren gut gelaunt und plauderten – alle, bis auf ein älteres Paar am Nebentisch. Die beiden saßen nebeneinander statt sich gegenüber und starrten trübsinnig aus dem Fenster. Wie zwei Wachsfiguren sahen die beiden aus.
RHZ09/DEZ.20797 RZ, 23.12.2009
e. Winterschwatz Glitzersterne und Zukunftspläne Die Feiertage sind vorbei, die Weihnachtspflichten erfüllt. Gefeiert habe ich mit meiner Familie. Jetzt verbrauche ich mein Weihnachtsgeld. Gerade war ich *in Zürich* einkaufen.
A08/JAN.00408 St. Galler Tagblatt, 04.01.2008, S. 38; Winterschwatz

Was sich zunächst beim sog. Absentiv (vom Typ (1)) darstellt als die Prädikation einer durch die VP bezeichneten Handlung eines Subjekts – was den Gedanken nahe legt, es

[3] In diesem Zusammenhang sei vielleicht die folgende Spitze erlaubt: Wenn ein möglicher Fragekontext den Maßstab für die (semantische) Charakterisierung der Konstruktion abgibt, könnte man aus dem Umstand, dass die Konstruktion auch als Antwort auf eine Frage nach der Tätigkeit jederzeit tauglich ist, den Schluss ziehen, die Konstruktion *aktitiv* zu taufen.

handele sich hierbei um eine spezifische Form der *verbalen* Prädikation bzw. eine Prädikation, bei der der Infinitiv das Hauptprädikat sein soll –, legen die Daten in (9) nur in der Analyse nahe, in der die Lokalausdrücke adverbiale Funktion tragen. Damit einher geht die Annahme, bei *sein* handele es sich um ein (regulär) tempusbildendes Auxiliar; nur dies ist mit traditionellen Annahmen der Subkategorisierung von Verben verträglich. Auxiliar-*sein* (status)regiert allerdings den 3. Status (10)a (vgl. Bech 1955/57) oder in modalen Kontexten den 2. Status (10)b (vgl. Rapp und Wöllstein 2009) – nicht jedoch den 1. Status.

(10) a. Theo ist angekommen.
b. Theo ist zu verhaften. / Maria hat Theo zu verhaften.

Kopula-*sein* subkategorisiert als prädikatives Komplement eine NP, AP oder eine PP – nicht jedoch eine VP.

(11) Alex ist Schiffbauer/unfähig/in Lemwerder/*ankommen.

Die Kategorisierung als Kopula-*sein* erhält jedoch ihre Rechtfertigung dadurch, dass statt *sein* (zumindest im Prinzip) auch die Wahl von *bleiben* möglich ist.

(12) a. David bleibt [$_{VP}$ noch ein bisschen Holz hacken].
b. David ist [$_{VP}$ noch ein bisschen Holz hacken] geblieben.

Darüber hinaus zeigt sich, dass für das sog. Absentivmuster charakteristisch ist, dass die explizite Prädikation – bei der Existenz einer VP – auf Lokative beschränkt ist (13)c.

(13) a. *Alex ist/war Schiffbauer [$_{VP}$ arbeiten].
b. *Alex ist/war unfähig [$_{VP}$ arbeiten].
c. Alex ist/war in Lemwerder [$_{VP}$ arbeiten].

Verknüpft man die Annahmen aus (10) – (12) miteinander und nimmt die Subkategorisierungsbedingung für Kopula-*sein* ernst (heißt: kein VP-Komplement in Prädikativkonstruktionen), dann hat dies klare Folgen im Hinblick auf die kategoriale Klassifizierung und die Subkategorisierung – *sein* muss im sog. Absentiv als Kopula-*sein* angesehen werden und man muss von einem nichtverbalen prädikativen Komplement ausgehen.

Kommen wir zur angeblich fehlenden Lokalisierung: Die Annahme einer *verbalen* Prädikation als syntaktische Basis dieser Konstruktion ist – wie (9) belegt – mit dem Faktum konfrontiert, dass eine Konstruktion wie in (1) stets und ohne Beschränkung die Einfügung eines lexikalischen Indexes für die Lokalisierung erlaubt (14) und darüber hinaus auf eben diese beschränkt ist (vgl. (13)c) und dort als lokales Adverbial zum Infinitiv oder als lokales Komplement der Kopula fungiert.

(14) a. David ist im Hof Holz hacken.
b. Alex ist im Dorf einkaufen.
c. Helena ist am Strand schwimmen.

So eingefügte Lokationsbestimmungen lassen zwei syntaktische Verortungen zu, die in (15) durch die Klammerung indiziert sind.

(15) a. David ist [$_{VP}$ im Hof Holz hacken].
b. David ist im Hof [$_{VP}$ Holz hacken].

In der (15)a gemäßen Strukturierung bildet die lokative PP eine Konstituente der VP. Sie kann damit als Komponente der verbalen Prädikation über das Subjekt aufgefasst werden. Nach der zweiten Strukturierung (15)b ergibt sich eine *Lokations-Prädikation* über das Subjekt, zu der die VP als ein weiteres Prädikat hinzutritt. Typischerweise ist eine Äußerung von (14)a mit zwei Intonationsmustern verträglich – so argumentieren Fortmann und Wöllstein (2012) weiter:

(16) a. David ist im /Hof Holz hacken.
     b. David ist im /Hof /Holz hacken.

Beide Varianten scheinen mit einem feinen Interpretationsunterschied zu korrespondieren. Mit (16)b ist (definitiv) ausgesagt, dass *David* sich *im Hof* befindet, wogegen (16)a eher die Aussage intendiert, der zufolge sich *David* an einem nicht weiter bestimmten Ort befindet und dort *im Hof Holz hackt*. Dieser Interpretationsunterschied ließe sich strukturell dahingehend deuten, dass der Lesart (16)b die Struktur (15)b und der Lesart (16)a die Struktur (15)a zugrunde liegt.

(16)b stellt demnach eine Intonationsweise dar, bei der eine explizite Lokations-Prädikation über das Subjekt gemacht wird, was strukturell aus (15)b dann auch hervorgeht. Wenn die Charakterisierung der Interpretation von (14)a zutrifft, dann gibt die Struktur (15)a jedoch nicht alle Aspekte dieser Interpretation wieder. Die Implikation einer nicht weiter bestimmten Lokation, die den Ort der Handlung – *der Hof*, in welchem das *Holz hacken* vor sich geht –, findet syntaktisch keinen Ausdruck. Der Aspekt einer doppelten Lokalisierung kann aber ohne weiteres wie in (17) expliziert und strukturell gefasst werden.

(17) Alex war in Lemwerder [$_{\text{VP}}$ auf der Werft arbeiten].

In beiden Fällen (13)c und (17) wird über das Subjekt eine Lokation prädiziert, deren Gehalt weiter in die Lokation des Infinitiv-Ereignisses eingeht.

Wenn also in (15)a in der Intonationsvariante (16)a eine implizite Prädikation einer unbestimmten Lokation inbegriffen ist, deren Bedingungen der einer expliziten wie in (16)b oder (17) gleichen, ließe sich dies durch eine Erweiterung der Struktur in (15)a um eine entsprechende Leer-Kategorie ausdrücken (18)a. Die strukturellen Parallelen liegen damit auf der Hand:

(18) a. David ist e_{LOC} [$_{\text{VP}}$ im Hof Holz hacken].
     b. David ist im Hof [$_{\text{VP}}$ Holz hacken].

Mit einer Strukturierung wie in (18) ist natürlich der Annahme einer *unmittelbaren* Prädikation der den Infinitiv einschließenden VP über das Subjekt der Boden entzogen (Fortmann und Wöllstein 2012). Die *Absentiv*-Konstruktion stellt somit eine explizite oder implizite Lokations-Prädikation dar, in der die VP nunmehr als ein Adjunkt fungiert. Wie kann nun die Rechtfertigung einer Strukturstelle mit lokaler Ausprägung aussehen?

Wir beobachten, dass ausschließlich Lokationen als prädikative Komplemente in den Strukturen möglich sind (19)a vs. (19)b, c: Dass das implizite prädikative Komplement eben diese lokale Ausprägung hat, scheint für die Strukturen (18)a mit e_{LOC} dann zwingend:

(19) a. David ist im Hof [$_{VP}$ Holz hacken].
b. *David ist Förster [$_{VP}$ Holz hacken].
c. *David ist stark genug [$_{VP}$ Holz hacken].

Interessanterweise können mit *um-zu-* und (z.T. auch mit) *zu*-Konstruktionen die prädikativen Komplemente NP und AP auftreten (20)b, c; beide können jedoch die leere Lokation bzw. ein leeres prädikatives Komplement nicht lizensieren, bzw. nicht mit einem solchen auftreten (21)b, c:

(20) a. David ist im Hof [$_{VP}$ um Holz zu hacken] / [$_{VP}$ Holz zu hacken].
b. David ist Förster [$_{VP}$ um Holz zu hacken] / *[$_{VP}$ Holz zu hacken].
c. David ist stark genug [$_{VP}$ um Holz zu hacken] / [$_{VP}$ Holz zu hacken].[4]

(21) a. David ist e_{LOC} [$_{VP}$ Holz hacken].
b. *David ist e_{LOC} [$_{VP}$ um Holz zu hacken].
c. *David ist e_{LOC} [$_{VP}$ Holz zu hacken].

Als Zwischenfazit kann festgestellt werden, dass es sich beim sog. Absentiv nicht um eine verbale Prädikation über das Subjekt handeln kann, als vielmehr um eine Lokalisierungsprädikation über das Subjekt, zu der eine VP als weitere Prädikation hinzutritt. Hinzu kommt die Beobachtung, dass ausschließlich das Auftreten von *sein* zusammen mit einem Element vom semantischen Typ eines Lokationsausdrucks grammatisch ist; entgegen dem synchron isolierten Status der Form „NP_{NOM} + *sein* + Infinitiv“ und entgegen den Auffassungen in der Literatur dazu können weitere grammatische Mittel identifiziert werden. Betrachten wir dazu den Status und die Semantik des reinen Infinitivs.

4. Status und Semantik des reinen Infinitivs: Finalitätshypothese

In diesem Abschnitt wird es darum gehen, den Status des reinen Infinitivs als Adjunkt mit semantisch finaler Ausprägung zu begründen und Parallelen resp. Disparallelen von *um-zu-*, *zu-* und einfachem, reinen Infinitiv herauszustreichen. Dabei bildet die Finalitätshypothese (FH) von Fortmann und Wöllstein (2012) hier den Ausgangspunkt weiterer Überlegungen zum Status des reinen Infinitivs:

(22) Finalitätshypothese (FH): Prädikativkonstruktionen des Typs (19)a und (21)a bilden eine Prädikativkonstruktion lokaler Ausprägung und semantisch finalem Adjunkt.

Lexikalisch ausgedrückt wird Finalität bei Infinitiven im Deutschen synchron durch *um-zu*; ohne *um* kann auch *zu* allein Finalität grammatisch markieren (23) – belegt im Korpus durch (23)'.

---

4 Die Beschränkung auf Individuenprädikate bei den prädikativen Adjektiven bei finaler Modifikation ist bislang ungeklärt. Stadienprädikate sind nicht möglich: David ist *stark* [$_{VP}$ *um* Holz *zu* hacken]/[$_{VP}$ Holz *zu* hacken].

(23) a. [$_{CP}$ Präd-Subj + sein + XP_{LOC} [$_{XP}$ um + zu + Infinitiv]]
b. [$_{CP}$ David ist auf dem Hof [$_{XP}$ um Holz zu hacken]]

(23)' a. Die anderen Parteien hätten also noch Zeit, ebenfalls jemanden ins Rennen zu schicken.
A97/SEP.21872 St. Galler Tagblatt, 03.09.1997, Ressort: TB-OT
b. Der «Künstler» reist schon seit Jahren rund um die Welt. 35 Jahre ist er mit einer Gitarre von Stadt zu Stadt gezogen und hat Lieder von Berühmtheiten aus der Popszene interpretiert. Doch nun fühlt er sich zu alt, jeden Tag bis zu acht Stunden zu singen und spielen.
A98/NOV.71127 St. Galler Tagblatt, 07.11.1998, Ressort: AT-HER (Abk.); Künstler oder Bettler?

Die Prädikativkonstruktionen des Typs (23) sind mit (24) und (25) formal verwandt, drücken jedoch Finalität *grammatisch* aus.

(24) a. [$_{CP}$ Präd-Subj + sein + XP_{LOC} [$_{XP}$ zu + Infinitiv]]
b. [$_{CP}$ David ist auf dem Hof [$_{XP}$ Holz zu hacken]]

(25) a. [$_{CP}$ Präd-Subj + sein + XP_{LOC}/e_{LOC} [$_{VP}$ Infinitiv]]
b. [$_{CP}$ David ist (auf dem Hof) [$_{VP}$ Holz hacken]]

Frei verwendbar, d.h. ohne jegliche Beschränkungen betreffend das prädikative Subjekt, den Infinitiv und das prädikative Komplement, ist die *um-zu*-Konstruktion; *zu* und auch der reine Infinitiv benötigen eine Lokation – *zu* sogar die overte, vgl. erneut (19) – (21). Wie (25) illustriert, kann das prädikative Komplement XP_{LOC} overt wie auch covert e_{LOC} realisiert sein. FH hat bei Fortmann und Wöllstein (2012) zwei klare (strukturelle) Implikationen (26):

(26) a. Die Konstruktion weist immer eine (coverte/overte) Lokalisationsprädikation auf.
b. Syntaktisch ist die Verbalprojektion ein finales, infinites Adjunkt.

Finale Adjunkte lexikalischer Ausprägung (mit *um zu* oder *zu*) nehmen niemals Bezug auf den aktuellen Zustand der Welt, vielmehr formulieren sie den Zweck bzw. das Ziel, die den Sachverhalt im Bezugssatz begründen. In diesem Sinne nicht-referenziell verankert sind Ausdrücke dann, wenn sie nicht in direkter Weise auf den aktuellen Zustand der Welt Bezug nehmen. Zwar besitzt der morphologische Marker *-en* keine Finitheitsmerkmale, hat aber stets eine modale Interpretation, wenn er regiert von Modalverben oder frei als Wurzelinfinitiv vorkommt. Um nun zu begründen, dass es sich beim finalen infiniten Adjunkt um ein semantisches Substitut für Finalkonstruktionen handelt, wird gezeigt, dass der Infinitiv keineswegs nur eine Grundform ist.

4.1. Vom angeblichen Fehlen eines overten Trägers semantischer Eigenschaften

In den indoeuropäischen Sprachen wurden Richtung, Ziel und Zweck durch Kasusmarker (Dativ, Akkusativ und Lokativ) ausgedrückt (Haspelmath 1989: 291ff.). Typologisch kann davon ausgegangen werden, dass für das Deutsche kein Alleingang bei der Grammatikalisierung der Markierung von Ziel bzw. Zweck (= Finalität) postuliert werden kann, sondern das Deutsche – wie auch andere Sprachen – scheint hier einen universalen Grammatikalisierungspfad von purposiven Elementen zu Infinitiven vollzogen zu haben (vgl. Haspelmath 1989: 292 und 304–308 zum Griechischen). In diesem Zusammenhang weist auch Disterheft (1981) auf die indoeuropäischen Wurzeln von Infinitiven hin: Die Infinitive sind aus nomina actionis abgeleitet und haben vorzugsweise eine finale Interpretation, dies jedenfalls wohl immer dann, wenn sie nicht als Komplemente zu analysieren sind.

Im Gegenwartsdeutschen (GwD) werden Ziel und Zweck (einer Handlung im weitesten Sinne) in nichtfiniten Kontexten durch *um-zu* und (eingeschränkt) durch *zu* ausgedrückt (vgl. u.a. Brandt und Rosengren 1983, Vliegen 2002, 2004, Zifonun et al. 1997: 1428, 2290ff., 2318). Diachron ist dabei im Deutschen jedoch nicht erst der Marker ahd. *zi* oder mhd. *zu* oder aber Formen der Präposition *umb/umbe* (Demske 2010: 29f.) sondern das Morphem bzw. der Infinitivmarker *-en* für die Kennzeichnung von Finalität zuständig, der diachron Träger einer finalen Semantik ist (Curme 1922, Haspelmath 1989) mit synchron weiterhin modaler Semantik (Rapp und Wöllstein 2009, 2012). Paul (1920: 290;§330), Behaghel (1924: S.410; §202) und ganz deutlich Curme (1922: 270) führen den reinen Infinitiv, resp. den Infinitivmarker *-en*, auf den Akkusativ des Ziels zurück; damit war *-en* ursprünglich mit modaler Semantik finaler Ausprägung ausgestattet – weswegen die Bezeichnung des (reinen) Infinitivs als „Grundform" irreführend ist (Bech 1955/57: 13ff., Haspelmath 1989: 287). Dass der reine Infinitiv darüber hinaus unregiert auch synchron noch als Adjunkt fungieren kann, wird in der Literatur nicht diskutiert. Bemerkenswert ist in diesem Zusammenhang ein Hinweis von Ickler (2010).

Bis zum GwD vollzieht sich die Entwicklung der lexikalischen Finalitätsmarkierung – hier als *Lexikalische Substitution* bezeichnet – grob gezeichnet wie folgt:

(27) Lexikalische Substitution bei der Finalitätsmarkierung:

einfacher Infinitiv	→	*zu*-Infinitiv	→	*um zu*-Infinitiv
-en	→	*zu* + *-en*	→	*um* + *zu* + *-en*

Allgemein geteilt wird die Überzeugung, dass diejenigen Kontexte, in denen der reine Infinitiv erscheint, ausschließlich modal sind; (a) regiert durch Modalverben (28)a und ausschließlich kohärent konstruiert und (b) unregiert und frei (28)b immer mit modaler Semantik (und entweder *infinit-direktiver* oder *infinit-deliberativer* Satzmodus) (vgl. Reis 2003: 162f., Rapp und Wöllstein 2009: 166) – entgegen dem *zu*-Infinitiv, der nie frei vorkommen kann (28)c und auch in nicht-modalen Kontexten auftritt, bspw. regiert von faktiven Verben (28)d.

(28) a. Er muss/soll/dürfte/... diesmal dabei sein.[5]
b. (Warum) Urlaub haben!/Einmal noch Venedig sehen!/Nochmal 20 sein!
c. *Einmal noch Rom zu sehen!
d. Er bedauert, dabei sein zu müssen.

Im Folgenden betrachten wir die Formen „*sein* + XP + Infinitiv", „*sein* + XP + *zu*-Infinitiv" und „*sein* + XP + *um* + *zu*-Infinitiv" bzgl. ihrer formalen Verwandtschaft, wobei das infini-

5 Nicht diskutiert wird in diesem Zusammenhang der reine Infinitiv, der regiert von Vollverben bestimmten Typs in AcI-Konstruktionen auftritt; s. dazu Rapp und Wöllstein (2009: 162f.).

tivische Adjunkt Finalität nicht *lexikalisch* sondern *grammatisch* ausdrückt. Der einfache adverbiale Infinitiv in seiner spezifischen Umgebung ist – trotz seiner synchronen Isoliertheit – mit finaler Semantik ausgestattet.

(29) Semantische Substitution bei der Finalitätsmarkierung:
einfacher Infinitiv ← *zu*-Infinitiv ← *um zu*-Infinitiv

4.2. Korrespondierende Intentionalität

Der sog. Absentiv zeigt typische Beschränkungen in der Wahl des Subjekts (30) und des Infinitivs (30)'. Diese Beschränkungen begegnen uns sowohl bei overter wie bei coverter Lokations-Prädikation (übrigens gilt Gleiches auch für *um-zu*):

(30) Subjekt-Beschränkungen
a. *Der Ofen ist (im Zimmer) uns einheizen.
b. *Der Ofen ist im Zimmer, um uns einzuheizen.
c. *Der Keil ist (im Stamm) das Holz spalten.
d. *Der Keil ist im Stamm, um das Holz zu spalten.

(30)' Infinitiv-Beschränkungen
a. ??Hans ist (im Wald) sich vor Geistern fürchten.
b. ??Hans ist im Wald, um sich vor Geistern zu fürchten.
c. *Theo ist (im Bett) aufwachen.
d. *Theo ist im Bett, um aufzuwachen.

Wenn aber beide – Subjekt und Infinitiv – eine intentionale Semantik aufweisen (31)a bzw. durch Zuschreibung eine solche erhalten können (31)b und damit folglich bezüglich Intentionalität korrespondieren, wird die Reduktion der lexikalischen Ausdrucksmittel für die Finalität durch die Restriktionen beim prädikativen Subjekt und beim infinitivischen Adjunkt scheinbar „kompensiert".

(31) a. Alex ist das Getreide einbringen.
b. ?Die Mähmaschine ist das Getreide einbringen.

Der Gehalt der formalen Relation *Finalität* bliebe so erhalten, aber der mögliche Bedeutungsumfang der involvierten Einheiten wird eingeschränkt: Subjekt- und Verb-Restriktion auf Intentionalität.

4.3. Korrespondierende Beschränkungen für das prädikative Komplement[6]

Infinitivische Adjunkte treten im GwD eingeleitet durch die Konnektoren *ohne, anstatt* oder *um* immer unter Beteiligung des 2. Status *zu* auf und sind immer satzwertig (= CP). Einzig der finale Konnektor bzw. lexikalische Finalitätsmarker *um* (30) ist fakultativ (aber synchron mit Gebrauchsbeschränkungen verbunden; vgl. Zifonun et al. 1997: 1427–1440). Die

[6] Nicht diskutiert werden in diesem Zusammenhang Konstruktionen des Typs *Der Bohrer ist geeignet/leistungsfähig genug, (um) Schlösser zu zerstören.* (*um*)-*zu* Konstruktionen benötigen eine eigene Behandlung insbesondere wegen ihres besonderen Status zwischen Komplement und Adjunkt; vgl. hierzu auch Vliegen (2004).

Beobachtung zu Varianten infiniter Finalkonstruktionen in (29) – (31) zeigen aber neben den Beschränkungen das Subjekt und den Infinitiv betreffend jeweils auch spezifische Anforderungen bzw. Beschränkungen an das prädikative Komplement der Kopula bei lexikalisch ausgedrückter Finalität (32) vs. grammatisch ausgedrückter Finalität (33) und (34).

Wir beobachten beim Erscheinen der Marker *um* und *zu* in (32) (= [+*um*+*zu*]) keine Beschränkung auf ein Lokationsprädikat PP_{LOC} (32)a, b, c; nicht möglich ist dagegen ein leeres Prädikat (32)d.

(32) a. [$_{CP}$ Hans ist [$_{PP}$ in München], [$_{CP}$ um seine politischen Ziele durchzusetzen]].
b. [$_{CP}$ Hans ist [$_{NP}$ Bürgermeister], [$_{CP}$ um seine politischen Ziele durchzusetzen]].
c. [$_{CP}$ David ist [$_{AP}$ pünktlich/(nicht) alt genug/zu jung], [$_{CP}$ um Holz zu hacken]].
d. *[$_{CP}$ Irene ist [$_{XP}$ ∅], [$_{CP}$ um ihre Mutter zu besuchen]].

Beim Nichterscheinen des Markers *um* in (33) (= [-*um*+*zu*]) beobachten wir die Beschränkung auf ein Lokationsprädikat PP_{LOC} (33)a vs. (33)b, c, das wie auch bei [+*um*+*zu*] in (32)d nicht leer sein darf. Die Grammatikalität bzw. Verteilung von (33)b, c ist synchron schwierig zu beurteilen (hier müssten Akzeptabilitäts- und quantitative (Korpus-)Analysen Aufschluss geben). Auch ist entscheidend welchen Typs das Adjektiv in solchen Konstruktionen ist; Hinlänglichkeits- und Nezessitätskontexte (s. (31)c–(33)c) sind grammatisch, dagegen lassen sich Adjektive, die als unveränderliche Eigenschaft des prädikativen Subjekts gelten können – also nicht temporärer Natur sind –, nicht final modifizieren; skalierte Kontexte, die über einen „idealen Mittelwert" hinausreichen, (*nicht X genug, zu X*) weisen darüber hinaus das finale Adjunkt als nicht-realisierbar aus (was übrigens für finale Kontexte ungewöhnlich ist, weil sie i.d.R. als potentiell realisierbar gelten, also ihr Wahrheitswert prinzipiell offen ist; vgl. Sáebo (1991: 625), Wöllstein 2009: 93ff.).

(33) a. [$_{CP}$ Hans ist [$_{PP}$ in Augsburg], [$_{CP}$ seine Mutter zu besuchen]].
b. ??[$_{CP}$ Hans ist [$_{NP}$ Bürgermeister], [$_{CP}$ seine politischen Ziele durchzusetzen]].
c. [$_{CP}$ David ist [$_{AP}$ *pünktlich/(nicht) alt genug/zu jung], [$_{CP}$ Holz zu hacken]]. (vgl. auch Fußnote 5)
d. *[$_{CP}$ Irene ist [$_{XP}$ ∅], [$_{CP}$ ihre Mutter zu besuchen]].

Beim Nichterscheinen beider Marker *um* und *zu* in (34) (= [-*um*-*zu*]) beobachten wir die Beschränkung auf ein Lokationsprädikat PP_{LOC} (34)a vs. (34)b; entgegen (32)c und (33)c darf es bei [-*um*-*zu*] in (34)c leer sein.

(34) a. [$_{CP}$ Irene ist [$_{PP}$ in Augsburg], [$_{VP}$ ihre Mutter besuchen]].
b. *[$_{CP}$ Hans ist [$_{NP}$ Bürgermeister], [$_{VP}$ seine politischen Ziele durchsetzen]].
c. *[$_{CP}$ David ist [$_{AP}$ pünktlich/(nicht) alt genug/zu jung], [$_{CP}$ Holz hacken]].
d. [$_{CP}$ Irene ist [$_{XP}$ ∅] [$_{VP}$ ihre Mutter besuchen]].

Dies zusammengeführt mit Abschnitt 2 zur Rechtfertigung einer leeren Strukturstelle mit lokaler Ausprägung, vgl. (19) – (21), ergibt für (32)c, (33)c und (34)c, dass XP beschränkt ist auf ein leeres Lokationsprädikat e_{LOC}. Seine Lizenzierung wird hier nicht weiter vertieft; es sei nur der generelle Hinweis gegeben, dass eine VP und nicht eine CP (Proposition) – wie in den Beispielen (32) und (33) aufgrund des Typs *Ereignis* verortbar ist. Das Denotat der VP stellt eine Argumentstelle (= Ereignisargument im Davidsonischen Sinn) bereit, über das eine Lokation prädizieren kann; unabhängig, ob overt oder covert, das Ereignisargument wird immer mit der assertierten Konstruktion identifiziert – nur Ereignisse und nicht Propositionen können lokalisiert werden. Zusammengefasst ergibt sich das folgende Bild korrespondierender Beschränkungen für das overte prädikative Komplement (35) und das coverte (36):

(35) Overte prädikative Komplemente:

	ADJUNKT		
PRÄDIKATIVES KOMPLEMENT	*um zu*	*zu*	*reiner Infinitiv*
NP	+	-	-
AP	+	+/-	-
PP_{LOC}	+	+	+

Nur Lokationsprädikate sind mit allen Typen finaler Adjunkte möglich – grau unterlegt in (35) und nur der reine Infinitiv ist mit einer leeren Lokation möglich (36); daraus ergibt sich die Lizenzierung für e_{LOC}.

(36) Covertes prädikatives Lokationskomplement:

	ADJUNKT		
PRÄDIKATIVES KOMPLEMENT	*um zu*	*zu*	*reiner Infinitiv*
e_{LOC}	-	-	+

4.4. Deutung und Funktion der lexikalischen Marker *um* und *zu*

Das Vorzeichen von ±*um* und ±*zu* korreliert mit der Grammatikalität von (32) – (34). Der Marker *um* (bei [+*um*/+*zu*]) markiert lexikalisch Intentionalität und erlaubt a) nicht-intentionale Subjektreferenten (37)b und b) nicht-intentionale Verben im finalen Adjunkt (37)d; die Bedingung scheint nur zu sein, dass die Agenserschließung prinzipiell möglich sein muss; vgl. auch (31)b:

(37) a. *Der Korken ist in der Flasche den Wein schützen.
b. Der Korken ist in der Flasche, (um) den Wein zu schützen.
c. *Hans ist im Wald dem Fuchs begegnen.
d. Hans ist im Wald, (um) dem Fuchs zu begegnen.

Konstruktionen, die (*um*)-*zu*-enthalten, haben grundsätzlich keinen zugänglichen Wahrheitswert (38)a; für den finalen reinen Infinitiv gilt das auch. Auf Faktivität wird nur dann geschlossen, wenn die Ereignisstruktur nicht komplex ist (38)b; ist sie dagegen komplex, können Teile des Ereignisses negiert werden, ohne dass der Gesamtsatz ungrammatisch wird (39):

(38) a. Sie war in Augsburg, (um) ihre Mutter zu besuchen, aber diese war leider verreist.
b. *Sie war in Augsburg ihre Mutter besuchen, aber diese war leider verreist.

(39) Theo war Hornhechte angeln, aber er hat keine gefangen.

Das Fehlen des Markers *um* (bei [*-um/+zu*]) (= nicht lexikalisch ausgedrückte Finalität) erlaubt ausschließlich ein Lokationsprädikat (33)b, c – ist jedoch eingeschränkt auf die overte Lokation (33)a (oben begründet durch seinen semantischen Typ „Proposition“). Das Fehlen beider Marker *um* und *zu* (bei [*-um/-zu*]) erlaubt ein covertes Lokationsprädikat; was *um-zu* in der Finalkonstruktion leistet, leistet im sog. Absentiv (plus modale Interpretation des Infinitivs) *ausschließlich* die Intentionalität von Verb und prädikativem Subjekt im Zusammenwirken mit der modalen Interpretation des Infinitivs. Zusätzlich trägt *um* die bouletische Komponente bei (Wöllstein 2009); *zu* liefert die nicht-faktische Komponente – hier kongruieren *um* und *zu* (Wöllstein 2008, Rapp und Wöllstein 2009). Die Final-Interpretation des sog. Absentiv [*-um/-zu*] folgt aus der Kombination: a) modale Interpretation des Infinitivs und b) Intentionalität des prädikativen Subjekts (gleichzeitig auch das mit dem Infinitiv identifizierten Subjekts) und des infiniten Verbs:

(40)

	FREIE MODIFIKATION KEINE BESCHRÄNKUNG GGÜ. INTENTIONALEM SUBJEKT/INFINITEM VERB	LOKATIONSPRÄDIKAT overt	 covert
um zu	+	+	-
zu	-	+	-
reiner Infntiv	-	+	+

4.5. Syntax des finalen reinen Infinitivs

Syntaktisch ist die Verbalprojektion ein finales, infinites Adjunkt; eine (ggf. zu rechtfertigende) *um-zu*-Ellipse kann ausgeschlossen werden, da die grammatischen Eigenschaften und Beschränkungen für alle finalen Ausdrucksformen unter der Annahme einer Ellipsenhypothese übereinstimmen müssen, was sie nicht tun (39), (40). Dass es sich beim finalen infiniten Adjunkt auch nicht um eine CP handelt (sondern um eine VP, deren semantischer Typ einen Lokationsausdruck lizenzieren kann), darauf weist externe Evidenz hin: Der 1. Status kann nicht höher projizieren als VP. Denn selbst nominativische Ausdrücke, die eine IP rechtfertigen würden, sind keine tatsächlichen Subjekte: Reis (1995: 148ff.) legt überzeugend dar, dass die Nominative in Wurzelinfinitiven nicht als tatsächliche Subjekte zu verstehen sind, sondern über die Adressatenmenge quantifizieren; konsequenterweise sind hier nur Quantoren und Pluralia (41), nicht aber (identifizierende) Individualausdrücke möglich – auch nicht im sog. Absentiv (42):

(41) a. Alle mal herkommen!
b. Keiner herschauen!
c. Radfahrer absteigen!
d. *Paul absteigen!

(42) a. Wir sind/waren in Berlin, *alle/jeder* Sue gratulieren.
b. *Wir sind/waren in Berlin, *die Linguisten* Sue gratulieren.

Es ist deshalb davon auszugehen, dass ggf. auftretende Nominativphrasen auch hier keine echte Subjektfunktion haben, sondern außerhalb des Rektionsbereichs von V°/*v*° in der non-A-Position SpecF auftreten und dort den Adressatenbereich einschränken; vgl. Rapp und Wöllstein (2009: 165f.):

(42) Wir sind in Berlin [$_{FP}$ [$_{SpecF}$ alle [$_{F'}$ [$_{F°}$ [$_{VP}$ Sue gratulieren]]]]].

Der linksperiphere Marker *zu* kann sowohl in einer VP- (nur eingebettet von modalen Verben) als auch in einer CP-Struktur auftreten (Rapp und Wöllstein 2009: 172ff., 2012: 7ff.). Als unregierter Finalsatz ist er inkohärent und bildet eine CP. CP-Strukturen erlauben – aufgrund ihres Typs „Proposition" – keine lokale Verankerung, weswegen nur die overte Lokation grammatisch ist:

(43) Wir sind *(in Berlin) [$_{CP}$ ... [$_{VP}$ Sue zu gratulieren]].

Zu der Diskussion der Syntax (Kohärenz/Inkohärenz u.a.) des sog. Absentivs und der Einordung der Verhältnisse in (44) – bei overtem Lokationsausdruck ist die Nachstellung der VP möglich (44)a, bleibt die Lokations-Prädikation aber implizit, ist keine Nachstellung möglich (44)c – verweise ich auf Fortmann & Wöllstein (2012):

(44) a. ..., dass David im Wald ist, [$_{VP}$ Holz hacken]
b. ..., dass David im Wald [$_{VP}$ Holz hacken] ist
c. ..., *dass David ist, [$_{VP}$ Holz hacken]

Die Ungrammatikalität von (44)c legt nahe, dass implizite Lokations-Prädikationen entweder nicht komplex sind oder von einer Komplexität, wie wir sie in obligatorisch kohärenten Konstruktionen kennen.

Das infinitivische Adjunkt [*-um/-zu*] definiert als semantisches Substitut der lexikalischen Finalkonstruktion Ziele oder Zwecke. Findet Finalität nicht lexikalisch seinen Ausdruck sondern grammatisch – wie es durch den sog. Absentiv mit seiner Beschränkung geschieht, so bleibt in einem nächsten Schritt die Erklärung für die Absenz-Interpretation.

5. Finalität und Absenz

Zentrale Eigenschaft aller finalen/purposiven Konstruktionen ist, dass sie durch die im internen Konnekt q ausgedrückte Proposition Ziele oder Zwecke definieren (45) (vgl. auch Sǽbo 1991: 625), die *willentlich* herbeigeführt werden müssen und über Zuschreibung der Intention bzw. der zweckgerichteten Selbstständigkeit des prädikativen und des „infiniten" Subjekts im sog. Absentiv erfolgen. Darüber hinaus liefert *um* im infiniten Kontext die bouletische Bedeutungskomponente Wunsch/Wille/Ziel auszudrücken.

(45) a. David$_i$ ist im Hof [$_{XP}$ *um* PRO$_i$ Holz *zu* hacken]
p *q*

Das Verhältnis zwischen *p* und *q* wird als eine hinreichende Bedingungsrelation analysiert in dem Sinne dass: *wenn p wahr ist und q wahr werden kann und p wegen des Wunsches/Willens/Ziels, dass q* (vgl. Wöllstein 2009: 96):

(46) p & q & (Wunsch/Wille/Ziel) q o→ p
(o→ = hinreichende Bedingungsrelation)

Mit dem sog. Absentiv ist die Interpretation verbunden, dass sich das prädikative Subjekt nicht an einem erwartbaren oder üblichen Ort aufhält, sondern am Ort der Verbalhandlung, die im finalen Adjunkt ausgedrückt wird. Dabei kann der Ort der Verbalhandlung implizit bleiben. Die Absenz-Interpretation kann nun in zwei Schritten auf der Basis der logisch semantischen Struktur kausaler Verhältnisse finaler Konstruktionen (Zifonun et al. 1991: 2292ff.) pragmatisch abgeleitet werden: a) konditionale Verstärkung (47) und b) durch die aufhebenden reduktiven Schlussweise des modus tollens (48):

(47) konditionale Verstärkung: final ⇒ konditional
q o→ p
⇒ p → q

Unter Konditionalverstärkung wird implikatiert, dass wenn *David im Wald ist,* dann *hackt er dort Holz.* Aus den Voraussetzungen *nicht q* (= Holz hacken) und *wenn p, dann q* kann auf *nicht p* geschlossen werden, was Folgendes bedeutet: wenn er nicht Holz hackt, dann ist er nicht im Wald, bzw. an dem Ort der Verbalhandlung, die auch overt nicht ausgedrückt sein muss.

(48) Schlussfigur *modus tollens*
a. Prämissen: p → q
¬q
b. Konklusion ¬p

Die Schlussfigur mit $\neg q$ dann $\neg p$ bezogen auf das Lokalitäts-Prädikat führt zur Verneinung der Lokations-Prädikation *p David ist im Wald* (overter Ort der Verbalhandlung) und in *David hackt Holz* (coverter Ort der Verbalhandlung). Absenz ist somit in zwei Schritten implikatierbar: Wenn David nicht Holz hacken wäre, wäre er an einem erwartbaren Ort (sonst davon abwesend). Vermutlich liegt die Sache aber noch viel „einfacher", da nämlich die Anwesenheit von oder das Beschäftigsein an einem Ort immer mit der Annahme der Absenz von einem anderen Ort verknüpft ist.

Vor dem gesamten diskutierten Hintergrund möchte ich nochmals die Frage aufgreifen, warum Absenz überhaupt ein sprachliches Primitivum sein sollte und als sprachübergreifende Kategorie zur Verfügung steht: Angesichts der gegen die bestehenden Analysen und für eine Lokations-Prädikation mit finalem Adjunkt vorgebrachten Argumente, scheinen insbesondere aus typologisch-historischer Perspektive weitere Untersuchungen mehr als angebracht: U.a. die von Curme (1922), Disterheft (1981) und Haspelmath (1989) gemachten sprachübergreifenden Beobachtungen zur Entwicklung der Infinitive aus nominalen Finalitätsmarker scheinen hier vielversprechend: Finalität scheint hier der ausschlaggebende Faktor für die sprachübergreifenden Ähnlichkeiten zu sein.

6. Zusammenfassung und Fazit

Der sog. Absentiv ist als eine Prädikativkonstruktion aufzufassen, was der Ansicht der einschlägigen Arbeiten neueren Datums meist entspricht. Entgegen der in der Literatur vertretenen Ansicht wird Folgendes vorgeschlagen:

- Beim sog. Absentiv handelt es sich nicht um eine Verbal-Prädikation, sondern um eine Lokations-Prädikation: Das vermeintliche VP-Prädikat ist tatsächlich nur ein infinites Adjunkt zu einer Lokation, die im Deutschen zwar covert bleiben darf, bei identischer syntaktischer Struktur jedoch jederzeit ihren expliziten Ausdruck finden kann, nämlich entweder phrasal als Orts-/Richtungs-PP oder lexikalisch als Lokaladverb.
- Die infinite Adjunktphrase ist ihrerseits die Schwundform einer zugrundeliegenden *um-zu*-Konstruktion mit finaler Semantik. Die für den sog. Absentiv nachweisbaren semantischen Selektionsrestriktionen (Subjekt- und Infinitivbeschränkungen) sind keineswegs spezifisch für einen vermeintlich eigenen Konstruktionstyp *Absentiv*; sie folgen vielmehr zwanglos.
- Die absentive Interpretation ergibt sich durch pragmatisches Kalkül.

Derzeit noch ungeklärt ist die exakte Modellierung des Nexus, in der das Infinitiv-Adjunkt zum Lokationsprädikat bzw. zur Prädikativkonstruktion steht. So ist der Grad der syntaktischen Integration noch nicht bestimmt, und auch für die dafür anzunehmende syntaktische Struktur kommen mehrere Möglichkeiten infrage: Es könnte sich um eine reine Kontrollstruktur handeln, vielleicht um eine Koordinationsstruktur, möglicherweise auch um einen Fall von Sekundärprädikation. Weitere Evidenz ist aus konstruktionsvergleichenden Abwägungen zu ziehen und natürlich insbesondere unter sprachtypologischen Aspekten erwartbar. Als vorläufiges Ergebnis lässt sich festhalten: Für den sog. Absentiv im Deutschen kann (und sollte!) auf die Annahme eines spezifischen Konstruktionstyps und/oder die Anreicherung des Lexikons durch konstruktionstypspezifische Doubletten bereits bestehender Einträge verzichtet werden, denn Syntax, Semantik und Pragmatik folgen transparent aus allgemeinen grammatischen Prinzipien.

Bibliographie

Abraham, W. (2008): Absentive arguments on the absentive: An exercise in silent syntax. Grammatical category or just pragmatic inference? *Language Typology and Universals (STUF)* 61: 358–374.

Bech, G. (1955/57): *Studien über das deutsche verbum infinitum* (Bd. I–II). Kopenhagen: Munksgaard.

Behaghel, O. (1924): *Deutsche Syntax. Eine geschichtliche Darstellung. Bd. II.* Die Wortklassen und Wortformen. B. Adverbium. C. Verbum (=Germanische Bibliothek 1.1.10. 2). Heidelberg: Winter, 303–372.

Blatz, F. (1900): *Neuhochdeutsche Grammatik. Zweiter Bd.: Satzlehre (Syntax).* Karlsruhe.

Curme, G. O. (1922): *A Grammar of the German Language*. Second Revised Edition. [Ninth printing 1964]. New York: Ungar.

Brandt, M. und I. Rosengren (1983): Das deutsche Finalsatzgefüge in kontrastiver Sicht. *Studia Linguistica* 37: 146–160.

Dahl, Ö. (2000): *Tense and aspect in the languages of Europe*. Berlin/New York: de Gruyter.

Davidson, D. (1967): The logical form of action sentences. In: N. Rescher (Hg.), *The logic of decision and action*. Pittsburgh: University of Pittsburgh Press, 81–95.

Demske, U. (2011): Finale Marker in Infinitivkonstruktionen – Wandel und Variation. In: H. Christen, F. Patocka und E. Ziegler (Hgg.), *Struktur, Gebrauch und Wahrnehmung von Dialekt*. Wien: Praesens Verlag, 29–46.

Disterheft, D. (1981): Remarks on the History of the Indo-European Infinitive. *Folia Linguistica Historica* 2: 3–34.

DUDEN (2005): *Die Grammatik*. Bd.4, 7. Auflage. Mannheim: Brockhaus Verlag.

DUDEN (2005): *Die Grammatik*. Bd.4, 7. Auflage. Völlig neu erarbeitete und erweiterte Auflage. Mannheim u. a.: Dudenverlag.

DUDEN (2006): *Richtiges und gutes Deutsch. Wörterbuch der sprachlichen Zweifelsfälle*. 6. Aufl. Mannheim u.a.: Dudenverlag.

DUDEN (2009): *Die Grammatik: unentbehrlich für richtiges Deutsch*. 8. überarbeitete Auflage. Mannheim u. a.: Dudenverlag.

Ebert, K. H. (1996): Progressive aspect in German and Dutch. *Interdisciplinary Journal for Germanic Languages and Semiotic Analysis* 1: 41–62.

Ebert, K. H. (2000): Progressive markers in Germanic languages. In: Ö. Dahl (Hg.), *Tense and aspect in the languages of Europe*. Berlin/New York: de Gruyter, 605–653.

Eisenberg, P. (1999): *Grundriß der deutschen Grammatik II: Der Satz*. Stuttgart: Metzler.

Fortmann, C. und A. Wöllstein (2012/ in preparation): The absentive construction in German.

de Groot, C. (1995): De absentief in het Nederlands: een grammaticale categorie. *Forum der Letteren* 36: 1–18.

de Groot, C. (2000): The absentive. In: Ö. Dahl (Hg.), *Tense and aspect in the languages of Europe*. Berlin/New York: de Gruyter, 693–719.

de Groot, C. (2001): Functional Grammar and the non-lexical expression of absence. In: I. Kenesei und R. M. Harnish (Hgg.), *Perspectives on semantics, pragmatics, and discourse: A festschrift for Ferenc Kiefer*. Amsterdam: Philadelphia, 3–20.

Haslinger, I. (2007): *The Syntactic Location of Events*. PhD-Thesis, LOT Dissertation Series.

Haspelmath, M. (1989): From purposive to infinitive – a universal path of grammaticization. *Folia Linguistica Historica* 10: 287–310.

Hentschel, E. und P. Vogel (Hgg.) (2009): *Deutsche Morphologie*. Berlin/New York: de Gruyter.

Hoffmann, L. (2007): *Handbuch der deutschen Wortarten*. Berlin/ New York: de Gruyter.

Ickler, T. (2010): http://www.sprachforschung.org/ickler/index.php?show=news&id=1278 (Letzter Stand vom 10-9-2012).

Jacobs, J. (2001): The dimensions of topic-comment. *Linguistics* 39: 641–681.

König, S. (2009): Alle sind Deutschland ... außer Fritz Eckenga – der ist einkaufen! Der Absentiv in der deutschen Gegenwartssprache. In: E. Winkler (Hg.), *Konstruktionelle Varianz bei Verben* (=OPAL-Sonderheft 4/2009), 42–74.

Krause, O. (1997): Progressiv-Konstruktion im Deutschen im Vergleich mit dem Niederländischen, Englischen und Italienischen. *Zeitschrift für Sprachtypologie und Universalienforschung (STUF)* 50: 48–82.

Krause, O. (2001): *Progressiv im Deutschen: Eine empirische Untersuchung im Kontrast mit Niederländisch und Englisch*. Unveröffentlichte Dissertation, Universität Hannover.

Krause, O. (2002): *Progressiv im Deutschen: Eine empirische Untersuchung im Kontrast mit Niederländisch und Englisch* (=Reihe Linguistische Arbeiten 462). Tübingen: Niemeyer.

Maienborn, C. (2001): On the Position and Interpretation of Locative Modifiers. *Natural Language Semantics* 9: 191–240.

Maienborn, C. (2003): *Die logische Form von Kopula-Sätzen* (=Studia grammatica 56). Berlin: Akademie Verlag.

Paul, H. (1920): *Deutsche Grammatik*. Band IV. Syntax (Zweite Hälfte). Halle: Niemeyer, 93–136.

Rapp, I. (1996): Zustand? Passiv? – Überlegungen zum sogenannten „Zustandspassiv". *Zeitschrift für Sprachwissenschaft* 15: 231–265.

Rapp, I. und A. Wöllstein (2007): *Absentiv und Adsentiv: Instanzen von Topic-Comment-Strukturen – ereignisstrukturelle und pragmatische Beschränkungen*. Unveröffentlichtes Manuskript, Universität Tübingen.

Rapp, I. und A. Wöllstein (2009): Infinite Strukturen: selbständig, koordiniert und subordiniert. In: V. Ehrich, I. Reich und M. Reis (Hgg.), *Koordination und Subordination im Deutschen* (=Sonderheft Linguistische Berichte). Hamburg: Buske.

Rapp, I. und A. Wöllstein (2012): Satzwertige zu-Infinitive. Erscheint in: H. Altmann, J. Meibauer und M. Steinbach (Hgg.), *Handbuch der Satztypen*. Berlin/New York: de Gruyter.

Reis, M. (1995): Extractions from verb-second clauses in German? In U. Lutz und J. Pafel (Hgg.), *On extraction and extraposition in German*. Amsterdam: John Benjamins, 45–88

Reis, M. (2003): On the form and interpretation of German Wh-infinitives. *Journal of Germanic Linguistics* 15 (2): 155–201.

Sáebo, K. J. (1991): Causal and Purposive Clauses. In: A. v. Stechow und D. Wunderlich (Hgg.), *Semantik. Ein internationales Handbuch der zeitgenössischen Forschung* (=Handbücher zur Sprach- und Kommunikationswissenschaft 6). Berlin/New York: de Gruyter, 623–631.

Vliegen, M. (2004): Die *om te*-Konstruktion im Niederländischen und die *um zu*-Konstruktion im Deutschen. Ein Vorschlag zur Bedeutungsbeschreibung. *Leuvense Bijdragen* 93, 179–220.

Vogel, P. (2005): *Wir sind dann essen! Der Absentiv im Deutschen und anderen Sprachen*. Unveröffentlichtes Manuskript, Universität Bern.

Vogel, P. (2007): Anna ist essen! Neue Überlegungen zum Absentiv in den europäischen Sprachen mit einem Exkurs zum Deutschen. In: L. Geist und B. Rothstein (Hgg.), *Kopulaverben und Kopulasätze: Intersprachliche und Intrasprachliche Aspekte*. Tübingen: Niemeyer, 253–284.

Vogel, P. (2009): Absentiv. In: E. Hentschel und P. Vogel (Hgg.), *Deutsche Morphologie*. Berlin/New York: de Gruyter.

Wöllstein, A. (2005): *Die Verlaufsform ist am kommen.* Habilitationsvortrag, Universität Köln.

Wöllstein, A. (2007): *Einordnung der Form am + reiner Infinitiv in das Bechsche System der Status*. Unveröffentlichtes Manuskript, Bergische Universität Wuppertal.

Wöllstein, A. (2008): *Konzepte der Satzkonnexion*. Tübingen: Stauffenburg.

Wöllstein, A. (2009): *Grammatische Mittel sprachlicher Konzepte in der Informationsstruktur*. (StuTS, Universität Bochum)

Zifonun, G. et al. (Hg.) (1997): *Grammatik der Deutschen Sprache*, 3 Bde (Schriften des Instituts für Deutsche Sprache). Berlin/New York: de Gruyter.

Semantische Kongruenz

Elisabeth Löbel

1. Einleitung

In der langen Tradition zur Beschreibung von formaler Kongruenz (*constructio ad formam*) wird generell zwischen drei Domänen unterschieden: (i) Kongruenz zwischen Prädikat und Argument(en) (z. B. die Verb-Subjekt-Kongruenz), (ii) Kongruenz innerhalb der NP/DP (Kongruenz zwischen dem Nomen und Determinierern, Adjektiven usw.) sowie (iii) Kongruenz zwischen Pronomen und Antezedens, die im Gegensatz zu (i) und (ii) auch über die Satzgrenze hinaus möglich ist und daher in der Forschung teilweise nicht mehr unter Kongruenz, sondern unter Anapher subsumiert wird. Die für Kongruenz relevanten Kategorien Person, Genus und Numerus stimmen jedoch unter bestimmten Bedingungen nicht notwendigerweise überein, so dass zwischen dem Auslöser der Kongruenz und seiner mit ihm kongruierenden lexikalischen Einheit(en) Merkmalskonflikte entstehen bzw. entstehen können. Diese „semantische" Kongruenz (*constructio ad sensum*) steht nicht in gleichem Maße im Zentrum des theoretischen Interesses in der Sprachwissenschaft wie die formale bzw. syntaktische Kongruenz, nicht zuletzt deshalb, da sie zahlreiche Variationen bzw. Spielarten erlaubt, die abhängig von der jeweiligen Sprache einen mehr oder weniger großen Stellenwert innehaben. In diesem Kontext unmittelbar einschlägig sind die Arbeiten von Corbett, der ausgehend von Corbett (1979, 1983) eine auf einer breiten typologischen Basis beruhende Systematisierung in Form der Kongruenzhierarchie vorgeschlagen hat (Corbett (1991) für Genus, Corbett (2000) für Numerus sowie allgemein zur Kongruenz Corbett (2006)). Er wendet sich explizit gegen die traditionelle oben erwähnte Dreiteilung in unterschiedliche syntaktische Domänen und stellt fest, dass „ ... these three parts of the problem are linked in interesting ways, and that it makes sense to treat them together, rather than trying to draw unmotivated boundaries between them" (Corbett 2006: 28). Im Folgenden wird diese Hierarchie dargestellt, anhand von ausgewählten Sprachen illustriert und auf einige Probleme hingewiesen.

2. Die Kongruenzhierarchie

Die sowohl für Numerus als auch Genus geltende Kongruenzhierarchie wird in Corbett (2006: 207) wie in (1) dargestellt (Nummerierung von mir, E.L.):

(1) Agreement Hierarchy
Attributive > predicate > relative pronoun > personal pronoun
1 2 3 4
„These four positions represent successively less canonical agreement [...]. For any controller that permits alternative agreements, as we move rightwards along the Agreement Hierarchy, the likelihood of agreement with greater semantic justification will increase monotonically (that is, with no intervening decrease)."

Diese Kongruenzhierarchie repräsentiert abnehmenden syntaktischen Zusammenhang zwischen dem Kongruenzauslöser N (*controller*) und den kongruierenden Elementen (*targets*). Je enger der Zusammenhang zwischen dem Bezugsnomen und den kongruierenden Elementen ist, desto mehr überwiegen syntaktische Faktoren; je loser dagegen der Zusammenhang, desto mehr können semantische Faktoren für Kongruenz ausschlaggebend sein. Letzteres gilt insbesondere für die anaphorische Wiederaufnahme durch Personalpronomina.

Wie schon erwähnt, korreliert diese Hierarchie nicht mit der traditionellen Dreiteilung in NP/DP, Satz und satzübergreifende Anapher. Auffällig sind jedoch die folgenden drei Aspekte:

(i) Die Positionen 1 und 3 präsentieren den Bereich der NP/DP, die Positionen 2 und 4 gehen darüber hinaus. Ferner fehlt bei Position 1 (‚attributive') eine explizite Differenzierung zwischen Attribution im engeren Sinne und Determination, was sicher damit zusammenhängt, dass diese Hierarchie vorwiegend an slawischen Sprachen entwickelt wurde, insbesondere dem (artikellosen) Russischen.
(ii) Der zweite Aspekt betrifft den Status der in dieser Hierarchie genannten Kategorien. Corbett (2006: 207) selbst spricht vorsichtig von „Positionen" („ [...] what is important here is the relative places of the four positions"). Betrachtet man die verwendeten Begriffe jedoch genauer, fällt auf, dass es sich bei den Positionen 1 und 2 um syntaktische *Funktionen* handelt (Attribut und Prädikat), bei den Positionen 3 und 4 jedoch um lexikalische *Kategorien* (Relativ- und Personalpronomen). Korreliert man diese Beobachtung mit dem NP/DP-internen und dem NP/DP-externen Bereich, stellt man fest, dass in Bezug auf Kongruenz im NP/DP-internen Bereich zum einen eine syntaktische Funktion (Attribut), gleichzeitig aber auch eine lexikalische Kategorie (Relativpronomen)[1] relevant ist. Analoges gilt für den NP/DP-externen Bereich, bei Position 2 liegt die syntaktische Funktion Prädikat vor, in Position 4 jedoch die lexikalische Kategorie Personalpronomen.
(iii) Der dritte Aspekt betrifft den unterschiedlichen Bezugspunkt der Kongruenz. Worauf sich ein Personalpronomen in der hier relevanten anaphorischen Verwendung bezieht, ist weder ein Nomen noch eine NP/DP, sondern ein *Satzglied* wie Subjekt oder Objekt, d.h. eine DP im engeren Sinne, eine Determiniererphrase (ausführlich hierzu Olsen 1991). Dies gilt auch für das Prädikat, denn ein Prädikat kongruiert ja nicht mit einem Nomen bzw. einer NP/DP, sondern mit seinem Subjekt, d.h. ebenfalls einem Satz-

[1] Corbett (ibid.) selbst weist auf den geringeren Stellenwert des Relativpronomens hin: „Note also that the relative pronoun position is the least important, since many languages do not build relative clauses with a pronoun."

glied. Der Bezugspunkt für ein adjektivisches Attribut ist hingegen das *Nomen*, d.h. eine lexikalische Kategorie.

Die Kongruenzhierarchie ist vielfach sprachspezifisch präzisiert worden. Eine erste Differenzierung stammt von Corbett (1983) selbst, indem sowohl für die attributive Position als auch für die beiden Typen von Pronomina eine Unterscheidung zwischen Nominativ und obliquem Kasus vorgenommen wurde; die Position Prädikat wurde ebenfalls entsprechend der von Comrie (1975) aufgestellten Prädikatshierarchie differenziert (vgl. Punkt 3 in (2)). Darauf basierend wurden, um nur einige Beispiele zu nennen, von Cornish (1986: 210) für das Französische weitere Differenzierungen vorgenommen, so dass ihm zufolge die Kongruenzhierarchie aus den folgenden einzelnen Teilhierarchien besteht:

(2)	1. Attributive:	article > determiner
	2. Attributive:	prenominal adjective > postnominal adjective > appositional adjective
	3. Predicate:	finite verb > participle > adjective > noun
	4. Articulator:	syntactic pronoun (possessives, reciprocal, reflexive, and restrictive pronouns)
	5. Pronoun:	non-restrictive relative pronoun > anaphoric personal pronoun > deictic personal/demonstrative pronoun

Neben Französisch als Beispiel für eine Artikelsprache sei noch die Elaboration der Kongruenzhierarchie speziell für das Russische als Beispiel für eine artikellose Sprache erwähnt (Weiss 1993):

(3)	attr.$_{\text{obl}}$	<	attr.$_{\text{nom}}$	<	prädikativ	<	postpositive Apposition	<	Relativ-pronomen	<	Personalpronomen oder Null
	1		2		3		4		5		6

Position 1 wird durch das attributive Adjektiv in einem obliquen Kasus vertreten, Position 2 durch das attributive Adjektiv im Nominativ, und Position 4 steht für die postpositive Stellung eines Adjektivs.

Im Folgenden wird Corbetts Kongruenzhierarchie (abgekürzt KH) für Genus (Kap. 3) und Numerus (Kap. 4) am Beispiel ausgewählter Sprachen näher beschrieben und auf die einzelnen Positionen ausführlicher eingegangen.

3. Semantische Kongruenz im Genus

3.1. Genus und hybride Nomina

Die Ansicht, dass die Kategorie Genus eine im Lexikon festgelegte Eigenschaft ist, die arbiträr vergeben wird und daher relativ „funktionsarm" ist (Köpke und Zubin 2009: 132), hat sich nicht zuletzt durch die Arbeiten von Corbett zur KH verändert. Dahl (2000: 106) unterscheidet zwischen lexikalischem und referenziellem Genus (Sexus), d.h. neben dem Lexikon ist die referierende NP/DP und damit die Syntax für Kongruenz ausschlaggebend. Standardbeispiel im Deutschen ist das Nomen *Mädchen* (Genus: Neutrum, Sexus: weiblich).

Durch diese Verlagerung in die Syntax wird „das Genus dann in sehr vielen Fällen pragmatisch vergeben und ist nicht mehr eine durchgängige Eigenschaft des Lexikons" (Köpke und Zubin 2009: 132). Mit anderen Worten: Neben dem Lexikon und damit auch der Morphologie sind für Kongruenz sowohl die Syntax als auch die Pragmatik gleichermaßen relevant.

In diesem Kontext sind insbesondere Nomina mit „common gender" (*genus communis*) wie frz. *professeur* (*Lehrer(in)*) zu nennen. Corbett (1991: 225ff.) spricht hier von „hybriden" Nomina, was am Beispiel von *vrač* (*Arzt/Ärztin*) (maskulines Genus) im Russischen illustriert wird:

(4)	a.	vrač	prišel-Ø	'The doctor came.'
		doctor	came-MASC	
	b.	vrač	prišl-a	'The doctor came.'
		doctor	came-FEM	

(Corbett 1991: 231)

Unter der Maßgabe, dass *vrač* (*Arzt/Ärztin*) auf eine Frau referiert, wählten in einer Befragung die Informanten für das verbale Prädikat zu 51,7 % die feminine Kongruenz. Die englische Übersetzung zeigt hingegen interessanterweise, dass keine formale Unterscheidung vorliegt und somit die Referenz in beiden Beispielen ambig bleibt, weil im Englischen Genus nur bei Pronomina (*he*, *she*, *it*) formal unterschieden wird.[2]

3.2. Semantische Kongruenz im Deutschen

Eine für das Deutsche angepasste und um Possessiva und deiktische Pronomina erweiterte KH wird in Köpke und Zubin (2009: 146) vorgeschlagen:

(5) grammatikalisch ◄——————————————► konzeptuell

Determinierer, Attribut	Relativpronomen usw.[3]	Possessivpronomen	Personalpronomen	Deiktisches Pronomen (exophorisch)

Während den Verfassern zufolge Corbetts KH vom syntaktischen Typus des Targets ausgeht, schlagen sie vor, dass sich „die pragmatische Kongruenz [...] mit wachsender Entfernung des Targets vom kontrollierenden Nomen durchsetzt" (Köpke und Zubin 2009: 145) und daher folgende „psycholinguistische Skalierung" aufgestellt werden kann:

[2] Allgemein zeigt sich Corbett (1991) zufolge im Russischen, dass auch bei Referenz auf eine weibliche Person bei Eigenschaften als Arzt (gut, kompetent, etc.) die maskuline, bei Eigenschaften der Person (hübsch, attraktiv, etc.) hingegen die feminine Kongruenz gewählt wird.

[3] „NP mit syntaktisch getilgtem Kopf (*das eine Mädchen ... das/die andere*), Quantor mit partitiver Phrase (*eines/eine der ... Mädchen*)", s. Köpke und Zubin (ibid.).

„Auslöser-Aktivierungsprinzip: Je mehr die Aktivierung eines syntaktisch steuernden Auslösers (Nomens) im Bearbeitungsgedächtnis des Sprechers abnimmt, desto eher kann eine pragmatische Projektion (also pragmatische Kongruenz) das vom syntaktischen Auslöser ausgehende Genusmerkmal (also grammatische Kongruenz) ausstechen.“

(Köpcke und Zubin 2009: 146)

Diese KH kann an dem hybriden Nomen *Mädchen* (Genus: Neutrum, Sexus: weiblich) in (6) illustriert werden (nur die mit *das Mädchen* referenzidentische Lesart der Pronomina ist relevant):

(6) a. Das Mädchen$_i$, das/*die mit seiner$_i$/$^{??}$ihrer$_i$ Puppe spielt.
b. Das Mädchen$_i$ spielt mit seiner$_i$/ihrer$_i$ Puppe.
c. Das Mädchen$_i$ sitzt ganz allein in der Ecke.
c‘. Es$_i$ spielt mit seiner$_i$/ihrer$_i$ Puppe.
c‘‘. Sie$_i$ spielt mit *seiner$_i$ /ihrer$_i$ Puppe.

Sowohl bei dem Determinierer als auch dem Relativpronomen ist ausschließlich syntaktische Kongruenz im Neutrum möglich, das Possessivum *seiner* in (6)a ist wesentlich akzeptabler als das feminine *ihrer*, in (6)b erlaubt das Possessivum jedoch sowohl syntaktische als auch semantische Kongruenz. Die Alternativen bei der anaphorischen Wiederaufnahme in (6)c zeigen einen interessanten Unterschied: Syntaktische Kongruenz (das Pronomen *es*) erlaubt beide Alternativen des Possessivum (6)c‘. Bei semantischer Kongruenz hingegen (das Pronomen *sie*) ist nur das ebenfalls feminine Possessivum *ihrer* möglich, eine Rückkehr zur syntaktischen Kongruenz ist unter der hier relevanten referenzidentischen Lesart nicht erlaubt, was genau der in Corbett für die KH unter (1) genannten Beschränkung („semantic agreement will increase monotonically, (that is, with no intervening decrease)“) entspricht.

Die für Köpke und Zubin (2009: 146) ausschlaggebende, wachsende Entfernung des Targets vom Auslöser der Kongruenz und damit die lineare Distanz entspricht zumindest im Deutschen nicht den Fakten, wie die Beispiele in (7) mit enger (7)a und loser Apposition (7)b illustrieren:

(7) a. Das Mädchen$_i$ Barbara, das$_i$/die$_i$ mit seiner$_i$/ihrer$_i$ Puppe spielt
b. Das Mädchen$_i$, es$_i$/sie$_i$ heißt Barbara, spielt mit seiner$_i$/ihrer$_i$ Puppe.

Bei der engen Apposition (*Barbara*) in (7)a ist auch beim Relativpronomen semantische Kongruenz möglich. Man könnte hier einwenden, dass durch den Einschub des Namens *Barbara* eine größere Distanz zum Auslöser *das Mädchen* vorliegt. Beispiel (7)b zeigt jedoch, dass nicht Distanz, sondern syntaktische Gebundenheit bzw. *Fügungsenge*[4] relevant ist; die lose Apposition ist, wie diese Bezeichnung schon suggeriert, nicht eng in den syntaktischen Zusammenhang eingebunden. Dies korreliert auch mit dem in (7)a aufgeführten Relativsatz: Aufgrund der Apposition *Barbara* ist dieser nur nichtrestriktiv interpretierbar, es liegt ein ‚appositiver‘ Relativsatz vor.

---

4 Begriff nach Lehmann (1984: 208), der diesen Begriff im Zusammenhang mit der losen bzw. engen Attribution verwendet. Ausführlich hierzu auch Löbel (1986: 100ff.).

Dass in älteren Sprachstufen des Deutschen semantische Kongruenz beim Relativpronomen einen größeren Stellenwert als im heutigen Deutsch hatte, zeigen die Untersuchungen von Fleischer (2012) zum Verhalten des Nomens ahd. *wīb* (*Weib*), was mit den grammatischen Eigenschaften des Relativpronomens begründet wird:

> „Einerseits weist das Relativpronomen auf einen etablierten Diskursreferenten zurück und hat somit einen anaphorischen Gehalt, andererseits stellt der Relativsatz ein Attribut zu diesem Diskursreferenten dar [...]. Die Tatsache, dass hier diachron die größten Schwankungen auftreten, kann als symptomatisch dafür angesehen werden, dass die Kongruenz des Relativpronomens sowohl anaphorische als auch attributive Züge aufweist."
>
> (Fleischer 2012: 24f.)

Generell ließe sich für das Standardbeispiel *Mädchen* einwenden, dass es sich bei diesem Nomen um eine lexikalisierte Diminutivbildung handelt und semantische Kongruenz für derartige Bildungen nicht produktiv ist. Wie folgende Beispiele anhand von *der Bruder* vs. *das Brüderchen* und *die Decke* vs. *das Deckchen* zeigen, ist semantische Kongruenz durchaus möglich, sofern es sich um einen Referenten mit dem Merkmal [+human] handelt:

(8) a. Sie hat ein Brüderchen bekommen. Es/Er soll Herbert heißen.
    b. Sie hat ein Deckchen gekauft. Es/*Sie ist aus Brüsseler Spitze.

Wie schon erwähnt, wird Genus im Englischen nur bei Pronomina formal unterschieden, das Merkmal [+/- human] ist jedoch für das pronominale System ebenfalls relevant, und zwar beim Relativpronomen (*who* vs. *which*), wie die Beispiele in (9) zeigen:

(9) a. The volcano *who* just left the room was Bill's kid.
    b. The soldiers *which* were made of lead were thrown away.

(Barlow 1988)

Eine Differenzierung wie in (9) ist im Deutschen nicht möglich; ein Satz analog zu (9)b wie *Der Soldat, der dort hinten steht.* ist außerhalb des Kontexts ambig, eine Disambiguierung ist nur aufgrund zusätzlicher Attribute und den semantischen Selektionsrestriktionen des Verbs bzw. des Prädikats möglich.

Hier kommt die eingangs erwähnte Unterscheidung zwischen lexikalischem und referenziellem Genus (Dahl 2000: 106) ins Spiel: Die Verwendung von *soldiers* in (9)b zeigt dies deutlich, während bei Metaphern wie *volcano* in (9)a strittig ist, ob dies noch unter semantische Kongruenz zu fassen ist.[5]

Dass man auch in Sprachen, in denen Genus nicht wie im Deutschen vorwiegend arbiträr, sondern nach semantischen Zuweisungsregeln zugewiesen wird, zusätzlich noch von semantischer Kongruenz sprechen kann, lässt sich in einer typologisch völlig anderen Sprache zeigen, dem Swahili.

---

[5] Auch in constraint-basierten Ansätzen wie HPSG (Pollard und Sag 1994) werden Beispiele für metonymische Beziehungen wie *The hashbrowns at table nine is angry*, die einen bestimmten konzeptuellen Rahmen (hier: Restaurant) voraussetzen, zusammen mit Nomina vom Typ *committee* unter „reference transfer" subsumiert, was allerdings nicht semantische Kongruenz im Genus, sondern im Numerus betrifft (s. Abschnitt 4).

3.3. Swahili

Swahili, eine Bantu-Sprache mit einem ausgeprägten, semantisch motivierten System von Nominalklassen, subsumiert Corbett (1991: 43) unter den Sprachen mit „extensive gender systems". Dies zeigt, dass für ihn kein Unterschied besteht zwischen Genus im engeren Sinne (zwei bis vier nominale Klassen) und Nominalklassensystemen (bis zu 20 verschiedene Klassen). Dieser Unterschied ist ihm zufolge rein quantitativer Natur, ausschlaggebend für Genus ist Kongruenz: „[...] the determining criterion of gender is agreement. [...] Thus many languages described as having 'noun classes' fall within our study. The number of genders is not limited to three: four is common and twenty is possible" (Corbett 1991: 5).

Die Relevanz der Nominalklassenpräfixe kann an folgendem Beispiel illustriert werden (die Zahlen stehen für unterschiedliche Nominalklassen, s.u.):

(10) a. M-swahili ‚der Swahili' (Mensch)
1
b. Ki-swahili ‚das Swahili' (Sprache)
7
c. U-swahili ‚Swahili-Land' (vgl. auch ‚U-ganda')
11

(Löbel 1997: 87ff.)

Stark vereinfacht (da es insbesondere zu den semantischen Klassen zahlreiche Ausnahmen gibt) lässt sich dieses „erweiterte" Genussystem wie in (11) darstellen, wobei ungerade Zahlen der traditionellen Bantu-Forschung entsprechend für Singular, gerade Zahlen für Plural stehen (ausführlich hierzu Corbett (1991: 47), vgl. auch Löbel (1997: 89ff.)):

(11)

Nominalklasse	morphologische Form am Nomen	Kongruenz Verb	
1/2	m-/wa-	a-/wa-	(Menschen)
3/4	m-/mi-	u-/i-	(Pflanzen, Geister)
5/6	Ø ~ji-/ma-	li-/ya-	(Früchte, Augmentativa u.a.)
7/8	ki-/vi-	ki-/vi	(kleine Objekte, Diminutiva)
9/10	N-/N-	i-/zi	(Tiere)
11/10	u-/N-	u-/zi-	(lange Objekte, Abstrakta)

Wie jedes Genussystem hat auch dieses einen semantischen Kern, d.h. semantische Kriterien haben Vorrang vor morphologischen Kriterien, was anhand des Präfixes 7/8 (*ki-/vi-*) illustriert werden kann. Zunächst gilt die semantische Zuweisungsregel „Diminutives belong to gender 7/8 (*ki-toto* ‚baby'), [...] remaining animates belong to gender 1/2" (Corbett 1991: 47). Zusätzlich gibt es folgende morphologische Zuweisungsregel, falls die semantische nicht greift: „[...] morphological class 7/8 (*ki-/vi-*) → gender 7/8" (Corbett ibid.). Entsprechend liegt in (12)a die semantische Zuweisungsregel vor, die Diminutivbildung *kitoto* ‚Baby' kongruiert mit Klasse 7 (Singular), während die in (12)b ebenfalls nach Klasse 7 vorliegende Kongruenz der morphologischen Zuweisungsregel entspricht:

(12) a. kitoto hiki ki-na-lala
7child 7this 7-pres-sleep
'This tiny child is sleeping.'

(Carstens 1991: 22)

b. kikapu kikubwa kimoja kilianguka
7basket 7large 7one 7fell
'One large basket fell.'

(Corbett 1991: 43)

Folgt man den morphologischen Zuweisungsregeln, ist (13)a ungrammatisch. Da der Referent von *kiboko* ‚Flusspferd' belebt ist, ist Kongruenz nach Klasse 1 („remaining animates") (13)b obligatorisch:

(13) a. *kiboko ki-kubwa ki-meanguka [Klasse 7 N[-belebt]]
hippopotamus 7-big 7-has.fallen
'The big hippopotamus has fallen.'

(Bokamba 1985: 17)

b. kiboko m-kubwa a-meanguka [Klasse 1 N[+belebt]]
hippopotamus 1-big 1-has.fallen
'The big hippopotamus has fallen.'

(Corbett 1991: 48)

Beispiel (13)a „is unacceptable, unless the hippopotamus is a toy, that is to say, is not animate" (Bokamba 1985: 16–17); „this point emphasizes the semantic nature of the assignment rule in question. In Swahili the rule applies to all animates [...]" (Corbett 1991: 48). Dies heißt im Klartext, dass (13)a nicht ungrammatisch ist, sondern hier das schon eingangs erwähnte „referenzielle Genus" (vgl. auch Beispiel (9)b) ausschlaggebend ist. Der Referent in (13)a ist kein Flusspferd, sondern ein (unbelebtes) Spielzeug, und danach richtet sich die Kongruenz. Mit anderen Worten: Die „formale" Kongruenz in (13)a entpuppt sich streng genommen als semantische Kongruenz, d.h., dass trotz der vorliegenden semantischen Zuweisungsregeln auch im Swahili zusätzlich noch von semantischer Kongruenz gesprochen werden kann, da das Nomen *kiboko* (*Flusspferd*) zwei Lesarten erlaubt. Die kongruierenden Elemente und damit die overten formalen Markierungen sind für die Lesart des jeweiligen Nomens ausschlaggebend. Welche Rolle diese Markierung generell für das Lexikon des Swahili spielt, zeigt noch folgendes, bezeichnenderweise aus einem Lehrbuch stammendes Beispiel:

(14) a. n-dege a-ruka. N[+belebt]
5 1-fliegt
'Der Vogel fliegt.'
b. n-dege i-naruka N[-belebt]
5 5-fliegt
'Das Flugzeug fliegt.'

(Brauner und Herms 1979: 119)

Bevor auf die semantische Kongruenz im Numerus im nächsten Abschnitt (Kap. 4) näher eingegangen wird, sei hier der Vollständigkeit halber darauf hingewiesen, dass dieses Phänomen auch im Swahili vorliegt:

(15) a.	mkutano	u-meamua	N[-belebt]
	3	3	
	'die Versammlung beschloss'		
b.	mkutano	wa-meamua	N[+human, Plural]
	3	2	
	'die Versammlung beschloss'		

(Brauner 1979: 427f.)

Beispiel (15)a entspricht den morphologischen Zuweisungsregeln, d.h. morphologische Kongruenz nach Nominalklasse 3 (Singular N[-belebt]) signalisiert kollektive Referenz, in (15)b hingegen liegt mit Nominalklasse 2 (Plural N[+human]) semantische Kongruenz und somit distributive Referenz (auf die Mitglieder der Versammlung) vor.

4. Semantische Kongruenz im Numerus

Die in (1) aufgestellte KH für Genus und deren Beschränkungen gilt auch für Numerus (Corbett 2000: 189f.):

(16) (=(1)) Kongruenzhierarchie für Numerus

> attributive > predicate > relative pronoun > personal pronoun
>
> „For any controller that permits alternative agreement forms, as we move rightwards along the Agreement Hierarchy, the likelihood of agreement forms with greater semantic justification will increase monotonically (that is, with no intervening decrease)."

Wie schon in (15) am Beispiel des Swahili gezeigt, nimmt die nominale Subklasse der Kollektiva als Kongruenzauslöser mit ihrer zum Teil möglichen distributiven vs. kollektiven Lesart einen besonderen Stellenwert bei dieser Hierarchie ein, worauf wir im folgenden Abschnitt näher eingehen wollen.

4.1. Kollektiva

Corbett (2006: 206f.) illustriert die KH für Numerus am Nomen *committee*, dem Standardbeispiel für semantische Kongruenz im Numerus im Englischen: „[...] syntactic (singular) or semantic (plural) agreement is possible for all agreement targets, except attributive modifiers, where only syntactic agreement is acceptable" (ibid.):

(17) a. this committee .../*these committee
b. The committee has/have decided.
c. the committee, which has decided .../the committee, who have decided ...
d. The committee ... It .../They ...

Semantische Kongruenz ist bekanntlich im Englischen möglich, da *committee* eine Kollektion bezeichnet (Singular, kollektive Lesart), gleichzeitig aber auch in der Bedeutung von *committee* enthalten ist, dass diese Institution aus Mitgliedern besteht (Plural, distributive Lesart).

Nomina vom Typ *committee* „are often called 'collectives' but [...] this is an overused term, so [...] we will use the term 'corporate'" (Corbett 2000: 188). Bei diesen „Körperschaftsnomina" lässt sich eine Korrelation zur Belebtheitshierarchie herstellen, die genau genommen aus drei Unterhierarchien besteht:

(18) Belebtheitshierarchie (nach Corbett (2000: 56f.))
speaker > addressee > 3rd person > kin > human > animate > inanimate
1. Personenhierarchie (erste > zweite > dritte Person)
2. Nominale Hierarchie (Pronomina > Nomina)
3. Nominale Subklassen (human > belebt > nicht-belebt)

Semantische Kongruenz korreliert Corbett zufolge im Englischen mit den nominalen Subklassen: Während diese bei N[+human] wie *committee* sehr häufig vorkommt, wird sie bei N[+belebt] wie *herd* weniger häufig verwendet, und bei N[-belebt] wie *forrest* ist nur syntaktische Kongruenz möglich.

Während es in Bezug auf *committee* keine Parallele zum Deutschen gibt, verhalten sich Englisch und Deutsch in (19) analog, das nominale Prädikat *early riser* (*Frühaufsteher*) erlaubt lediglich distributive, aber keine kollektive Referenz. Der Kongruenzauslöser ist also nicht das Subjekt mit dem Nomen *family* (*Familie*) als Kopf, sondern die Art des Prädikats (hierzu Urbas (1993)):

(19) a. My family are early risers.
b. Meine Familie sind Frühaufsteher.

Vorschläge, Nomina wie *committee* bzw. *family* im Lexikon unterspezifiziert zu lassen, um Merkmalskonflikte zu vermeiden (u.a. Ortmann (1992)), bieten keine eindeutige Lösung, da auch im Englischen semantische Kongruenz nur erlaubt ist, wenn das ein Kollektivum dieses Typs enthaltende Subjekt *definit* ist:

(20) a. A committee has/*have decided.
b. The committee which has/*who have decided ...

Wie (20)b zeigt, spielt auch die Art des Relativsatzes eine Rolle: Corbetts Beispiele in (17)c *the committee, which has decided .../the committee, who have decided ...* erlauben semantische Kongruenz nur unter der Maßgabe, dass der Relativsatz *nicht-restriktiv* ist, was durch das Komma signalisiert wird. Definitheit und Restriktivität spielen also in Bezug auf semantische Kongruenz eine entscheidende Rolle – ein Aspekt, der meines Wissens in der Literatur nicht genügend berücksichtigt wird.

Die Unterscheidung zwischen restriktivem und nichtrestriktivem Relativsatz ist auch im Deutschen relevant, allerdings nicht für kollektive Nomina, sondern für Kollektivkonstruktionen, wie (21) zeigt. Während beim nichtrestriktiven Relativsatz in (21)a sowohl syntaktische als auch semantische Kongruenz möglich ist, ist der Relativsatz in (21)b aufgrund des definiten Artikels in *der Strauß Blumen* nur restriktiv interpretierbar:

(21) a. Ein Strauß Blumen, über den/die sie sich bestimmt freuen würde, ...
b. Der Strauß Blumen, über den/*die sie sich sehr gefreut hat, ...
(Löbel 1986: 98ff.)

Der Vergleich von Kollektivkonstruktionen im Deutschen und Englischen ist Thema des nächsten Abschnitts.

4.2. Kollektivkonstruktionen

Für semantische Kongruenz im Numerus sind Kollektivkonstruktionen besonders relevant, wie auch folgende Beispiele (DUDEN Grammatik 2006: 1020) zeigen:

(22) a. Eine *Reihe* von Studenten *war* (auch: *waren*) bereits Parteimitglied.
b. Eine riesige Herde Schafe *war* (auch: *waren*) das Pfand.
c. Eine Menge Äpfel *lag/lagen* unter dem Baum.

„Wenn einer Sammelbezeichnung im Singular das Attribut im Plural folgt, ist standardsprachlich sowohl der Singular (nach der grammatischen Grundregel) als auch der Plural (Konstruktion nach dem Sinn) zulässig" (DUDEN Grammatik 2006: 1022). Während in (22) appositive Konstruktionen vorliegen, zeigt (23), dass semantische Kongruenz auch bei eindeutigen Genitivattributen möglich ist, wie die deutsche Übersetzung des Beispiels aus dem Swahili (Brauner 1979: 427) zeigt, wobei das Präfix *wa-* die Nominalklasse 2 (Plural für [N+human]) bezeichnet (GS = grammatisches Subjekt, LS = logisches Subjekt). Deutsch und Swahili verhalten sich also in dieser Hinsicht parallel (vgl. Löbel 1997: 96f.), das logische Subjekt mit N[+human] erlaubt semantische Kongruenz:

(23)

Baadhi	ya	*wa*-tu	*wa*-likwenda	Msumbiji.
Teil	der	Kl.2-Leute	Kl.2-gingen	Mosambik.
(GS)		(LS)		

'Ein Teil der Leute (einige Leute) ging (gingen) nach Mosambik.'
(Brauner 1979: 427)

Unmittelbar einschlägig für den Vergleich von Deutsch und Englisch ist eine Untersuchung von Berg (1998). Mit 46 Muttersprachlern des Deutschen und 57 Muttersprachlern des amerikanischen Englisch wurde die Kongruenz des verbalen Prädikats mit Kollektivkonstruktionen vom Typ *a group of researchers* (*eine Gruppe von Forschern*) als Subjekt untersucht. Einige repräsentative Ergebnisse sind in (24) dargestellt:

(24) Kongruenz des verbalen Prädikats im Deutschen und Englischen

		Englisch Sg. : Pl.	Deutsch Sg. : Pl.
a.	a number of critical issues 'eine Anzahl heikler Themen'	4 : 50	30 : 16
b.	a bunch of flowers 'ein Strauß Blumen'	29 : 26	45 : 1
c.	a heap of old papers 'ein Stapel alter Zeitungen'	25 : 28	42 : 2
d.	a group of researchers 'eine Gruppe von Forschern'	10 : 45	32 : 14
e.	a host of patients 'eine Schar von Patienten'	7 : 41	44 : 2
f.	a series of reports 'eine Reihe von Berichten'	6 : 40	28 : 18

(Berg 1998: 51f.)

Der Unterschied zwischen beiden Sprachen in Bezug auf diese Beispiele ist offensichtlich, im Deutschen ist syntaktische Kongruenz (Singular) vorherrschend, im Englischen semantische Kongruenz (Plural): „All of them favor singular agreement in German and almost all of them favor plural agreement in English. [...] The English data fall all along the range from an overwhelming predominance of the semantic principle to an equilibrium of the semantic and syntactic principles. This balance is found in *a bunch of flowers* and *a heap of old papers*" (Berg 1998: 54). Ausschlaggebend für das Gleichgewicht in (24)b und (24)c ist „the salience of the singular meaning associated with the head noun", *bunch* (*Strauß*) und *heap* (*Stapel* bzw. *Haufen*) haben mehr ‚Gestaltqualität' im Vergleich zu *a number of* (*eine Anzahl von*) in (24)a, bei dem eher die Funktion eines Quantifizierers vorliegt. Dieses Kriterium ist den vorliegenden Daten zufolge für Kongruenz im Englischen relevant, jedoch nicht für Kongruenz im Deutschen.

Berg (1998: 66f.) erklärt den zwischen Deutsch und Englisch vorliegenden Unterschied mit dem unterschiedlichen Stellenwert der morphosyntaktischen Komponente in beiden Sprachen: „At the heart of the agreement decision is the morpho-syntactic component. When this component is weak, the syntactic force has to yield to the semantic force [...]. However, when this component is strong, the syntactic force will easily override the semantic force [...]." Ausschlaggebend für die Semantizität des Englischen ist neben einer rigiden Wortstellung insbesondere die nur gering ausgeprägte Flexionsmorphologie (*poor inflectional morphology*, ibid.).

Die Untersuchungen von Berg (1998) sind ein schönes Beispiel dafür, dass auch in eng verwandten Sprachen wie Deutsch und Englisch die semantische Kongruenz einen unterschiedlich hohen Stellenwert haben kann.

5. Schlussfolgerungen

In der Regel stimmen die Merkmale zwischen einem Kongruenzauslöser und den mit ihm kongruierenden Elementen überein, es liegt syntaktische Kongruenz vor. Kommt es jedoch zu Merkmalskonflikten, da „nach dem Sinn" (*constructio ad sensum*) kongruiert wird, liegt semantische Kongruenz vor. Die hierfür relevanten universalen Gesetzmäßigkeiten hat Corbett mit seiner Kongruenzhierarchie in (1) (in (25) wiederholt) aufgestellt. Diese Hierarchie enthält, wie eingangs erwähnt, sowohl syntaktische Funktionen (Positionen 1 und 2) als auch lexikalische Kategorien (Positionen 3 und 4), die Positionen 1 und 3 sind NP/DP-intern, 2 und 4 hingegen NP/DP-extern, die Bezugsebenen sind für Position 1 eine lexikalische Kategorie (N) und für die anderen Positionen syntaktische Kategorien (VP, NP, S).

(25) Kongruenzhierarchie nach Corbett für Genus und Numerus
attributive > predicate > relative pronoun > personal pronoun
1 2 3 4

Als Alternative für die hier schwerpunktmäßig untersuchten Sprachen Deutsch und Englisch schlage ich in (26) eine KH vor, die nicht zuletzt aus Gründen der typologischen Vergleichbarkeit einheitlich auf semantischen Funktionen beruht:

(26) Determination < Modifikation < Restriktivität < Prädikat < Anapher

Diese KH ist um die Position der Determination erweitert, da die Unterscheidung zwischen definiter und indefiniter NP/DP für semantische Kongruenz eine entscheidende Rolle spielt, wie die Beispiele unter (20)a und (21)a zeigen. Die enge Korrelation zwischen Definitheit und Restriktivität zeigt sich am Relativpronomen, das Corbett zufolge unter typologischer Perspektive am „wenigsten wichtig" ist (vgl. Fn.1 sowie (20)b und (21)b). Das Relativpronomen kann sogar in dieser Hierarchie als ein Wendepunkt angesehen werden, da es nicht nur attributive Eigenschaften aufweist, sondern auch eine Art „Mini-Anapher" darstellt. Für beide Sprachen relevant ist die Unterscheidung zwischen restriktivem und nicht-restriktivem, „appositiven" Relativsatz ((7)b sowie (17)c), wobei semantische Kongruenz auf die nicht-restriktive Variante beschränkt ist, die wiederum weniger stark in den syntaktischen Zusammenhang eingebunden ist als die restriktive Variante. Das kann als Indiz dafür gewertet werden, dass nicht nur lineare Distanz für semantische Kongruenz ausschlaggebend ist (vgl. (5)), sondern syntaktische Fügungsenge bzw. Gebundenheit. Possessiva (6) und Personalpronomina (wie in (8)) können unter Anapher subsumiert werden.

Es wurde auch darauf hingewiesen, dass nicht nur Eigenschaften von N in seiner Funktion (i) als Subjekt für semantische Kongruenz relevant sind, sondern auch (ii) die Art des nominalen Prädikats. Für (i) sind, wie allseits bekannt, im Englischen das Merkmal [+human] (vgl. (9)) und im Swahili das Merkmal [+belebt] (vgl. (13)) relevant, aber auch im Deutschen sind diese Merkmale für die anaphorische Wiederaufnahme von Diminutivbildungen (vgl. (8)) ausschlaggebend. Für (ii) gilt, wie (19) zeigt, dass das Prädikatsnomen nur eine distributive Lesart erlaubt, semantische Kongruenz daher sogar obligatorisch ist.

Inwiefern die in (26) auf semantischen Funktionen basierende KH auch für andere typologisch unterschiedliche Sprachen Gültigkeit hat, bleibt weiterer Forschung überlassen.

Corbetts Analysen beruhen auf mehreren hundert Sprachen, und in diesem Zusammenhang ist besonders interessant, dass das Englische in Bezug auf Kongruenz auch unter dieser breiten typologischen Perspektive eine besondere Rolle spielt: „Its agreement system is at the typological extreme, particularly in the role of semantics; it should certainly not determine our approach, but it will prove very useful as a familiar language which exhibits *an exotic agreement system*“ (Corbett 2006: 32, Hervorhebung von mir, E.L.).

Bibliographie

Barlow, M. (1988): *A situated theory of agreement.* Unpublished Diss., Stanford: Stanford University.

Berg, T. (1998): The resolution of number conflicts in English and German agreement patterns. *Linguistics* 36: 41–70.

Bokamba, E. G. (1985): Verbal agreement as a noncyclic rule in Bantu. In: D. Goywaerts (Hg.), *African linguistics: Essays in memory of M.W.K. Semikenke.* Amsterdam: Benjamins, 9–54.

Brauner, S. (1979): Aktuelle Tendenzen der Entwicklung der Konkordanzbeziehungen im Swahili. *Zeitschrift für Phonetik, Sprachwissenschaft und Kommunikationsforschung* (ZPSK) 32: 422–428.

Brauner, S. und I. Herms (Hgg.) (1989): *Lehrbuch des modernen Swahili.* Leipzig: VEB Verlag Enzyklopädie.

Carstens, V. (1991): *The morphology and syntax of determiner phrases in Kiswahili.* Unpublished Diss., UCLA.

Comrie, B. (1975): Polite plurals and predicate agreement. *Language* 51: 406–418.

Corbett, G. (1979): The agreement hierarchy. *Journal of Linguistics* 15: 203–224.

Corbett, G. (1983): *Hierarchies, targets and controllers: Agreement patterns in Slavic.* London: Croom Helm.

Corbett, G. (1991): *Gender.* Cambridge: Cambridge University Press.

Corbett, G. (2000): *Number.* Cambridge: Cambridge University Press.

Corbett, G. (2006): *Agreement.* Cambridge: Cambridge University Press.

Cornish, F. (1986): *Anaphoric relations in English and French. A discourse perspective.* London: Croom Helm.

Dahl, Ö. (2000): Animacy and the notion of semantic gender. In: B. Unterbeck u.a. (Hgg.), *Gender in grammar and cognition. Approaches to gender.* Berlin/New York: de Gruyter, 99–115.

Dudenredaktion (Hg.) (2006): *Duden. Die Grammatik.* 7. Auflage. Mannheim: Dudenverlag. (= Duden 4).

Fleischer, J. (2012): *Grammatische und semantische Kongruenz in der Geschichte des Deutschen: Eine diachrone Studie zu den Kongruenzformen von ahd. wīb, nhd. Weib.* Manuskript (danach zitiert). Erscheint in: PBB.

Köpcke, K.M. und D. A. Zubin (2009): Genus. In: E. Hentschel und P. M. Vogel (Hgg.), *Deutsche Morphologie* (De Gruyter Lexikon). Berlin/New York: de Gruyter, 132–154.

Lehmann, C. (1984): *Der Relativsatz. Typologie seiner Strukturen, Theorie seiner Funktionen, Kompendium seiner Grammatik.* Tübingen: Narr.

Löbel, E. (1986): *Apposition und Komposition in der Quantifizierung. Syntaktische, semantische und morphologische Aspekte quantifizierender Nomina im Deutschen.* (=*Linguistische Arbeiten* 166). Tübingen: Niemeyer.

Löbel, E. (1997): Numerus: Funktionale Kategorie vs. syntaktische Funktion. In: E. Löbel und G. Rauh (Hgg.), *Lexikalische Kategorien und Merkmale.* (=*Linguistische Arbeiten* 366) Tübingen: Niemeyer, 87–123.

Löbel, E. (2009): Numerus. In: E. Hentschel und P. M. Vogel (Hgg.), *Deutsche Morphologie* (De Gruyter Lexikon). Berlin/New York: de Gruyter, 260–270.

Olsen, S. (1991): Die deutsche Nominalphrase als Determinansphrase. In: S. Olsen und G. Fanselow (Hgg.), *DET, COMP und INFL.* Tübingen: Niemeyer, 35–56.

Ortmann, A. (1992): Zur Auflösung von Merkmalskonflikten unter Kongruenz. Arbeiten des SFB 282. *Theorie des Lexikons* 24. Düsseldorf: Heinrich Heine Universität.

Pollard, C. und I. A. Sag (1994): *Head-driven Phrase Structure Grammar.* Chicago: University of Chicago Press.

Urbas, M. (1993): Numeruskongruenz und Numeruskonflikte in Kopulasätzen. Arbeiten des SFB 282. *Theorie des Lexikons* 38. Düsseldorf: Heinrich Heine Universität.

Weiss, D.(1993): How many sexes are there? Reflections on natural and grammatical gender in contemporary Polish and Russian. In: R. Laskowski und G. Hentschel (Hgg.), *Studies in Polish inflectional morphology and syntax. Synchronic and diachronic problems.* München: Sager, 71–105.

Selektion und Interpretation morpho-syntaktischer Einheiten*

Ilse Zimmermann

1. Zielstellung

Es geht um die Rolle morpho-syntaktischer und semantischer Information lexikalischer Einheiten in der Laut-Bedeutungs-Zuordnung sprachlicher Äußerungen. Anhand von Substantiven und Verben des Russischen wird erörtert, welche morpho-syntaktischen Merkmale und Bedeutungsanteile sie als Lexikoneinheiten haben und in die Syntax und Semantik von Sätzen einbringen. Für Kasus-, Numerus-, Tempus- und Modusflexive wird angenommen, dass ihre semantische Interpretation verzögert – mit Hilfe von leeren Köpfen – erfolgt (s. Zimmermann 1990). Die zu betrachtenden Flexive sind im Beispiel (1)a hervorgehoben. (1)b gibt die grammatisch determinierte Bedeutung von (1)a an, die Bedeutungsanteile leerer Kategorien sind markiert.

(1) a. V Potsdame vosstanavliva**et**sja gorodskoj dvorec kvalificirovann**ymi** rabоč**imi**.
in Potsdam wird wiedererrichtet (das) Stadtschloss (von) qualifizierten Arbeitern
b. **ASSERT** **^∃s [[~[t <** $\mathbf{t^0}$**]]** ∧ [[**∃!y** [[STADTSCHLOSS y] ∧ [[t ⊆ τ(s)] ∧
[s INST [WIEDERERRICHTEN y x]]]] ∧ **∃z** [[[**|z| ≥ 2]** ∧ [[ARBEITER z] ∧
[QUALIFIZIERT z]]] ∧ **[**$\mathbf{R_{adv}}$ **z s**]]] ∧ [loc(s) ⊂ POTSDAM]]]

2. Grammatiktheoretische Grundannahmen

Die Analyse bewegt sich im Rahmen eines minimalistischen Konzepts der Laut-Bedeutungs-Zuordnung. Wesentlich dabei ist die Unterscheidung von grammatisch determinierter Bedeutungsrepräsentation SF und ihrer Interpretation auf der Ebene der konzeptuellen Struktur CS (s. Bierwisch und Lang 1987, Dölling 1997, Bierwisch 2007, Lang 2011).

Eine ganz zentrale Rolle in der Laut-Bedeutungs-Zuordnung kommt dem Lexikon zu, und zwar für die Interrelierung phonologischer, morpho-syntaktischer und semantischer Struktureinheiten. Die Arbeit verfolgt ein lexikalistisches Morphologiekonzept, dem zufolge

---

* Für hilfreiche Diskussion danke ich Johannes Dölling, Elena Gorishneva, Radek Šimik und den Teilnehmern des Kolloquiums zur slavistischen Linguistik an der Georg-August-Universität Göttingen, wo ich am 27.6.2012 wesentliche Teile dieser Arbeit vorgetragen habe.

derivierte und flektierte Wortformen im Lexikon repräsentiert sind und als elementare Bausteine in die Syntax eingehen (z.B. (2)-(3)).[1]

(2) $[_{N+max}\,[_{N}$ raboč] **imi**]

(3) $[_{V+max}\,[_{V+max}\,[_{V}\,[_{V}\,[_{V}$ voz [stanavl']] ivaj] **et**] sja]

Das Flexiv *-imi* in (2) markiert den Instrumental. Das Flexiv *-et* in (3) kennzeichnet die dritte Person Singular des Indikativs im Präsens.

Mit Pitsch (2012) nehme ich an, dass Flexive, sofern sie mit Bedeutungsanteilen assoziiert sind, nur als deren Schatten anzusehen sind. Die jeweilige Bedeutung selbst kommt erst durch leere Köpfe ins Spiel, die das flektierte Wort c-kommandieren und bestimmte morpho-syntaktische Merkmale desselben c-selegieren.

Syntaktische Kategorien X^i ($0 \leq i \leq$ '') sind Projektionen lexikalischer und funktionaler Kategorien. Modifikatoren schließen sich an passende Modifikanden als Adjunkte an. Das heißt, die Merkmale des Modifikanden setzen sich durch; vgl. Chomsky 2011, der sich diesbezüglich nicht festlegt. (4)a und (4)b geben für Sätze und Nominalgruppen die angenommenen Strukturschichten an.[2]

(4) Syntaktische Basisstrukturen
a. (PP) CP ModP TP PolP vP* VP
b. DP NumP NP

Bezüglich der Bedeutung lexikalischer Einheiten zeigen (5) und (6) in allgemeiner Form die Argumentstruktur und die Prädikat-Argument-Struktur von Substantiven und Adjektiven sowie von Verben.

(5) Schema der Bedeutungsstruktur von Substantiven und Adjektiven
$\lambda x_n \ldots \lambda x_1 [\ldots x_n \ldots x_1 \ldots]$

λx_1 ist die referentielle Argumentstelle von Substantiven. In referierenden Substantivgruppen wird sie durch die funktionale Kategorie D gebunden.

(6) Schema der Bedeutungsstruktur von Verben
$\lambda x_n \ldots \lambda x_1 \lambda s\, [[t\ R_{asp} \supseteq/\subseteq \tau(s)] \wedge [s\ \text{INST}\, [\ldots x_n \ldots x_1 \ldots]]]$
mit $\tau \in \langle e,e\rangle$, R_{asp}, $\supseteq$, $\subseteq\, \in \langle e,\langle e,t\rangle\rangle$, INST $\in \langle t,\langle e,t\rangle\rangle$

λx_i ($1 \leq i \leq n$) sind die Partizipantenargumentstellen.[3] λs ist die referentielle, auf Situationen Bezug nehmende Argumentstelle von Verben. Das Topikzeitargument t ist das hierarchisch höchste Argument von Verben und kann durch Tempus und/oder temporale Modifikatoren spezifiziert werden. Es ist durch den Aspekt auf die Situationszeit $\tau(s)$ bezogen. (6) macht deutlich, dass Aspekt inhärenter Bestandteil der Bedeutungsstruktur von Verben ist.

---

1 αmax bezeichnet wortstrukturelle Projektionen.

2 Haider (2010) sieht keine Evidenz, zwischen CP und vP irgendwelche funktionalen Strukturetagen anzunehmen.

3 Von unpersönlichen Verben wie *smerkat'sja* (*dämmern)* wird hier abgesehen.

Kategoriale Selektion (c-selection) ist durch Indizierung von Argumentstellen repräsentiert, z.B. $\lambda x_{<+R+P>}$ als Kasusanforderung[4] an einen dativischen nichtstrukturellen Argumentausdruck wie bei *pacientu* (*dem Patienten*) als Objekt von *pomogat'* (*helfen*). Die Erfüllung solcher Anforderungen gilt als erfolgreiches feature checking. Argumentstellen für strukturelle Argumente haben keine Indizes. Die betreffenden Anforderungen sind vorhersagbar (s. Zimmermann 2002).

Es wird mit phonologisch leeren Köpfen gerechnet, die Bedeutungsanteile liefern und bestimmte morpho-syntaktische Merkmale selegieren, die Affixen lexikalischer Köpfe oder Partikeln zugeordnet sein können. Außerdem werden semantische Templates (*type shifts*) in der Verknüpfung von Bedeutungskomponenten angenommen.

3. Die Analyse

Die folgende Analyse konzentriert sich zunächst auf den Beispielsatz (1), dessen Syntax in (1)c angegeben ist. Alle darin figurierenden leeren Kategorien und die hervorgehobenen Flexive werden beleuchtet werden.

(1) c. [$_{CP}$ [$_{PP}$ V Potsdame]$_i$ [$_{C'}$ ∅ [$_{ModP}$ ∅ [$_{TP}$ ∅ [$_{PolP}$ ∅ [$_{vP}$ [$_{vP}$ [$_{vP}$ vosstanavliva**ets**ja$_j$ [$_{VP}$ [$_{DP}$ [$_{D'}$ ∅ [$_{NumP}$ ∅ [$_{NP}$[$_{AP}$ gorodskoj][$_{NP}$ dvorec]]]]] [$_{V'}$ t$_j$]]] [$_{PP}$ ∅ [$_{DP}$ [$_{D'}$ ∅ [$_{NumP}$ ∅ [$_{NP}$[$_{AP}$ kvalificirovann**ymi**][$_{NP}$ rabo**č**imi]]]]]] t$_i$]]]]]][5]

3.1. Adverbielle Kasus

Wie bekommt die Instrumentalphrase *kvalificirovannymi rabočimi* in (1) ihre modifikatorische adverbielle Bedeutung (vgl. Zimmermann 2003)?

Kasusflexive an sich haben keine Bedeutung. Eine Instrumentalphrase kann im Russischen ohne weiteres als obliques Komplement von Verben wie z.B. *zanimat'sja* (*sich beschäftigen mit*) auftreten. Im Beispiel (1) jedoch hat die Instrumentalphrase adverbielle Bedeutung. Diese erhält sie durch eine phonologisch leere Präposition. Bedeutungshaltige Präpositionen sind Relationsausdrücke, die Terme als Komplement haben. Die NP muss semantisch entsprechend angepasst werden. Das bewerkstelligt ein Zeroartikel. Schließlich müssen in der hier betrachteten NP noch Modifikator und Modifikand verknüpft werden, was durch ein Template geschieht. Und die Pluralbedeutung der NP muss berücksichtigt werden und wird durch einen funktionalen Zerokopf ins Spiel gebracht.

Die Ingredienzien des Modifikators *kvalificirovannymi rabočimi* sind in (7)–(12) angegeben, (13) ist die resultierende Bedeutungsstruktur.

(7) Syntax
[$_{PP}$ ∅ [$_{DP}$ ∅ [$_{NumP}$ ∅ [$_{NP}$ [$_{AP}$ kvalificirovannymi][$_{NP}$ rabočimi]]]]]

---

[4] Die russischen Kasus werden nach Jakobson durch die Merkmale αR(ichtung), βP(eripherie), γU(mfang) unterschieden (s. Zimmermann 2002).

[5] In SpecC figurierende Einheiten und finite Verben werden in ihrer Basisposition interpretiert.

(8) Der lexikalische Kopf *rabočimi*[6]

a. /raboč/; αV+N–max; λx [ARBEITER x]

b. /-imi/; +pl+P–R–U+max; $\lambda P_{<\alpha V+N>}$ [P]

Das Pluralsuffix *-imi* bringt das morpho-syntaktische Merkmal +pl, die Kasusmerkmale +P–R–U und die wortstrukturelle Information +max ein und selegiert einen nominalen Stamm, ohne dessen Bedeutung zu verändern.

(9) Modifikationstemplate[7]

TS_{MODIF}: $\lambda Q_{2(<agr>)\alpha}\, \lambda Q_{1(<agr>)\beta}\, \lambda x\, [[Q_1\, x] \wedge [Q_2\, x]]$

mit $Q_1, Q_2 \in$ <e,t> und $\alpha = + \rightarrow \beta = +$

agr steht abkürzend für Genus-, Numerus- und Kasusmerkmale.

Das Modikationstemplate verknüpft die Bedeutungen des Modifikators Q_2 und des Modifikanden Q_1 und verlangt zwischen ihnen Kongruenz bezüglich Genus, Kasus, Numerus, sofern der Modifikator solche Kongruenzmerkmale hat. Das ist in dem hier analysierten Beispiel der Fall.

(10) Pluralbedeutung

/∅/; +Num; $\lambda P_{<+plur+N>}\, \lambda x\, [[|x| \geq 2] \wedge [P\, x]]$

mit $P \in$ <e,t>, $\geq \in$ <e,<e,t>>

Bevor die NP mit einem Determinierer verbunden wird, kommt ihre Numerusbedeutung zur Geltung. Die funktionale Zeroeinheit selegiert ein mit +plur+N gekennzeichnetes Komplement und fügt seiner SF die Pluralbedeutung hinzu.

(11) Zeroartikel

/∅/; +Dαdef; $\lambda P_1 \lambda P_2 \exists(!)_\alpha\, x\, [[P_1\, x] \wedge [P_2\, x]]$

mit $P_1, P_2 \in$ <e,t>

Der Zeroartikel überführt die NumP-Bedeutung in einen generalisierten Quantor, der als Argument fungieren kann.

(12) Adverbielle Zeropräposition

/∅/; –V–N; $\lambda y_{<+P>}\, \lambda x\, [R_{adv}\, y\, x]$

mit $R_{adv} \in$ <e,<e,t>> und $R_{adv} \in$ {AGENS, MITTEL, ...}

Die Zeropräposition liefert eine anonyme adverbielle Relation, die in CS kontextabhängig als Agens, Mittel usw. spezifiziert werden kann. Der Argumentstellenindex <+P> ist die Kasusanforderung an die Instrumentalphrase.

(13) Die SF des adverbiellen Modifikators

||kvalificirovannymi rabočimi|| = $\lambda x\, \exists z\, [[[|z| \geq 2] \wedge$ [[ARBEITER z] $\wedge$ [QUALIFIZIERT z]]] $\wedge$ $[R_{adv}\, z\, x]]$

---

6 Das Nomen *rabočij* (*Arbeiter*) kann adjektivisch und substantivisch gebraucht werden. Es hat eine adjektivische Flexion, genau wie *kvalificirovannyj* (*qualifiziert*).

7 Siehe Zimmermann (1992).

In CS wird bei agentiven Verben wie in (1) der Parameter R_{adv} des Modifikators mit A-GENS spezifiziert und der Parameter x des passivierten Verbs mit z identifiziert.

3.2. Aspekt, Tempus und Modus

Finite Verbformen wie in (1) kommen mit TAM-Kennzeichnungen und entsprechenden morpho-syntaktischen Merkmalen aus dem Lexikon.

(14) $[_{V+max} [_{V+max} [_{V} [_{V} [_{V}$ voz [stanavl']] ivaj] et] sja]; +V–N–pf–prät–imp–konj;
$\lambda y_{<I-II-pl>} \lambda s$ [[t $\subseteq \tau(s)$] $\wedge$ [s INST [WIEDERERRICHTEN y x]]]

Das externe Argument x von *vosstanavlivat'* ist durch das Reflexivannex *sja* blockiert.[8] λy wird in (1) durch die DP *gorodskoj dvorec* spezifiziert. Die Argumentstelle λs für die bezeichnete Situation steht als Ansatzpunkt für die Modifikationen *kvalificirovannymi rabočimi* und *v Potsdame* zur Verfügung.

Im Gegensatz zu Tempus und Modus ist die Aspektbedeutung in der SF der angegebenen Verbform repräsentiert.[9] Die Interpretation des Tempus- und Modusflexivs erfolgt aus Skopusgründen verzögert.

Das Suffix *-et* der Verbform *vosstanavlivaetsja* ist im Lexikon folgendermaßen repräsentiert (vgl. Pitsch 2012):

(15) /-et/; –prät–imp–konj+max; $\lambda P_{<+V-N\alpha pf>}\ \lambda x_{<-I-II-pl>}\ \lambda s$ [P x s]

Das Suffix versieht das bezüglich Aspekt spezifizierte Verb mit Tempus- und Modusmerkmalen sowie mit Person- und Numerusmerkmalen, bezüglich derer das externe Argument des Verbs zu kongruieren hat.[10] Außer den von *-et* gelieferten Merkmalen und dem ergänzten Suffix ändert sich an der betroffenen Verbform nichts. Tempus- und Modusbedeutungsanteile kommen erst durch funktionale Operatoren hinzu, die auf die Tempus- und Modusmerkmale selektiv Bezug nehmen.

Mit all diesen Komponenten gehen die Konstituenten in die Syntax ein. Es ergibt sich die vP des Beispiels (1) (zur Syntax s. (1)c).

(16) Die SF von vP
||vP|| = λs [[∃!y [[STADTSCHLOSS y] ∧ [[t $\subseteq \tau(s)$] ∧ [s INST [WIEDERERICHTEN y x]]]] ∧ ∃z [[[ARBEITER z] ∧ [QUALIFIZIERT z]] ∧ [R_{adv} z s]]] ∧ [loc(s) ⊂ POTSDAM]]

Bei affirmativen Sätzen wie in (1) liefert der Zerokopf der die vP dominierenden Polaritätsphrase keinen zusätzlichen Bedeutungsbeitrag. Bei negierten Sätzen kommt die Negation –

---

8 Die bei imperfektiven Verben durch das Reflexivannex angezeigte Passivierung des Verbs findet im Lexikon statt.

9 Das bedeutet, dass der Parameter R_{asp} durch die Aspektaffixe als ⊇- bzw.⊆-Relation zwischen t und τ(s) bereits auf der Wortebene spezifiziert wird. Bei Nominalisierungen wie *vosstanovlenie* (*Wiederrichtung*) bleibt R_{asp} unspezifiziert und geht als Parameter in CS ein.

10 Ich nehme nicht an, dass Person- und Numeruskongruenz und Nominativlizensierung in IP (oder in TP bzw. ModP) erfolgen.

als verzögerte Interpretation der an V adjungierten Partikel *ne* (s. unten) – hinzu und nimmt die vP-Bedeutung in ihren Skopus.

(17) /∅/; +Pol; $\lambda P_{(<+neg>)\alpha}\lambda s(\sim)_\alpha$ [P s]
mit $\sim \in$ <t,t>, $P \in$ <e,t>

In affirmativen Sätzen ist die SF der PolP[11] mit der SF von vP identisch.

Die leeren funktionalen Köpfe von TP, ModP und CP, die PolP in ihren Skopus nehmen, bringen spezifische Bedeutungskomponenten in die Satzstruktur ein und c-selegieren ihr jeweiliges Komplement, und zwar Merkmale, die dessen lexikalischer Kopf aus dem Lexikon mitbringt oder ihm durch Partikel wie die Negation *ne* hinzugefügt sind. Die mit diesen Merkmalen assoziierten Morpheme werden durch die Bedeutung des jeweiligen funktionalen Kopfs verzögert semantisch interpretiert.

Der funktionale Tempusoperator basiert auf einem der Lexikoneinträge in (18).

(18) Tempus
a. /∅/; +T; $\lambda P_{<-\alpha\text{prät}-\text{konj}>}\lambda t\ [[(\sim)_\alpha\ [t < t^0]] \wedge [P\ t]]$
mit $P \in$ <e,t>, $< \in$ <e,<e,t>>
b. /∅/; +T; $\lambda P_{<+\text{konj}>}\lambda t$ [P t]

Tempus nimmt Bezug auf die Topikzeit t in Relation zur Äußerungszeit t^0 (s. Reichenbach 1947, Klein 1994). Die Topikzeit wird durch den Aspekt zur Ereigniszeit in Beziehung gesetzt (s. (6)). An die Argumentstelle λt können temporale Modifikatoren angeknüpft werden. Die in (18)a angegebene Relation zwischen t und t^0 ist mit dem morpho-syntaktischen Merkmalen +/–prät–konj korreliert und deckt die Bedeutung der entsprechenden Flexive perfektiver wie imperfektiver Verben ab.[12] (18)b mit Bezug auf das morpho-syntaktische Merkmal +konj trägt der Tatsache Rechnung, dass der Konjunktiv im Russischen keine Tempusbedeutung signalisiert.[13]

Um die SF von T auf dessen Komplement anwenden zu können oder temporale Modifikatoren von TP mittels des Modifikationstemplates (9) integrieren zu können, muss auf die SF von PolP die Lambdaabstraktion (19) angewendet werden.

(19) TS_{LA}: $\lambda p \lambda t$ [p]

Die TP ist das Komplement des funktionalen Kopfes Mod. (20) repräsentiert seinen Lexikoneintrag für den Indikativ (s. Zimmermann 2009, 2010).

---

[11] PolP mit und ohne Negation ist die typische Adjunktionsstelle für Satzadverbien wie *verojatno* (*wahrscheinlich*) oder *kak izvestno* (*wie bekannt/bekanntlich*).

[12] Für perfektive Verben gilt das Bedeutungspostulat (i), das präsentische Interpretation ausschließt.
(i) $\forall P \forall s \forall t\ [[[t \supseteq \tau(s)] \wedge [P\ s]] \rightarrow [[\sim[t \supseteq t^0]] \wedge [[t \supseteq \tau(s)] \wedge [P\ s]]]]$
Für imperfektive Verben kommt in CS aktuelles bzw. nichtaktuelles Präsens wie auch nichtanalytisches Futur als Interpretation in Frage, wie z.B. in *Čto ty delaješ' segodnja večerom?* (*Was machst du heute Abend?*).

[13] Zur Quelle der morpho-syntaktischen Merkmale +prät und +konj siehe unten.

(20) Modus: der Indikativ
$/\varnothing/$; +Mod; $\lambda P_{<\text{-imp-konj}>}\exists s\ [P\ s\ t]$
mit $P \in <e,<e,t>>$

Modus bzw. C oder intensionale Prädikate stellen den Bezug auf Welten w her, die je nach Kontext zu charakteristischen mentalen Modellen gehören, z.B. $[w \in M_{\text{epist/desid}}\ sp]$ für den Indikativ bzw. Imperativ in Hauptsätzen (s. Lohnstein 2000). (20) gibt die unmarkierte, indikativische Modusbedeutung an, durch die die temporale Argumentstelle blockiert und das referentielle Argument s existenzquantifiziert wird.

(21) ist der Lexikoneintrag für den funktionalen Kopf C in Hauptsätzen. Er charakterisiert den assertiven Illokutionstyp.

(21) Illokutionstyp: Assertion
$/\varnothing/$; +C+force–quest; $\lambda p_{<\text{–imp}>}$ [ASSERT $^\wedge$p]
mit ASSERT $\in <<s,t>,a>$, $^\wedge \in <t,<s,t>>$
und $[^\wedge p] \equiv \lambda w\ [[^\wedge p]\ w]$ bzw. $\lambda w\ [w \in {}^\wedge p]$ und $w \in s$

Mit Krifka (2001) nehme ich an, dass Hauptsätze dem semantischen Typ a angehören und Sprechakttypen bezeichnen. Der assertive Operator ASSERT intensionalisiert sein propositionales Komplement.

Da der in (14) angegebene lexikalische Kopf *vosstanavlivaetsja* die Merkmale –prät–imp–konj hat, sind die selektionalen Anforderungen der funktionalen Köpfe (18), (20) und (21) für Tempus, Modus und Illokutionstyp erfüllt und es ergibt sich die in (1)b repräsentierte SF von (1).

(1) b. **ASSERT** $^\wedge$**∃s [[~[t < t⁰]]** ∧ [[∃!y [[STADTSCHLOSS y] ∧ [[t ⊆ τ(s)] ∧
[s INST [WIEDERERRICHTEN y x]]]] ∧ **∃z [[[|z| ≥ 2]** ∧ [[ARBEITER z] ∧
[QUALIFIZIERT z]]] ∧ **[R_{adv} z s]**]] ∧ [loc(s) ⊂ POTSDAM]]]

Die in (1)b enthaltenen Parameter in Gestalt ungebundener Variablen, t, x und R_{adv}, werden in CS existenzquantifiziert bzw. spezifiziert.

Die Bedeutungspostulate (22)a und (22)b liefern in CS den Bezug auf dem Illokutionstyp ASSERT entsprechende mentale Modelle des Sprechers (vgl. Truckenbrodt 2006 a, b).

(22) a. $\forall^\wedge p\ [[\text{ASSERT}\ ^\wedge p] \rightarrow [^\wedge p \cap M_{EP}\ sp]]$
b. $\forall^\wedge p\ [[\text{ASSERT}\ ^\wedge p] \rightarrow \exists w'[[w' \in M_{VOLIT}\ sp] \wedge [w' \in {}^\wedge p \cap CG]]]$

Für Assertionen gilt, dass die assertierte Proposition dem epistemischen Modell des Sprechers angehört und er möchte, dass sie auch dem common ground CG angehört.

Das Gesagte zeigt sich auch in dem Beispiel (23) mit einer Temporalbestimmung, der Negation und einer präteritalen Verbform im Indikativ.

(23) a. **Pri GDR** gorodskoj dvorec **ne** vosstanavlivalsja.
in der DDR (das) Stadtschloss nicht wurde wiedererrichtet
b. $[_{CP}$ Pri GDR$_i$ $[_{C'}\varnothing$ $[_{ModP}\ \varnothing$ $[_{TP}$ t$_i$ $[_{TP}\ \varnothing$ $[_{PolP}$ $[_{DP}\ \varnothing$ $[_{NP}$ gorodskoj dvorec]]$_j$ $[_{PolP}\ \varnothing$ $[_{VP}$ t$_j$
$[_{V}$ ne $[_{V}$ vostanavlivalsja]]]]]]]]]]
c. ASSERT $^\wedge$∃s [[**[t < t⁰]** ∧ [∃!y [[STADTSCHLOSS y] ∧ [~[[t ⊆ τ(s)] ∧ [s INST
[WIEDERERRICHTEN y x]]]]]] ∧ **[t ⊆ τ(GDR)]**]

(23)b und (23)c sind die syntaktische und semantische Struktur des Beispiels und zeigen die angenommenen Skopusverhältnisse der Komponenten. Der temporale Modifikator nimmt als Adjunkt von TP das Präteritum, das an PolP adjungierte Subjekt und die Negation in seinen Skopus.[14] Seine SF ist in (24) angegeben.

(24) Die Temporalangabe
$||\text{pri GDR}|| = \lambda t\ [t \subseteq \tau(\text{DDR})]$

(24) besagt, dass die Topikzeit t in der Existenzzeit der DDR unecht enthalten ist.

Durch das Modifikationstemplate (9) ergibt sich die Verknüpfung dieses Modifikators mit der Bedeutung des Modifikanden, der TP mit dem funktionalen Kopf T. Dessen Bedeutung ist in (18)a repräsentiert und ist an die morpho-syntaktischen Merkmale +prät–konj geknüpft, die durch das Suffix *-l* der finiten Verbform *vosstanavlivalsja* eingebracht werden (s. (25)).

(25) /-l/; +prätαkonj–max; $\lambda P_{<+V-N>}$ [P]

Dieses Formativ ist semantisch eine identische Abbildung. Nur im Indikativ wird das Suffix *-l* in T präterital interpretiert (s. (18)a).[15]

3.3. Der Konjunktiv

Der russische Konjunktiv ist in Isačenko (1962) und in der Akademiegrammatik (RG 1980) ausführlich beschrieben. Die folgende Analyse ist wesentlich angeregt durch Kratzer (1992a, b). Es wird der Beispielsatz (26)a betrachtet, dessen syntaktische Struktur (26)b und (26)b' unterschiedliche Positionen der Konjunktivpartikel *by* deutlich macht. Die hervorgehobenen Struktureinheiten sind Schwerpunkt der folgenden Analyse.

(26) a. **Pri GDR by**$_{\alpha}$ gorodskoj dvorec ne vosstanavliva**l**sja **by**$_{-\alpha}$.
in der DDR (das) Stadtschloss nicht würde wiedererrichtet werden
b. $[_{CP}$ Pri GDR$_i$ $[_{C'}$ ∅ $[_{ModP}$ t$_i$ $[_{ModP}$ ∅ $[_{TP}$ ∅ $[_{PolP}$ $[_{DP}$ ∅ $[_{NP}$ gorodskoj dvorec]]$_j$ $[_{PolP}$ ∅
$[_{VP}$ t$_j$ $[_{V'}$ $[_{V}$ $[_{V}$ ne $[_{V}$ vostanavlivalsja]] by]]]]]]]]]]
b'. $[_{CP}$ Pri GDR$_i$ $[_{C'}$ ∅ $[_{ModP}$ t$_i$ $[_{ModP}$ by $[_{TP}$ ∅ $[_{PolP}$ $[_{DP}$ ∅ $[_{NP}$ gorodskoj dvorec]]$_j$ $[_{PolP}$ ∅
$[_{VP}$ t$_j$ $[_{V'}$ $[_{V}$ ne $[_{V}$ vostanavlivalsja]]]]]]]]]]

Die in SpecC platzierte PP *pri GDR* wird hier als Adjunkt von ModP konditional interpretiert.

Die Partikel *by* kennzeichnet im Russischen zusammen mit der Präteritalform des finiten Verbs oder mit dem Infinitiv den Konjunktiv.[16] Sie tritt enklitisch zum finiten Verb oder

---

[14] Sätze wie *V ijune dolgo ne šël dožd'* (*Im Juni hat es lange nicht geregnet*) verdeutlichen die Skopusverhältnisse von TP und PolP besonders deutlich. Es geht in diesem Beispiel um eine Situation des Nichtregnens, die im Juni bestand und lange dauerte.

[15] Das Suffix *-l* in (25) ist sprachhistorisch ein Partizipialformativ, an das Genus- und Numerussuffixe angefügt werden.

[16] Kombinationen der Partikel *by* mit noch anderen Verbformen sind hier nicht berücksichtigt.

figuriert als Kopf von ModP, wo sie auch interpretiert wird und an C bzw. an eine XP klitisiert.

(27) Modus: der Konjunktiv
/*by*/∅/, C/XP__; +Mod; $\lambda P_{<+\text{prät+konj/-fin-part}>}$ $\exists s$ [P s t]; ~[^$\exists s$ [P s t] $\cap$ M_{EP} u]
mit P $\in$ <e,<e,t>>

Der Konjunktiv fügt an die Indikativbedeutung (s. (20)) ~[^$\exists s$ [P s t] $\cap$ M_{EP} u] als Präsupposition an, die besagt, dass dem epistemischen Modell des modalen Subjekts u die Proposition ^$\exists s$ [P s t] nicht angehört. Dieser funktionale Konjunktivkopf ist als +Mod kategorisiert und selegiert entweder ein finites Komplement mit den morpho-syntaktischen Merkmalen +prät+konj oder eine Infinitivphrase wie in der finalen PP *dlja togo čtoby vosstanovit' gorodskoj dvorec* (*um das Stadtschloss wiederzuerrichten*), wo das Konjunktivformativ *by* an die Konjunktion *čto* klitisiert ist. Solche Infinitivkomplemente bleiben im Folgenden außer Betracht.

Das Zeroformativ in (27) tritt auf, wenn die Partikel *by* dem finiten Verb adjungiert wird (s. (26)b) und die präteritale Verbform mit der Kennzeichnung +prät+konj selegiert. Die semantische Interpretation der Partikel *by* findet dann verzögert, in ModP, statt. (28) beinhaltet den Lexikoneintrag der Konjunktivpartikel *by*, die ein Verb als phonologischen Wirt und eine flektierte Verbform mit der Kennzeichnung +prät+konj verlangt. Semantisch ist die Partikel leer.

(28) /by/, V__; $\lambda P_{<+\text{prät+konj+max}>}$ [P]

Da TP im Konjunktiv keine Tempusbedeutung beisteuert, wird der temporale Bezug ausschließlich kontextuell hergestellt. Die Präteritalform des Verbs bedeutet im Konjunktiv nicht Präteritum, s. (18)b. Im Beispiel (26) liefern der Modifikator *pri GDR* und unser Weltwissen die richtige Interpretation.

Für die konditionale Lesart des Modifikators ist das besondere Template (29) erforderlich, das auf die Topikzeit Bezug nimmt.[17]

(29) $TS_{MODIF'}$: $\lambda Q_1 \lambda Q_2 \forall t\ [[Q_1\ t] \rightarrow [Q_2\ t]]$
mit Q_1, $Q_2 \in$ <e,t>

Zusammen mit den leeren Köpfen Mod und C ergibt sich die SF (26)c'.

(26) c'. ASSERT ^$\forall t$ [[t $\subseteq$ τ(DDR)] $\rightarrow$ $\exists s \exists ! y$ [[STADTSCHLOSS y] $\wedge$ [~[[t $\subseteq$ τ(s)$\wedge$ [s INST [WIEDERERRICHTEN y x]]]]]]; ~[^$\exists s \exists ! y$ [[STADTSCHLOSS y] $\wedge$ [~[[t $\subseteq$ τ(s)] $\wedge$ [s INST [WIEDERERRICHTEN y x]]]]] $\cap$ M_{EP} sp]

Da die DDR nicht mehr existiert, das Stadtschloss gerade wiedererrichtet wird und die durch den Konjunktiv ausgedrückte Präsupposition auf den Sprecher zutrifft, gilt für ihn die CS (30),

(30) $\forall w$ [[w $\in$ M_{epist} sp] $\rightarrow$ [w $\in$ ^$\forall t \exists s$ [[~[t < t^0]] $\wedge$ [[$\exists ! y$ [[STADTSCHLOSS y] $\wedge$ [[t $\subseteq$ τ(s)] $\wedge$ [s INST [WIEDERERRICHTEN y x]]]]$_p$ $\rightarrow$ ~[t $\subseteq$ τ(DDR)]$_q$]]

[17] Damit Q_2 in (29) Prädikatstatus hat, muss auf die SF des Modifikanden TS_{LA} (s. (17)) angewendet werden.

wobei p mit der Präsensbedeutung[18] und ~q dem Weltwissen des Sprechers entsprechen und sich [p → ~ q] daraus und aus der Assertion (23) [q → ~p'] mit p' ohne Tempuscharakterisierung ableiten lässt. Der Konjunktiv in (23) zeigt diese Nichtkorrespondenz zwischen SF und CS in Bezug auf p in allgemeiner Form an. Bezüglich q ist sie nicht ausgedrückt.

Der konditionale Nebensatz in (27) mit dem Konjunktiv drückt dagegen die betreffende Nichtkorrespondenz mit dem epistemischen Modell des Sprechers aus. (28) ist die SF dieses Satzgefüges. (29) beinhaltet den Lexikoneintrag für die konditionale Konjunktion *esli* (*wenn*).

(27) Esli **by**$_{\alpha}$ GDR eščë suščestvova**l**a by$_{-\alpha}$, gorodskoj dvorec ne vosstanavliva**l**sja **by**.
wenn (die) DDR noch existieren würde, das Stadtschloss nicht wiedererrichtet werden würde

(28) ASSERT ^∀t∃t' [[t ⊆ t'] ∧ ∃s' [[t' ⊆ τ(s')] ∧ [s' INST [EXISTIEREN DDR]]]] → ∃s∃!y [[STADTSCHLOSS y] ∧ ~[[[[t ⊆ τ(s)] ∧ [s INST [WIEDERERICHTEN y x]]]]; ~[^∃t∃s∃!y [[STADTSCHLOSS y] ∧ ~[[[t ⊆ τ(s)] ∧ [s INST [WIEDERERRICHTEN y x]]]]] ∩ M_{EP} sp] ∧ ~[^∃t'∃s' [[t' ⊆ τ(s')] ∧ [s' INST [EXISTIEREN DDR]]] ∩ M_{EP} sp]

(29) /esli/; –V–N+C; $\lambda P_{1<\alpha konj>}\lambda P_{2<\alpha konj>}\forall t\exists t'$ [[t ⊆ t'] ∧ [P_1 t']] → [P_2 t]
mit $P_1, P_2 \in$ <e,t>

Wie das Template (26) bezieht die Konjunktion *esli* zwei Prädikate auf die Topikzeit t und allquantifiziert diese Variable. Die beiden Prädikate kongruieren im Modus.[19] Syntaktisch ist die Konjunktion als Fusion aus P und C kategorisiert. Ihr Komplement ist ModP. Die beiden jeweils durch den Konjunktiv der Teilsätze hinzugefügten Präsuppositionen machen klar, in Bezug auf welche Komponenten des Satzgefüges Dissenz bezüglich dessen, was der Sprecher weiß, besteht, nämlich dass die DDR nicht mehr existiert und dass das Stadtschloss wiedererrichtet wird.

4. Zusammenfassung und Ausblick

In der Analyse bewährt sich deutlich die Unterscheidung von SF und CS. Neu an der Analyse gegenüber meinen früheren Arbeiten sind der Bezug auf Welten, die Behandlung des Konjunktivs und der Negation im Russischen und die Vereinheitlichung verzögerter semantischer Interpretation morpho-syntaktischer Formative im nominalen und verbalen Bereich. Die angenommenen leeren Köpfe sind eine Konsequenz der Repräsentation von Wortformen im Lexikon. Die Arbeit folgt der Annahme, dass Flexive Lieferanten von morpho-syn-

---

[18] Die präsentische Interpretation der Konjunktivform *vosstanavlivalsja by*, die selbst nicht Tempusunterschiede signalisiert, ist wegen des imperfektiven Aspekts in CS möglich.

[19] In Zimmermann (2009) wird angeführt, dass wie im Deutschen auch in slawischen Sprachen imperativische Propositionen anstelle des konditionalen Nebensatzes auftreten können.

taktischen Merkmalen sind, die durch Operatoren selegiert und semantisch interpretiert werden. Auch für bestimmte Partikeln trifft dies zu.

Der Ausarbeitung harren die anderen Illokutionstypen, weitere konditionale Ausdruckstypen, die Selektion von Komplementsätzen mit dem Konjunktiv, die allgemeinen Funktionsweisen der Negation, die Parallelitäten von verbalem Modus und Determinierern sowie die Prüfung der Möglichkeiten, mit einer Syntax fast ohne leere funktionale Kategorien wie bei Haider (2010) zurechtzukommen.

Die vorgeschlagene, auf das Russische bezogene Analyse schließt nicht aus, dass sie im Prinzip auch für andere Sprachen – je nach deren morpho-syntaktischen Gegebenheiten – Gültigkeit haben kann.

Ich widme diese Arbeit Susan Olsen, mit der mich mehr als zwei Jahrzehnte enge Freundschaft und viel gemeinsames Nachdenken über die durch komplexe Wörter signalisierten syntaktischen und semantischen Informationen und über die unverzichtbare Unterscheidung zwischen SF und CS verbinden.

Bibliographie

Bierwisch, M. (2007): Semantic Form as interface. In: A. Späth (Hg.), *Interfaces and interface conditions* [Language, Context, and Cognition 6], Berlin/New York: de Gruyter, 1–32.

Bierwisch, M. und E. Lang (Hgg.) (1987): *Grammatische und konzeptuelle Aspekte von Dimensionsadjektiven* [Studia grammatica 25+26], Berlin: Akademie-Verlag. English version 1989: *Dimensional adjectives: Grammatical structure and conceptual interpretation* [Springer Series in Language and Communication 26], Berlin/Heidelberg/New York: Springer-Verlag.

Brandt, M., M. Reis, I. Rosengren und I. Zimmermann (1992): Satztyp, Satzmodus und Illokution. In: I. Rosengren (Hg.), *Satz und Illokution* [Linguistische Arbeiten 278], Band 1. Tübingen: Niemeyer, 1–90.

Dölling, J. (1997): Semantic Form and abductive fixation of parameters. In: R. van der Sandt, R. Blutner und M. Bierwisch (Hgg.), *From underspecification to interpretation*. Working Papers of the Institute of Logic and Linguistics Heidelberg, 113–139.

Chomsky, N. (2012): Problems of projection. Erscheint in: *Lingua*.

Haider, H. (2010): *The syntax of German*. Cambridge: CUP.

Isačenko, A. V. (1962): *Die russische Sprache der Gegenwart. Formenlehre*. Halle (Saale): VEB Max Niemeyer Verlag.

Klein, W. (1994): *Time in language*. London/New York: Routledge.

Kratzer, A. (1991a): Modality. In: A. von Stechow und D. Wunderlich (Hgg.), *Semantik. Ein internationales Handbuch der zeitgenössischen Forschung* [Handbücher zur Sprach- und Kommunikationswissenschaft 6], Berlin/New York: de Gruyter, 639–650.

Kratzer, A. (1991b): Conditionals. In: A. von Stechow und D. Wunderlich (Hgg.), *Semantik. Ein internationales Handbuch der zeitgenössischen Forschung* [Handbücher zur Sprach- und Kommunikationswissenschaft 6], Berlin/New York: de Gruyter, 651–656.

Krifka, M. (2001): Quantifying into question acts. *Natural Language Semantics* 9 (1): 1–40.

Lang, E. (2011): Two-level semantics: Semantic Form and Conceptual Structure. In: C. Maienborn, K. von Heusinger und P. Portner (Hgg.), *Semantics* [HSK 33.1]. Berlin/New York: de Gruyter, 709–740.

Lohnstein, H. (2000): *Satzmodus – kompositionell. Zur Parametrisierung der Modusphrase im Deutschen* [Studia grammatica 49]. Berlin: Akademie Verlag.

Pitsch, H. (2012): Verb stems in Russian and BYT'. Erscheint in: U. Junghanns, D. Fehrmann, D. Lenertová und H. Pitsch (Hgg.), *Formal Slavic Linguistics. Proceedings of FDSL 9, Göttingen 2011* [Linguistics International], Frankfurt/M.: Peter Lang.

Reichenbach, H. (1947): *Elements of symbolic logic.* New York: The Free Press.

RG (1980): *Russkaja grammatica*, I & II, N. Ju. Švedova (glavnyj redaktor). Moskva: Hauka.

Truckenbrodt, H. (2006a): On the semantic motivation of syntactic verb movement to C in German. *Theoretical Linguistics* 32 (3): 257–306.

Truckenbrodt, H. (2006b): Replies to comments by Gärtner, Plunze and Zimmermann, Portner, Potts, Reis and Zaefferer. *Theoretical Linguistics* 32 (3): 387-410.

Zimmermann, I. (1988): Wohin mit den Affixen? In: W. Motsch (Hg.), The contribution of word-structure theories to the study of word formation, *Linguistische Studien, Reihe A* 179: 157–188.

Zimmermann, I. (1990): Zur Legitimierung leerer Köpfe. In: A. Steube (Hg.), Syntaktische Repräsentationen mit leeren Kategorien oder Proformen und ihre semantischen Interpretationen, *Linguistische Studien, Reihe A* 206: 75–90.

Zimmermann, I. (1992): Der Skopus von Modifikatoren. In: I. Zimmermann und A. Strigin (Hgg.), *Fügungspotenzen. Zum 60. Geburtstag von Manfred Bierwisch* [Studia grammatica 34], Berlin: Akademie Verlag, 251–279.

Zimmermann, I. (2002): Structural cases in Russian. In: I. Kaufmann und B. Stiebels (Hgg.), *More than words. A Festschrift for Dieter Wunderlich* [Studia grammatica 53], Berlin: Akademie Verlag, 275–298.

Zimmermann, I. (2003): On the semantics of cases. In: U. Junghanns und L. Szucsich (Hgg.), *Syntactic structures and morphological information*. Berlin/New York: de Gruyter, 341–380.

Zimmermann, I. (2009): Satzmodus. In: S. Kempgen, P. Kosta, T. Berger und K. Gutschmidt (Hgg.), *Die slavischen Sprachen. Ein internationales Handbuch zu ihrer Struktur, ihrer Geschichte und ihrer Erforschung*, Band 1. Berlin/New York: de Gruyter, 484–505.

Zimmermann, I. (2010): *Where are the worlds?* Handout. International conference to honor Manfred Bierwisch, ZAS Berlin.

Secondary stress in morphologically complex words in Faroese: A word game*

Nicole Dehé and Allison Wetterlin

1. Introduction: Word stress in Faroese

Word stress, and in particular the distribution of secondary stress in Insular Scandinavian has yet to be systematically studied and the phonetic correlates in production and perception have yet to be identified (this was noted for Icelandic by Zonneveld et al. 1999: 570 and new studies have not been added since then). The present paper reports on a pilot study that was designed to systematically ascertain the correlates of word stress in Icelandic and Faroese, starting out with Faroese.

In the literature, we find the basic Faroese word stress rules summarised as in (1) (see Thráinsson et al. 2004: 28).

(1) Basic word stress rules in Faroese
  a. Primary stress falls on the first syllable in all native Faroese words.
  b. There is a stress alternation rule which places a weak secondary stress on every other syllable.
  c. The first syllable of the second part of compound words gets secondary stress.

According to these rules, word stress in Faroese is very similar to that of its close relative Icelandic. First of all, like Icelandic, Faroese has retained the typical Germanic word stress pattern such that (the majority of) native words have primary stress on the initial syllable of a word (cf. also Lockwood 1977: 8, Barnes and Weyhe 1994: 196, Árnason 2011: 275 and references given there). Secondly, according to (1)b, Faroese also has alternating secondary stress, as illustrated below in (2)a (see also Árnason 1985 and 2011). Secondary stress is said to be rhythmically motivated in both languages. It follows a strengthening rule (Árnason 1985 for Icelandic), which creates alternating stress starting from the primary stress on the first syllable (see (3)a–c). This rhythmic rule has the consequence that secondary stress can also fall on inflectional suffixes. For example, Icelandic *'ung#barn,ið* in (3)b has secondary stress on the suffixed definite article *-ið*, while *barn* 'child' is weakened. This is not a trait found in the other Germanic languages, and in the context of Icelandic the

* This research was made possible by an AFF grant from the University of Konstanz. We would like to express our thanks to the Faculty of Faroese at the University of the Faroe Islands for their support and the use of their facilities. Special thanks go to Guðrið Poulsen and all the participants for their interest and endurance.

assumption has not remained undisputed (see Gussmann 1985, Hayes 1995). However, it appears as if Faroese also has alternating secondary stress which can fall on suffixed definite articles as observed by Árnason (2011); see his examples in (4).[1]

(2) Word stress in Faroese[2]

	STRESS PATTERN	EXAMPLE	GLOSS
a.	ˈσ σ # ˌσ σ	ˈgrinda#ˌhvalur	'pilot whale'
		ˈonga#ˌstaðni	(no#place) 'nowhere'
b.	ˈσ # ˌσ	ˈÍs#ˌland	'Iceland'
c.	ˈσ # ˌσ σ	ˈís#ˌlendskur	'Icelandic'
		ˈtil#ˌbiðja	(to#pray) 'worship'
d.	ˈσ σ σ # ˌσ σ	ˈkjallara#ˌbúgvi	'cellar dweller'

(3) Word stress in Icelandic

	STRESS PATTERN	EXAMPLE	GLOSS
a.	ˈσ σ # ˌσ σ	ˈferða#ˌmaður	(travel-GEN.PL#man) 'tourist'
b.	ˈσ # σ ˌσ	ˈung#barnˌið	(young#child$_{DEF}$)'infant, baby'
c.	ˈσ # σ ˌσ	ˈborð#plaˌta	(table#plate) 'table top'
d.	ˈσ σ σ # ˌσ σ	ˈkartöflu#ˌflögur	(potato#flakes) 'potato crisps'

(4) Alternating stress in Faroese: secondary stress on the suffixed definite article (examples from Árnason 2011: 96, 276)

	STRESS PATTERN	EXAMPLE	GLOSS
a.	ˈσ σ ˌσ	ˈbátiˌnum	'boat.the$_{DAT}$'
b.	ˈσ σ ˌσ	ˈhúsiˌnum	'house.the$_{DAT}$'
c.	ˈσ σ ˌσ	ˈbygdiˌna	'village.the$_{ACC}$'

In Icelandic, the rhythmic rule wins over morphological structure such that in compounds with monosyllabic first components, the secondary stress is on the second syllable of the second morphological component (instead of initial stress in the second component; see (3)c). Faroese differs from Icelandic in this respect. In compounds or otherwise morphologically complex words with monosyllabic first components, Faroese follows the compound stress rule in (1)c. As Thráinsson et al. (2004: 28) explain, the compound rule wins out over the alternating stress rule, creating words with primary and secondary stress on adjacent syllables (see (2)b, c).

One exception to alternating stress in both Faroese and Icelandic is given in (2)d and (3)d, respectively, where due to the morphological structure (a trisyllabic first component), two unstressed syllables intervene between primary and secondary stress, following the compound stress rule in (1)c.

[1] Throughout the paper, the following symbols are used: single superscripted (ˈ) or subscripted (ˌ) vertical lines preceding the syllable indicate main (primary) and secondary stress, respectively. A sigma σ denotes a syllable and a hash mark # indicates a boundary between the components of morphological compounds, = indicates a functional morpheme boundary (inflection).

[2] The examples are taken from Thráinsson et al. (2004: 28) and Lockwood (1977: 8).

Another important difference between Icelandic and Faroese is that it is much more common for words to have non-initial primary stress in Faroese than in Icelandic; see, for example, Lockwood (1977: 8), Barnes and Weyhe (1994: 196), Zonneveld et al. (1999: 583). This is true for loanwords (see (5)) as well as native Faroese words, e.g., compound adverbs (see (6)).

Another relevant property of Faroese is that "certain forms may vacillate between right-strong and left-strong patterns" (Zonneveld et al. 1999: 583), for example, a compound such as *burðar#vektir* 'birth#weight' may be realised either as *'burðar,vektir* or *,burðar'vektir*.

(5) Non-initial primary stress in non-native Faroese words;
examples from Barnes and Weyhe (1994: 196), Árnason (2011: 278)
a. stu'dentur 'student'
b. ameri'kanari 'an American'
c. poli'ti 'police'

(6) Non-initial primary stress in native Faroese words;
examples from Zonneveld et al. (1999: 583), Árnason (2011: 277)
a. harum'framt 'furthermore'; lit: 'here-about#further'
b. ser'stakliga 'specially'; lit: 'each#individually'
c. aftu'rum 'behind'; lit: 'after#about'

Relatively little is known about the phonetic cues to word stress in Faroese and in particular to the cues for secondary stress. Across languages most of the relevant literature on stress focusses more on the difference between stressed and unstressed syllables than on the difference between primary and secondary stress (see the recent discussion in Plag, Kunter and Schramm 2011). Generally speaking, phonetic cues to stress found for various languages include syllable and segment duration, vowel quality, pitch movement, and intensity. For German, Kleber and Klipphahn (2006) did not find any phonetic evidence for rhythmical secondary stress in their study, which compared the acoustic correlates of vowel duration, intensity, and F0 among others for syllables with primary stress, secondary stress, and no stress. However, some experimental evidence has been provided specifically for phonetic cues to secondary stress in other languages. For example, pitch movement and amplitude peak have been identified as cues to word-initial secondary stress in Spanish (Prieto and van Santen 1996).

More specifically for Insular Scandinavian, durational and F0 cues are likely to be candidates for signalling stress. In particular, the syllabic nucleus is described as being lengthened under stress in Icelandic (e.g., Haugen 1958, Zonneveld et al. 1999: 568) and Faroese (Árnason 2011), i.e., lengthening of the vowel in open syllables, and the final consonant in closed syllables with non-extrametrical final consonants. Unlike the syllable nucleus, the role of the syllable onset is not prominent in the literature, thus nothing is known about whether there is also lengthening of the syllable onset under stress.

In Icelandic, aspiration of intervocalic stops may also be a possible indicator of (secondary) stress. The two main varieties of Icelandic behave differently in this respect. The "hard" (northern) variety has aspirated stops between vowels in non-stress positions, e.g., in words like *taka* (['tʰaː.k⁽ʰ⁾a] 'to take') and *bátur* (['pau.t⁽ʰ⁾Yr̥] 'boat'). On the other hand, aspiration of stops in the "soft" (southern) varieties of Icelandic indicates foot-initial position, thus stress position; in this variety, stops in the onset of unstressed syllables are unaspirated (Thráinsson and Árnason 1992, Árnason 2011). Similarly, according to Árnason (2011), northern varieties of Faroese tend to have aspiration (postaspiration or preaspiration) in word internal position (and then only after non-high vowels), whereas southern varieties have unaspirated medial stops. However, according to Árnason (2011: 119–20), there is "quite a bit of variation" regarding soft/hard dialects and aspiration in Faroese "and the picture is not entirely clear". The soft/hard distinction "as far as it applies to internal onsets, is only based on preaspiration. Thus aspiration in internal onsets is only marginal in Faroese" (see also Thráinsson et al. 2004). However, this has never been tested systematically.

Furthermore, reduction/deletion processes common in both Icelandic and Faroese are sensitive to the difference between unstressed syllables and syllables with some degree of stress such that they may apply to the former but not the latter (e.g., Zonneveld et al. 1999: 570, Árnason 2011: 276).[3]

Another cue to secondary stress in Icelandic mentioned in the literature is pitch movement. Zonneveld et al. (1999: 570) maintain that syllables with secondary stress can attract pitch accents; pitch movement would be associated with the relevant syllable. This is related to a claim made by Dehé (2009) that syllables with secondary stress can be associated with phrase accents, i.e., a tonal target after the last pitch accent in an intermediate phrase.

The aims of the study reported on here are as follows: (i) to ascertain the location of secondary stress in production and perception, (ii) to identify the most prominent phonetic parameters related to secondary stress in production and perception, and (iii) to compare secondary stress on lexical and functional morphemes.

2. The experiment

In order to approach the research questions outlined above in a way that would enable us to ultimately compare Icelandic and Faroese data, a pilot word game was designed in which words were conveyed by one participant to another only by using the syllables *ta ta ta* or *na na na*. Production data were elicited to investigate the phonetic cues indicating stress, and perception was relevant under the assumption that if a word is produced and subsequently recognised, the phonetic cues employed by the speaker conveyed the stress pattern successfully. The sequences *ta ta ta* and *na na na* were used in order to control the segmental environment. More specifically, they were chosen for the following reasons: in *ta ta ta*, the segmental make-up was ideal to test closure duration (onset plosive), voice onset time

[3] However, note that in Icelandic, syllables which would be predicted to have rhythmically determined secondary stress at word level may be lost at sentence level due to Final Vowel Deletion (FVD), a rule which deletes a word-final vowel before an initial vowel on the following word. For example, in (x) below, the final syllable of *barninu* would carry secondary stress according to (1)b, but can be deleted in the given context. (See Dehé 2008 for details.)

(x)	María	gaf	barninu	epli.
	Maria	gave	child.the	apple

(VOT)/aspiration and vowel duration; in *na na na*, the segmental make-up was ideal to test vowel duration, onset consonant duration, and, due to continuous voicing, pitch movement.

2.1. Stimuli design and methods

Eighty-eight morphologically complex Faroese words were found, considering different morphological and rhythmic patterns. Twenty-two functioned as target words and 66 were distracters. The target words fall into the groups exemplified in Table 1. Word group (a) consists of compounds with mono-syllabic first components; primary stress is on the first syllable, secondary stress is predicted to be on the second syllable according to the compound rule given above in (1)c. Groups (b–g) consist of morphologically complex words with disyllabic first components. In this group, primary stress is on the word-initial syllable, and secondary stress is on the first syllable of the second morphological component; however, if the second component does not follow the native stress-initial pattern, secondary stress may be elsewhere (see (f) in Table 1). The word *bikarið* in group (d) only has an inflectional morphological boundary separating the second and third syllable. In group (h), the first lexical component of each word consisted of three syllables, the first one bearing primary stress; secondary stress was on the fourth syllable, i.e., the first syllable of the second component according to (1)c. Groups (i–k) had non-initial primary stress with varying positions of both primary and secondary stress. The predictions with regard to stress positions will be explained in more detail below.

WORD GROUP	MORPHOLOGICAL AND RHYTHMIC STRUCTURE	EXAMPLES	GLOSS
a.	ˈσ # ˌσ σ	tin#pípa	'tin whistle'
	ˈσ # ˌσ=σ	ung#ross=ið	'young horse$_{DEF}$'
b.	ˈσ σ # ˌσ	ommu#barn	(grandmother#child) 'grandchild'
c.	(ˈσ # σ) # ˌσ	(reyð#vín)#glas	'red wine glass'
d.	ˈσ σ=ˌσ	bikar=ið	'beaker$_{DEF}$'
	ˈσ σ ˌσ	kenn-ar-i	'teach-er'
e.	ˈσ σ # ˌσ σ	róma#køka	'cream cake'
f.	ˈσ σ # σ ˌσ σ	skrivi#maskina	(write#machine) 'typewriter'
g.	ˈσ σ # (ˌσ # ˌσ σ)	fúta#skriv#stova	(bailiff$_{GEN}$#write#room) 'bailiff's office'
h.	(ˈσ # σ σ) # ˌσ σ	(sam#ferðar)#maður	(together#travels$_{GEN}$#man) 'travelling companion'
	ˈσ σ σ # ˌσ σ	litingar#pottur	(colouring#pot) 'dyepot'
i.	σ ˈσ σ # ˌσ	adressu#bók	'address book'
j.	ˌσ σ ˈσ	telefon	'telephone'
k.	ˌσ σ ˈσ σ	politistur	'police officer'

Table 1: Example words illustrating morphological and rhythmical patterns

2.2. Participants

The experiment was carried out with 34 participants (17 pairs) in July 2011 by the authors in three locations on the Faroe Islands. The participants were between 19 and 60 years of age; they were four male and 30 female native speakers of Faroese. Sixteen participants (8 pairs) were tested in Tórshavn (Streymoy Island) at the University of the Faroe Islands, sixteen (8 pairs) at a local school in Miðvagi (Vágur Island), and two participants (one pair) at a private home in Vágur (Suðuroy Island).

2.3. Procedure

Two participants (A and B) were each seated in front of a computer screen, that could not be seen by the other participant (see left-hand panel of Figure 1). The participants received written and oral instructions in Faroese as to the procedure of the game. The game commenced as one word appeared on participant A's screen and a list of four words (in pseudo-randomised order) appeared on participants B's screen (see right-hand panel of Figure 1). These four words included the target word, i.e., the word on participant A's screen (*skrivimaskina* 'σ σ # σ ˌσ σ in Figure 1), and three other words. These three words differed from the target in length (one syllable too few or too many; not more than one distracter per trial; *bókamessa* 'σ σ # ˌσ σ in Figure 1), and/or rhythmical pattern (position of primary or secondary stress; at least two distracters per trial; *ónøktiligur* and *sømdarpeningur*, both 'σ σ # ˌσ σ ˌσ, in Figure 1). None of the three distracters had the same morphological or rhythmic structure as the target. Participant A was instructed to convey the word on the screen to B solely using the syllables *tatata* in such a way that B would be able to guess which word it was. Participant A was not allowed to say the actual word at any time, but was only allowed to say *ta ta ta* or later *na na na* using as many *ta*-s or *na*-s as needed. Each *ta* corresponded to one syllable of the target word. After hearing the *tatata*-sequence, Participant B tried to figure out which word it was, then asked A to repeat the word, this time using *nanana*. After hearing the *nanana* variation, participant B considered the words in the list again and made a guess. The participants moved on to the next trial when the word was correctly identified. Three guesses were allowed. If B did not recognise the word, participant A revealed the target word and then moved on to the next word. The participants changed roles at half time, i.e., after 11 words.

TWO PARTICIPANTS PLAYING THE WORD GAME	COMPUTER SCREENS: DEPICTING WHAT EACH PARTICIPANT SEES

Participant A

skrivimaskina

Participant B

ónøktiligur
skrivimaskina
sømdarpeningur
bókamessa

Figure 1: Word game; left-hand panel: two participants playing the word game; right-hand panel: computer screens for one trial as seen by participant A on the left and participant B on the right (glosses: *ónøktiligur* 'who never gets enough; impossible to satisfy'; *skrivi-maskina* 'typewriter'; *ˈsømdarpeningur* 'honorary pension'; *bókamessa* 'book fair')

2.4. Recordings

All word game sessions were recorded using two Microtrack II (M-Audio) recorders and two Rode NT-5 condenser microphones. All recordings were then edited into individual sound files and analysed in Praat (Boersma and Weenink 2012).

2.5. Analysis

A minimum of 22 *tatata*s and *nanana*s (2 speakers, 11 words each) were extracted per pair, plus repetitions. The *tatata*- and *nanana*-sequences were annotated for the following landmarks, as illustrated in Figures 2 and 3; *tatata*: closure duration (cd), voice onset time (vot), and vowel duration (v) for each syllable (σ); note that the beginning of the very first cd was set arbitrarily because closure duration cannot be identified at the beginning of an utterance; *nanana*: consonant (c) and vowel (v) duration for each syllable (σ). In Figures 2 and 3, the numbers indicate the number of the syllable, e.g., v4 is the duration of the vowel in the fourth syllable.

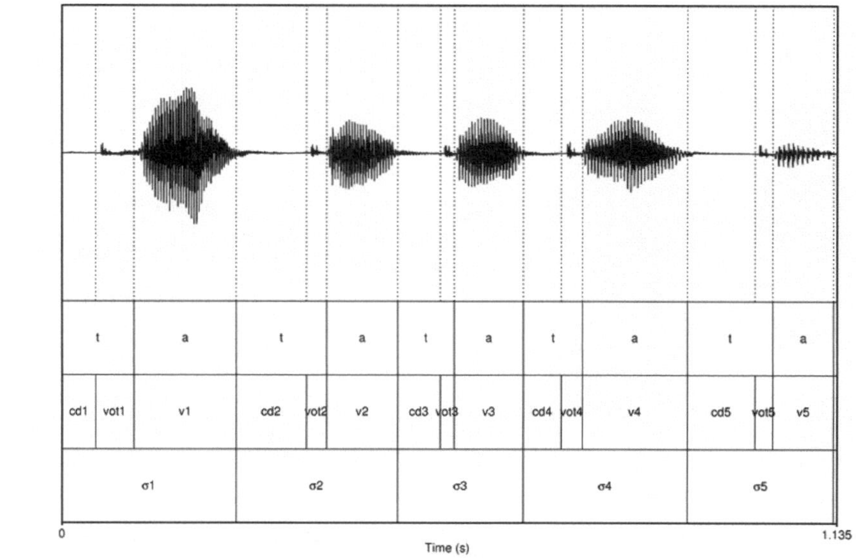

Figure 2: Annotated sound file of a *tatata* sequence (Speaker M14) conveying *skrivimaskina* ('type writer')

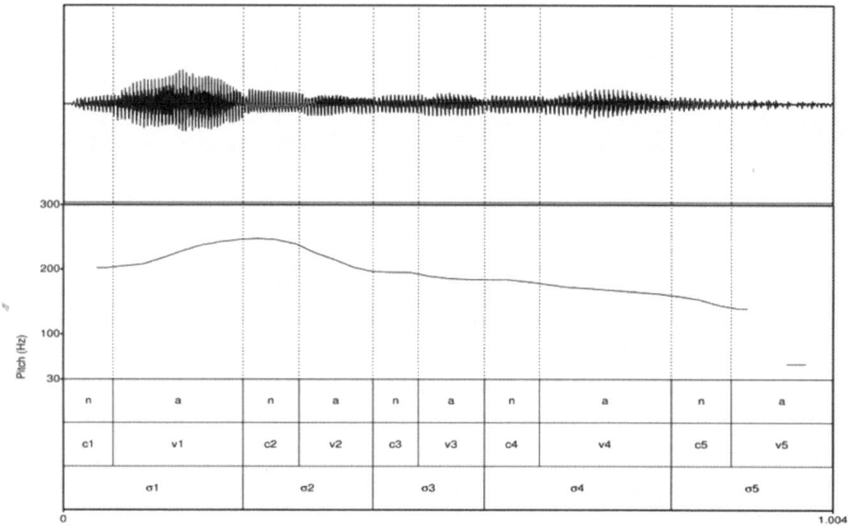

Figure 3: Annotated sound file of a *nanana* sequence (Speaker M14) conveying *skrivimaskina* ('type writer')

2.6. Results and discussion

As is well known amongst phonology and phonetics lecturers, not all students are readily able to hear and correctly convey word stress even if they make intuitive use of it in both production and perception of their native language. Therefore we were anticipating that some pairs would not work out well in the word game. Since we were to find out how stress is produced as well as the acoustic correlates that are important to identify stress, we only included words in the analysis that were correctly identified. Moreover, we only took correctly identified words from participants who were able to correctly identify more than 64% of the test words. The main results are reported on in this section.

The results are given in milliseconds and are grouped according to number of syllables for easier comparison and listed according to average VOT (Tables 2 and 6) and vowel duration (V) (Tables 3 and 7) for the *ta ta ta* tokens, and according to vowel duration (V) (Tables 4 and 8) and consonant duration (C) (Tables 5 and 9) for the *na na na* tokens. The word groups (a–k) in Tables 2 through 9 are identical to those in Table 1 above. We begin with the results for a set of trisyllabic words with varying morphological structures (Tables 2 through 5 organised according to morphological patterns and phonetic parameters). Recall that if secondary stress is rhythmically motivated (compare (1)b and the Icelandic pattern), then secondary stress should be placed on the third syllable across the board, i.e., for all words regardless of the morphological structure. If, on the other hand, secondary stress follows the compound rule in (1)c, then it should be realised on the second syllable in the words of group (a) in Tables 2 through 5, but on the third syllable in the tokens for group (b). Group (c) consists of a morphologically complex first constituent *reyð#vín* 'red wine' and *glas* 'glass', thus both rhythmically and morphologically motivated secondary stress would be expected on the third syllable. However, according to the compound rule in (1)c, a secondary stress might also occur on the second syllable. In group (d), the word *bikarið* differs from *kennari* morphologically in that it includes the suffixed definite article *-ið*, while *kennari* is a derivative with the masculine agentive suffix *-ar-i* 'teach-er'. However, this made no difference in any of the measurements, thus their results are grouped together. Rhythmically, if Faroese is similar to what is reported for Icelandic, secondary stress should be on the third syllables in these examples, i.e. on the suffixed definite article in *bikarið*.[4]

4 In the tables below, shaded cells indicate values which correspond to positions of secondary stress as predicted according to (1); in case of conflict between (1)b and (1)c, predictions are according to the compound rule in (1)c.

	WORD GROUP	EXAMPLES	TOKENS	AVERAGE VOT σ1	AVERAGE VOT σ2	AVERAGE VOT σ3
a.	'σ # ˌσ σ	tinpípa	12	63.4	42	37.1
b.	'σ σ # ˌσ	ommubarn	8	55.5	34.8	40.2
c.	'σ-σ # ˌσ	reyðvínglas	4	68.5	37.7	52.1
d.	'σ σ= ˌσ	bikarið	12	51.6	37.2	37.8
	'σ σ ˌσ	kennari				

Table 2: Average voice onset time (VOT) of syllable onset /t/ in msec; *ta ta ta*: 3 syllable words

	WORD GROUP	EXAMPLES	TOKENS	AVERAGE V σ1	AVERAGE V σ2	AVERAGE V σ3
a.	'σ # ˌσ σ	tinpípa	12	214.8	121.5	114
b.	'σ σ # ˌσ	ommubarn	8	137.2	106.7	160
c.	'σ-σ # ˌσ	reyðvínglas	4	195.8	135.1	134.7
d.	'σ σ= ˌσ	bikarið	12	156.1	127.8	115.5
	'σ σ ˌσ	kennari				

Table 3: Average vowel duration (V) in msec; *ta ta ta*: 3 syllable words

	WORD GROUP	EXAMPLES	TOKENS	AVERAGE V σ1	AVERAGE V σ2	AVERAGE V σ3
a.	'σ # ˌσ σ	tinpípa	12	253.5	136	126.8
b.	'σ σ # ˌσ	ommubarn	8	122.4	105	127
c.	'σ-σ # ˌσ	reyðvínglas	4	270	179.6	116.3
d.	'σ σ= ˌσ	bikarið	12	226.5	113.4	114.9
	'σ σ ˌσ	kennari				

Table 4: Average vowel duration (V) in msec; *na na na*: 3 syllable words

	WORD GROUP	EXAMPLES	TOKENS	AVERAGE C σ1	AVERAGE C σ2	AVERAGE C σ3
a.	'σ # ˌσ σ	tinpípa	8	97.1	112.6	81.3
b.	'σ σ # ˌσ	ommubarn	8	56.5	82	77.6
c.	'σ-σ # ˌσ	reyðvínglas	4	117	89.5	115.2
d.	'σ σ= ˌσ	bikarið	12	54.4	58	91.8
	'σ σ ˌσ	kennari				

Table 5: Average consonant duration (C) in msec; *na na na*: 3 syllable words

VOT (Table 2)

The average duration of the VOT of the onset consonants on each syllable of the trisyllabic *tatata* words in Table 2 correlates with the morphological structure. In groups (a–c) the VOT for the onset of the syllables following the morpheme boundary is greater than that of the unstressed syllable. This is our first hint at secondary stress and it is true regardless of whether primary and secondary stress are on adjacent syllables (group a) or not (groups b and c). When no lexical morpheme boundary is present (group d), the VOT of the onset of the second and third syllable do not differ, thus giving us our first indications that there is no rhythmical stress on the third syllable (e.g., the suffixed definite article) of these words.

Vowel duration (Tables 3 and 4)

The average vowel durations for the *tatata* and *nanana* tokens reported in Tables 3 and 4, respectively, behave similarly. We find that vowels are longer in syllables directly following a morphological boundary than in unstressed syllables in groups (a) and (b). However, it should be noted that in group (b) the duration of the vowel following the morphological boundary in words such as *ommu#barn* is even longer than that of the stressed syllable. This may be a case of a vacillating stress pattern. In group (c) (*[reyð#vín]#glas*), vowel duration does not differentiate between the second and third syllables in the *tatata* tokens – it is only significantly longer in the syllable bearing main stress. This reflects the conflict noted above: the morphological rule predicts secondary stress both on the second and third syllable due to the complex morphological structure, while the rhythmical rule only suggests secondary stress on the third syllable. The same result was found for the *nanana* tokens of the category without a lexical morpheme boundary in (d). For the *nanana* tokens of *[reyð#vín]#glas* as well as for the *tatata* tokens of group (d) vowel duration decreases with distance to the main stressed syllable where it is the longest for the first syllable, again giving us no indication of rhythmical secondary stress on the third syllable.

Consonant duration (Table 5)

The average consonant durations for the *nanana*s show the least amount of correspondence to morpheme boundaries. In groups (a) and (c) consonants of the main stressed syllable and after a morpheme boundary are the longest. For group (b), the syllable not predicted to bear stress either because of a morpheme boundary or because of word rhythm has the longest consonant. In group (d), consonant duration is greatest in the word final syllable, which would correspond to rhythmical stress on every other syllable. However, since this finding does not comply with the findings for VOT and vowel duration, which otherwise seem to be more reliable correspondents of stress positions, we will not interpret consonant duration here as a cue to secondary stress on the third syllable.

The next set of results we report on is for compounds of four or five syllables length with disyllabic and trisyllabic first constituents (groups e–h in Tables 6–9 below), as well as words with non-initial primary stress (groups i–k in Tables 6–9). The tables again summarise the mean durational values. For compounds with disyllabic first components and initial primary stress in both components (groups e and g) the compound rule and alternating stress rule make identical predictions. Secondary stress should be realized on the first syllable of the second component, i.e. on the third syllable. In group (g), an additional secondary stress should either fall on the fifth syllable according to the stress alternation rule in (1)b, or, indicated here, on the fourth syllable according to the compound rule in (1)c. In group (f), a secondary stress is predicted on the fourth syllable due to non-initial primary stress in the second component. In compounds with trisyllabic first components and native stress pattern (group h), the secondary stress should follow the compound rule in (1)c and fall on the fourth syllable of the compound winning over the alternating stress rule. The stress patterns of the words in groups (i–k) follow their morphological make-up such that *adressubók* is predicted to have secondary stress on the fourth syllable *bók* along with non-native primary stress on the second syllable of the first component. For the remaining two words (j and k) we predict secondary stress on the first syllable for rhythmical reasons; non-native primary stress is on the third syllable in these words.

	Word group	Examples	tokens	Average VOT σ1	Average VOT σ2	Average VOT σ3	Average VOT σ4	Average VOT σ5
e.	'σ σ # ˌσ σ	rómakøka	17	51.5	42	42.5	40.0	
f.	'σ σ # σ ˌσ σ	skrivimaskina	5	47	34.1	39.5	39.2	41.0
g.	'σ σ # (ˌσ #ˌσ σ)	fútaskrivstova	5	52.3	47.0	65.3	41.2	45
h.	'σ-σ σ # ˌσ σ / 'σ σ σ # ˌσ σ	samferðarmaður / litingarpottur	12	68	51.1	36.7	46.8	39.2
i.	σ 'σ σ # ˌσ	adressubók	4	63.3	60	55	54.5	
j.	ˌσ σ 'σ	telefon	6	47	26.6	50.3		
k.	ˌσ σ 'σ σ	politistur	2	55	28.9	65	40.5	

Table 6: Voice onset time (VOT) of syllable onset /t/ in msec; *ta ta ta:* 4 and 5 syllable words

	Word group	Examples	Tokens	Average V σ1	Average V σ2	Average V σ3	Average V σ4	Average V σ5
e.	'σ σ # ˌσ σ	rómakøka	17	167.5	150.4	154.5	116.6	
f.	'σ σ # σ ˌσ σ	skrivimaskina	5	128.3	101.2	105.6	149.7	105
g.	'σ σ # (ˌσ #ˌσ σ)	fútaskrivstova	5	166.9	147.7	129.5	110	96.2
h.	'σ-σ σ # ˌσ σ / 'σ σ σ # ˌσ σ	samferðarmaður / litingarpottur	12	209.6	117.6	133.4	172	112
i.	σ 'σ σ # ˌσ	adressubók	4	160.3	200	138.8	106.2	
j.	ˌσ σ 'σ	telefon	6	71.8	86.2	233.8		
k.	ˌσ σ 'σ σ	politistur	2	79.8	82.7	144.3	102.5	

Table 7: Vowel duration (V) in msec; *ta ta ta:* 4 and 5 syllable words

	Word group	Examples	Tokens	Average V σ1	Average V σ2	Average V σ3	Average V σ4	Average V σ5
e.	'σ σ # ˌσ σ	rómakøka	11	186	142	170	110	
f.	'σ σ # σ ˌσ σ	skrivimaskina	4	165.8	134.8	115.9	186.8	124.1
g.	'σ σ # (ˌσ #ˌσ σ)	fútaskrivstova	4	251.4	178.5	149.7	131.8	112.7
h.	'σ-σ σ # ˌσ σ / 'σ σ σ # ˌσ σ	samferðarmaður / litingarpottur	9	227.4	163.4	148.6	194	114.2
i.	σ 'σ σ # ˌσ	adressubók	4	177	221.1	147	132	
j.	ˌσ σ 'σ	telefon	5	93.9	83.7	224.4		
k.	ˌσ σ 'σ σ	politistur	2	106.2	91.1	176.1	90.2	

Table 8: Vowel duration (V) in msec; *na na na*: 4 and 5 syllable words

	Word group	Examples	tokens	Average C σ1	Average C σ2	Average C σ3	Average C σ4	Average C σ5
e.	ˈσ σ # ˌσ σ	rómakøka	13	64.3	92.4	93.0	83.3	
f.	ˈσ σ # σ ˌσ σ	skrivimaskina	4	66.3	73.6	59	72	77.3
g.	ˈσ σ # (ˌσ #ˌσ σ)	fútaskrivstova	4	60.81	83.4	71.6	97.6	108.1
h.	ˈσ-σ σ # ˌσ σ / ˈσ σ σ # ˌσ σ	samferðarmaður / litingarpottur	9	73	101.2	83	92.1	89.8
i.	σ ˈσ σ # ˌσ	adressubók	4	54.3	96.1	86.4	111.7	
j.	ˌσ σ ˈσ	telefon	5	78	57.5	79.2		
k.	ˌσ σ ˈσ σ	politistur	2	37	54.3	69.2	75.5	

Table 9: Consonant duration (C) in msec; *na na na*: 4 and 5 syllable words

VOT (Table 6)

The average VOT values for this second set of words clearly indicate that VOT is used as a cue for primary stress. Secondary stress, however, only correlates with VOT duration in four (g, h, j, k) out of the seven groups. In groups (e) and (g), the morphological and rhythmical secondary stress prefer the third syllable. However, in groups (e) and (f) the main stressed syllable has a very high VOT value compared to all the other syllables where there is no differentiation in VOT. The words in group (g), on the other hand, do appear to mark the third syllable with some prominence since it has the longest average VOT of the word. It is even longer than the primary stressed syllable. In group (h), for which secondary stress is predicted to fall on the fourth syllable according to the compound rule, the VOT is indeed longer on this syllable than on the preceding and following ones, thus making it stand out from its surroundings in this way. In group (i) (*adressubók*), VOT duration does not reflect the predictions with regard to either primary or secondary stress positions. However, for the two remaining groups (j) and (k), VOT duration does reflect the predicted stress patterns such that the syllables carrying primary stress have the longest VOT averages and the second longest VOT values are on the word initial syllables, for which secondary stress is predicted following rhythmic alternation.

Vowel duration (Tables 7 and 8)

The average vowel duration in both the *tatata* and *nanana* tokens produced comparable results, clearly suggesting that vowel duration can be considered a correlate of both primary and secondary stress. In group (e), where the word stress rules (rhythm and morphology) predict primary stress on the initial syllable and secondary stress on the third syllable, this is reflected in the duration values. The vowel of the first syllable is longest, followed by the vowel of the third syllable, which in turn is longer than the second and fourth syllable (even if this effect is stronger for *nanana* than for *tatata*). In group (f), the second morphological component (*maskina*) demands non-native stress on its second syllable, and this is indeed reflected in the vowel duration, which is the longest for this syllable for both the *tatata* and *nanana* tokens. One possible explanation is vacillating stress patterns, another is that non-native stress is marked more clearly. This latter explanation would be corroborated by the results for group (i) (*adressubók*), where the vowel of the second syllable, which bears non-native primary stress, is clearly longer than all other vowels, without secondary stress being reflected in vowel duration. In group (g), vowel duration behaves similar to VOT duration, such that it does reflect primary but not secondary stress, perhaps due to the conflict between alternating rhythm and morphological stress in the second component of the compound (similar to *reyðvínglas* above). Group (h) follows very clearly the predicted pattern: primary stress (first syllable) is reflected in the longest vowel duration, followed by the second longest vowel duration in the fourth syllable, which bears secondary stress according to the compound rule. In groups (j) and (k), non-native primary stress is marked by longest vowel durations, while initial secondary stress is marked by second longest vowel duration in *nanana*s but not *tatata*s.

Consonant duration (Table 9)

As for the trisyllabic words, consonant duration of the *nanana* tokens does not reflect the predictions with respect to word stress. It only correlates with primary stress in the groups with non-native stress. Here (groups i–k) either the longest (for j) or second longest consonants (for i and k) are found in the onset of this syllable. Again, this reflects that non-native stress is marked more clearly, even by this duration parameter, which does not otherwise seem to participate in the marking of stress.

Pitch movement

Finally, across all word groups, a systematic analysis with regard to pitch movement has yet to be done. However, upon first impression we do not find any results suggesting pitch as a phonetic cue to secondary stress. As can be seen in Figure 3 above, a local pitch peak can be found on the first *na* representing the syllable bearing primary stress. Secondary stress is predicted to occur on the fourth syllable (see (2)d in Table 1). However, while the fourth *na* in Figure 3 is clearly lengthened, no notable pitch movement other than continuation of the overall downward trend can be observed. This is despite the fact that stress is in a non-native position here (second syllable of *maskina*), which is otherwise marked very clearly. This example is representative of the pattern which we seem to find for pitch movement across our data.

2.7. Summary of results

To summarise the results, we will return to the aims of this pilot study given at the end of Section 1 above and repeated here for convenience: (i) to ascertain the location of secondary stress in production and perception, (ii) to identify the most prominent phonetic parameters related to secondary stress in production and perception, and (iii) to compare secondary stress on lexical and functional morphemes.

First, the location of secondary stress in production and perception was tested in such a way that only those productions of *tatata*s and *nanana*s were included in the analysis that were correctly identified by the other participant. The results include no surprises, i.e. the stress rules in (1) were confirmed for Faroese. Secondary stresses were phonetically implemented in the predicted positions or they were not implemented at all. In positions where there is a conflict between the rhythmical rule in (1)b and the morphological compound rule in (1)c, the compound rule wins (groups a and h). If there is no conflict, the secondary stress is not always implemented (groups c and e). Non-native stress is usually clearly marked, whether it is a primary stress or a secondary stress position (groups i–k and also group f for vowel duration). Notice once again that the results reported on here are not for real words in real conversation and that the object of the game was to convey the words to the other participant to guess, hence the speech was possibly exaggerated at least for some tokens and certainly in repetitions. However, since secondary stress in Faroese has yet to be systematically studied, to reliably ascertain the position of secondary stress exaggeration was welcome.

Second, the most prominent phonetic parameters related to secondary stress are vowel duration (Tables 3, 4, 7 and 8) and VOT/aspiration (Tables 2 and 6). Pitch does not seem to play a role (cf. Figure 3). The duration of the initial consonant in *nananas* does not seem to be a reliable parameter in any way, thus we will not interpret it with regard to secondary stress (see the discussion of Tables 5 and 9 above). Remember in this context that only marginal aspiration is reported in the literature for internal onsets in Faroese. Looking at the values in the tables above and given that VOT corresponds to secondary stress positions in Faroese, aspiration may be marginal in internal onset positions, but it may also be strengthened and used to indicate word stress positions.

Third, looking at secondary stress associated with lexical and functional morphemes, no lengthening was found for inflectional suffixes in our Faroese data (e.g., *-ið* in *bikarið* in group d). The assumption of alternating stress realised also on syllables corresponding to inflectional affixes could therefore not be corroborated. Future research will have to directly compare inflectional and derivational suffixes in an even more balanced design.

3. Conclusion and outlook

Regarding the location of secondary stress the Faroese results comply by and large with what we know from the literature. Faroese has alternating stress, but where morphology and rhythm conflict (e.g., morphological compounds with mono-syllabic first component) the compound rule wins. As for phonetic parameters, vowel duration has been identified as the most prominent cue to stress so far, together with VOT. Regarding the question of secondary stress associated with inflectional affixes, no lengthening effects were found for inflectional suffixes in our Faroese data. Moreover, although a systematic analysis of the *na* syllables has yet to be done, pitch movement does not seem to be a promising cue to secondary stress. However, to elicit pitch movement/pitch accents associated with syllables bearing secondary stress, the target words will be placed in an appropriate context in a future study. Overall, more data is needed to address the open questions that came up in the previous sections. In particular, in a follow-up we will include closed syllables in the word game, specifically with postvocalic preaspiration since we know that preaspiration in this position and syllable-closing consonants may be lengthened under stress in Icelandic (e.g., Árnason 2011, Árnason and Schäfer 2012) and possibly Faroese, although preaspiration behaves differently in the two languages (see Árnason 2011 for discussion). Furthermore, an even more balanced design and more tokens will put us in a position to follow up the differences between inflectional and derivational suffixes, and it will also allow us to systematically test the individual factors (e.g., stress position, alternating rhythm, position of morphological boundaries, nature of morphological boundaries (word formation vs. inflection; compounding vs. derivation)) for each phonetic parameter statistically. In addition, we will conduct an Icelandic word game for comparison. Ideally, words will be chosen which have the same morphological patterns as those used in Faroese, or the same lexical elements where possible. Also, the Icelandic target syllables will be as closely related to the Faroese ones as possible, i.e., Icelandic *ta* [tʰaː] and *na* [naː] as open syllables, along with closed syllables with post-vocalic preaspiration (e.g., *patt* [pʰaht] or *tipl* [tʰɪhpl̥]). The comparison between the results of the experiments for the two languages will then put us in a position to answer the questions about differences in secondary stress positions in Icelandic and Faroese, as well as the relevant phonetic cues.

Bibliography

Árnason, K. (1985): Icelandic word stress and metrical phonology. *Studia Linguistica* 39: 93–129.
Árnason, K. (2011): *The phonology of Icelandic and Faroese*. Oxford: Oxford University Press.
Árnason, K. and M. Schäfer (2012): A stress test for segmenthood. Paper presented at the *11th International Conference of Nordic and General Linguistics*, 18–20 April 2012, University of Freiburg.
Barnes, M. P. and E. Weyhe (1994): Faroese. In: E.König and J. van der Auwera (eds.), *The Germanic languages*. London/New York: Routledge, 190–218.
Boersma, P. and D. Weenink (2012): *Praat: doing phonetics by computer* [Computer program]. Version 5.3.04. http://www.praat.org/
Dehé, N. (2008): To delete or not to delete: The contexts of Icelandic final vowel deletion. *Lingua* 118: 732–753.
Dehé, N. (2009): An intonational grammar for Icelandic. *Nordic Journal of Linguistics* 32: 5–34.
Gussmann, E. (1985): The morphology of a phonological rule: Icelandic vowel length. In: E. Gussmann (ed.), *Phono-morphology: Studies in the interaction of phonology and morphology*. Lublin: RW KUL, 75–94.
Haugen, E. (1958): The phonemics of Modern Icelandic. *Language* 34: 55–88.
Hayes, B. (1995): *Metrical stress theory: Principles and case studies*. Chicago: The University of Chicago Press.
Kleber, F. and N. Klipphahn (2006): An acoustic investigation of secondary stress in German. *Arbeitsberichte des Instituts für Phonetik und digitale Sprachverarbeitung der Universität Kiel (AIPUK)* 37: 1–18.
Lockwood, H. (1977): *An introduction to Modern Faroese*. Tórshavn: Føroya Skúlabókagrunnur.
Plag, I., G. Kunter and M. Schramm (2011): Acoustic correlates of primary and secondary stress in North American English. *Journal of Phonetics* 39: 362–374.
Prieto, P. and J. van Santen (1996): Secondary stress in Spanish: some experimental evidence. In: C. Parodi, C. Quicoli, M. Saltarelli and M.L. Zubizaretta (eds.), *Aspects of Romance linguistics*. Washington, DC: Georgetown University Press, 337–356.
Thráinsson, H. and K. Árnason (1992): Phonological variation in 20th century Icelandic. *Íslenskt mál* 14: 89–128.
Thráinsson, H., H. P. Peterson, J. Jacobsen and Z. S. Hansen (eds.) (2004): *Faroese: An overview and reference grammar*. Tórshavn: Føroya Fróðskaparfelag.
Zonneveld, W., M. Trommelen, M. Jessen, C. Rice, G. Bruce and K. Árnason (1999): Wordstress in West-Germanic and North-Germanic languages. In: H. van der Hulst (ed.), *Eurotyp 4: Word Prosodic Systems in the Languages of Europe*. Berlin/New York: de Gruyter, 477–603.

On participles of German verbs borrowed from English

Heinz Vater

1. Preliminary remarks

Every day we are confronted with articles in German newspapers and journals (like *Die Sprachwelt*) with complaints about the growing number of anglicisms in German and the frequent use of English words and expressions within German texts. Many authors warn against the flooding of German with English elements. One of them, Mathias Schreiber, even speaks of "poisened magma" that is on the point of burying German culture.[1]

I do not belong to those critics of the English influence on the German language. For centuries, German was exposed to the influence of other languages, mainly Latin and French, and stayed intact; you can even say that these influences contributed to an enrichment of the German language. I agree with Jürgen Spitzmüller (2007: 195), who says that a language does not consist of one identity only but is composed of many identities.[2] Besides, you have to consider the fact that there are many things, equipment, and processes for which no native words are available (cf. Stickel 1984). For me, the only problem to be investigated (and handled in practice) is the way in which foreign words and expressions are integrated into the German language.

1 "Schrecklichstes [...] Symptom der kranken Sprache [...] ist jenes modische Pseudo-Englisch, das täglich aus den offenbar weitgehend gehirnfreien Labors der Werbeagenturen, Marketing-Profis, Computer-Verkäufer, Technik-Anbieter, Popmusik-Produzenten [...], aber auch aus Behörden, wissenschaftlichen Institutionen, Massenmedien und den Rede-Schreibstuben der Politiker [...] quillt wie zähfließender, giftiger Magma-Brei, der ganze Kulturlandschaften unter sich begräbt." (Schreiber 2006: 185). Paulwitz (2010) fears that German, by getting mixed with English, will turn to a "monkey-language".

2 "[...] eine Gesellschaft zeichnet sich nicht zuletzt auch durch das Mit- und Gegeneinander verschiedener Einstellungen und Werthaltungen aus. Es gibt nicht nur, wie es auch gerade im Anglizismendiskurs immer wieder dargestellt wird, *eine* Identität, der gegenüber alles andere ein Identitätsverlust wäre. In einer Gesellschaft existieren, interagieren und kollidieren eine ganze Menge teilweise sehr unterschiedlicher kollektiver Identitäten." Spitzmüller (2007) also points to the fact that new products or (international) institutions often inherit terms coined in a foreign country. Zifonun (2000) mentions additional reasons for the use of anglicisms (like speech economy, prestige, variation of expression and tabooing). Cf. also Carstensen (1965).

An "anglicism" can – according to Fischer (1980: 19) – be defined as an English word or an English phrase or abbreviation used in another language or as the product of a process obtained in a language under the influence of the English language.[3]

An interesting paper by Dagmar Hausmann (2006) has the title "*Downgeloaded* und *geforwardet*".[4] The paper treats problems connected with past participles of verbs borrowed from English and their morphological integration into the German language.[5] The two participles in the title of this article demonstrate two different positions of the affix *-ge-*; it is inserted in *downgeloaded* but prefixed in *geforwardet.*[6] Why do speakers of German make this distinction? The question when *ge-* precedes the verb stem and when it is inserted in it cannot easily be answered, since several morphological facts play a role (e.g., composition vs. prefixation or formation with verbal particles, cf. Vater 2002[4], 2008). According to Hausmann (2006) prefixed verbs (with main accent on the word base) are not divided (cf. *Ich verkaufe das Haus/habe das Haus verkauft*), whereas particle verbs – with main accent on the particle – are divided by the prefix *-ge-* in the participle and by *-zu-* in the infinitive: *Ich rufe dich an*; *ich habe dich angerufen, ich habe versucht dich anzurufen*. But that is not the whole truth. Her complicated classificatory system (with six main groups and several subgroups, cf. Hausmann (2006: 53-64)) does not really mirror the decisive facts. I suggest a different system – not quite elaborated yet – that takes care of the morphological facts in a simpler and possibly more convincing way.

2. German past participles

First we have to glance over the methods of participle formation in German, i.e., the ways in which participles of native German verbs are formed. In German, past participles can be divided into three classes concerning their behavior towards *-ge-*:

---

3 "Der Anglizismus [...] kann [...] beschrieben werden als ein englisches Wort, eine englische Wendung oder eine englische Abkürzung in einer anderen Sprache oder als das Produkt einer unter englischsprachlichem Einfluß stattgefundenen Veränderung eines anderssprachlichen Wort- oder Wortgruppenkörpers in morphologischer, semantischer, syntaktischer, orthographischer, lautlicher und frequenzmäßiger Hinsicht [...]."

4 The different spelling of the endings (*-ed* vs. *-et*) is no longer relevant (cf. Hausmann 2006).

5 In the following, the term "participle" is used referring to past participles exclusively.

6 The affix *-ge-* is a genuine prefix in cases like *geforwardet*; in cases like *downgeloadet* it could be called an "infix" (cf. Fleischer/Barz 1995[2]: 33); this position (which occurs frequently in Latin, even within root morphemes) is rarely used in German. In cases like *down-ge-load-et*, *-ge-* is inserted in a complex verb, between the two main constituents of the verb, cf. the native verb forms *ab-ge-gang-en*, *aus-ge-lauf-en*, *mit-ge-zähl-t*, *rad-ge-fahr-en* (the final flexives *-en* resp. *-t* mark the participle, cooperating with the infix *-ge-*).

GROUP	SUBGROUP	INFINITIVE	PERFECT PARTICIPLE
I	a	erleben	erlebt
	b	marschieren	marschiert
II	a	geben	gegeben
	b1	frühstücken	gefrühstückt
	b2	mutmaßen	gemutmaßt
III	a	abraten	abgeraten
	b1	fremdgehen	fremdgegangen
	b2	eislaufen	eisgelaufen
	b3	walzfräsen	Walzgefräst

Table 1: Formation of past participles

Group I consists of verbs that do not get a prefix *ge-* because they already have a prefix (like *besuchen* or *erleben*) in (a), or have final stress like the verbs in (b) (e.g., *marschieren*).[7] Group II contains simple verbs (a) and complex verbs that cannot easily be divided; differently from *fremdgehen* you cannot divide *frühstücken* in IIb1 into *früh* and *stücken*; it is derived from the noun *Frühstück*, which is an idiomatic compound: whereas *Hochhaus* ('high house', *highrise)* is a high house, *Frühstück* (*breakfast*) is not a "frühes Stück" ('early piece').[8] The same is true of verbal compounds having nouns as their first constituents (IIb2), like *mutmaßen* (*to conjecture*); again, it cannot be divided into *mut* and *maßen* and is idiomatic, its meaning not being predictable from its constituents.[9]

Group III contains (a) particle verbs, i.e., verbs with a particle as first component, and (b) divisible verbal compounds, i.e., complex verbs of the types A+V (b1) and N+V (b2). There are many verbal particles in German, e.g., *ab-*, *an-*, *auf-*, *aus-*, *bei-*, *durch-*, *mit-*, *über-*, *unter-*, *weg-*, *zu-*, *zusammen-* etc.; subgroup IIIa is quite large and utterly productive. It has to be mentioned that many linguists dealing with word formation in German in a more traditional way (like Fleischer and Barz 1995[2], cf. also Eisenberg 1998: 244) count particles as prefixes, acknowledging that prefixes do not constitute a homogeneous group. Fleischer and Barz (1995[2]: 294) divide prefixes into two groups: (a) non-divisible ("non-distancable") prefixes like *be-*, *ent-*, *er-* and *ver-*; (b) divisible prefixes *like ab-*, *an*, *auf-*, *aus-*, *bei-*, *dar-*, *durch-*, *ein-*, *los-*, *nach-*, *über-*, *um-*, *unter-*, *vor-*, *wider-* and *zu-*. The members of the second group cannot really be called prefixes, since they do not behave like genuine prefixes: they are firmly combined only with verbal infinitives (cf. *ab-fahr-en*); in all finite forms and in participles they are divided from the verbal root: *fährt ... ab*, *abgefahren*. Corresponding to Bussmann (2008[4]: 509f), Olsen (1995, 1997, 1998) and Hausmann (2006), I use the term "particle" for these elements. I would also classify *hinter-*, *voll-* and *wieder-* – treated as

7 Neef (1996: 236) gives a slightly more exact explanation: "Erlaubt als erste Silben sind unbetonte Silben (*belebt*) wie auch solche, die einen tertiären Akzent tragen (*mißglückt*, *diskutiert*)."

8 Wiese (1996: 94) mentions besides *frühstücken* and *ohrfeigen* also *wallfahrten* and *kennzeichnen* as examples of complex verbs with this kind of structure. The (fairly old) verbs *mutmaßen* and *nasführen* obviously also belong to this group; in their participles *ge-* is prefixed: *genasführt* (cf. *WDG* Bd. 4: 2579 und 2612).

9 *Mut* in *mutmaßen* has about the same meaning as English *mood* (with which it is genetically related).

compound constituents by Fleischer and Barz (1995^2: 294) – as particles.[10] Table 2 contains a few examples of German particle verbs.

INFINITIVE	PAST PARTICIPLE
abwerfen	abgeworfen
anrufen	angerufen
auffordern	aufgefordert
auswählen	ausgewählt
durchstöbern	durchgestöbert
mitkommen	mitgekommen
weggehen	weggegangen
zuschneiden	zugeschnitten

Table 2: Particle verbs

IIIb is a fairly large group, subdivided in IIIb1 A+V-compounds like *kranklachen*, IIIb2 N+V-compounds like *eislaufen*, and IIIb3 V+V-compounds.[11] Complex verbs of the types A+V or N+V are quite often idiomatized; *fremdgehen* does not mean 'to go/walk in a strange way' but *to have an affair*, in Am. Eng. *to have a hanky-panky*; *staubsaugen* (*to vacuum*) does not mean 'to inhale dust' but 'to use a vacuum cleaner'.[12] Table 3 lists some examples of A+V:

INFINITIVE	PAST PARTICIPLE	INFINITIVE	PAST PARTICIPLE
fernsteuern	ferngesteuert	richtigstellen	richtiggestellt
fertigmachen	fertiggemacht	schönreden	schöngeredet
freischalten	freigeschaltet	schwarzsehen	schwarzgesehen
fremdgehen	fremdgegangen	weiterbilden	weitergebildet
geheimhalten	geheimgehalten	wundliegen	wundgelegen
gesundpflegen	gesundgepflegt	zufriedenstellen	zufriedengestellt
gutschreiben	gutgeschrieben	kaputtmachen	kaputtgemacht

Table 3: A+V compounds

Combinations of a noun and a verb (N+V) seem to be more problematic. Here, many Germans are often insecure concerning the position of *ge-*; do you say *staubgesaugt* or *gestaub-*

[10] There are elements that can be used in both ways, as prefixes (in firm combination with verb stems) and as particles (i.e., divisible from the verb stems); thus, *über* occurs as prefix in *übersetzen* (*to translate*; main stress on the verb stem) and as particle in *übersetzen* (*to cross over a river*; participle: *übergesetzt*).

[11] The V+V subgroup contains very few verbs, mostly used in technological context, e.g., *walzfräsen* ('to mill-cut') and *schweißbrennen* (*to weld*). Duden (1995^2, Vol. 8) does not mention these verbs. Fleischer and Barz (1995^2: 295) mention some V+V examples like *grinskeuchen*, used mainly in fiction. They point to the fact (loc. cit. (297)) that the A+V type is the biggest subgroup. On the other hand, the N+V subgroup is not as weak as the V+V subgroup and seems to be quite productive.

[12] Besides A+V verbs there are combinations of pref+A+V: *verschlimmbessern* (*to make something worse by improving it*) is an example of this type; it seems to function like normal prefix verbs. And there are combinations of an adjective with a prefixed verb (A+pref+V) like *fernbedienen*.

saugt (i.e., *vacuumed*)? Besides, there does not seem to be a strict borderline between compounds of the N+V type and verb phrases.[13]

INFINITIVE	PAST PARTICIPLE
danksagen	dankgesagt
haushalten	hausgehalten
kopfstehen	kopfgestanden
lobpreisen	lobgepriesen[14]
lustwandeln	lustgewandelt/gelustwandelt
preisgeben	preisgegeben
probefahren	probegefahren
radfahren	radgefahren
sandstrahlen	sandgestrahlt/gesandstrahlt
seiltanzen	seilgetanzt
standhalten	standgehalten
staubsaugen	staubgesaugt /gestaubsaugt[15]
zwangsansiedeln	zwangsangesiedelt

Table 4: N+V compounds

According to Fleischer and Barz (1995^2: 296) this group is small and not productive. But I noticed that it seems to become more productive, especially in participles like *blutgetränkt* ('blood-soaked') and *hitzegewohnt* ('used to heat').[16] It happens frequently in German (and in other languages) that a word formation pattern that was not productive for a long time, gets productive again.[17] In Google I found e.g., *fisch ofen gedünstet* ('fish steamed in the oven'), where at least *ofengedünstet*, probably also *fischofengedünstet*, being compounds of the N+V type, should be written together. On the other hand, there are also compounds of the type N+V with the N-constituent behaving like a prefix, i.e., without *ge*-insertion (e.g., *erleben – erlebt*):

---

13 "Zwischen Komposita dieses Typs und entsprechenden Wortgruppen bestehen fließende Übergänge. Neben *kopfstehen*, *radfahren* stehen *Schlange stehen*, *Auto fahren*, *Bock springen*, *Gefahr laufen*, *Feuer fangen* als Wortgruppen." (Fleischer and Barz 1995^2: 297).

14 This participle – like others of this kind – sounds strange and seems to be avoided by speakers of German.

15 Eisenberg (1998: 226) remarks: "Die Form *gestaubsaugt* ist nur dann möglich, wenn der substantivische Bestandteil untrennbar mit dem Verb verbunden ist wie in *gemaßregelt*, *gehandhabt* usw." (cf. also Hausmann 2006: 24). Most people avoid forming the participle (and the perfect tense) of *staubsaugen*, saying something like *ich musste staubsaugen* ('I had to vacuum') rather than *ich habe staubgesaugt/gestaubsaugt*.

16 According to Hausmann (2006: 19) V+V compounds are extremely rare, whereas N+V as well as A+V occur fairly often and are productive.

17 This happened e.g., with the suffix *-e* (in *Wärme*, *Röte* etc.) that lost its productivity, often being replaced by *-heit* (cf. *Schönheit* vs. *Schöne*), but "woke up" recently to new productivity, cf. *Anmache* (ordinary for *seduction*), *Abzocke* (ordinary for *leaving sb. pennyless*), *Auslege* (*laying out cards in a card game*).

(1) Und wenn dann dort auch noch *luxussaniert* wird [...]
(Martin Klesmann, Die Mischung macht es, *BLZ*, 19.8.10: 17)

Among the N+V verbs you will also find some where the N is combined with a particle verb; these are obviously treated like normal particle verbs, with *-ge-* inserted after the particle:

(2) Tibetische Nomaden sollen nicht *zwangsangesiedelt* werden.
(www.igfm-muenchen.de/tibet/ftc/2010/UN-Tib-Nomaden_23-12)

The very small group of V+V compounds (IIIb3) is mainly used in the infinitive, rarely in finite forms and participles. I could not find any remark in grammars of German telling you how to form the past participles of these verbs, but I found the following example in the internet:

(3) Stirnräder walzgefräst und geschliffen.
(advertisement by the firm Neugert, seen May 15, 2012)

3. Participles of verbs borrowed from English

Verbs borrowed from English can be classified according to the system presented in section 2; they acquire adjectival flexives when used as modifiers to nouns, like native German participles (cf. (4) and (5)). Verbs like *promoten* or *designen*, containing a prefix (in this case of Latin origin), belong to group I; they don't get a *ge*-prefix in their participles:

(4) Gleichfalls mit einem einfachen Joystick auf einem perfekt designten Podest macht Olaf Val im Atelier für Multimedia und Performance das Spiel mit dem Licht einer simplen Glühbirne zum Ereignis.
(J. Kisters, Raum aus Klängen, *KStA*, 20.7.01: 8)

Verbs with the Eng. suffix *-ize* (that correspond to German latinisms ending in *-ier-en*) seem usually to be transformed to verbs with the suffix *-ier-*, already existing in German. I found only one example of *womanized* in a German context, which behaves (as expected) like German verbs with the suffix *-ier*, i.e., getting no *ge-* in the participle (subgroup Ib):

(5) Womanized im Maxxim heißt einmal im Monat Zutritt nur Frauen ('Womanized in 'Maxxim' means once a month only admission for women.').
(www.berlinonline.de).

Simple verbs like *dopen* ('to dope') or *floppen* ('to flop') take the prefix *ge-*, as expected, like native German verbs (cf. IIa, Table 1); in modifier position (within an NP), adjective flexives are added in modifier positions like in (7):

(6) Vielleicht lag es daran, dass [...] sein Elektro-Album „Rudebox" *gefloppt* war [...][18]
(Markus Schneider, Männer mit Knubbeln, *BLZ*, 27.8.10: 28)

(7) Gruner + Jahr [...] war [...] mit [...] der zur ostdeutschen „Zeit" *gedopten* „Wochenpost" auf die Nase gefallen [...]
(Kathr. Rohnstock, Mentalität, *FAZ* 10.7.99: IV)

A+V verbs are treated like native German verbs of the subclass IIb1 (cf. *frühstücken*), since they are derivations of nominal compounds rather than verbal compounds (cf. above):

(8) Ich habe mich drum gekümmert und den Namen „AntiAntifa" *geblackmailt*.
(www.the-warrior-clan.de/printview.php?board=1&topic=279, April 23, 2009)

N+V verbs like *bookmarken* ('to bookmark') and *facebooken* ('to facebook') which are not verbal compounds are treated like native German *mutmaßen* in IIb2:

(9) Wenn ich früher etwas Schönes oder Komisches gefunden habe, habe ich es *gebookmarkt*, also einer Liste mit Lesezeichen für Websites hinzugefügt.
(Peter Glaser, Es gibt ihn doch! Ein später Triumph für Loriot und ein Ärgernis für die Sittenwächter von Facebook: Der Schwanzhund, *BLZ* 8.3.2012: 24)

(10) Jede Sekunde wird getwittert, *gefacebookt*, hin und wieder [...] gesimst.
(*blu*, Febr. 2010: 3, Intro)

Interestingly enough, the subclass IIb experienced an expansion by the influx of verbs of English origin like *forwarden* (*to forward*), having two recognizable constituents fused so closely that they are not separable anymore; their participles are prefixed by *ge-*: *geforwardet*.

(11) Wie wird eine Anfrage richtig geforwardet?
(www.rootforum.org/forum/viewtopic.php?f=107&t=48809, April 29, 2008)

Group III comprises verbs that either contain an (English) preposition or particle that can be separated from the root in German (group III.a, cf. *updaten*)[19] or two recognizable and separable N+V-components like in *babysitten* (group IIIb2); I could not find any examples of the V+V-type (cf. Table 1 above). In all these verbs *-ge-* is inserted between the two components: *babygesittet* (cf. Table 5).

---

18 Considering the orthography, participles of verbs borrowed from English look more like their English origins than the corresponding infinitives, which have to be spelled with double consonants in cases like *floppen*, *shoppen*, *joggen*, *pinnen*, where the English infinitives have only one consonant (cf. Eisenberg (2012^2: 242).

19 Hausmann (2006: 47) remarks that the English particle *up* sounds like the German particle *ab* and is sometimes replaced by it, e.g., in the verbs *updaten* and *upgraden* (which are occasionally spelled *abdaten*, *abgraden*). Duden (2006^{24}: 1059) and Duden (2007^9: 1069) do not list the *ab*-spellings.

With particle verbs there are two possibilities: Whereas the producer of (12) treats the verb *downloaden* like the German verb *herunterladen* (with the past participle *heruntergeladen*), i.e., separable, the producer of (13) treats it as inseparable and lets the prefix *ge-* precede the stem (like in *geforwardet*). Likewise, with the verb *updaten* (here classified as group IIIa) I found the form *upgedatet* – which I think is the form preferred by most German speakers –, but also the alternative form *geupdatet*:[20]

(12) a505chs.exe von ftp.adobe.com kann nicht *downgeloaded* werden.
(*Internet-Explorer* on the Siemens-Fujitsu-Computer, Apr. 16, 2002, 6 pm.)

(13) Installiert *gedownloadete* Updates und schaltet den Computer aus.
(announcement in Windows XP)

(14) So, ich hab gestern mal meine Browser *upgedatet* und hab jetzt Firefox 2.0 und IE 7.0.
(Josef D., 12.11.2006, 11:25; gefunden bei Google)

(15) Denn natürlich hatte er seine Hits von gestern [...] nicht einfach so kopiert. Er hatte sie gewissermaßen *geupdatet*.
(Jenny Hoch, Unten nackt – oben ganz der Papa: Baselitz' „Russenbilder". www.spiegel.de/kultur, 15.11.07)

It seems that the speaker's/writer's sensation whether he or she has to do with a German or a foreign word, plays a role. Hybrids ("semi-anglicisms") like *einchecken* ('to check in') seem to prove this supposition:

(16) *Eingecheckt* hatte Justin Timberlake im Hotel Intercontinental.
(*KStA*, 11.6.07: 30)

It should be mentioned that the remaining verb forms (finite forms and infinitives) behave completely in accordance with the native German pattern; like with German particle verbs, *zu* is inserted between the particle and the infinitival verb form (cf. (17)) and the particle is separated from the verb stem in finite forms (cf. (18)):

(17) [...] hatten die Zuschauer [...] schon reichlich Gelegenheit, sich auf Hölderlins elegischen Tonfall *einzugrooven*.
(Chr. Bos, Es gilt das gesprochene Wort, *KStA*, 25.2.08: 22)

(18) Über ein Passwort *loggt* er *sich* auf der Internetseite der Schule *ein*.
(Alice Ahlers, Penne mit Passwort, *KStA*, 7.3.08: 8)

Speakers of German obviously consider *einchecken*, *einloggen* etc. to be divisible German part-icle verbs. The same is true of *auscasten* ('to cast out') and *ausflippen* ('to flip out,

[20] Duden, *RGD* (2007[6]: 919) gives the following description: "Das Verb *updaten* (*aktualisieren*) wird teils als Präfixverb mit untrennbarem Bestandteil *up*, teils als Verb mit Verbzusatz (erster Bestandteil trennbar) gebraucht: *ich update*, [...] *sie hat upgedatet* [...]." This is not consequent; with *hat upgedatet* you would also expect *date up* (cf. *höre auf*). For *downloaden* Hausmann (2006) lists only *downgeloadet*.

freak out'); here again, the participles have been formed according to the IIIa-pattern (like German *ausrasten*, a verb with approximately the same meaning as *ausflippen*):

(19) *Ausgecastet* – DSDS verliert, die Dienstagserien kippen, [...]: RTL zeigt plötzlich Schwäche – das ist problematisch, weil es nicht in anderen Zeitformen auftritt
(Title of the article by Peer Schader, *BLZ*, 18.5.12: 26)

(20) Als die auf dem T-Shirt Body Angels gelesen hat, hat sie nicht nur die Nase gerümpft, sie ist richtig *ausgeflippt*.
(U. Kreikebaum, Komische Sprüche [...], *KStA* 24./25.3.07: 37)

We probably can formulate a rule:

> The more speakers/writers of German consider at least one of the components of a complex verb as being German, the more they will treat that verb as a native complex verb.

Concerning the IIIb1-type, I could not find any examples of A+V compounds; all A+V combinations I found like *blackmailen* and *highlighten* seem to belong to the IIb1-subclass.[21] There are enough examples of the IIIb2-type (the N+V subgroup) like *babysitten* (cf. (21)), *breakdancen*, *kitesurfen*, *mountainbiken*, *snowboarden* (listed in Hausmann 2006: 55). Parallel to the problems concerning the assignment of German verbs like *staubsaugen* to groups II or III (cf. *gestaubsaugt/staubgesaugt* in Table 4), there are obviously corresponding problems with verbs borrowed from English. Although most speakers of German would form the participle like in (21), there are some that would prefer *gebabysittet* (cf. (22)) or would not know how to form the participle like in the case of *staubsaugen* (cf. fn. 15).

(21) 100000 Dank an alle die *babygesittet* haben!
(www.notmoms.de, April 9, 2008)

(22) Morgen wird doch net *gebabysittet* (tolles Wort) [...]
(www.tagtt.de/archive, May 2, 2012)

In Table 5, the anglicisms have been integrated into the subclassificational system of German verb formation (with infinitives and past participles indicated).

[21] I found *gehighlightet* on the internet (under www.dict.cc/?s=gehighlightet). Cf. also *geblackmailt* in (7).

GROUP	SUBGROUP	INFINITIVE	PERFECT PARTICIPLE
I	a	erleben	erlebt
		promoten	promotet
	b	inspizieren	inspiziert
		womanizen	womanized
II	a	geben	gegeben
		dope	gedopt
	b1	frühstücken	gefrühstückt
		blackmailen	geblackmailt
	b2	mutmaßen	gemutmaßt
	b3	baysitten	gebabysittet[22]
		./.	./. [23]
		forwarden	geforwardet
III	a	abraten	abgeraten
		updaten	upgedatet
	b1	fremdgehen	fremdgegangen
		./.	./.
	b2	kopfstehen	kopfgestanden
		babysitten	babygesittet

Table 5: Subclassification

It turns out that all complex verbs of English origin are basically treated the same way as native German complex verbs, with two exceptions:

- Among the particle verbs, there is a subgroup of verbs prefixing *ge-*, like in *geforwardet*, whereas the bulk of particle verbs behaves like German particle verbs, infixing *-ge-* like in *outgecheckt*; quite often you will find both options like in *gedownloadet* vs. *downgeloaded*; *geupdatet* vs. *upgedatet*.[24]
- All verbs of the A+V type of English origin seem to be treated as non-divisible (cf. *geblackmailt*); I could not find any examples of verbs infixing *-ge-* like in native German A+V compounds like *fremdgegangen* (cf. chapter 2) and *gleichgeschaltet* ('forced into line'). Concerning these verbs (as also concerning some inflectional aspects of verbs of the other subgroups) further research is necessary.

22 The German Dictionary on the internet indicates under *babysitten* in "Suchbegriff Verben" the perfect and plusquamperfect forms *habe/hatte gebabysittet* (checked on May 14, 2012).

23 According to the Duden grammar (2006[7]: 447), all particle verbs are divisible, with infixed *-ge-* (i.e., group IIIa, cf. *abraten*). Here verbs with English prepositions or particles like *for* or *out* are not taken account of.

24 Participles of English origin are sometimes spelled with final *-d*, but more and more often with *-t* (cf. the remarks below and Hausmann 2006: 42f). Langner (1995) treats only the spelling of derivational suffixes borrowed from English but does not take inflectional suffixes like *-(e)t* and *-en* marking German past participles into account.

4. Summary

I agree with the final statement by Hausmann (2006: 65), stating that the influx of many English words has not led to a "loss of structure" (*Strukturverlust*) of the German language; speakers of German are trying successfully to integrate words borrowed from English into the morphological system of German. This is also true of the formation of participles: Verbs taken from English are assigned to the three subclasses of German participles: I. participles without *-ge-* (*promotet*), II. participles with prefixed *ge-* (*geblackmailt*), III. participles with infixed *-ge-* (*upgedated, babygesittet*). Slight deviations concern particle verbs that prefix *ge-* (*geforwardet*) and the lack of group IIIb1 A+V compounds (**blackgemailt*, **quickgemillt*) that would correspond to the native German pattern exemplified by *fremdgegangen* (see Table 5). I have not said very much about the orthography of verbal anglicisms but I can refer the reader to Hausmann (2006), who found that the English participle flexive *-ed* has been replaced more and more often by German -(*e*)*t*, this way indicating German final devoicing.[25] Spellings like *downgeloaded* give way to spellings like *downgeloadet*. Eisenberg (2001: 185) mentions that phonological integration processes are often accompanied by graphematic integration.

The fact that English word material is getting more and more integrated into the German language can also be witnessed by semi-anglicisms like *einchecken, eingrooven, einloggen* und *ausflippen* in (15)–(18) as well as Germanized forms like *abdaten* and *abgraden* (cf. Hausmann 2006: 47). There are even verbs composed of a German prefix (*be-*, *er-*, *ver-* etc.) combined with an English verbal stem, the most popular one being *ergoogeln*:

(23) Schon in der Schule *ergoogeln* sich die Kinder ihre Referate.
(Interview, *Spiegel* 12.2.07: 146)

Thus, verbs of English origin are getting increasingly integrated into the inflectional system of German verbs, in about the same way as Latin and French verbs were integrated into the morphological system of German during many centuries.

Bibliography

Carstensen, B. (1965): *Englische Einflüsse auf die deutsche Sprache nach 1945*. Heidelberg: Winter.

Duden (1995[2]): *Das große Wörterbuch der deutschen Sprache*. In 8 Bänden. Mannheim: Dudenverlag.

Duden (2006[7]): *Die Grammatik. Unentbehrlich für richtiges Deutsch*. [Autoren: Peter Eisenberg, Peter Gallmann, Cathrine Fabricius-Hansen u.a.]. Mannheim / Leipzig / Wien / Zürich: Dudenverlag. (= Duden Bd. 4).

[25] It has to be mentioned that in word stems final devoicing is almost never marked, cf. *Leid* [lajt], *Krieg* [kri:k].

Duden (2006[24]): *Die deutsche Rechtschreibung*. Mannheim: Dudenverlag (= Duden Bd. 1).

Duden (2007[6]): *Richtiges und gutes Deutsch. Wörterbuch der sprachlichen Zweifelsfälle.* (Duden 9). Mannheim/Leipzig/Wien/Zürich: Dudenverlag. Abgekürzt als *RGD*.

Duden (2007[9]): *Das Fremdwörterbuch*. Mannheim: Dudenverlag (= Duden Bd. 5).

Eisenberg, P. (1998): *Grundriss der deutschen Grammatik*. Vol. 1: *Das Wort*. Stuttgart: Metzler.

Eisenberg, P. (2001): Die grammatische Integration von Fremdwörtern. Was fängt das Deutsche mit seinen Latinismen und Anglizismen an? In: G. Stickel (ed.), *Neues und Fremdes im deutschen Wortschatz. Aktueller lexikalischer Wandel*. Jahrbuch 2000 des Instituts für Deutsche Sprache. Berlin: de Gruyter, 183–209.

Eisenberg, P. (2012[2]): *Das Fremdwort im Deutschen*. Berlin/New York: de Gruyter.

Fischer, U. (1980): *Der Einfluß des Englischen auf den deutschen Wortschatz im Bereich von Essen und Trinken, dargestellt anhand schweizerischer Quellen*. Frankfurt am Main: Peter Lang (= *Europ. Hochschulschriften. Deutsche Sprache und Literatur*, Bd. 372).

Fleischer, W. und I. Barz (1992, 1995[2]): *Wortbildung der deutschen Gegenwartssprache*. Tübingen: Niemeyer.

Hausmann, D. (2006): *"Downgeloaded" und "geforwardet" – Sprecherverhalten in morphologischen Zweifelsfällen am Beispiel des Sprachgebrauch im Internet*. Universität zu Köln: Inst. f. Linguistik (= *Arbeitspapier* Nr. 50).

Langner, H. C. (1995): *Die Schreibung englischer Entlehnungen im Deutschen. Eine Untersuchung zur Orthographie von Anglizismen in den letzten hundert Jahren, dargestellt an Hand des Dudens*. Frankfurt: Peter Lang.

Neef, M. (1996): *Wortdesign. Eine deklarative Analyse der deutschen Verbflexion*. Tübingen: Stauffenburg (SdG 52).

Olsen, S. (1995): Partikelverben im deutsch-englischen Vergleich. In: Lang, E. and G. Zifonun (eds.), *Deutsch – typologisch*. Berlin: de Gruyter (= *IdS, Jahrbuch 1995*), 261–288.

Olsen, S. (1997): Der Dativ bei Partikelverben. In: C. Dürscheid, K. H. Ramers and M. Schwarz (eds.), *Sprache im Fokus. Festschrift für Heinz Vater zum 65. Geburtstag*. Tübingen: Niemeyer, 307–328.

Olsen, S. (1998): *Semantische und konzeptuelle Aspekte der Partikelbildung mit ein*. Tübingen: Stauffenburg.

Paulwitz, T. (2010): Wird Deutsch zur Affensprache? *Deutsche Sprachwelt*, spring 2010: 1.

Schreiber, M. (2006): Deutsch for sale. *Der Spiegel* 40 (2.10.2006): 182–198.

Spitzmüller, J. (2007): Sprache und Identität: Warum die Anglizismen die Gemüter erhitzen. *Muttersprache* 117, 3: 185–198.

Stickel, G. (1984): Einstellungen zu Anglizismen. *Göppinger Arbeiten zur Germanistik* 423: 279-310.

Stickel, G. (1999): *Sprache – Sprachwissenschaft – Öffentlichkeit*. Berlin/New York: de Gruyter (= *Institut für deutsche Sprache, Jahrbuch* 1998).

Vater, H. (1994, 2002[4]): *Einführung in die Sprachwissenschaft*. München: Fink (= *UTB* 1799).

Vater, H. (2008): Zur morphologischen Integration von Anglizismen im Deutschen. *Deutschunterricht für Ungarn* 23. (1-2): 13–40.

Wiese, R. (1996): *The Phonology of German*. Oxford: Clarendon.

Zifonun, G. (2000): Grammatische Integration jugendsprachlicher Anglizismen. *Der Deutschunterricht* 52, 4: 69–79.

Abbreviations

A	=	adjective
N	=	noun
V	=	verb
pref	=	prefix

Abbreviated bibliographical indications

BLZ	=	*Berliner Zeitung*. Berlin: Berliner Verlag GmbH
KStA	=	*Kölner Stadtanzeiger*. Kölnische Zeitung seit 1802. Köln: Neven DuMont.
Spiegel	=	*Der Spiegel. Das deutsche Nachrichten-Magazin*. Hamburg: Spiegel-Verlag.
WDG	=	Klappenbach, Ruth and Steinitz, Wolfgang (eds.) (1968^2). *Wörterbuch der deutschen Gegenwartssprache*. Berlin: Akademie-Verlag.

Morphological code-mixing: The case of Zulu agreement in English*

Heike Tappe

1. Introduction

Multilingual and bilingual societies are a growing reality in the world; in fact, current research indicates that speakers of two or more languages outnumber monolingual speakers (Grosjean 2010). Hence there is a growing interest in linguistic processes and representations in multi- and bilingual speakers[1]. The multilingual mind poses a number of challenges to linguistic research. It may even be the 'test-bed' for our assumptions about language production and language comprehension models and ultimately our assumptions about the language faculty (Francis 2011).

The current paper presents a synopsis of one set of such challenges by bringing together crucial observations on code-mixing (in particular intra-sentential code-mixing between Zulu and English) from fields as diverse as sociolinguistics, psycholinguistics, language acquisition research, syntax, morphology, and the neurosciences. My objectives are threefold: My first objective is to conduct a 'stock-taking' exercise that juxtaposes selected findings and ideas from vastly different fields of linguistic research. My second objective is to provide examples from Zulu/English code-mixes that might be informative with respect to morphological processes and representations in a multilingual speaker. Finally, my third objective is to provide a 'shopping list' of research items that might be missing or be on too low a supply in our research 'cupboard'.

1.1. Mixed sentences and mixed words

Code-switching, code-mixing, lexical insertion and lexical borrowing are terms that describe various types of situations in which a bi- or multilingual speaker uses her two languages within one discourse.

The term code-switching is predominantly used for situations of inter-sentential changes in language use, like e.g., in sentence (1) below. Torres (1992) asserts that code-switching (unlike code-mixing) is encouraged by changes in the social situation like for example the appearance of a new interlocutor who does not speak the current discourse language.

---

* I am indebted to Dr. Langa Khumalo and Matthew Lasich who read a pre-final draft of this paper. All errors and shortcomings are mine.

1 Henceforth I will use the term 'multilingual' to cover both speakers of two and speakers of more than two languages.

(1) He said he was going to church. Aber ich glaube das nicht.[2]
'But I do not believe this.'

In contrast the term *code-mixing* is generally used for intra-sentential language mixes (see, e.g., Bhatt 1997: 223) like in (2)a, or, for intra-lexeme language mixes like in (2)b (see also Vater (this volume)):

(2) a. Die verrücktesten Studenten may be most fun to work with.[3]
'The craziest students ...'
b. Ich habe Dir die email geforwarded
Ich habe Dir die email geforwarded
I have you the email $\text{prefix}_{\text{perfect marker}}$

The term *lexical insertion* is mostly reserved for instances, where an utterance is largely in one language and one lexeme from another available language is inserted, see example (3).

(3) Ich geh dann mal zum faculty board.
I go then $\text{once}_{\text{discourse marker}}$ to $\text{the}_{\text{contracted form}}$
'I am going to the faculty board just now.'

Lexical borrowings share all features of lexical insertions; the only difference between the two is that lexical borrowings are conventionalized lexical insertions that have become part of the lexicon of the guest language, examples are provided in (4)a to (4)d. Since lexical borrowings have the status of conventionalized lexemes in the guest language, they may be used by monolingual and multilingual speakers alike.

(4) a. I am having a déjà vu.
b. He has lots of savoir faire.
c. She is a real gourmet.
d. My child is going to a Waldorf kindergarten.

The types of mixed language usage in the examples 1–3 are verbal strategies that may be employed by multilingual speakers for a variety of reasons; these "[...] depend on the interlocutor (age, sex, social position), the topic of conversation, and the environment in which the interaction occurs" (Coronel-Molina and Rodríguez-Mondoñedo 2012: 3). Grosjean (1982) summarized some of the functions of code-mixed speech as: filling a lexical gap, specifying the addressee or excluding someone from a conversation, changing the role of the interlocutor, asserting ethnic identity or quoting someone, and qualifying a message or portraying emotions.

Even though language purists may regard language mixes as signs of insufficient language competence, multilingual speakers seem to have "[...] clear and unambiguous intuitions of what is, and also what is not, a possible code-switched utterance" (Bhatt 1997: 223–224); i.e., it has been attested that code-switching and code-mixing follow grammatical rules (Baker and Jones 1998: 60–61).

[2] Lexical items from guest language are presented in italics.
[3] According to e.g., Callahan (2002: 8) the noun phrase 'die verrücktesten Studenten' constitutes a German 'embedded language island' in an English matrix language sentence (compare the analogous example from Delgado (1982: 66–67) cited by Callahan.

These statements raise a variety of questions; in particular with regards to the architecture of the multilingual language production and comprehension system like, e.g.: How is a non-linguistic speaker intention (i.e., a pre-verbal message, Levelt 1989: 9) realized as a language-mixed linguistic utterance? How do two grammatical systems interact to produce a grammatical yet mixed utterance? How do morphological rules from one language (which operate in the mental lexicon of this language) access and manipulate lexical material from the mental lexicon of the other language?

For the past three decades research on the multilingual mind has largely been dedicated on determining how multilingual speakers manage to keep their languages separate. "This bias is a remnant of the view that a bilingual is essentially two monolinguals in one brain […]" (Schmid 2010: 3). However, language mixes may be rather the rule than the exception in discourses among multilingual speakers who have more than one language in common (e.g., Heredia and Altarriba 2001: 164). Hence Schmid (2010) argues that we need to shift our research efforts towards understanding linguistic multi-competence.

For Schmid the term 'linguistic multi-competence' describes an architecture of the language production and comprehension system that integrates the mental grammars of a multilingual speaker into one architecture: "Bilingual knowledge, competence and proficiency are not made up of separate or separable subsystems (L1, L2, …) but they consist of one holistic and dynamic system within which every change has ramifications throughout all subsystems (e.g., De Bot, [Lowie and Verspoor][4] 2007)." (Schmid 2010: 1). Schmid's phrasing is reminiscent of the 'third system' idea that holds that in multilinguals we might find an 'integrated language system'. A similar thought is verbalized by Deumert (2005) in the context of research on contact languages: "Languages in contact are shaped not only by the dynamics of internal, evolutive language change, but also by processes of linguistic convergence and language mixing which continuously interrupt the stabilization of fixed form-meaning pairings, and challenge the structuralist conceptions of language as a closed, unitary, finite rule-system. Contact languages are fluid systems with 'soft' rather than hard edges […]" (Deumert 2005: 114).

The current contribution discusses the idea of fluidity of 'languages in contact' in a South African context, in particular the contact situation between varieties of South African English and Zulu spoken in Durban, the third largest South African city, situated in the province of KwaZulu-Natal. The main research questions are: Which assumptions do we have to make about the multilingual language processing system so that it can 'cope' with fluid language mixing between two languages from vastly different language families? How safe are we to assume that speakers have separate language systems if the languages in question are contact languages that have to be used in conjunction for the speakers to be able to function in all aspects of the society? In the following I will first sketch the language situation in South Africa with a particular focus on the roles of English and Zulu in KwaZulu-Natal and Durban. I will then discuss a selection of code-mixed Zulu-English utterances against current research findings on code-mixing from various disciplines.

4 De Bot's co-authors added.

2. Multilingualism in South Africa

South Africa recognizes eleven official languages – Afrikaans, English, Ndebele, Northern Sotho, Sotho, Swati, Tsonga, Tswana, Venda, Xhosa and Zulu – and endeavours to give every citizen the right to participate in all aspects of the society in his or her own home language. Approximately 24% of South Africans are home language speakers of Zulu. This makes Zulu the most common home language in the country. In addition Zulu is (at least partially) mutually intelligible with Xhosa, Swati and Ndebele, which all belong to the Nguni language group.

According to the census data from 2001, only eight to nine per cent of South Africans are home language speakers of English, however, in the aftermath of Western colonization and the Apartheid regime English has become the lingua franca in large parts of the country. English enables communication across racial and ethnic borders (the 2001 census estimates that about 45% of the country's population have some competence in spoken English) and in most parts of the country English is the language of commerce, education and academia, the media and jurisprudence. Obviously, the dominant status of English is also strengthened by its role as an international lingua franca i.e., in international media, commerce and academia. This means that while English is clearly a minority language in South Africa, it is the language with the highest prestige and hence the language with the greatest number of second language speakers.

2.1. Zulu and English in Durban

Durban, the third largest city in South Africa, is situated in the province of KwaZulu-Natal (KZN), which hosts both the greatest number of English speakers and the greatest number of Zulu speakers of all South African provinces: The vast majority of Zulu speakers (72%) reside in KwaZulu-Natal, where it is the home language to about 82% of the provincial population (numbers according to the 2001 census), while about one-third of KwaZulu-Natal's inhabitants are English home language speakers (8.2% countrywide, 34.9% in KwaZulu-Natal, respectively, according to the 2001 census). According to these figures and in keeping with the fact that the province hosts the two most important languages in South Africa, Zulu-English bilingualism should be common in KwaZulu-Natal. Indeed the majority of the province's inhabitants are bilingual; yet, bilingualism is unequally distributed among English and Zulu home language speakers. The majority of Zulu home language speakers have some degree of command of English. This, however, does not hold for English home languages speakers, most of whom have little or no command of Zulu.

This inequality is mainly due to the fact that English is the dominant language in the province (and in the country) as mentioned above. In addition, the dominance of English is reflected and reinforced by the schooling system because overall English is the dominant language of learning and teaching (LOLT) in the country (LOLT-report 2007). Most single medium of instruction schools are schools with English as the medium of instruction (see table 1 for the respective figures). An additional 13,000 schools (approximately 51% of all schools in South Africa) were classified as dual medium of instruction schools in 2007, 2,300 of which combine English and Afrikaans as the medium of instruction, while the remaining schools almost exclusively combine English with one African language. These numbers demonstrate the dominance of English as a medium of instruction.[5]

MEDIUM OF INSTRUCTION	SINGLE MEDIUM OF INSTRUCTION SCHOOLS IN SOUTH AFRICA
Afrikaans	1,174
English	4,342
isiNdebele	1
isiXhosa	29
isiZulu	41
Sepedi	8
Sesotho	0
Setswana	22
Siswati	22
Setswana	0
Tshivenda	2
Xitsonga	24
Total	5,643

Table 1: Number of single medium schools by LOLT in 2007
Department of Education: 1998 to 2007 Annual School Survey
(Department of basic education 2010: 24)

Even in rural high schools that are classified as single medium instruction schools at least the grades 10–12 are mostly taught in English because in the National Senior Certificate Examination (the South African university entrance exam) all learning areas – with the exception of the languages – are examined either in English or in Afrikaans. However, in comparison to English, Afrikaans plays a significantly smaller role in KZN (Appelraju 2010: 75). Appalraju points out that especially in rural schools in KZN learners are taught and examined in the secondary language, which entails that their LOLT is a language that they have little exposure to and that their teachers are often not very fluent in (Appalraju 2010: 76). She assumes that the implementation of the prescribed dual medium instruction (i.e., the move from Zulu as a medium of instruction to Zulu and English, or, English alone) may lead to subtractive bilingualism, because Zulu is thus gradually replaced by a hegemonic additional language, which is almost always English in KwaZulu-Natal (Appalraju 2010: 76).

This assumption is born out of the observation that teaching materials are pre-dominantly in English and that – not only in the area of educational/ academic/ scientific content – terminology development in Zulu has either not (yet) taken place, or, is progressing very slowly. Generally Zulu exhibits a large number of lexical gaps, which are particularly tangible to language users who live in urban environments where, first, the language contact situation is

[5] It seems to have been impossible to categorize the remaining 7.357 schools as either single or as dual medium of instruction school. In all likelihood these are schools which offer dual medium instruction in the first four (or more) grades and gradually switch to single medium of instruction thereafter. Regrettably, it is unclear from the cited report whether this is what the reader is intended to infer.

more marked than in rural areas and, second, the work space requires vocabulary that is often not available in Zulu and where, third, access to international media and entertainment (cinemas, casinos, etc.) is more easily available than in rural environments. Thus, in particular in urban environments the task of functioning in all areas of society in Zulu alone becomes difficult. This observation is shared by Webb and Sure, who state that in urban environments many South African citizens do not have adequate opportunities to use their native languages (Webb and Sure 2000: 89).[6]

3. Intrasentential language mixing: Background information

The close and constant contact and competition situation between the two languages, Zulu and English, also leads to perpetual lexical intrusion from the hegemonic languages – primarily from English but also from Afrikaans – even in situations where there is no lexical gap in the host language (Zulu).

In informal conversations, students with Zulu as their home language remarked that many Zulu expressions feel less 'economical' than the English translation equivalents. This holds, for example, for Zulu numerals, which in comparison to their English counterparts appear rather long. Compare the equivalents in (5)a and (5)b as well as those in (6)a and (6)b:

(5) a. two thousand three hundred and fifty three
b. 'izinkulungwane ezimbili namakhulu amathathu namashumi amahlanu nantathu'

(6) a. cell phone
b. 'umakhalekhwikhwini'

Literally translated (5)b means: 'Thousands that-are-two and hundreds-that-are-three and tens-that-are-five and three'. For much the same reasons that lexemes for numerals are frequently borrowed from English, the standard Zulu lexeme for *cell phone*, namely, *umakhalekhwikhwini* (which literally means 'the screaming in the pocket') is currently mostly used in Zulu language classes for second language learners and has widely been replaced by the shorter *icell* in actual conversations.

While the examples in (5) and (6) may be explained by a certain 'round-about-ness' of the standard Zulu lexemes, table 2 lists a number of representative examples of instances where an English lexeme has been inserted into Zulu even though a standard Zulu expression is available and where the inserted word is not necessarily shorter than the existing lexeme in standard Zulu.

6 However, the study of Magagula (2009) shows no significant difference in the amount and frequency of use of 'urban' Zulu between rural and urban high-school students in KwaZulu-Natal, which indicates that 'urban' Zulu with its high occurrence of code-mixing may indeed be ubiquitous.

ENGLISH	INSERTED LEXEME	STANDARD ZULU LEXEME
clinic	iclinic	umtholampilo
gate	igeythi	isango
permission	ipermission	imvume
licence	ilayicensi	imvume yokushayela

Table 2: English lexemes inserted into a modern Zulu variety

(Magagula 2009: 5 and 34)

In sum, lexical gaps and lexical competition, in combination with sociolinguistic reasons[7] make intra-sentential code-mixing ubiquitous – especially in urban environments. This observation is shared by the website *The languages of South Africa*, which lists the below example of an intra-sentential language mix between three languages: The utterance in (7) has Zulu as the matrix-language and intra-sentential mixes from both English (in italics) and Afrikaans (underlined).[8]

(7) a. IChiefs isidle nge*referee's optional time, otherwise*ngabe ihambe<u>sleg</u>.

b. 'Chiefs [a local soccer team] has beaten us owing to the referee's optional time, otherwise they could have lost.'[9]

(*The languages of South Africa* webpage, original example from Mfusi 1989: 31)

c.

I-	Chiefs	i-	si-	dl	-e	nge-
PRE-PREFIX$_{NC5}$	Chiefs	SC/SM$_5$	US$_{OM}$	beat$_{VERB\ ROOT}$	SUFFIX$_{SP}$	NM

referee's optional time, otherwise	-ngabe	i-	hamb	-e	sleg
	perhaps	SC$_7$	go$_{VERB\ ROOT}$	PAST$_{SUB}$	bad

Even though the example in (7) is extreme with respect to the extent of mixing it contains, such utterances do occur and the frequent usage of English lexical insertions combined with morphological changes is abundant in modern, urban varieties of Zulu.

3.1. Zulu English code-mixing: General strategies & theoretical background

When discussing code-mixing between English and Zulu in the context of a 'third system' hypothesis, one has to take into consideration the fact that standard Zulu has a number of English loan words that are considered part of the lexicon of standard Zulu. Examples of such English loan words, which have almost exclusively been borrowed because of a lexical gap, are listed in table 3.

---

7 In addition to the sociolinguistic factors outlined above, see, e.g., Mesthrie's 2002: 204 argument that the standard varieties of African languages are associated with the rural areas and hence 'backw '

8 NC = morphological noun class marker, SC/SM = subject concord/ subject marker (morpheme marking subject agreement), OM = object marker, SP = Simple past tense marker, NM = negative modal, PAST$_{SUB}$ = Past tense plus subjunctive mood marker

9 The translation rendered at the website is not quite accurate and has been corrected.

ENGLISH	ZULU
cake	ikhekhe
coffee	ikhofi
bucket	ibhakede
curriculum	icurriculumu

Table 3: Established English loan words in standard Zulu (singular words)

The examples in table 3 exemplify a canonical morphological process of assimilating a lexeme from another language into a Zulu sentence frame that is the most productive process for 'foreign noun integration' in Zulu morphology. What happens is that a foreign noun receives the noun class marker *i(li)-* of noun class 5–which is held to be the 'default' noun class in Zulu (see discussion below)–and is phonologically, morphologically and orthographically assimilated into Zulu but changing, e.g., sequences of consonant clusters so as to adhere to the tonal patterns of Zulu. In Zulu grammatical morphology relating to noun classes is prefixed to both nouns and verbs: In the majority of Bantu languages, subject-verb agreement is expressed by prefixing a subject marker (SM) to the verb stem. This subject marker agrees with the noun class features of the preverbal[10] subject; cf. table 4 for an overview of the noun classes in Zulu[11].

CLASS (SINGULAR CLASSES)	CLASS (PLURAL CLASSES)
1 u(m)	2 aba
1a u	2a oo
3 um	4 imi-
5 i(li)-	6 ama
7 isi-	8 izi-
9 iN	10 iziN-/iiN
11 u(lu)-	
14 ubu-	
15 uku-	
16 u(lu)-	

Table 4: Zulu noun classes[12]

Noun class 5 (for singulars) and noun class 6 (for plurals, see table 5 for examples) have consistently been identified in the literature as 'default' noun classes; i.e., classes that for-

10 In structures with subject-verb inversion there is no morphological agreement between the subject and the verb (cf. e.g., Zeller 2008).

11 Prefixes in brackets are not always realized as a morphological noun class marker on the noun but are morphologically realized somewhere else in the 'system', e.g., as an object concord. In the present case the object concord for noun class 1 is -m- as in *Ngiyamthanda* (*I love him/her*). *Ngi* = 1pers sing pronoun, *-ya-* = verb alternation marker (i.e., 'disjoint', see e.g., Güldemann 2003), *-m-* = object concord: *-thand* = verb root; *-a* = present tense, indicative, active marker.

12 The common convention introduced by Meinhof (1906) which I am following here results in a gap between class 11 and class 14. The gap corresponds to two classes in Nguni languages which are absent in Zulu. The three locative classes 16, 17 and 18 are also absent in table 4 because in Nguni languages (in contrast to other Bantu languages) these are only realised in a few adverbial expressions.

eign nouns would most frequently be assimilated into (e.g., Koopman 2000). Van der Spuy (2010: 300) identifies noun class 6 as the default class that foreign nouns are inserted into because according to him *(a)ma-* is the form used for a productive gender[13] in Zulu and noun class 6 only contains borrowed nouns.

ENGLISH	ZULU
breadrolls	amabreadrolls
salads	amasaladi

Table 5: Established English loan words in standard Zulu (plural words)

Some researchers argue that the preference for noun class 5 as the default noun class might be semantically motivated because noun class 5 is the semantically most underspecified noun class; it is often described as containing nouns that refer to 'miscellaneous' types of objects. Even though there seems to be a semantic classification of Zulu noun classes, such a classification can only be upheld for a very small subset of the lexicon.[14]

The more prevalent processes at work during the assimilation of loan words into Zulu noun classes are morphologically and phonologically motivated. Schnoebelen (2005) identifies the following – interrelated – general processes: First, "minimise the amount of change a noun undergoes in the assimilation process" (Schoebelen 2005: 4) and thus, second, use a noun class that has a morphologically relatively unmarked prefix (Schoebelen 2005: 4). Noun classes 1, 1a, 2, 2a as well as noun class 5 are morphologically unmarked in comparison. However, classes 1, 1a, 2, and 2a come with the semantic constraint of being 'nouns to denote people, kinships and professions' and hence borrowing and insertions into these classes is largely restricted to nouns that fall into the semantic 'scope' of these noun classes, hence seemingly making noun class 5 the default class for borrowings and insertions. There are obviously exceptions to this general trend as is evidenced by the examples in table 6; these exemplify that in the past nouns that denote things which are 'closely associated with people' were also borrowed into noun class 1a (with a plural derived into noun class 2a)[15].

ENGLISH	STANDARD ZULU
lettuce	uletisi
collar	ukhololo

Table 6: Established English loan words in standard Zulu (plural words)

Taraldsen (2010) and other Bantuists (e.g., van der Spuy 2010) point out that the Zulu noun class prefixes are hierarchically structured. As mentioned earlier the initial vowel is most

[13] Later in his article, van der Spuy (2010: 312) rejects the very notion of *gender* for Zulu, however. He rather argues that Zulu nouns are marked for [class], [sub-class] and [plural].

[14] This holds with the exception of the noun classes 1, 1a, 2 and 2b which almost exclusively contain nouns referring to persons (noun class 1 and 2) or kinship terms, nouns referring to professions and proper names (noun class 1a and 2b).

[15] There is some regularity in how singular and plural noun classes relate in Zulu, e.g., usually a noun from noun class 1 *umuntu* (*person*) will have its plural in class 2, i.e., *abantu* (*people*). See the pairing indicated in table (4). However, there is some flexibility in the system, for example, some class 1 nouns denoting nationality in fact form their plurals in class 6 rather than in class 2: *umZulu* (*a Zulu person*), *amaZulu* (*several Zulu persons, the Zulus*) (cf. Taraldsen 2010: 1524).

commonly analysed as a pre-prefix (often called the 'augment') that forms a morpho-syntactically independent part of the nominal prefix which functions like a D-type head (see Taraldsen 2010: 5 for a discussion of supporting arguments for this assumption). Taraldsen's radical decomposition approach to the morpho-syntax of Nguni noun class prefixes and concords rests on a superset assumption, namely that layers of functional heads are nested in one another, and the additional assumption that one morpheme may lexicalise 'non-trivial spans of heads', i.e., more than a single morpho-syntactic head. His analysis captures the empirical observation that nominal prefixes in Nguni languages always contain more heads than morphemes and that lexicalisation in general 'targets spans rather than single terminals' (Taraldsen 2010: 18). Against the background of this assumption his analysis can adequately explain the fact that the lexicalisation patterns for the functional heads within the noun class concord and agreement system are not identical across the different noun classes.

The outcome of his distributional analysis of noun class prefixes and concords across a wide variety of Bantu languages is summarised in his template for the morpho-syntax of Nguni noun class prefixes and concords, here reproduced in (9), in which the A-layer contains the functional head regulating noun class features (i.e., lexically 'filled' by the augment), the SC-layer contains the functional head regulating subject concord, the OC layer contains the functional head regulating object concord, the AC layer contains the functional head regulating adjectival concord, and the I layer contains two functional heads regulating lexicalisation patterns within the scope of negation and for vocatives: In both cases the augment (pre-prefix) is typically dropped (which is regulated by the 'lowest' functional head represented in (9), i.e., Q), but for some noun classes (e.g., NC10 for Zulu) the higher head W can be lexicalised, see examples in table 7.

(9) [A-layer A [SC-layer Xn [OC-layer Yn [AC-layer Zn [I-layer Wn Qn [root]]]]]

NOUN CLASS	STANDARD ZULU	ENGLISH
Vocative singular--NC9	hamba, (*i)nja!	go dog
Vocative plural-- NC10	hambani, zinja!	go dogs

Table 7: Vocatives in noun class 9 and noun class 10

Taraldsen (2010: 16) summarises his decision for this radical de-compositional analysis as:

> "I [initially] interpreted the disappearance of the initial vowel as a reflex of A not being added to the N-projection in certain syntactically defined contexts. But on the backdrop of the results obtained in the intervening sections, it becomes clear that in these contexts, a number of other heads must be absent as well."

The significance of Taraldsen's analysis for the current context is that it clarifies the complexity of the Zulu noun class concord and agreement system, as summarised in table (8).

	PREFIX	SC	OC	AC1	AC2	DEM
CLASS 1	umu-	u-, a-, e-	m-	m-	m-	lo
CLASS 2	aba-	ba-, be,	ba-	ba-	ba-	laba
CLASS 3	um-	u-	u-	m-	m-	lo
CLASS 4	imi-	i-	i-	mi-	mi-	le
CLASS 5	i(li)	li-	li-	li-	li-	leli
CLASS 6	ama-	a-, e-	a-	ma-	ma-	la
CLASS 7	isi-	si-	si	si-	si-	lesi
CLASS 8	izi-	zi-	zi-	ziN-	zi-	lezi
CLASS 9	iN-	i-	i-	iN-	yi-	le
CLASS 10	iziN-	zi-	zi-	ziN-	zi-	lezi
CLASS 11	u(lu)-	lu-	lu-	lu-	lu-	lolu
CLASS 14	ubu-	bu-	bu-	bu-	bu-	lobu
CLASS 15	uku-	ku-	ku-	ku-	ku-	loku

Table 8: Zulu noun class concord and agreement system[16]

4. The empirical data

In the following I will present selected data from spontaneous intra-sentential code-mixing between English and Zulu. The data presented here originate from Magagula's (2009) socio-linguistic Masters' thesis.[17] Magagula collected spontaneous insertions from students in two urban and in two rural schools[18] with predominantly Zulu mother tongue learners and teachers in KwaZulu-Natal with the aim to assess the prevalence of a new variety/ new varieties of Zulu.[19] Her data is based on 100 written text samples [20]produced by equal numbers of female and male learners in grades 10 and 12. Emergent Zulu varieties are characterised by ubiquitous code-mixing and some as yet under-researched morpho-syntactic differences from Standard Zulu.

16 In the interest of space I leave out noun classes 1a, 2a which do not add any additional insight.

17 All the data in the following paragraphs are from Magagula (2009), who studied the emergence of a mixed Zulu-English variety in KwaZulu-Natal from a purely sociolinguistic perspective. The data were collected both in urban and in rural schools in KwaZulu-Natal. Students were asked to write a short personal account about their experiences at school. For details on the data collection consult Magagula (2009: 40–45).

18 The rural schools are situated in the Nongoma area in Zululand; the urban schools are situated in the KwaMathuka township in the eThekwini municipality.

19 South African sociolinguists have identified a number of Zulu varieties. In the interest of keeping matters simple I will not go into any detail in the current context. I also will not use any of the terms that have been used to describe any of these varieties because I want to keep the discussion and description of the data as general as possible. See, e.g., Lafont (2005), Finnlayson and Madiba (2002), Madiba (2001) and Slabbert and Myers-Scotton (1997).

20 Learners were asked to write – in Zulu – a short essay (no shorter than one page) on soccer and a short letter to a friend about their December school reports.

New varieties of Zulu are often termed 'urban' because the language contact situation in urban environments leads to greater competition between languages (see outlined above); however, Magagula could not establish a significant difference between urban and rural students with respect to the extent of 'spontaneous insertion' they are engaged in. This is in line with Appalraju's (2010) findings, whose empirical research was conducted solely in rural schools and who found that even in rural areas of KwaZulu-Natal students' competence in Standard Zulu was rather limited. The credibility of these results is strengthened by the fact that both data collections were carried out in school environments. Standard Zulu (also called 'Deep Zulu') is the 'norm', i.e., the register most appropriate for an academic environment.

The study reiterates the commonly made observation that (in particular young) Zulu speakers habitually insert English words into Zulu. It is sometimes assumed that this happens in cases of lexical gaps in Zulu. However, in none of the cases that Magagula (2009) recorded the insertion was motivated by a lexical gap in the Zulu language, which suggests that the participants' individual mental lexicons might have these gaps rather than the Zulu language, or, that the learners chose not to use the Zulu terms because they habitually speak in a mixed variety for socio-linguistic reasons. Many of the spontaneous insertions were in fact re-insertions; i.e., words that were originally assimilated from English into Zulu are here replaced by spontaneous insertions. Much in line with findings from other studies, the spontaneous insertions found by Magagula (2009) favour integrating English singular nouns into noun class 5 (or, in some cases potentially into a newly developing noun class 9a, see discussion below) and English plural nouns into noun class 6. Most importantly in the current context the data indicate the following: First, the spontaneous insertions show a smaller degree of phonological and morphological assimilation than older loans. Second, spontaneous insertions receive Zulu prefixes, e.g., the English determiner is replaced by a number of nested functional heads[21]; I have found only one instance of a switch where the spontaneous insertion was inserted into Zulu without receiving Zulu morphology (see example (b) *Agasti* in table 10 below). As a consequence there seems to be some competition for 'headship' between the two languages in some phrases as if the head noun's 'language identity' is not unanimously clear at all times. This idea needs more empirical support than I can provide here; it is congruent with a 'third system hypothesis' as proposed by Deumert (2005) and Schmid (2010), namely a system where all components are highly interrelated. Some of the examples I found in Magagula's corpus seem to suggest that through the process of continuous and ubiquitous spontaneous insertion the rich Zulu noun class concord and agreement system as outlined above might undergo a corrosion process. I hypothesise that such a process might be driven by the direct competition (maybe within an integrated 'third system') of the rather impoverished nano-syntax of the English noun 'agreement system' and the rich nano-syntax of the Nguni noun class prefixes and concords. This process of constant competition is strengthened by sociolinguistic factors outlined above, in particular the early transition to English as a medium of teaching and learning, which might lead to an impoverished Zulu lexicon, and the low prestige of Standard Zulu especially among younger speakers.

---

[21] Compare Taraldsen's (2010) analysis presented above.

The data from Magagula's corpus clearly demonstrate that the students under investigation rely heavily on spontaneous insertions. It comes rather as a surprise that some students felt compelled to insert English words into Zulu even for colour terms and names for months (see tables 9 and 10).

	ENGLISH	SPONTANEOUS INSERTIONS	STANDARD ZULU
a.	blue	oblue	oyisibhakabhaka
b.	green	obugreen	obuluhlaza
c.	yellow	oyellow	ophuzu
d.	yellow card	iyellow card	ikhadi eliphuzu

Table 9: Colour terms

Example (d) in table 9 indicates that the spontaneous insertion *yellow card* seems to have been treated as a compound (with the English head last word order). The compound receives the default noun class 5 prefix, which is congruent with the noun class of the Standard Zulu *-khadi* which is an earlier, assimilated loan (*ikhadi eliphuzu* literally means 'the card that is yellow'). In accordance with this analysis the inserted head noun *card* in *iyellow card* dictates the word order inside the inserted phrase (see the Head-Syntax Principle[22], Bhatt 1997: 17). This analysis is supported by example (13.12) in table 13 below, *ifirst aid* (*usizo lokuqala*, in standard Zulu, which literally means 'the help that is first'). In both cases we find an 'island' of English word order/ syntax in a Zulu sentence, however, this 'island' is prefixed by a Zulu morpheme.

	ENGLISH	SPONTANEOUS INSERTIONS	STANDARD ZULU
a.	June	UJuni	UNhlolanja
b.	August	Agasti	UNcwaba
c.	September	USeptember	KuMandulo
d.	November	UNovember	KuLwezi
e.	December	UDesemba	UZibandlela

Table 10: Names for months

As already mentioned above, the example (b) in table 10 is the only example in Magagula's corpus of a spontaneous insertion without Zulu prefixing. This might be due to the fact that the English noun *August* starts with a vowel. Zulu phonology does not allow vowel sequences[23]. However, the word *August* has been spontaneously assimilated into Zulu in terms of its phonological and morphological structure, which again indicates a system with highly interrelated processing between the two languages in question.

As outlined in paragraph 3.1, the noun classes 1, 1a, 2 and 2a are the default noun classes for personal names, terms referring to people, kinship terms and terms for professions. The examples in table 11 demonstrate that spontaneous insertion into Zulu in Magagula's data in general observes this semantic constraint; surprisingly there is an exception, see example

22 "HEAD-SYNTAX (HS): Grammatical properties (e.g., case, directionality of government, etc.) of the language of the head must be respected within its 'minimal domain' (à la Chomsky, 1993)." (Bhatt 1997: 17).

23 It would have been interesting to see how the nouns *April* and *October* would have been inserted as they are also vowel commencing. However, these are missing in the data corpus available.

(11)e. This is indicative of the strong tendency to assign the default-prefix *i-* when inserting English nouns into Zulu.

	ENGLISH	SPONTANEOUS INSERTION	STANDARD ZULU
a.	referee	ureferee	unompempe
b.	goalkeeper	ugoalkhipha	unozinti
c.	captain	ukapteni	umphathi webhola
d.	coach	ucoashi	umqeqeshi
e.	manager	imeneja	umphathi

Table 11: Singular terms for people/ professions

Similarly, the plural nouns in table 12 illustrate that in spontaneous insertions, there is a tendency to apply the plural noun class marker of noun class 6 (examples (12)b and (12)c) which seems to be competing with the canonical plural marker for professions and 'types of people', which would be *aba-* (which is the noun class marker for noun class 2b). And, obviously, the standard Zulu equivalents belong to noun class 2b as would be expected.

	ENGLISH	SPONTANEOUS INSERTION	STANDARD ZULU
a.	under 23s	aba-under 23s	abangaphansi kwama-23
b.	defenders	amadifenda	abavimbi
c.	sponsors	amasponsors	abaxhasi

Table 12: Plural terms for people/ professions

The examples in table 13 demonstrate the prevalence of the spontaneous insertion of English words into Zulu by attaching the default prefix *i-*. This process clearly happens irrespective of the noun class of the standard Zulu noun, which indicates that the insertion or sometimes re-insertion into noun class 5 does not follow the noun class categorisation patterns of standard Zulu; i.e., nouns are inserted into noun class 5 irrespective of the noun class that the standard Zulu equivalent is in. This is clear evidence that the spontaneous insertions are not determined by semantic processes.

Examples (13.28) and (13.29) are the only examples in Magagula's corpus that give a 'morphological hint' lending itself to Canonici's (1996) hypothesis that we could be witnessing the emergence of a new noun class, i.e., noun class 9a, (remember noun class 9's noun class marker is *iN-*). The subject concord for noun class 9 is *i-* (cf. table 8). Canonici observes: "There seems to be a growing new class of borrowed nouns in Zulu which simply prefix /i-/ (without the nasal) to the foreign noun stem. These 'new' nouns follow the inflectional pattern of Cl 9, except for a new locative form that prefixes /kwi-/." (Canonici 1996: 22)

The emergence of a new noun class 9a that uses *i(N)-* as noun class marker and *i-* as subject concord might further drive the morphological simplification that seems to be under way in modern (mixed) Zulu varieties. Unfortunately Magagula did not record full sentences and hence (many) concords and other agreement markers are absent in her data collection and I have no further data available at this moment in time. Future research into spontaneous code-mixing needs to record the whole agreement system to get a better understanding of the issue; however the data available from Magagula's corpus (in particular the examples in tables 15, 16 and 17) demonstrate that the participants in her study simplified the Zulu morphology quite considerably and there are a number of identifiable tendencies in the morphological corrosion process. However, given that we do not have clear evidence for a noun class 9a in the available corpus, I will henceforth follow the assumption that spontaneous insertions with an *i-* prefix belong in noun class 5.

The examples (13.21)–(13.24) are noteworthy in this respect: In the examples (13.23) and (13.24) the spontaneous insertion process 'respects' a morphological constrain in Zulu, i.e., consonant clusters cannot begin with *s-*. However, this very constraint is violated in examples (13.21) and (13.22).

Moreover, Zulu names for languages canonically belong to noun class 7 and accordingly take the noun class marker *isi-*; however, in Magagula's corpus we find examples (13.38) and (13.39), i.e., nouns denoting languages with the noun class marker of noun class 5. These examples violate a very strong constraint of Zulu noun class prefixing and hence provide evidence for morphological 'corrosion'.

	ENGLISH	SPONTANEOUS INSERTIONS	STANDARD ZULU
1.	magazine	imagazine	iphephabhukhu
2.	Physical Science	iPhysical Science	iSayensi
3.	break	ibreak	inhlabakhefu
4.	half time	ihalf time	ingxenye yesikhathi
5.	wall	iwall	udonga
6.	first aid	ifirst aid	usizo lokuqala
7.	winter	iwinter	ubusika
8.	direction	idirection	umgudu
9.	library	ilibrary	umtapo wolwazi
10.	order	i-order	ukuqoqeka
11.	Business Studies	iBusiness studies	iziFundo Zomnotho
12.	Maths	iMaths	iziBalo
13.	Economics	i-Economics	ezoMnotho (*ezo* = about)
14.	Natural Science	iNatural Science	ezeMvelo (*eze* = about)
15.	Technology	iTechnology	ezoBuchwepheshe
16.	Geography	iGeography	ezeZwe
17.	Biology	iBiology	ezeMvelo
18.	Life Orientation	i-LO	ezeMpilo
19.	dictionary	idictionary	isichazimazwi
20.	secondary school	isecondary	isikole samabanga aphakeme
21.	score	iscore	umklomela
22.	stadium	istadium	inkundla yebhola
23.	spade	isipade	i-fosholo
24.	scheme	isikimu	iqembu
25.	lamb	ilambu	isibani
26.	talent	ithalente	isiphiwo
27.	lead pencil	ipencila	umsizi
28.	newspaper	inyuziphepa	iphephandaba
29.	dish	indishi	isitsha

30.	bench	ibhentshi	isiqgiki
31.	pen	ipeni	usiba lokuloba
32.	final	ifaneli	ukuphela konyaka
33.	win	iwini	ukunqoba
34.	goal	igoli	inqaku
35.	week	iviki	isonto
36.	class	iklasi	igumbi lokufundela
37.	toilet	itoilethi	indlu yangasese NC9
38.	English	i-Inglishi	i*si*Ngisi
39.	Afrikaans	i-Afrikaans	i*si*Bhunu

Table 13: English words spontaneously inserted into Zulu (singular)

The examples in table (13) above and in table (14) below also show that in a large number of spontaneous insertions the morphological structure of the guest nouns remains intact, see examples (13.1)–(13.22), (14.40–14.46) as well as examples (14.52–14.58). This means that to a large extent the spontaneous insertions in Magagula's corpus are not assimilated into Zulu morphology and phonology.

For the remaining example in table (13) and (14) we see minimal changes in the morphological structure. Mostly the changes amount to adding a final vowel in order to assimilate the spontaneous insertion into the tonal structure of Zulu (examples (13.24)–(13.38) and examples (14.47–14.51). In only a few cases there are further 'internal' changes to the words, some of which might also be accounted for by the process of phoneme to grapheme 'transmission' (i.e., the students write the word as they 'hear' it following Zulu orthographical rules). This hypothesis does, however, need further examination.

	ENGLISH	SPONTANEOUS INSERTIONS	STANDARD ZULU
40.	exercise books	ama-exercise	amabhuku okubhalela
41.	goals	amagoal	amanqaku
42.	finals	amafinal	amanqamu
43.	clubs	amaclub	amaqembu
44.	poems	amapoem	izinkondlo
45.	minutes	amaminute	imizuzu
46.	movies	amamovie	izithombe
47.	penalties	amaphenalthi	izijezo
48.	goals	amagoli	amanqaku
49.	taxis	amatekisi	amakhumbi
50.	holidays	amaholide	izinhlabakhefu
51.	teams	amathimu	amaqembu
52.	fouls	amafouls	amaphutha
53.	questions	amaquestions	imibuzo
54.	colours	amacolours	imibala
55.	lessons	amalessons	izifundo
56.	problems	amaproblems	izinkinga
57.	weekends	amaweekends	izimpelasonto
58.	shorts	amashorts	isikhindi (sing)

Table 14: English nouns spontaneously inserted into Zulu (plural)

If we juxtapose the examples (14.40)–(14.51) with the examples (14.52–14.58) we see that for the majority of the examples the spontaneous insertion process 'acknowledges' the fact that the prefix *ama-* contains the morpho-syntactic feature [+plural]. However, in the second set of spontaneous insertions this is clearly not the case; examples (14.52)–(14.58) are doubly marked for plural with both the Zulu prefixing *ama-* and the English plural suffix *-s*. This might be another piece of evidence for a close interaction between the two linguistic systems, which in these cases leads to redundant feature assignment.

Table 15 illustrates that in only two cases in Magagula's corpus English nouns are spontaneously inserted into noun classes other than noun class 5. The underlying logic is in line with older borrowings that put English loans into noun class 2a and 2b if they denoted professions and entities that are closely associated with people). Example (a) in table 15 inserts the English noun *mistresses* into the same noun class (i.e., 2b, *o-*) which gets assimilated and simplified during the process. This is similar to the processes underlying the borrowing of the earlier loan *othishakazi* (o-thisha-kazi = NC 2b, assimilated the noun *teacher* and added the Zulu suffix *–kazi* (*female*)). Example (b) replaces the morphologically rich *umsebenzi* (NC 2a, *work*) *was-e-khaya* (*which is-in-haus/ home*) with a spontaneous insertion of the non-assimilated English noun into a Zulu noun phrase. The last example (c) is especially surprising because Magagula provides as the standard Zulu equivalent *e-li-lodwa* (*that/ who is one*) which displays noun class 5 agreement morphology, hence it would have followed a noun in NC5 (in Zulu phrases *-lodwa* follows the noun and the object concord, here *-li-* agrees with the preceding noun). In contrast, the spontaneous insertion *uwani* exhibits NC1 morphology and omits the morpheme *e-,* which is highly irregular as it seems to have been used in a morpho-syntactic slot that would have been filled with *elilodwa* in standard Zulu as Magagula suggests (Magagula 2009: 49).[24]

	ENGLISH	SPONTANEOUS INSERTIONS	STANDARD ZULU
a.	mistresses	omisi	othishelakazi
b.	homework	uhomework	umsebenzi wasekhaya
c.	one	uwani	elilodwa

Table 15: Spontaneous insertions into other noun classes

Table 16 and 17 illustrate that the process of spontaneous insertion of English words into Zulu by attaching Zulu morphemes to English words is not restricted to nominal insertions. The examples in table 16 demonstrate that similar processes are at work in spontaneous verb insertions. In the examples below I mark in bold the verb insertions and the equivalent standard Zulu verb stems. It is apparent that the English verbs are mostly inserted leaving the Zulu morpho-syntactic 'environment' intact. Three verbs, (a) to (c) in table 16, are assimilated into Zulu phonology and orthography. In examples (a) and (b) the assimilated Englsih verb receives the Zulu suffix *-ile* which encodes recent past. The suffix in (c) *-e* may encode either the imperative, the subjunctive mood, or the recent past so this example's English translation by Magagula relates to the standard Zulu equivalent rather than to the English insertion, which suggests that maybe in the context of the text the present tense would have been more appropriate than the recent past.

24 Unfortunately, Magagula does not provide the whole sentence in her data.

In the examples (d) to (f) non-assimilated English verbs are inserted into the Zulu morpho-syntactic frame. In (d) and (e) the verb receives the suffix *-a* signalling simple present.

Example (f) shows that morphological simplification that supersedes the grammatical rules of the host language may also happen in the case of verb insertions. Here the verb *cope* remains unchanged during insertion even though Zulu grammar demands that in negated sentences the verb receives the suffix *-i.*[25]

The example (g) may look like a verb insertion because the morpheme *-be* could be English; however, *-be* in Zulu is a subjunctive verb equivalent to the English *may be.* Thus, *ngibe* is most probably the Zulu verb and thus the English insertion concerns the adverb *early* only. I included this example here because it illustrates a trend towards avoiding expressing states of affairs in Zulu, when the Zulu-English code-mix offers a shorter alternative.

	ENGLISH	SPONTANEOUS INSERTIONS	STANDARD ZULU
a.	they have gymned	ba*jim*ile	ba*zilolong*ile[26]
b.	I have failed	ngi*fey*ile	ngingaa*phumelel*i[27]
c.	they lose	li*luze*	li*hlulw*e[28]
d.	Nana is washing clothes	uNana u*wash*a izingubo	uNana u*hlanz*a izingubo
e.	I understand.	ngiya-*understand*a	ngiya*qond*a
f.	I do not cope	angi*cope*	angi*melan*i
g.	I am early	ngibe *early*	ngi*fike* ngesikhathi[29]

Table 16: Verbs and adverbs

The general trend towards morphological simplification in the mixed code is also evident in locative expressions (see table 17). In Zulu, the locative function IN is doubly marked; first, by the prefix *e-* and second, by the suffix *-ini* or *-eni* depending on the phonological and morphological structure of the noun in question. As is evidenced in table 17 when English expressions are inserted into a Zulu prepositional phrase, these morphological processes may be simplified: Only the examples (a) and (b) receive both locative markings. All other examples treat the prefix *e-* like the English *in (the)* and simply prefix it to the English nouns. This is particularly noteworthy in example (f) where the standard Zulu equivalent to the English phrase *at the beach* forms the locative according to a different set of rules altogether, yielding *olwandle.*

---

[25] Negation is doubly marked in Zulu sentences: First, the affix *a-* precedes the subject pronoun, e.g., *angi-* (*ngi-* 'I') or the subject concord, e.g., *aba-, ali-,* etc. Second, the verb suffix *-i* is attached to the verb, e.g., *angikuthandi* (*I do not like it*): *a-* = negation marker, *ngi-* 'I', *-ku-* = 'it$_{NC15}$', *-thand-* 'love, like', *-i* = negation.

[26] *Bazilolongile* translates to *ba-* 'they$_{NC2}$', *-zilolong-*'exercise', *-ile* = recent past tense.

[27] *Ngingaphumeleli* translates to *ngi* 'I', *nga* 'not' (participle mood negative), *phumelel* 'come out, succeed, win', *-a* = negation marker

[28] The suffix *-we* marks the passive in Zulu. Literally translated *lihlulwe* means 'they$_{NC5}$ were beaten'.

[29] *Ngifike ngesikhathi* translates to *ngi-* 'I', *-fik-e* 'arrive-subjunctive', *nge-* (*nga* and *i* → *nge*) 'with/ on', *(i)sikhati* 'time'.

	ENGLISH	SPONTANEOUS INSERTIONS	STANDARD ZULU
a.	in class	*E*clas*ini*	*e*gunj*ini* lokufundela
b.	in the kitchen	*E*kitch*eni*	*e*xhib*eni*
c.	in the cinema	*E*cinema	*e*zithomb*eni*
d.	in the library	*E*library	*e*mtatsh*eni* wolwazi
e.	in town	*E*town	*e*dolobh*eni*
f.	at the beach	*E*beach	olwandle

Table 17: Locative expressions

5. General discussion

The data presented in this paper are in many ways limited. First, they only represent a rather limited corpus and second the corpus as presented by Magagula (2009) only contains a few complete sentences, hence, the data do not exhibit the full concord and agreement system in Zulu as represented in table 8 above.

However, there is evidence for some morpho-syntactic trends. It is clearly apparent that for intra-sentential mixes involving noun phrases (examples in tables 10–15) the participants in Magagula's (2009) socio-linguistic study preferred lexical-functional mixes where the determiner is provided by the host language Zulu. There was no single instance where a complete English D+NP was inserted into a Zulu sentence. This seems to be consistent with an extended version of the *Grammatical Features Spell-Out Hypothesis* (Liceras, Spradlin and Fernández Fuertes 2005, Liceras, Fernández Fuertes, Perales, Pérez-Tattam, and Spradlin 2008). The hypothesis states that a bilingual (child) has access to one functional abstract lexicon and that in the process of activating features of two grammars, code-mixing choices favour the functional categories containing highly 'grammaticized' features (Liceras et al. 2008: 831). Given that noun class 5 (and maybe noun class 9, compare the discussion above) provide these highly 'grammaticized' features and are at the same time neither semantically nor morphologically marked there is an overwhelming trend to insert English nouns into this class (or these classes).

Such processes of 'convergence' are central to code-mixing (see e.g., Sánchez 2012: 514). Convergence processes allow the two languages spoken by a bilingual individual to agree on the set of structural (Myers-Scotton 2002)[30] and functional[31] (Sánchez 2012) properties to be used in mixed utterances and manifest themselves in the mapping of formal functional features onto morphology or phonology.

Overall, the data presented here suggest that the participants' mental lexicon might be best represented by a *Bilingual Interactive Activation (BIA)* model, akin to the model developed by Dijkstra and colleagues (see, e.g., Dijkstra and van Heuven 2002) for multilingual

30 "As a mechanism, convergence is the process that promotes a splitting of abstract lexical structure in one variety and its combining with such abstract lexical structure from another variety, often resulting in a restructuring of grammatical relations and even surface-level grammatical morphemes from the stronger group in the equation." (Myers-Scotton 2002: 164).

31 'Functional' meaning 'concerning morpho-syntactic functional categories'.

lexical access; what is required is a lexicon in which morphemes are inter-connected within and across the two languages, with excitatory and inhibitory bidirectional connections between the lemma level and the lexeme level.

Much in line with an interactive model of the bilingual mental lexicon, Kirsnet, Lalor, and Hird (1993) suggest that the strength of interlinking among lexical items of pairs of languages might be steered by similarities and shared features of said languages (e.g., with respect to the number of cognate words, or a shared orthographic system). In the current case the participants are L1 Zulu speakers with English as their L2. Given that their two languages are typologically vastly different, it might well be that the specific sociolinguistic background outlined above leads to co-activation (inhibition and excitation) of their two languages in the mental lexicon, rather than being characterised by similarities between the two languages under consideration. I think it would be fruitful to combine insights from sociolinguistic research (e.g., Deumert, 2005) with research on lexical organisation in the multilingual mind and with research on spontaneous code-mixing to gain deeper insight into the possibilities and limits of the multilingual language processing system.
Such a line of research would contribute to understanding how sociolinguistic and individual variables may interact with the component of *executive control* (see, e.g., Rodriguez-Fornells, Rotte, Heinze, Noesselt and Muente 2002 and Rodriguez-Fornells, van der Lugt, Rotte, Britti, Heinze and Muente 2005) in multilingual language processing. I suspect that emotive factors and factors related to the socio-psychological construction of hybrid identities that seem to contribute to language change in language contact situations (see e.g., Ansaldo 2010) may also play a role in language activation patterns.

In addition it is to be expected that the current South African schooling system along with language choices by parents and educators are currently leading to an ongoing subtractive bilingualism where many young South Africans are no longer proficient in the standard varieties of the African languages. This may give rise to a 'third system' as envisioned by, e.g., Schmid (2010) with less language separation than we might canonically expect in balanced bilinguals. The apparent corrosion of the Zulu morphology that has been discussed throughout this paper may be seen as evidence for this hypothesis. To test such a hypothesis with a population like the one whose data are reported on in the current contribution it would be insightful to measure the computational 'cost' of code-mixing along the lines of Costa and Santesteban's research paradigm (2004).

Bibliography

Ansaldo, U. (2010): Identity alignment and language creation in multilingual communities. *Language Sciences* 32: 615–623.

Appalraju, D.P. (2010): *Emerging bilingualism in rural secondary schools in KwaZulu-Natal: The impact of educational policies on learners and their communities*. Unpublished PhD thesis, University of KwaZulu-Natal, Durban, South Africa. Accessible from the World Wide Web at: http://hdl.handle.net/10413/840 (last access: 1st of June 2012, 12:35).

Baker, C. and S.P. Jones (eds.) (1998): *Encyclopedia of bilingualism and bilingual education*. Clevedon, UK: Multilingual Matters.

Bhatt, R.M. (1997): Code-switching, constraints, and optimal grammars. *Lingua 102*: 223–251.

Broeder, P., G. Extra and J. Maartens (2002): Multilingualism in South Africa with a focus on KwaZulu-Natal and Metropolitan Durban. *Project for the study of alternative education in South Africa* (PRAESA) occasional papers No. 7. Accessible from the World Wide Web at: http://web.uct.ac.za/depts/praesa/OCCPapers.htm (last access: 3rd of June 2012, 12:20).

Callahan, L. (2002): The Matrix Language Frame model and Spanish/English codeswitching in fiction. *Language and communication* 22: 1–16.

Canonici, N. (1996): *Zulu grammatical structure*. Durban: University of Natal.

Coronel-Molina, S.M. and M. Rodríguez-Mondoñedo (2012): Introduction: Language contact in the Andes and Universal Grammar. *Lingua* 122: 447–460.

Costa, A. and M. Santesteban (2004): Lexical access in bilingual speech production: Evidence from language switching in highly proficient bilinguals and L2 learners. *Journal of Memory and Language* 50: 491–511.

De Bot, K., W. Lowie and M. Verspoor (2007): A Dynamic Systems Theory approach to second language acquisition. (Keynote article). *Bilingualism: Language and cognition* 10 (1): 7–21.

Department of Basic education, Republic of South Africa (2010): *The status of the language of learning and teaching (LOLT) in schools: A quantitative overview*. Accessible from the World Wide Web at: http://advocacyaid.com/ecdnewsflash/LOLT_REPORT_1.pdf (last access: 3rd of June 2012, 12: 31).

Deumert, A. (2005): The unbearable lightness of being bilingual: English–Afrikaans language contact in South Africa. *Language Sciences* 27: 113–135.

Dijkstra, A., and W.J.B. van Heuven (2002): The architecture of the bilingual word recognition system: From identification to decision. *Bilingualism: Language and Cognition* 5: 175–197.

Finnlayson, R. and M. Madiba (2002): The intellectualisisation of indigenous languages of South Africa: Challenges and prospects. *Current issues in language planning* 3: 40–61.

Francis, N. (2011): Imbalances in bilingual development: A key to understanding the faculty of language. *Language Sciences* 33: 76–89.

Goral, M., E.S. Levy, L.K. Obler and E. Cohen (2006): Cross-language lexical connections in the mental lexicon: Evidence from a case of trilingual aphasia. *Brain and Language* 98: 235–247.

Grosjean, F. 1982: *Life with two languages: An introduction to bilingualism*. Cambridge, MA: Harvard University Press.

Grosjean, F. (2010): *Bilingual: Life and reality*. Cambridge, MA: Harvard University Press.

Güldemann, T. (2003): Present progressive vis-à-vis predication focus in Bantu: A verbal category between semantics and pragmatics. *Studies in Language* 27 (2): 323–360.

Heredia, R.R. and J. Altarriba (2001): Bilingual language mixing: Why do bilinguals code-switch? *Current Directions in Psychological Science* 10: 164–168.

Kirsnet, K., E. Lalor and K. Hird (1993): The bilingual lexicon: Exercise, meaning, and morphology. In: R. Schreuder and B. Weltens (eds.), *The bilingual lexicon*. Amsterdam: John Benjamins, 215–246.

Koopman, A. (2000): *Zulu language change.* Howick: Bervitas.

Lafon, M. (2005): The future of isiZulu lies in Gauteng: The importance of taking into account urban varieties for the promotion of African languages, with special reference to isiZulu. Issues for debate. In: V. Webb, A. Deumert and B. Lepota (eds.), *The standardisation of African languages in South Africa*. Report on the workshop held at the University of Pretoria 30 June–1 July 2005. Pretoria: University of Pretoria. Accessible from the World Wide Web at: http: //hal=uni-diderot.archives-ouvertes.fr (last access: 5th of July, 12:17).

Levelt, W. (1989): *Speaking. From intention to articulation*. Cambridge, MA: MIT Press.

Liceras, J.M., K.T. Spradlin and R. Fernández Fuertes (2005): Bilingual early functional–lexical mixing and the activation of formal features. *International Journal of Bilingualism* 9(2): 227–252.

Liceras, J. M., R. Fernández Fuertes, S. Perales, R. Pérez-Tattam and K.T. Spradlin (2008): Gender and gender agreement in bilingual native and non-native grammars: A view from child and adult functional–lexical mixings. *Lingua* 118: 827–851.

Madiba, M. (2001): Towards a model for terminology modernization in the African languages of South Africa. *Language Matters* 32: 53–57.

Magagula, C.S. (2009): *Standard versus non-standard IsiZulu: A comparative study between urban and rural learners' performance and attitude.* Unpublished Masters thesis, University of KwaZulu-Natal, Durban, South Africa. Accessible from the World Wide Web at: http://researchspace.ukzn.ac.za/xmlui/handle/10413/273?show=full (last access: 20th of July 2012; 9: 30).

Mati, X. (2004): *Using code switching as a strategy for education.* Paper presented at the AEAA Conference. Accessible from the World Wide Web at: (last access: 20th of July 2012; 9: 30).

Meinhof, C. (1906): *Grundzüge einer vergleichenden Grammatik der Bantusprachen*. Berlin: Reimer.

Mesthrie, R. (2002): *Language in South Africa*. Cambridge, MA: Cambridge University Press.

Mfusi, M.J.H. (1989): *Soweto Zulu Slang: A sociolinguistic study*. Honours essay. University of South Africa.

Myers-Scotton, C. (2002): *Contact Linguistics: Bilingual encounters and grammatical outcomes.* Oxford: Oxford University press.

Poarch, G.J. and J.G. van Hell (2012): Cross-language activation in children's speech production: Evidence from second language learners, bilinguals, and trilinguals. *Journal of Experimental Child Psychology* 111: 419–438.

Rodriguez-Fornells, A., M. Rotte, H.J. Heinze, T. Noesselt and T.F. Muente (2002): Brain potential and functional MRI evidence for how to handle two languages with one brain. *Nature* 415: 1026–1029.

Rodriguez-Fornells, A., A. van der Lugt, M. Rotte, B. Britti, H.J. Heinze and T.F Muente (2005): Second language interferes with word production in fluent bilinguals: Brain potential and Functional imaging evidence. *Journal of Cognitive Neuroscience* 17: 422–433.

Sánchez, L. (2012): Convergence in syntax/morphology mapping strategies: Evidence from Quechua–Spanish code mixing. *Lingua* 122: 511–528.

Slabbert, S. and C. Myers-Scotton (1997): The structure of Tsootsitaal and Iscamtho: Code switching and group identity in South African townships. *Linguistics* 34: 317–342.

Schmid, M.S. (2010): *Language, multilingualism and integration.* Project sketch. Accessible from the World Wide Web at:http://www.rug.nl/staff/m.s.schmid/Language%20multi lingualism% 20integration.pdf. (last access: 6th of June 2012, 10: 08).

Schoebelen, T. (2005): *The shape of things to come.* The nominal morphology of Zulu loan words. Accessible from the World Wide Web at: www.stanford.edu/~tylers/notes/papers/ Zulu_ loans_Schoebelen.pdf (last access: 23rd July 2012, 15:46).

Statistics South Africa (2001): *Census 2001.* Accessible from the World Wide Web at: http://www.statssa.gov.za/census01/html/default.asp (last access: 3rd of July 2012, 14: 03).

Taraldsen, K.T. (2010): The nanosyntax of Nguni noun class prefixes and concords. *Lingua* 120: 1522–1548.

The languages of South Africa. Webpage. Accessible from the World Wide Web at http://www.southafrica.info/about/people/language.htm (last access: 1st of June 2012; 10:45).

Torres, L. (1992): Code-mixing as a narrative strategy in a bilingual community. *World Englishes* 11: 83–193.

Van der Spuy, A. (2010): Generating Zulu noun class morphology. *Language Matters: Studies in the Languages of Africa* 41(2): 294–314.

Webb, V. and K. Sure 2000: *African voices: An introduction to the languages and linguistics of Africa.* New York: Oxford University Pres.

Zeller, J. (2008): The subject marker in Bantu as an antifocus marker. Stellenbosch Papers in *Linguistics* 38: 221–254.

English – synthetic, analytic and synthetic again? Are we going round in circles? The cases of the reduced auxiliaries *have* and *will**

Lothar Peter

1. Introduction

It is a commonplace in historical linguistics that the English language, at fairly rapid speed, developed from a predominantly synthetic language type in the early stages of Old English to a predominantly analytic language type in the period of Early Modern English, which is also the current status.

For quite some time in the 19th and 20th centuries linguists assumed that there was no place for new productive patterns in English creating synthetic structures. Nevertheless, this underlying assumption sometimes intermingled with conflicting findings by the linguists holding the view. A typical example of the awareness of this disagreement is Vachek's remark (1961: 10) in his detailed discussion of the analytic trend of English that "… a fairly large number of problems calls for examination, despite the fact that in the grammatical plane of English the drift from the synthetic to the analytical type of grammatical structure is quite obvious", which has the following specification in a corresponding note: "This does not mean, of course, that synthetic language means do not exist in ModE alongside of analytical ones; it only means that the former are no more productive in ModE …". In other words, he claims that new synthetic elements will not appear in the structure of English.

A first notion of a circle or cycle concerning the use of synthetic and analytic linguistic means arises in Jespersen (1917), in which he discusses the issue of long-term change of negation and establishes different stages of its historical development (ibid.: 4–14). A recent systematic treatment of this aspect can be found, e.g., in Mosegaard Hansen (2011).

In the course of modern linguistics and its various orientations over approximately the last thirty years, however, we repeatedly find publications opining that the emergence of synthetic elements, obviously, has continued to exist until today.

Among those linguists, we find Danchev and van Gelderen with views based on general empirical observations. Danchev (1992: 36) discusses links between a contact situation and a potential increase in analyticity arising therefrom. He concludes (ibid.), with regard to the historical development of English, that "[i]t might be said that whereas the dominant typological feature of Middle English is provided by the marked trend towards analyticity, the Modern English period is characterized both by *continuing analyticity* and *reemerging syn-*

* The author is indebted to Frank Polzenhagen for helpful comments on an earlier version of this chapter.

theticity" and compares this phenomenon of a "drift" with a pendulum between analyticity and syntheticity in longer historical periods.

Van Gelderen (2006: 284), in her textbook on the history of English, suggests an established "linguistic cycle" and expects languages to move, almost automatically, it would appear, from synthetic to analytic, and to synthetic again. Her argumentation is based on, for instance, examples of function words (i.e., words having syntactic function) that appear to have merged with phonetically reduced juxtaposed function words, yielding a merger in a quasi-word form, cf., e.g., *shoulda* (underlined for the reduced auxiliary *have*). In van Gelderen (2011) she elaborates a theoretical model of cyclical historical change, arguing that "cycles are the result of reanalysis by the language learner" (ibid.: 4). In the context of grammaticalisation, she states:

> The best-known examples of lexical elements changing to grammatical ones are verbs being reanalyzed as auxiliaries and prepositions as complementizers. There are also grammatical elements that are reanalyzed into more grammatical ones. These changes necessitate renewal and the entire process is sometimes referred to as a *linguistic cycle*. (ibid.: 5–6)

With regard to the syntheticity-analyticity correlation in historical change, we find a number of publications that are based on a mainly quantitative, though in certain aspects also qualitative, analysis of corpora of English texts. They aim to document (predominantly) real-time ongoing language change (cf., e.g., Leech et al. 2009), historical change (cf., e.g., Szmrecsanyi 2012, in press), real-time and apparent-time change in combination (cf., e.g., Mair 2006), or illustrate typological morpho-syntactic variability in current varieties of English (Szmrecsanyi 2009). The first three publications record an increasing use of synthetic linguistic means. Szmrecsanyi (2012: 663) concludes after an analysis of token frequencies of analytic and synthetic linguistic means in long-term diachronic change:

> An analysis of frequency fluctuation in individual markers further revealed that while in the big picture, twentieth-century English is quantitatively almost back to the analyticity-syntheticity coordinates defining twelfth-century English, modern analyticity and syntheticity seem qualitatively different from their Early English counterparts. For example, determiners have become increasingly important as an analytic category, but pronouns have been on the decline. Conversely, the possessive marker used to be (but is no more) an important synthetic marker, whereas inflected adjectives are on the rise.

The general observation is easy to agree with. However, our observation is that the possessive marker seems to be spreading, now occurring in combinations with nouns or nominal phrases until recently blocked by semantic restrictions.

Szmrecsanyi also offers a cause for the (quantitatively) increasing use of synthetic means and states with regard to the advantage of *'s* (as a genitive marker and clitic) over an *of*-phrase

> […] syntheticity is more output-economical than analyticity is because synthetic markers are typically more compact than analytic markers. (Szmrecsanyi 2009: 323)

In view of reduced auxiliaries such as *would*, however, when they are reduced to just one sound, one wonders whether this is a sweeping statement. Many such studies, almost inherently, have the problem to pin down and separate as well correlate developments at the two levels of expression, spoken and written, mainly due to lack of speech data.

This issue of the two media is also reflected in van Gelderen's (2008) example (see above, no exact source given):

(1) I shoulda known that.

The spelling of this sentence is equivalent to:

(2) I should have known that. (also cf. I should've known that.)

It thus reflects an early instance of the use of the auxiliary *have* and its phonetic treatment in the given linguistic context. In an earlier publication van Gelderen (1998, online version, no page) has the analogous structure:

(3) I shoulda/shouldav gone.

In respect to this pattern, she argues, "the auxiliary *-ve* is a clitic and needs to incorporate into another head". In van Gelderen (2008: 284), she comments that mergers like *shoulda* started to come into existence around 1450 and, according to her, "the auxiliary *have* has become an affix". The use of the term *affix* here relates to an inflectional morpheme. It is obvious that forms like *shoulda* or *shouldav* are:

- The result of the emergence of new analytic means in Middle English, i.e., function words, as in the case of the auxiliaries *should* and *have*, the latter being different now from the main verb *have*;
- As soon as it comes into use, due to its status and function and its lexical non-relevance, it is phonetically treated accordingly, i.e., reduced – a process running parallel with its stabilisation as a morpho-syntactic element.
- The orthographic form *shoulda* is the written representation only of this development: The auxiliary *have* occurs in a weakened form and – as in the example – appears to form a unit with the preceding word *should*.[1]

The present paper examines weakened auxiliaries with the aim to see if van Gelderen's and others' positions are applicable to auxiliaries like *have* or other function words with regard to Present-Day English. For reasons of time and space, of course, the analysis will be restricted in scope. It will therefore only study the auxiliary *have* and the auxiliary *will* (the latter in its function to express future reference) in their weakened forms, in which they, as part of certain complex verb forms, express morpho-syntactic oppositions with other verbal forms. It shall further be restricted to cases in which no other auxiliary is part of the verbal form.

This is to provide arguments for their phonological, morphological and morpho-syntactic interpretation, which, in turn, is supposed to answer the question whether the mergers can

---

[1] We cannot be sure that the vocalic form indicated by the spelling *should<u>a</u>* correctly represents the pronunciation resulting from the weakening of *have*. It may be interpreted as /-ə/ or /-ɐ/. In Present-Day English, however, it is not a likely option.

be classified as a synthetic output of a linguistic process in the sense of qualitative consequences for the structure of verbal paradigms.

Further provisions that have to be made are:

- Owing to the aforementioned spelling-pronunciation issue, it is considered necessary to give priority to spoken English as the phenomenon mentioned above is change originating in the spoken language. Any record of written occurrences can only be thought of as a reflection of the former. Nonetheless, for reasons of readability and use in the literature, the orthographic form cannot be avoided.
- Geographical or social variation will not be studied. The basis of discussion is the realisations of auxiliaries in non-regional standard English English pronunciation, traditionally known as Received Pronunciation.

2. Phonological aspects of the reduction of auxiliaries

As stated above, a spelling like *shoulda* principally reflects the result of certain phonetic processes, i.e., those processes involved in the phonetic reduction of unstressed function words in English. We can deduce from such spellings in historical texts that reduction of function words and all its consequences have been a typical trait of English for ca. five centuries. In analogy, the same applies to the weakening of unstressed syllables (as inflectional morphemes) bearing inflectional information in Middle English, a comprehensive process yielding a loss of inflectional differentiation. This development led to, among other things, the collapse of the English nominal case and gender systems.

In Present-Day English English, almost all function words (prepositions, auxiliaries, pronouns, etc.) occurring in prosodically unmarked positions remain unaccented and, due to consequent lack of articulatory force, undergo weakening. As this happens in all utterances produced in linguistic/social contexts of non-formal degree, the English language has weakening to an extent that is not shared by other Germanic languages, e.g., German. The process is also apparent in all unstressed syllables of content words (words having lexical function).

For the groups of function words, many textbooks on English English phonetics and/or phonology have a listing of them in their reduced (or weak or unaccented) forms as, e.g., in Cruttenden (2008: 266–268). The weak forms here, as elsewhere, are often listed first and regarded as the usual form, the default case, so to speak.

For the structural auxiliary *will*, which is used to form a complex verb expressing future-time reference, for instance, we have the weak forms /wɪl/ (unstressed, but no reduction of /w/ and the vowel, e.g., at the beginning of an intonational phrase), /əl/ (in post-consonantal position) and /l̩/ (in post-vocalic position), and, in contrast, the strong form /wɪl/ (stressed). It must not be confused with the modal auxiliary *will*, which is a means expressing volition. Both, however, stem from the same Old English modal *willan*. Maybe, because the two are often confused, Cruttenden (and also Roach – see below) fails to mention the (structural) auxiliary *will*.

In analogy to *will*, the auxiliary *have* – not to be confused with the main verb *have* 'possess' – occurs in the weak forms /həv/, /əv/ and /v/, and in the strong form /hæv/, but also increasingly, among younger standard speakers, /hav/. However, the weak forms are more conspicuous only with regard to frequency. Qualitatively, the distribution of weak forms and their opposites, the strong forms, has to follow a set of general phonetic and prosodic principles. This set comprises:

(a) the position in the intonational phrase (related to rhythmical processing)
(b) the distinction between neutral (unemphatic speech) and emphatic speech
(c) the level of style (related to degree of formality, speech rate, etc.)
(d) contrasting and citing modes.

These principles are discussed in a detailed description of the use of weak and strong forms by Roach (2008, chapter 12).

Concerning (b), it seems that, at least in non-formal spoken English English in certain positions in the intonational phrase, there are systematic distinctions of affirmation and negation in neutral vs. emphatic speech, almost like in paradigmatic relation; cf., e.g., (3) and (4):

(3) He has seen (his uncle). [spelling unmarked regarding emphasis]
/hiz ˈsiːn/ vs. /hi ˈhæz ˌsiːn/

(4) He has not seen (his uncle).
/hi ˈhæzn ˈsiːn/ vs. /hiz ˈnɒt ˌsiːn/

The phonetic process of reduction may include the following components for *have* (as indicated by the contraction form *they've asked*):

As *have* is lexically not important, the word – monosyllabic in its strong/non-reduced form – only gets a low degree of force. Depending on the final phoneme of the preceding word, this leads to the consequence that it is reduced to three forms (see above) according to prosodic and phonemic position. Relevant sub-processes of reduction are the deletion of /h-/ in post-consonantal position and, furthermore, the deletion of the reduction vowel *schwa* in post-vocalic position.

Reduced auxiliaries are often represented in spellings that are called *contractions* or *contracted forms* (cf., e.g., *they've*, *he'll* or *she'd*). The latter are used to orthographically indicate the phonetic merger of, for example, personal pronouns and weak-form auxiliaries. However, there is no symmetry between phonetics/phonology on the one hand and orthography on the other: (1) Contracted forms are only used in informal orthography, implying a direct correlation for informal texts only. (2) Not all forms of reduction have an equivalent form of contraction; there is none, e.g., for /əv/. This is also discussed by Krug (2011: 556), concerning more English auxiliaries.

As a consequence of reduction, however, the reduced auxiliaries may lose their status of phonological autonomy as syllables or words. These mergers or fusions, of course, are in a way indicated by contractions such as *they've* and, also, *(the) kids've*. The fusion process is further strengthened in English by the phenomenon of liaison (linking of initial vowels of a word with the final sound of the preceding word) and, as a consequence, the blurring of morphological boundaries.

Consequently, a phonological interpretation of *they've* yields a monosyllabic unit and, correspondingly, *kids've* can be considered a disyllabic unit. Nevertheless, such a result, i.e., the fact that phonological units may be formed as a result of reduction, falls short of giving a complete answer to our major question, implying further clarification is needed esp. at morphological and morpho-syntactic levels.

Issues like the attachment of weak forms to other words (or phrases) are central to the notion of clitics. Studies pertaining to this concept reflect on typical interface issues. The importance of cliticization to the main issue of this paper is therefore studied in the following section.

3. Reduced auxiliaries as clitics

The phenomenon of attachment of weak forms to other words, or structures more complex than a word, deserves attention because it has implications on several linguistic levels and poses one of the classical interface problems, involving phonology, morphology and syntax. To start with, it raises the point of phonetic, phonological and morphological boundaries.

For quite some time, the phenomenon has been studied as cliticization predominantly in historical linguistics and comparative studies of, e.g., Romance and Slavonic languages.

Current general reference dictionaries show, after closer inspection, that the awareness of clitics being a relevant linguistic phenomenon has grown only slowly, and so has its theoretical and terminological refinement. This becomes evident when one takes a look at Bußmann 1996 (an English translation of a second German edition). Although it does deal with clitics and cliticization and has the entry "cliticization", it does not explain the term itself but refers the reader further to the entries "enclisis" and "proclesis". Here, we take the term *enclitic* as an example, also as it is of a greater importance for the problems under investigation in this paper. The definition given for *enclisis* is "[a]ttachment of a weakly stressed or unstressed word (enclitic) onto the preceding word, generally with simultaneous phonetic weakening, e.g., *I'm* for *I am* …"[2] The corresponding definition of *enclitic* is more cautious though as it uses "element" instead of "word" in defining it as a "[w]eakly stressed or unstressed element which attaches itself to a preceding stressed word …", leaving the status of the enclitic open. In Bußmann (2002: 192), we find for "Enklise" (= enclisis) the definition "attachment of an unstressed or weakly stressed word (enclitic) to the preceding word … [author's translation]". In strong contrast, the entry "Enklitikon" (= enclitic) on the same page uses the term morpheme ("weakly stressed morpheme"). So the readers find themselves in a terminological muddle.

Furthermore, Crystal (2008: 80) explains *clitic* as a "form which resembles a word, but cannot stand on its own as a normal utterance, being phonologically dependent upon a neighbouring word (its *host*) in a construction", which implies that he adds one new aspect to the definition, the concept of "host".

---

2 Note that the written form, i.e., the orthographic representation of the contraction, is used.

The reason for the relatively undifferentiated and sometimes confusing treatment of the terms and concepts in these reference works obviously lies in the complexity of the matter (cf. Sections 2 and 3).

Among the early detailed discussions of clitics with a relevance to the English language in general and English auxiliary verbs in particular are Zwicky (1977), Zwicky and Pullum (1983) and Spencer (1991), all with a generativist orientation. Zwicky considers weak forms of English function words (e.g., auxiliaries and certain pronouns)

> [c]ases where a free morpheme, when unaccented, may be phonologically reduced, the resultant form being phonologically subordinated to a neighboring word. Cliticization of this sort is usually associated with stylistic conditions [...] (Zwicky 1977: 5)

He classifies them as having "ordinary syntax (the reduced forms occur in the same positions as the full forms)", suggesting the term *simple clitics* for them (ibid.: 6). He also gives a general definition of simple clitics as "any word that can appear unaccented has the potential to cliticize to a neighboring word" (ibid.: 9) and summarises that "simple clitics show the phonological behavior of affixes of the first type, or # type" (ibid.: 29), i.e., of inflectional morphemes.

We find further clarification for issues related to our initial mentioning of potentially new synthetic elements in Sections 2 and 3 in Zwicky and Pullum (1983; cf. esp. 502–506), who adopt the following stance (ibid.: 502–503):

> Two types of bound morphemes are found attached to (free) words in many languages: clitics and affixes, in particular inflectional affixes. English, for instance, has auxiliary verbs like *is*, *has*, and *have*, which may become clitic to words preceding them [...] English [...] has a few clear inflectional affixes, among them affixes expressing the plural for nouns (knights), the past for verbs (arrived), and the superlative for adjectives (fastest) [...]

With regard to reduced auxiliaries as clitics (i.e., enclitics), they also state (ibid.) that

> they are optional variants of full forms (*is*, *has*, *have*), and occur in the same positions in sentences as the corresponding full forms. Consequently, a major condition on the combinability of a word with one of these clitics is the ability of that word to occur with the appropriate full form in syntactic structures [...] word-clitic combinability is largely governed by SYNTACTIC considerations. The conditions governing the combinability of stems with affixes are of quite a different sort: they are MORPHOLOGICAL and/or LEXICAL in character, being concerned with the substructure of a finite set of words.

They further specify (ibid.: 504–506) that *'s* (cf. *is* as full form), *'s* (*has*), and *'ve* (*have*) differ from the inflectional affixes *-er*, *-ed* and *-est* completely concerning the following criteria:

- Degree of selection between the clitics and the hosts is low as opposed to inflectional endings being relatively specific in selecting their stem (e.g., *-ed* attaching to verbal stems only);
- No arbitrary gaps in host-clitic combinations contrasting with (occasional) gaps in inflectional paradigms (e.g., non-existence of a past participle of the verb *stride*);
- Hosts are morphonologically unaffected by the above mentioned clitics as opposed to "arbitrary groupings into paradigm sets, sub-regular and irregular for both stems and affixes, and suppletion" (cf. from among their examples *dice*, *slept* and *worst*);
- "No cases where the contribution of these clitics [mentioned above] to sentence meaning is not identical to the contribution of their associated full forms" in contrast to cases of inflected forms having idiosyncratic semantics;
- "No syntactic operations exist which treat a word combined with one of the clitics *'s* or *'ve* as a unit", whereas inflected words are treated as units by syntactic operations;
- Clitics can attach to already cliticized hosts (*I'd 've done*); the analogy is not true of inflectional endings.

In a detailed study of the ca. 60 English function words, Dixon (2007: 575) also distinguishes between clitics and affixes, and correspondingly, between clitic boundary and affix boundary. He has, e.g., *dog's* /dɒg=z/ (in *dog has*) with a clitic boundary and *dogs* /dɒg-z/ with an affix boundary.[3]

When discussing auxiliaries, he notes (ibid.: 590–591) that there is a difference between *had* and *would* in particular on the one hand and *should* and *could* on the other. The modal *would* (as the structural *had*) may occur in several forms of reductions in which they cliticize, with /d/ as the only obligatory element, whereas *should* and *could* have /ʃd/ and /kd/ as a minimal requirement. Apparently, although the three modals fill the same position in some complex verb forms, they can be considered to be able to express different modal concepts. Accordingly, they have to be kept distinctive. – From this, however, the questions arise, first, of whether this notion of a syllable (with two such consonants in marginal positions, without a vowel) is correct, and, second, whether *could* and *should* are clitics at all. At least the two auxiliaries are no prototypical representatives of their class.

The latter aspect of *could* and *should* is also discussed by Anderson (2008: 171). Here we are confronted with a different interpretation: The auxiliary *would* is discussed as having an idiosyncratic reduced form, and not *could* and *should*. However, the consequence of the statement, i.e., whether they are clitics, is not directly addressed. We only find, on the same page, a summarizing listing of reduced forms, with *could* and *should* not listed. This is accompanied by the statement: "An overall generalization is that the environments in which the reduced auxiliaries can occur are all ones where a corresponding full verb is possible as well".

Later Anderson (ibid.: 172) discusses the correlation between clitics and inflectional morphemes:

[3] I have changed Dixon's notation of the vowel of *dog* for the symbol agreed upon by all pronouncing dictionaries covering English English pronunciation.

> Exactly parallel facts [about *'s* clitics – L.P.] obtain for the relation between reduced auxiliary *'d* (representing *had* or *would*) and the regular past ending /-d/. It seems reasonable to conclude, then, that in structural terms the reduced auxiliaries are entirely analogous to these other grammatical elements, which are generally considered to be located in phonological structure as "syllable affixes" attached to the word to their left.

The assumption that *'d* is considered one and the same reduced auxiliary, no matter how many corresponding full verb forms there are, poses an additional problem, leading up to a mismatch of interpretation at clitic level and at the level of morpho-syntactic interpretation of the complex verb form (cf. Section 5).

After a comparative analysis of the syllable structure of affixed words, here inflected words (example *thirsts*), vs. combinations of host and reduced auxiliary in *Tim's leaving*, Anderson concludes that "the English reduced Auxiliaries are lexical variants of full forms, consisting of a single consonant. As such they are 'prosodically deficient', since a single consonant (especially an obstruent) cannot constitute a syllable in English ..." (ibid.: 172–173). This conclusion of lexical variation, however, collides with the aforementioned notion of clitics *'s* and *'d* representing more than one full form in each case.

Aside from the last aspect, recent publications show the progress made in the theoretical treatment of clitics. For the moment though, as it seems, the current concept of (en)clitics like *'ll* and *'ve* does not fully contribute to an understanding of all aspects involved.

In order to tackle the issue of a potential structural change in morphology and syntax mentioned in Section 1, the following questions have to be addressed:

- Did or do they start or even boost a drift towards more syntheticity of Present-Day English?
- Can such development be observed in an ongoing restructuring of certain verbal categories, e.g., Tense?

We attempt to answer the questions by examining the role of the auxiliaries in the building of certain morphological categories of the English verb. For the description of these categories we use an established theoretical model in a slightly modified version.

4. Grammaticalisation and (morpho-syntactic) paradigmaticalisation

Certain verbal patterns emerging in the (Late) Middle English or Early Modern English periods, as represented by e.g., *will ask* and *have asked* (cf. also *is asked*), with (structural) auxiliaries forming complex verb forms, are an interesting topic in the study of historical language change as well as Present-Day English. The full systemic impact of processes related to the grammaticalisation of *will* and *have*, however, can only be seen when they are discussed with regard to their (multiple) paradigmatic relations. In order to discuss these relations, the auxiliaries are also examined from a synchronic perspective. For an inclusion of the concept of grammaticalisation, see this section further below.

The concepts of "paradigmatic relations" and "paradigm" are of basic importance to our line of argumentation.

The term *paradigm* is not just understood as a list of somehow related forms of conjugation or declension but as a network of paradigmatic relations. We conceive of such paradigmatic relations, prototypically, as based on functional and formal oppositions pertaining to a morphological or, for Present-Day English rather, morpho-syntactic category (cf. e.g., Tense and Aspect in its traditional sense).

For the theoretical concept of the morpho-syntactic category we follow Lucko (1999: 273), who explicates that "[s]uch categories ... can conveniently be described as conforming to [a] ... model, which is based on a privative binary opposition and has its roots in the descriptive traditions of Prague School Linguistics ..."

The notion of oppositions or, in a more or less pre-theoretical way, inflectional contrasts has long been applied in the understanding of historical morphological categories, such as those of Old English. Cf. e.g., verbal tense and mood distinctions or noun contrasts of gender, case and number. They were all brought about by synthetic means, i.e., inflectional morphemes and ablaut. Over time, as we know, the structure of, e.g., the truly morphological category of Tense has changed to include analytic elements – auxiliaries. This results in structures going beyond the word level. The verb form *will ask* (expressing future-time reference) is therefore commonly perceived as a phrase forming an opposition with *asked* (past-time reference). Thus the purely morphological contrast between *asked* and *ask* (present-time reference) has been supplemented by the inclusion of a phrasal form, yielding a mixed, i.e., morpho-syntactic category structure. When analysing more complex verb forms like *will have been asked*, we see the interaction between analytic and synthetic means as well as between the word level and the phrase level.

The (reduced or unreduced) auxiliary *will*, for instance, in the morpho-syntactic opposition *ask* vs. *will ask* (also *shall ask*), as shown above, combines with a verbal infinitive to build a permanent phrase-like (analytic) form. This is why, for now and in view of these oppositions, but deviant from van Gelderen's assumption of affixation (see p. 285 of this paper), the only plausible question to be asked is whether reduced auxiliaries as parts of complex verb forms bring about new oppositions in the given set of verb forms.

Going back to the theoretical concept of morpho-syntactic category, we can conceive of the category as having an underlying categorial function in that the forms involved express an opposition between the specification of a basic concept, with regard to our three verb forms, a differentiation between present reference and, e.g., past reference. This specific differentiation, however, is part of a category structure relying on a more abstract categorial function; cf., e.g., Lucko (1999: 273). There is a general structure that can be applied to all morpho-syntactic categories. It contains a formally marked element as part of an opposition, specifying a certain categorial function. It has a counterpart element that looks different formally. Both members fulfil the categorial function in contrasting ways. The marked element gives a specification with regard to the concept, whereas the other expresses the negation of this specification. The following verb forms illustrate such a formal and functional opposition:

(5) *ask_* vs. *ask<u>ed</u>*

This contrast concerns the temporal relation between the moment of speaking and the speaker's point of interest. These two referential points are derived from the Reichenbach model of time and tense (Reichenbach 1947, 1956), in which three relevant points in time are distinguished: speech time (= moment of speaking), event time (= point in time or time interval at/in which an action/process/state occurs) and reference time (= time of interest or of orientation). The relation of the three to one another can be depicted on a timeline. Reichenbach's model was, in a slightly modified way, combined with the aforementioned concept of morpho-syntactic category by, e.g., Lucko (1990: 580–585).

Taking a closer look at the two verb forms above, we thus find that *asked* specifies the function as 'reference time before speech time' and *ask* (like *asks*) expresses the logical negation of this specification (but may also be used to abstract from the specification). Consequently and in contrast to this, the form *ask* has no formal marker related to the category in question. This form negates the specification; this negation, accordingly, can be paraphrased as 'reference time not before (or after) speech time', implying that the two points coincide.

As a consequence of the concept of privative binary opposition, the (abstract) function fulfilled by *asked* and *will ask*, respectively, is 'reference time before or after speech time', i.e., the two points in time must not coincide or overlap. The traditional name of this category is retained in this theoretical model as Tense.

In a similar way, we may describe the distinction between the verb forms *asked* in *they asked* and *have asked* in *they have asked*. In order to explain the opposition between the two we need, drawing from the Reichenbach model again, a different set of two positions on the timeline compared to the previous pair of verb forms. The opposition in question here is based on a causal and temporal relation between event time and reference time in the following ways:

(6) a. *have asked* = reference time after event time
b. *asked* = reference time coincident with event time

The specification 'reference time after event time' can be translated, in a semi-theoretical way, as "the speaker is interested in something resulting from and occurring after the event itself". From the implied result he/she "looks back" to the event causing the result. This "retrospective view" may be used to name the function of verb forms like *have asked* as RETROSPECTIVE. In contrast, the functional negation thereof ('reference time coincident with event time') expresses that "the speaker's interest is in (on) the event itself". The respective function is accordingly called COINCIDENT.

For more details and implications, e.g., the interpretation of the *be going to*-form as PROSPECTIVE, see Lucko (1990/1992, 1995) and Polzenhagen (2008), who name this categorial distinction CORRELATION.

In sum, these two formal and functional oppositions thus establish two morpho-syntactic categories of the Present-Day English verb, namely Tense and Correlation. With regard to these categories, the finite verb forms above are marked as follows:

ask	Present, Coincident
asked	Past, Coincident
have asked	Present, Retrospective
will ask	Future, Coincident

In the historical perspective, verb forms like *will ask* and *have asked* were novel forms of morpho-syntax in the period of Early Modern English. The existence of *will* and *have* at that time as function words was the result of a process of grammaticalisation. By grammaticalisation we understand, roughly, their change from content words to function words with all consequences for their phonetics and phonology, meaning, syntactic combinability, etc. (cf. e.g., Trask 2000: 141f. and Bußmann 1996: 196f.; for detailed discussions see Hopper and Traugott 2003, chapter 6, and Lehmann 2004).

The new aspect this paper wishes to examine is the combination of the dimensions of grammaticalisation and morpho-syntactic category. In doing so, we see, for the verb forms *will ask* and *have asked* to become members of the aforementioned categories, that they had to undergo different changes in several stages:

(a) Functional/semantic change from main verb to auxiliary verb;
(b) Consequently, their falling subject to phonetic processing (weakening);
(c) Stabilisation and regularisation of their use;
(d) Becoming an element of some specific opposition, and, thus of a paradigm, an orderly arranged set of oppositions – a process to be named "paradigmaticalisation".

For the purpose of this paper, *paradigmaticalisation* is used as a provisional term. The term can, according to (d), roughly, be defined, for verb forms like *will ask* and *have asked*, as a regular long-term occurrence in some privative binary opposition of form and function, expressing, in one way or the other, the underlying categorial distinction.

The fulfilment of paradigmaticalisation, i.e., completion as a process, can be used as a criterion for the assessment of reduced auxiliaries attached to preceding syntactic elements.

With regard to the categories of Tense and Correlation, we find no evidence of new oppositions arising from the use of the reduced auxiliaries *will* and *have*.

However, our starting-point was a different one. The consequence of van Gelderen's idea of affixation (see p. 285) extended to reduced *will* and *have* (as parts of the verb forms above) is that they must be considered grammatical morphemes attached to a noun or pronoun (or corresponding phrase). What are, then, the implications?

Following van Gelderen in her explanation of *shoulda*/*shouldav*, structures like *they've* and *kids've* would have to be interpreted as word forms of *they* and *kids*. This interpretation leads to a patterning of the noun and pronoun forms in question like:

(7)	I'll	I've	I'd
	you'll	you've	you'd
	…	…	…
	they'll	they've	they'd
	kids'll	kids've	kids'd

Apart from *kids* already being a word form of *kid*, such word forms cannot be distinguished in a workable typological description. Although the table looks like a regular pattern, the forms do not reflect formal/functional distinctions of the pronouns and the noun *kid(s)*, and are not part of a paradigm. Affixation, however, with regard to (morpho-syntactic) functional categories, that does not lead up to paradigmaticalisation is merely a formal extension of the host word. Cliticization here does not cause the existence of affixes.

As a consequence, the concept of syntheticity needs to be understood in the light of these findings. Not all formal extensions or fusions as clitics, here typologically restricted to English, end up being grammatical morphemes.

5. Conclusion

The aim of this paper was to investigate possible (qualitative) consequences of the use of reduced auxiliaries as enclitics with regard to their potential impact on English functional (grammatical) categories, in the sense that the categories involved become "more synthetic".

We conclude, mainly from Sections 3 and 4, that we only find counter-evidence for simple enclitics to have become inflectional morphemes. As reduced auxiliaries, having been in existence for centuries, they have not been able to form oppositions other than the ones known since late Middle English or Early Modern English. The reasons for this result seem to be:

- Extralinguistically, there is no (current) communicative or systemic need for further morpho-syntactic differentiation in the sub-paradigms in question, and
- intralinguistically, a lack of more potential material (i.e., function words) for reduction.

Taking a comparative look at English-related creoles or pidgins, however, we find new instances of grammaticalisation and paradigmaticalisation after their stabilisation and complexification. For example, in West African Pidgin English, at least in most of its varieties, the marker *bin* or *bi* (derived from English *been*) is used to express past-time reference e.g., in *a bi(n) si i(n) yesterday* 'I saw her/him yesterday' (cf. Peter and Wolf 2007: 15). One could thus assume that a contact situation of a certain type may effect systemic historical change of a contact language, i.e., operate as a driving force, which, in a way seems to confirm Danchev's and others' position regarding the aspect of contact (see Section 1).

Bibliography

Bußmann, H. (1996): *Routledge Dictionary of Language and Linguistics*. London/New York: Routledge.

Bußmann, H. (2002): *Lexikon der Sprachwissenschaft*. 3rd Edition. Stuttgart: Kröner.

Cruttenden, A. (2008): *Gimson's Pronunciation of English*. 7th Edition. London: Hodder Education.

Crystal, D. (2008): *A Dictionary of Linguistics and Phonetics*. 6th Edition. Oxford: Blackwell.

Danchev, A. (1992): The evidence for analytic and synthetic development in English. In: M. Rissanen, O. Ihalainen, T. Nevalainen and I. Taavitsainen (eds.), *History of Englishes: New Methods and Interpretations in Historical Linguistics*. Berlin/New York: de Gruyter, 25–41.

Dixon, R. M. W. (2007): Clitics in English. *English Studies* 88 (5): 574–600.

Gelderen, E. van (2011): *The Linguistic Cycle: Language Change and the Language Faculty*. New York: Oxford University Press.

Gelderen, E. van (2006): *A History of the English Language*. Amsterdam and Philadelphia: John Benjamins.

Gelderen, E. van (1998): Structure of Tense and Aspect. *Linguistic Analysis* 27: 138–165. [Online version: http://www.public.asu.edu/~gelderen/LA-HAVE.htm; 10 September, 2012]

Hopper, P. J. and E. Closs Traugott (eds.) (2003): *Grammaticalization*. 2nd Edition. Cambridge: Cambridge University Press.

Jespersen, O. (1917): *Negation in English and Other Languages*. Copenhagen: A. F. Høst.

Krug, M. (2011). Auxiliaries and grammaticalization. In: H. Narrog and B. Heine (eds.), *The Oxford Handbook of Grammaticalization*. New York: Oxford University Press., 547–558.

Leech, G., M. Hundt, C. Mair and N. Smith (eds.) (2009): *Change in Contemporary English: A Grammatical Study*. Cambridge: Cambridge University Press.

Lehmann, C. (2004): Theory and method in grammaticalization. *Zeitschrift für Germanistische Linguistik* 32 (2): 153–187.

Lucko, P. (1999): Morphological categories as interfaces between lexis and grammar. In: P. Lucko and U. Carls (eds.), *Form, Function and Variation in English – Studies in Honour of Klaus Hansen*. Frankfurt/M.: Peter Lang, 273–281.

Lucko, P. (1995): Between aspect, actionality and modality: The functions of the expanded form. In: W. Riehle and H. Keiper (eds.), *Anglistentag 1994 Graz. Proceedings*. [Proceedings of the Conference of the German Association of University Teachers of English XVI], 171–182.

Lucko, P. (1990/1992): Zur Morphologie der englischen Verben. Part I *Fremdsprachenunterricht* 43 (12): 580–585, Part II. *Fremdsprachenunterricht* 45 (5): 281–283.

Mair, C. (2006): *Twentieth-Century English: History, Variation and Standardization*. Cambridge: Cambridge University Press.

Mosegaard Hansen, M. B. (2011): Negative cycles and grammaticalization. In: H. Narrog and B. Heine (eds.), *The Oxford Handbook of Grammaticalization*. New York: Oxford University Press, 570–579.

Narrog, H. and B. Heine (eds.) (2011): *The Oxford Handbook of Grammaticalization*. New York: Oxford University Press.

Peter, L. and H. G. Wolf (2007): A comparison of the varieties of West African Pidgin English. *World Englishes* 26 (1): 3–21.

Polzenhagen, F. (2008): The so-called Tense-Aspect system of the English verb: A cognitive-functional view. In: H. G. Wolf, L. Peter and F. Polzenhagen (eds.), *Focus on Eng-*

lish: Linguistic structure, language variation and discursive use. Studies in honour of Peter Lucko. Leipzig: Leipziger Universitätsverlag, 219–246.

Reichenbach, H. (1947): *Elements of Symbolic Logic*. New York: Macmillan.

Reichenbach, H. (1956): *The Direction of Time*. Berkeley: University of California Press.

Roach, P. (2009): *English Phonetic and Phonology: A practical course*. 4th Edition. Cambridge: Cambridge University Press.

Spencer, A. (1991): *Morphological Theory*. Oxford: Basil Blackwell.

Szmrecsanyi, B. (2012, in press): Analyticity and Syntheticity in the History of English. In: T. Nevalainen and E. Closs Traugott (eds.), *The Oxford Handbook of the History of English*. New York: Oxford University Press, 654–665.

Szmrecsanyi, B. (2009): Typological parameters of intralingual variability: Grammatical analyticity versus syntheticity in varieties of English. *Language Variation and Change* 21: 319–353.

Trask, R. L. (2000): *The Dictionary of Historical and Comparative Linguistics*. Edinburgh: Edinburgh University Press.

Vachek, J. (1961): Some less familiar aspects of the analytical trend of English. *Brno Studies in English* 3: 9–74.

Wells, J. C. (2008): *Longman Pronunciation Dictionary*. 3rd Edition. Harlow/Essex: Pearson Education

Zwicky, A. M. (1977). *On Clitics*. Bloomington/Indiana: Indiana University Linguistics Club.

Zwicky, A. M. and G. K. Pullum (1983): Cliticization vs. inflection: English *n't*. *Language* 59: 502–513.

Corpus-based modeling of the semantic transparency of noun-noun compounds

Heike Zinsmeister

1. Introduction

Küchenmesser 'kitchen knife', *Milchgesicht* 'baby face' (literally 'milk face'), and *Dichterfreund* in the sense of 'poet and friend' exemplify three semantic types of noun-noun compounds in German, differing with regard to their semantic transparency. In *Küchenmesser*, both morphological main parts (*Küche* 'kitchen' and *Messer* 'knife') contribute directly to the meaning of the whole; the compound refers to a specific type of knife, namely a knife that is used in the location of a kitchen. *Küchenmesser* is thus semantically transparent: Its meaning is created compositionally from the meanings of its parts. The meaning of *Milchgesicht* is less obvious. Sometimes the word directly refers to a young-looking face, but this compound generally refers to a person attributed to have a youthful face. *Milchgesicht* referring to a person is semantically opaque, as its meaning is not directly compositionally determined from its parts: It does not refer to a specific type of face, but rather to a person. Finally, like *Küchenmesser*, *Dichterfreund* is semantically transparent, but differs in the way its meaning is composed from its parts. *Dichterfreund* in the intended meaning refers to a person who is both a friend and a poet. The compound meaning is a unification of the meanings denoted by *Dichter* and *Freund*.

The three semantic types illustrated by *Küchenmesser*, *Milchgesicht*, and *Dichterfreund*, respectively, correspond to three traditional semantic compound classes: (i) determinative (or endocentric), (ii) possessive (also *bahuvrihi* or exocentric), and (iii) copulative (or *dvandva*) compounds (Olsen 2000). As the alternative terminology in parentheses indicates, these concepts are based in part on the semantic description of Sanskrit compounds.

This paper presents a study that relates the traditional semantic classification of noun-noun compounds to corpus-based evidence.[1] We modify the classes by including all kinds

---

[1] I am very happy to contribute to this Festschrift for Sue Olsen. I learned a great deal from her as a student assistant in her Introduction to Linguistics course in Stuttgart – not only about linguistics but also about teaching in general. Since then, I have moved on to computational linguistics, and I would like to contribute to this volume from a corpus-linguistic perspective. Computational semantics is not my major research area. However, the study described in this paper builds on two previous publications of mine: one on noun-verb collocations with a focus on the semantic transparency of compounds (Zinsmeister and Heid 2004), and one in which I applied the same similarity measure used in this paper to investigate the semantic transparency of complex verbs (Zinsmeister and Smolka 2012). I would like to thank Claire Bacher for correcting my English. I am responsible for all errors that remain.

of lexicalized compounds in the second class, and thus distinguish between (i) compounds that are semantically transparent in the sense of determinative compounds, (ii) compounds that are not semantically transparent (such as possessive compounds, but also all other kinds of morphological noun-noun compounds with a lexicalized meaning that cannot be directly related to the compositional meaning of their parts), and (iii) compounds that are semantically transparent in the copulative sense. The main focus lies in the distinction between classes (i) and (ii), since instances of class (iii) are rather rare in the corpus.

Our corpus-based study is grounded in the approach of *Distributional Semantics,* which assumes that the meaning of a word can be modeled by collecting information about its distribution in a corpus (Firth 1957, Harris 1968, Marconi 1997). The distributional information is collected by examination of co-occurring words, structures, or relations. The sum of this contextual information can be viewed as a kind of mold, a container that shapes the meaning of the word in a characteristic fashion. This approach predicts that two semantically similar words will occur in similar contexts, i.e., they will have similar distributional properties. For our three semantic compound classes, we expect the characteristic distributional patterns for the compounds and their nominal parts to be related to their different semantic transparencies.

The chapter is organized as follows: Section 2 introduces noun-noun compounds in German with respect to their morphological structure and semantic classification. Section 3 sketches the basic ideas of Distributional Semantics and discusses skew divergence as a measure for distributional similarity. Section 4 describes our corpus-based study and discusses its results. Finally, Section 5 briefly concludes the chapter, proposing ideas for future research.

2. Noun-noun compounds in German

Compounding is a very productive word-formation process in German. In this paper, we investigate a particular type of compounding – namely, nominal compounds that are built from two nominal stems, such as *Küchenmesser* 'kitchen knife', *Milchgesicht* 'baby face', or *Dichterfreund* 'poet and friend', as discussed in the introduction.

Küchenmesser includes the filler element *-n-* in addition to its nominal stems *Küche* and *Messer.* Another example of a filler element is *-s-*, as seen in *Arbeitsstätte* 'workplace', which consists of the nominal stems *Arbeit* and *Stätte.* The form *Arbeits* is not part of the declension paradigm of *Arbeit*; this demonstrates that the filler element (here, *-s-*) is merely a filler and does not belong to the first stem of the compound. A negative filler can be seen in *Sachmittel* 'material expenses', which consists of the stems *Sach* and *Mittel. Sach* is the derivational stem of the noun *Sache,* which relates to *Sach* by *-e*-deletion. The derivational stem only occurs in derivations, never as an independent word.

The default orthographical representation of a German noun-noun compound is a single word in which the two noun stems are separated neither by a space nor by a hyphen, but only at times by filler elements such as those described above.[2]

[2] For a recent study on German compound filler elements, see Nübling and Szczepaniak (2011).

2.1. Morphological structure

Following Olsen (2000), we assume an endocentric morphological structure for noun-noun compounds in German:

> The traditional insight that syntagmas are grammatical "extensions" of one of their elements [...] is captured in current analyses of word structure by the notion head, which was introduced into morphological theory from syntactic theory by Williams, 1981: The head constituent determines the category and other morpho-syntactic properties of the complex word. This is accomplished by the percolation of features up to the node immediately dominating the head and its sister in a recursive fashion [...]. In English, German and Dutch, the head is on the right. (Olsen 2000: 204)

Diagram (1) demonstrates how the compound *Milchgesicht* 'baby face' inherits its morpho-syntactic features from its morphological head *Gesicht* 'face'. The categorial feature *N* (noun), like gender and number features (neuter singular), percolates from the head constituent to the mother node.

(1)

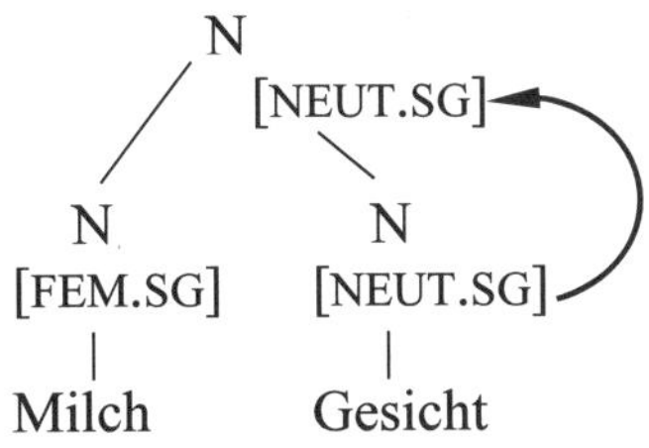

Motivated by the asymmetric morphological structure, in the rest of this chapter we will refer to the first noun stem in a noun-noun compound as the 'modifier noun' or 'modifier' and to the second noun stem as the 'head noun' or 'head', independent of the compound's meaning as a whole.

2.2. Semantic types

As introduced in Section 1, we distinguish between three different semantic compound types. The first type is traditionally referred to as a determinative (or endocentric) compound (cf. Olsen 2000). Its meaning is compositionally derived from the meanings of its parts: The meaning of the head noun denotes the type of referent, and the meaning of the modifier noun modifies this in some semantic relation to the head noun, such that it further specifies or modifies the meaning of the head noun. Dowty (1979) suggests modeling this meaning composition on the basis of the parts of the compound by means of the implicit relation 'is connected with'. Fanselow (1981a,b) spells out a list of basic relations that are independent from the lexical meanings of the nouns but are a fundamental part of the mental process of meaning creation itself, such as assuming a part-of relation or a causal relation between the meanings of the modifier and the head noun, or locating the referent of the head noun at a location denoted by the modifier noun. In addition to these basic relations, Fanselow also suggests a second type of relation that can arise from the meanings of the compound parts, which he dubs 'stereotypical relations'. For compounds with the head noun

Messer 'knife', for instance, the stereotypical relation would be that the modifier noun introduces an object that is typically cut by this type of knife, as in *Kuchenmesser* 'cake knife'. For the compound *Küchenmesser* 'kitchen knife', in contrast, the stereotypical relation does not apply; we instead employ the basic relation of locality. Most, if not all, determinative compounds are ambiguous between multiple possible interpretations; however, they tend to have a default interpretation. Determinative compounds are *semantically transparent,* in that their meaning is transparent with respect to the meaning of their head noun. In other words, they are semantically transparent because their meaning is similar to the meaning of their head noun.

The second semantic type is traditionally referred to as the possessive (also *bahuvrihi* or exocentric) compound. For practical reasons, we extend this class to include all morphological noun-noun compounds whose meanings cannot be compositionally derived from the meanings of their parts. The second class thus includes all noun-noun compounds that are lexicalized such that their meanings are opaque with respect to the meanings of their parts. They are *semantically opaque*, as their meanings are dissimilar from the meanings of their head nouns.[3]

The final semantic type is traditionally called the copulative (or *dvandva*) compound. This is the least frequent type of compound in German. In Fanselow's (1981b) definition, the meaning of a copulative compound is created by applying the basic relation 'AND' to the meanings of its parts. A copulative compound is thus doubly *semantically transparent*: Its meaning is similar both to the meaning of the head noun and to that of the modifier noun, implying that the meaning of the compound is a unification of the properties of its two parts.

2.3. Why are compounds interesting?

The distinction between semantically transparent and semantically opaque compounds is an interesting issue for cognitive linguists because it relates to issues of how and to what extent complex words enter the mental lexicon and the extent of interconnections between words of different kinds. In this paper, we will not specifically examine this aspect, instead referring the reader to the psycholinguistic literature, e.g., Marslen-Wilson (2007).

For lexicographers, it is important to know which compounds contribute a new meaning independent from the meanings of their head nouns. Semantically opaque compounds are more likely to receive their own lexicon entries than semantically transparent compounds are. An additional factor in this decision is whether a compound has been established in the speech community or whether it is just an occasional creative usage. Investigation of the online archive Wortwarte (cf. Lemnitzer 2007) demonstrates that the majority of newly coined words in the last decade have been nominal compounds, at least in the selection of online print media on which the archive is based.[4]

For computational linguists, lexical information is also a major issue. A lack of lexical coverage represents a bottleneck for many language-processing applications. Gaps in handwritten lexica are a common cause of diminished system performance. Automatic collec-

---

3 Some more fine-grained models distinguish the semantic transparency of compound parts from the transparency of the compound as a whole, e.g., Libben (1995).

4 Wortwarte: http://www.wortwarte.de/

tions of lexical information based on corpora can help to reduce this problem; however, when more complex information is required (for instance, frequency counts of verb-argument collocations such as *einen Zahn ziehen* 'pull a tooth'), even large corpora are often not extensive enough to provide sufficient instances to model the variety and combinatorial richness that exists in language. Statistical Machine Translation (SMT) is a prototypical language-processing application that is strongly dependent on corpus-derived lexical and contextual information. The bilingual lexical knowledge of SMT systems is harvested from word-aligned bilingual corpora consisting of original texts and their translations into another language. The words of the original texts are aligned with the corresponding words in the translated texts.

From these alignments, statistical machine translation tools learn probable translations for language pairs. Statistical machine translation systems produce better translations when they learn from aligned texts in which compounds are split into their parts (Fritzinger and Fraser 2010: 225).

Examples (2)a and (3)a below illustrate word alignment without compound splitting and word alignment with compound splitting, respectively. The model based on alignment (2)a cannot translate the unseen compound *Goldschatz* in (2)b, whereas the model based on (3)a is more flexible and has the means to translate the unseen word – given compound splitting of its input data as well.[5]

(2)	a. *Goldzahn* – *gold tooth*		align(*Goldzahn, gold*), align(*Goldzahn, tooth*)
	Schatz – *treasure*		align(*Schatz, treasure*)
	b. translate(*Goldschatz*) ?	→	*
(3)	a. *Gold+Zahn* – *gold tooth*		align(*Gold, gold*), align(*Zahn, tooth*)
	Schatz – *treasure*		align(*Schatz, treasure*)
	b. translate(*Gold+Schatz*)?	→	translate(*Gold, gold*)
			translate(*Schatz, treasure*)

What is remarkable in this example is that the second model has greater coverage, even though both translation models are based on the same amount of training data, i.e., the aligned data in (2)a and (3)a.

In sum, compound-splitting improves word-alignment performance, reducing the risk that a new complex word will not be translated, as it is likely that at least the head noun will have been seen in the word-aligned data. We assume that compound splitting for word alignment particularly improves system performance in cases in which the compound is semantically transparent. This is further motivation to develop methods for the robust, large-scale determination of the semantic transparency of compounds.

---

5 *Treasure of gold* might be a better translation for *Goldschatz*, but *gold treasure* gives a good idea of the word's meaning.

3. Distributional Semantics

The main contribution of this chapter is a corpus-based study focused on determining the transparency of a particular type of compound: German noun-noun compounds, as introduced in Section 2.1. To this end, we rely on the assumption that the meaning of a word is determined by its use. Translated into corpus-linguistic terms, this means that the meaning of a word is determined by its co-occurring words (Firth 1957, Harris 1968, Marconi 1997). Based on this assumption, we can conjecture that two words that share similar sets of co-occurring words will also be similar in meaning. This conjecture is the basis for distributional semantics in computational linguistics and is summarized in the Distributional Hypothesis (cf. Sahlgren 2008):

(4) *Distributional Hypothesis*:
There is a correlation between the distributional similarity of two linguistic items and their meaning similarity.

Assuming that the Distributional Hypothesis holds, we can utilize distributional information to estimate semantic information.

3.1 Distributional Similarity

Distribution refers to the corpus occurrences of a word, as determined by contextual information collected regarding these occurrences. In the simplest case, this contextual information consists of the summarized frequencies of the words that co-occur in the neighborhood of the target word.

The toy corpus in (5) provides occurrences of the noun *Zahn* 'tooth' and its compounds *Milchzahn* 'baby tooth' (literally 'milk tooth') and *Löwenzahn* 'dandelion' (literally 'lion tooth'). The neighborhood is set to a window of up to five words preceding and following the target word within the same sentence. Instead of counting co-occurrences of surface tokens, we will abstract to the lemmas of the context words, i.e., their base forms. It is not important to translate the corpus sentences here, since the meanings of the context words do not matter in this analysis. We could systematically replace the context words with differently colored shapes, and we would still be able calculate their distributional similarity to various target words.

(5) *A toy corpus with neighborhood windows of up to 5 tokens marked*:

a. ... da sie jetzt [erst angefangen hat ihre ersten *Milchzähne* zu verlieren].
b. Die [sechsjährige Katja verliert gleich zwei *Milchzähne* auf einmal].
c. [Als er seinen *Milchzahn* verliert, bekommt er es "von] der Zahnfee"
d. Wer lässt sich schon mitten in der [Nacht von seinem Großvater einen *Milchzahn* ziehen]?

e. [Wenn die *Milchzähne* früh gezogen werden müssen, besteht] die Gefahr, ...
f. Ned ist traurig [darüber, daß er seinen letzten *Zahn* verloren hat].
g. [... , um ihm etwa einen *Zahn* zu ziehen oder eine Kralle] zu verkürzen.

h. [So werden bei Zehnjährigen *Zähne* meist aus kieferorthopädischen Gründen gezogen].
i. Der Mund zieht sich in die Breite. [Scharfe, schwarze *Zähne* wachsen].
j. [Beim Stacheldrahtzaun wuchsen *Löwenzahn* und Brennnessel].
k. [Manchmal wächst ein *Löwenzahn* durch eine winzige Ritze aus] dem Asphalt.

The first context word in (5)a that counts is the adverbial *erst*, the second *anfangen*, and so forth. We count two instances of the lemma *erst* in (5)a, even though the second occurrence *(ersten)* is an ordinal number and not the adverbial; we do not disambiguate ambiguous lemmas. An example of an interesting context word is the verb *verlieren*, which co-occurs three times with *Milchzahn* (cf. (5)a,b,c), once with *Zahn* (cf. (5)f), and never with *Löwenzahn*.

A crucial point here is that we collect the co-occurrence counts systematically, presenting them in a common table with all three target nouns together. Each column in Table 1 represents the lemma of a target noun; each row the lemma of a context word. The cells are filled with the co-occurrence frequencies of the respective target noun and the corpus lemma as observed in the toy corpus. The distributions of the target nouns are then represented as the ordered lists of their co-occurrence counts; e.g., *Milchzahn* is represented by the 'code' *1 3 0 2 2 2 ... 0.*

		CO-OCCURRENCE COUNTS WITH		
	CONTEXT LEMMA	*Milchzahn*	*Zahn*	*Löwenzahn*
1	*ein*	1	2	2
2	*verlieren*	3	1	0
3	*wachsen*	0	1	2
4	*ziehen*	2	2	0
5	*sein*	2	1	0
6	*erst*	2	0	0
...	...	...	...	...
53	*beim*	0	0	1

Table 1: Co-occurrence counts from the toy corpus (random lemma order)

3.1.1. The standard Vector Space Model

Mathematically speaking, the distributions of the target nouns are vectors. The three vectors of *Milchzahn*, *Zahn*, and *Löwenzahn*, respectively, are depicted in (6). Each vector corresponds to one of the three co-occurrence columns in Table 1.

(6) *Vector representations*
a. *Milchzahn:* (1 3 0 2 2 2 ... 0)
b. *Zahn:* (2 1 1 2 1 0 ... 0)
c. *Löwenzahn:* (2 0 2 0 0 0 ... 1)

The interesting thing about vectors is that they can be combined in *vector space models* to predict the semantic similarity between the words that they represent (see Erk 2012 for a recent survey on vector space models). In such a vector space, each context word corresponds to a dimension, and the distribution of a target word is a vector in this multi-dimensional space. The similarity between two words can then be measured in terms of the distance between their vectors in the space.

In our toy corpus above, there are 53 different context lemmas (cf. Table 1), such that the corresponding vector space model will consist of 53 dimensions. It is not possible to imagine such a high-dimensional space; however, it is easy to understand the basic idea when the space is reduced to only two dimensions that conform to the common x- and y-axes of a simple graph.

To illustrate a two-dimensional vector space model, we consider only the first two context lemmas of Table 1, the co-occurrence frequencies of the context lemmas *ein* 'a' and *verlieren* 'lose'. To facilitate comprehension, (7) provides the corresponding vector representations.

(7) *Vector representations for the two-dimensional example*
  a. *Milchzahn:* (1 3)
  b. *Zahn:* (2 1)
  c. *Löwenzahn:* (2 0)

It is important to note that the toy distribution in (7) suggests that *Zahn* and *Löwenzahn* have a more similar distribution than *Zahn* and *Milchzahn*, contrary to what we would expect to see in a real corpus.

The vector space in Figure 1 is defined by the horizontal axis for the counts of *ein* and the vertical axis for the counts of *verlieren*. The vectors are plotted in the standard way: The vector for *Milchzahn*, for instance, ends at the point in space that corresponds to 1 on the x-axis (counts of *ein*), and 3 on the y-axis (counts of *verlieren*); the vector for *Zahn* ends at 2 on the x-axis and 1 on the y-axis.

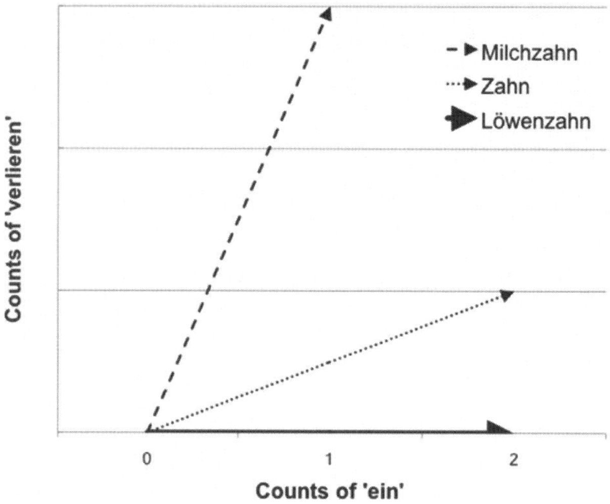

Figure 1: Vectors for the distributions of 'Milchzahn', 'Zahn' and 'Löwenzahn'

The similarity of two distributions is interpreted as the distance between their vectors. A common way to measure this distance is to calculate the cosine of the angle between the two vectors (e.g., Erk 2012: 637). If two vectors point in the same direction, meaning that the angle between them is 0°, then the cosine will be 1. Otherwise, the cosine will be less than 1; it will be -1 if the two vectors point in exactly opposite directions. In sum, the closer the cosine between two vectors is to 1, the more similar the two distributions are and thus the more semantically related the two target words are expected to be. The chart in Figure 1 confirms that the two-dimensional toy example exhibits an idiosyncratic result: The angle between *Zahn* and *Löwenzahn* is smaller than the angle between *Zahn* and *Milchzahn*. According to the Distributional Hypothesis, this would mean that the former pair is semantically more similar than the latter pair, contrary to common sense.

3.1.2. An alternative model

In this section, we will present an alternative model for calculating semantic similarity that was introduced by Lin (1999). It differs from the standard vector space model in terms of its basic elements, which determine the model dimensions, the scores that make up the vector values, and the similarity measure used to compare two distributions.

The basic elements in the standard model are the co-occurrence frequencies of context words. Context is defined as a window on the token string. Taking all context words into account results in a lot of noise; that is, irrelevant data that does not relate to the meaning of the nouns tends to obscure the actual meaning. We assume that verbs are good indicators for the meaning of a noun, as selectional restrictions of verbs indicate that the nouns that they select are similar to a certain extent. A window-based context does not always include the selecting verb of a noun. This is a more complicated problem for German than for English, due to German's head-final VP structure and less restrictive constituent order: In German, a nominal head and its selecting verb can occur at great distance from each other. In the alternative model, we make use of syntactically parsed data (cf. Baroni and Lenci 2010). That is, instead of blindly collecting adjacent words, we extract dependency parse patterns from the data: lexicalized dependency relations in the form of *Noun relation Verb,* e.g., *Noun is_subject_of Verb* or *Noun is_object_of Verb.* Table 2 summarizes the extraction result for our toy corpus in (5). Both *Milchzahn* and *Zahn* occur as objects of the verbs *verlieren* and *ziehen*, while *Zahn* and *Löwenzahn* both occur as subjects of *wachsen*.

RELATION	VERB	CO-OCCURRENCE COUNTS FOR		
		Milchzahn	*Zahn*	*Löwenzahn*
Object of	*verlieren*	3	1	0
	ziehen	2	2	0
Subject of	*wachsen*	0	1	2

Table 2: Dependency-parse pattern counts from the toy corpus

The use of raw frequency data has two drawbacks. One is that the general corpus frequency of a word has a strong impact on its distribution. A very common word such as *ein* 'a' is very likely to co-occur with many other words. Each individual co-occurrence instance with *ein* is therefore not as conclusive with regard to the distribution of the target word as a co-occurrence instance with a less-frequent word would be. Several alternative measures have been developed that take this bias into account (e.g., Lee 1999, 2001 and Evert 2005).[6] The second drawback is that raw frequencies do not generalize to unseen data. An alternative approach is to model the distribution by means of probabilities. Probabilities offer the advantage of weighting individual instances with respect to the overall corpus presence of the words. In addition, one can easily smooth the data such that unseen combinations are not completely 'out'; by assigning them a very small amount of the overall probability mass, they can still be taken into consideration.

RELATION	VERB	CO-OCCURRENCE PROBABILITIES FOR		
		Milchzahn	*Zahn*	*Löwenzahn*
Object of	*verlieren*	3/5 = 0.6	1/4 = 0.25	0
	ziehen	2/5 = 0.4	2/4 = 0.5	0
Subject of	*wachsen*	0	1/4 = 0.25	2/2 = 1
	Sum	1	1	1

Table 3: Probabilities for dependency-parse patterns (cf. Table 2)

(8) *Vector representations of the probability distributions*
  a. *Milchzahn:* (0.6 0.4 0)
  b. *Zahn:* (0.25 0.5 0.25)
  c. *Löwenzahn:* (0 0 1)

With regard to the similarity measure used to compare different distributions, we follow Lee (1999) who argues that similarity does not have to be a symmetric relation: "But the substitutability of one word for another need not [be] symmetric. For instance, 'fruit' may be the best possible approximation to 'apple', but the distribution of 'apple' may not be a suitable proxy for the distribution of 'fruit'" (Lee 1999: 30). Most similarity measures are symmetric, in the sense that they result in the same score independent of the direction of comparison. In investigating the similarity between compounds and their constituents, we expect it to be advantageous to use a similarity measure that is sensitive to the comparison direction. As a general tendency, compounds occur less frequently than their constituents in isolation, and they are less ambiguous and less polysemous than the simplex nouns.

In the alternative model, we represent the nouns by probability distributions over their lexicalized dependency relations (cf. Table 3). We compute the distance between a compound and its head or modifier noun with a variant of the Kullback-Leibler divergence $D(p||q)$. The Kullback-Leibler divergence (depicted in (9)) measures the difference between

---

6 See also the materials provided at http://www.cs.cornell.edu/home/llee/papers/cf.home.html (by Lilian Lee) and http://www.collocations.de/ (by Stefan Evert).

two probability distributions p and q by considering p as a kind of reference distribution and then summing up the divergence of q from p on a logarithmic scale.[7]

(9) $D(p||q) = \sum_i p_i \times \log \frac{p_i}{q_i}$

The basic idea of this measure is to quantify the average inefficiency of coding the distribution p by the other distribution q; it is asymmetric because it takes the first distribution as its reference point. In the extreme case in which p and q have the exact same distribution, D(p||q) would be zero, because the fraction p_i/q_i would be one for all dimensions and the logarithm of one is zero. If $p_i > q_i$, the logarithm value will be positive and D will increase; if $p_i < q_i$, the logarithm value will be negative and D will decrease. Since p is the reference distribution, D(p||q) will be positive after summing over all dimensions (except for the identity case discussed above).

The Kullback-Leibler divergence has a problem with dimensions for which q_i is zero, since division by zero is mathematically impossible. One exception is made by definition: Whenever p_i is zero, the quantity $0 \times \log(0/q_i)$ is interpreted as zero, independent of the value of q_i. As a consequence, the Kullback-Leibler divergence can only be applied to distributions for which p_i is zero whenever q_i is zero. For our toy example, this would mean that we could not use the distribution of *Zahn* as the reference distribution p for comparisons with the distributions of *Milchzahn* or *Löwenzahn*, because *Zahn* has positive probabilities for dimensions in which the other two nouns have zero probabilities. To overcome this restriction, Lee (1999, 2001) has introduced *skew divergence* as a variant of the Kullback-Leibler divergence. Instead of calculating the divergence using the observed probability distributions, this function smoothes the values of q, meaning that q will be positive for all dimensions for which p has a positive value. This is done by replacing q_i in (9) with the term $q_i^{smoothed}$ as defined in (10):

(10) $q_i^{smoothed} = w \times q_i + (1 - w) \times p_i$

The smoothed value combines the original probabilities of q_i with the corresponding probabilities of p_i. The weight *w* determines which fraction of q_i will be replaced by the corresponding fraction of p_i; it can take any constant value between zero and 1. In the following analysis, we will set *w* to 0.9 (cf. Schulte im Walde 2005). (11) presents the skew divergence scores for our toy example, taking the distribution of *Zahn* as the reference distribution:

(11) *Skew divergence scores for the toy example from Table 3 (w=0.9):*
a. D(p(*Zahn*)||q(*Milchzahn*)) ≈ 0.47
b. D(p(*Zahn*)||q(*Löwenzahn*)) ≈ 1.40

According to skew divergence, the distribution of *Milchzahn* diverges less from the distribution of *Zahn* in the toy example (D=0.47) than the distribution of *Löwenzahn* does (D=1.40), hence we analyze *Milchzahn* as being semantically closer to *Zahn* than *Löwenzahn* is to *Zahn*.

[7] Each distribution, p and q, must sum up to 1.

4. The study

In this section, we describe our corpus-based study, in which we model the semantic transparency of different types of noun-noun compounds (as introduced in Section 2.2.) by means of skew divergence (as described in the previous section).

4.1. Empirical setup

The textual base for our investigation was sdeWaC (Faaß et al. 2010),[8] a corpus of about 44 million sentences. This is a cleaned-up derivative of the larger, web-derived deWaC corpus (Baroni et al. 2009). Specifically, we made use of a dependency-parsed version of this corpus that had been parsed by the Bohnet parser (Bohnet 2010, Seeker and Kuhn 2012) and that also provided part-of speech annotation according to the STTS tagset (Schiller et al. 1999) and lemmatization.

The corpus served as the empirical base for the extraction of noun-noun compounds and their nominal components, and also for the collection of distributional information.

For the creation of the noun database, we first extracted all words that were annotated as common nouns in the corpus and analyzed them further using SMOR (Schmid et al. 2004), a morphological analyzer that covers the productive word formation processes of German – inflection, derivation, and compounding. Complex words were split into their lemmatized components, including those for which SMOR also offers a lexicalized, non-compositional entry (such as *Kindergarten* 'kindergarten' or *Lidschatten* 'eye shadow', which are more or less semantically opaque). In the current study, we only made use of compounds that were assigned simple noun-noun analysis by SMOR (often in addition to other analyses). Without further filtering, this procedure resulted in more than 1.1 million individual compound types. We refer to the number of compound types in which a noun occurs as a component as the noun's (head / modifier) family size (cf. Baayen et al. 1997). The most common modifier nouns, i.e., the nouns with the largest modifier family size, are *Land* 'country' (2,769 compound types), *Haupt* 'main / head' (2,687), and *Kind* 'child' (2,307). About 1,000 nouns only occur in one compound type as the modifier. *Argwohn* 'distrust' is one example: It is only observed in *Argwohngesicht* 'distrust face', which is a spontaneous creation and is completely transparent in meaning, as found in: *... und weg ist er. Natürlich nicht ohne sein dümmstes Argwohngesicht zum Besten zu geben.* ('... and off he goes. Of course not without showing his most stupid distrust face'). With respect to the head nouns, the most common nouns are *Bereich* 'area' (4,226 occurrences), *System* 'system' (3,082), and *Gruppe* 'group' (2,803). About 1,500 nouns only occur in one compound type as the head noun. Figure 2 depicts the skewed distribution of head family size; family size is plotted on the x-axis, the number of nouns on the y-axis. On the left are all the nouns with small family sizes (starting with about 1,500 at family size 1). On the right, we see individual data points for the nouns with large family sizes (e.g., *Bereich*, *System*, and *Gruppe*).

---

[8] sdeWaC is an acronym for 'Stuttgart DE Web as Corpus'.

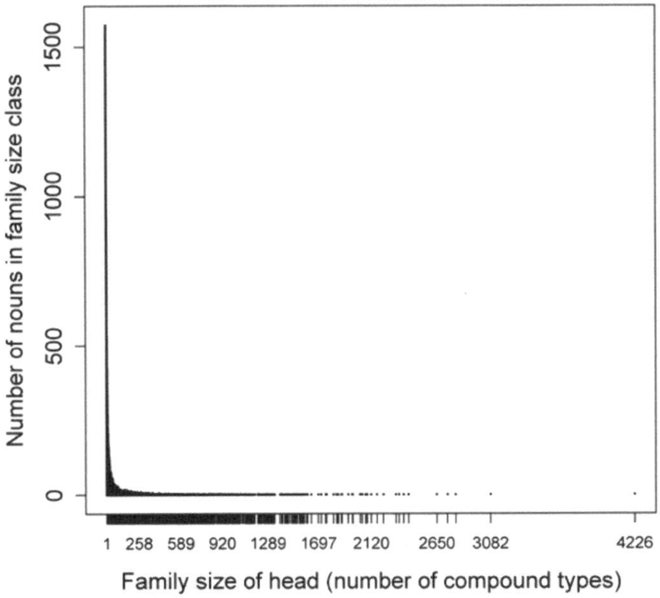

Figure 2: Compound family sizes of heads in sdeWaC

To create distribution vectors, we took lexicalized dependency relations into account, as was described in Section 3.1.2. The Bohnet parser has been trained on the CoNLL-X version of the TIGER corpus (Brants et al. 2004) and assigns dependency labels that correspond to functional edge labels in TIGER. We considered only those noun occurrences in which the noun was functioning as the immediate dependent of a verb, e.g., in the function of subject, accusative object, dative (an underspecified function in TIGER, comprising both dative objects and free datives), prepositional object, or modifier, to name the major categories.[9] The functional labels are subclassified by the lemma of the governing verb; that is, we counted co-occurrences with the relation '*wachsen*_subject' rather than 'subject' alone. For modifiers and prepositional objects, the labels also include information on the preposition and its case (if applicable). For example, the sentence *Außer dem Löwenzahn sehen wir ...* ('Besides the dandelion, we see ...') would result in a co-occurrence count for *Löwenzahn* with the relation '*sehen*_modifier_*außer*_dative'.

To process distributional similarity, we filtered the dataset by manually cleaning a subset of the lemmas, and by considering only noun types that occurred at least 30 times in the corpus. This left us with a database of 21,315 compound types. Furthermore, we did not include the modifier information, i.e., we ignored all instances in which the noun was related to the verb as a modifier. Evaluation of these decisions will require future analysis.

[9] We would like to thank Silke Scheible for providing subcategorization extraction for the parsed corpus.

4.2. Compound classes and distributional similarity

We predict that determiner compounds, possessive compounds, and copulative compounds will behave differently when their contexts are compared with those of their head nouns. Specifically, we make the following predictions with respect to their distributional similarities measured in terms of skew divergence D(p||q) (remember that low D indicates high similarity):

(12) *Determinative compounds:*
Head noun and compound will share many 'textual neighbors', i.e., they will have a high semantic similarity. The similarity of head and compound will exceed that of modifier and compound: D(c||h) will be low; D(c||h) will be lower than D(c||m).

(13) *Possessive compounds:*
Head noun and compound will not share many 'textual neighbors', i.e., they will have a low semantic similarity. The similarity of head and compound will not exceed the similarity of modifier and compound: D(c||h) will be high; D(c||h) will not be lower than D(c||m).

(14) *Copulative compounds:*
Head, modifier, and compound will share many 'textual neighbors', i.e., the compound will have a high similarity to both head and modifier: D(c||h) and D(c||m) will be low.

4.3. Results

In this section, we report the first results of our modeling of the different compound types by means of skew divergence.

The range of the score. The boxplots in Figure 3 visualize the skew divergence distributions D. These scores range from a minimum of 0.093, observed for the divergence of a head from its compound (cf. leftmost boxplot D(c||h)), to a maximum of 2.293, observed for the divergence of a compound from its modifier (cf. rightmost boxplot D(m||c)). The two boxplots on the left both model the divergence by taking the compound distribution as their reference point. Both have significantly lower scores than the corresponding boxplots on the right, which take the head or modifier distribution as their reference point. An explanation for this asymmetry could be that compounds are more restricted in meaning and do not correspond to all possible interpretations of their heads and modifiers. In terms of skew divergence, this means that compounds capture less of the distribution of their heads and modifiers than *vice versa*.

Correlations. An additional asymmetry became evident when we tested for correlations. D(h||c) and D(m||c) are both negatively correlated to the compound frequency (both rho≈-0.56 according to Spearman's rank correlation, $p<0.001$): the lower the frequency of the compound, the higher the D-score. As a consequence, interpreting D(h||c) or D(m||c) as a measure of similarity will tend to underestimate the similarity between modifier and compound for low-frequency compounds. For D(c||h) and D(c||m), we observe only very mild to no correlation with compound frequency (rho= -0.22, $p<0.001$, rho=-0.18, $p<0.001$). None of the scores correlates to the frequency of the head or modifier.

Given the observed correlations, D(h||c) and D(m||c) are suitable measures for the comparison of the similarity of a compound to its two component elements – if the compound *c* is kept constant. In general, however, it seems to be more advisable to use D(c||h) and D(c||m) to avoid the frequency-correlated bias, especially when different compounds are to be compared.

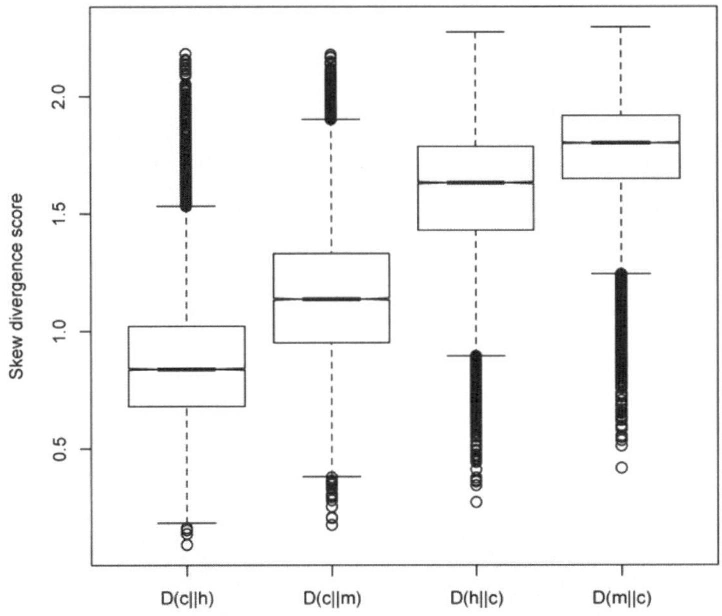

Figure 3: Boxplots for the distributions of skew divergence scores

Determinative compounds. Independent of the correlation described above, the boxplots in Figure 3 show that compounds are more similar to their heads than to their modifiers. This is exactly what characterizes determinative compounds. Given that determinative compounds constitute the largest group of compounds in German, it was to be expected that this property of determinative compounds would be reflected in the overall data.

Possessive compounds. We expected high scores for D(c||h) to reflect semantic opaqueness with respect to the head. For a small-scale manual evaluation, we filtered 105 compounds that passed certain heuristics (D(c||h)>1.6 and (D(c||h)- D(c||m))<0.3) and compared the proportions of possessive and determinative compounds in this 'possessive set' with their proportions in a set of 100 randomly sampled compounds. We identified 60 determinative compounds in the 'possessive' set[10] (i.e., compounds for which the question 'Is Compound a type of Head?' resulted in a positive answer) and 24 possessive compounds (for which the Compound was not a kind of Head), in addition to 14 processing errors (e.g., *Reimport* as *Reim+Port*). In the 'random set', we found 94 determinative compounds, 5 possessive compounds, 1 copulative compound, and no processing errors. The proportions of possessive compounds[11] and of determinative compounds[12] differ significantly between

[10] Plus 2 copulative compounds *Erdboden* 'soil' and *Haarschopf* 'shock of hair'.

[11] According to the proportion test, X=13.07, df=1, p<.0.001.

the 'possessive set' and the 'random set'. Examples of possessive compounds from the 'possessive set' include, *Blutbad* 'bloodbath', *Fallstrick* 'pitfall', and *Faltenwurf* 'drape'.

Copulative compounds. We expected that the 'double' similarity of copulative compounds would give rise to low scores for both $D(c||h)$ and $D(c||m)$. To evaluate this, we extracted 100 compounds that passed the filters of $D(c||h)<0.53$ and $D(c||m)<0.6$. At least 6 of these 100 candidates had a copulative interpretation ('Compound is a kind of Modifier and also a kind of Head'). Even if we identified a slightly larger number of compounds with a copulative reading, the results for the 'copulative set' do not differ significantly from the results for the 'random set'. There were many debatable cases in the evaluation sets. This suggests that our simple three-way classification is not sufficient to describe the compounds in an adequate way.

Example compound set. Finally, we briefly investigate the compound set of *Zahn* 'tooth' from our toy example. The chart in Figure 4 plots the divergence of the head (*Zahn*) from the compound on the x-axis and the divergence of the modifier from the compound on the y-axis. The dot-dash line indicates the area for which the head and modifier have the same amount of divergence from the compound. The dashed lines mark the mean values for the compound set of *Zahn*, and the dotted lines indicate the overall means of D. We predict determinative compounds to occur in the left-hand part of the chart (low $D(c||h)$), possessives in the (upper) right-hand part (high $D(c||h)$), and copulatives close to the dot-dash line ($D(c||h) = D(c||m)$), ideally in the left-hand half of the chart. *Eckzahn*, *Backenzahn*, *Milchzahn*, and *Giftzahn* all correctly cluster in the area where we expected to find determinative compounds. This also holds marginally for *Eckzähne* (a preprocessing error) and *Weisheitszahn*. *Löwenzahn* as a possessive compound is correctly situated in the right-hand half of the chart – although we would have expected it to appear higher in the chart, diverging more from its modifier noun. *Goldzahn* and *Stoßzahn* cluster together. This makes sense, as both compounds refer to items that have a monetary value.

[12] According to the proportion test, $X=30.75$, $df=1$, $p<0.001$.

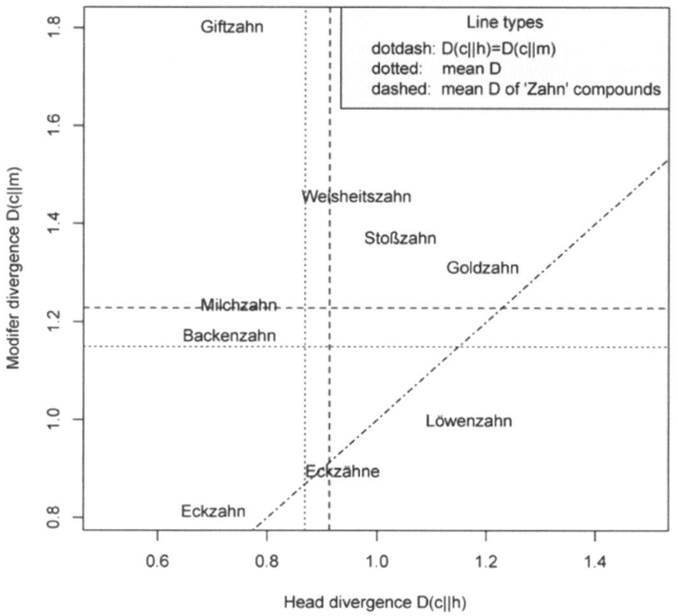

Figure 4: Head and modifier divergence for compounds of *Zahn* 'tooth'

5. Conclusion

This paper discusses the corpus-based modeling of three semantic noun-noun compound types – exemplified by *Küchenmesser* 'kitchen knife', *Milchgesicht* 'baby face' (literally 'milk face'), and *Dichterfreund* in the sense of 'poet and friend' – on the basis of their syntactic distributions. The main focus lies on describing skew divergence as a measure of distributional similarity. The corpus study presented in this chapter is essentially a pilot project; it permits first insight into the characteristics of the skew divergence score, but does not provide sufficient empirical evidence to allow the derivation of a conclusive model. More work is needed to better model the 'textual context', especially with regard to improving the parsing results and obtaining a more sophisticated feature extraction (e.g., including information, from syntactic modifiers, generalizing on lexical heads in terms of more abstract representation, etc.). In addition, future studies should include an objective evaluation set based on human transparency judgments and other experimental data such as human association norms (e.g., Schulte im Walde et al. 2012).

Bibliography

Baayen, R.H. (2008): *Analyzing linguistic data: A practical introduction to statistics using R*. Cambridge: Cambridge University Press.

Baayen, R.H., R. Lieber and R. Schreuder (1997): The morphological complexity of simplex nouns. *Linguistics* 35: 861–877.

Baroni, M., S. Bernardini, A. Ferraresi and E. Zanchetta (2009): The wacky wide web: A collection of very large linguistically processed web-crawled corpora. *Language Resources and Evaluation* 43(3): 209–222

Baroni, M. and A. Lenci (2010): Distributional memory: A general framework for corpus-based semantics. *Computational Linguistics* 36(4): 673–721.

Bohnet, B. (2010): Top accuracy and fast dependency parsing is not a contradiction. In: *Proceedings of the 23rd International Conference on Computational Linguistics (Coling 2010*), 89–97.

Brants, S., S. Dipper, P. Eisenberg, S. Hansen, E. König, W. Lezius, C. Rohrer, G. Smith and H. Uszkoreit (2004): TIGER: Linguistic interpretation of a German corpus. *Journal of Language and Computation* 2(4): 597–620.

Dowty, D. (1979): *Word meaning and Montague grammar*. Dordrecht: Reidel.

Erk, K. (2012): Vector space models of word meaning and phrase meaning: A survey. *Language and Linguistics Compass* 6(10): 635–653.

Evert, S. (2005): *The statistics of word cooccurrences: Word pairs and collocations*. PhD thesis. Institut für Maschinelle Sprachverarbeitung, Universität Stuttgart.

Faaß, G., U. Heid and H. Schmid (2010): Design and application of a gold standard for morphological analysis: SMOR in validation. In: *Proceedings of the 7th International Conference on Language Resources and Evaluation*, Valletta, Malta, 803–810.

Fanselow, G. (1981a): *Zur Syntax und Semantik der Nominalkomposition*. Tübingen: Niemeyer

Fanselow, G. (1981b): Neues von der Kompositafront oder zu drei Paradigmata in der Kompositionsgrammatik. *Studium Linguistik* 11: 43–57.

Firth, J.R. (1957): *Papers in linguistics 1934–51*. London: Longmans.

Fritzinger, F. and A. Fraser (2010): How to avoid burning ducks: Combining linguistic analysis and corpus statistics for German compound processing. In: *Proceedings of the ACL 2010 Joint Fifth Workshop on Statistical Machine Translation and Metrics MATR*, Uppsala. Sweden, 224–234.

Harris, Z.S. (1954): Distributional structure. *Word* 10:2/3, 146-162. (Reprinted in: Harris, Z.S. (1970): *Papers in structural and transformational linguistics*. Dordrecht: Reidel, 775–794).

Lee, L. (2001): On the effectiveness of the skew divergence for statistical language analysis. In: *Proceedings of Artificial Intelligence and Statistics (AISTATS)*, 65–72.

Lee, L. (1999): Measures of distributional similarity. In: *Proceedings of the Annual Meeting of the Association of Computational Linguistics (ACL)*, 25–32.

Lemnitzer, L. (2007): *Von Aldianer bis Zauselquote: Neue deutsche Wörter, woher sie kommen und wofür wir sie brauchen*. Tübingen: Narr.

Libben, G. (1998): Semantic transparency in the processing of compounds: Consequences for representation, processing, and impairment. *Brain and Language* 61: 30–44.

Marconi, D. (1997): *Lexical competence*. Cambridge, MA: MIT Press.

Marslen-Wilson, W.D. (2007): Morphological processes in language comprehension. In: G. Gaskell (ed.), *Oxford Handbook of Psycholinguistics*. Oxford: Oxford University Press, 175–193.

Murthag, F. (2005): *Correspondence analysis and data coding with JAVA and R*. Boca Raton, FL: Chapman & Hall/CRC.

Nübling, D. and R. Szczepaniak (2011): Merkmal(s?)analyse, Seminar(s?)arbeit und Essen(s?)ausgabe: Zweifelsfälle der Verfugung als Indikatoren für Sprachwandel. In: *Zeitschrift für Sprachwissenschaft 30*: 45–73.

Olsen, S. (2000): Article 87: Composition. In: G. Booij, C. Lehmann and J. Mugdan (eds.), *Morphology: A Handbook of Inflection and Word Formation*. Berlin: Walter de Gruyter, 2000, 897–916.

Sahlgren, M. (2008): The distributional hypothesis. *Rivista di Linguistica* 20 (1): 33–53.

Seeker, W. and J. Kuhn (2012): Making ellipses explicit in dependency conversion for a German treebank. In: *Proceedings of the 8th International Conference on Language Resources and Evaluation (LREC)*, 3132–3139.

Schiller, A., S. Teufel, C. Stöckert and C. Thielen (1999): *Guidelines für das Tagging deutscher Textcorpora mit STTS (Tech. Rep.)*. Stuttgart: Institut für maschinelle Sprachverarbeitung.

Schmid, H., A. Fitschen and U. Heid (2004): SMOR: A German computational morphology covering derivation, composition and inflection. In: *LREC '04: Proceedings of the 4th Conference on Language Resources and Evaluation*, 1263–1266.

Schulte im Walde, S. (2005): Exploring features to identify semantic nearest neighbours: A case study on German particle verbs. In: *Proceedings of the International Conference on Recent Advances in Natural Language Processing (RANLP),* 608–614.

Schulte im Walde, S., S. Borgwaldt and R. Jauch (2012): Association norms of German noun compounds. In: *Proceedings of the 8th International Conference on Language Resources and Evaluation (LREC)*, 632–639.

Williams, E. (1981): On the notions 'lexically related' and 'head of a word'. *Linguistic Inquiry* 12: 245–274.

Zinsmeister, H. and U. Heid (2004): Collocations of complex nouns: Evidence for lexicalisation. In: *Proceedings of KONVENS 2004*. Vienna, Austria.

Zinsmeister, H. and E. Smolka (2012): Corpus-based evidence for approximating semantic transparency of complex verbs. In: K. Würzner and E. Pohl (eds.): *Lexical Resources in Psycholinguistic Research. Potsdam Cognitive Science Series* (vol. 3). Potsdam: Universitätsverlag Potsdam, 45–59.

Why say *yes* in Joyce? Molly Bloom's *yes because* in the "Penelope" episode of *Ulysses*

Claudia Olk

The special status of the *yes* in the final episode of *Ulysses* is widely recognized.[1] *Yes* is both the first and the last word in the "Penelope" episode that concludes the textual odyssey of Joyce's masterpiece, and it occurs more than 80 times in the eight long sentences of Molly Bloom's soliloquy. Similar to her mythical counterpart, Penelope, Molly waits for her husband Leopold to return home from his wanderings, and she remains stationary, in her bed, as she recapitulates events of the novel, retells memories of her youth in Gibraltar, muses on her various erotic encounters and recalls scenes from her life with Leopold Bloom. In her reminiscences, Molly revisits experiences and places, and the soliloquy gestures towards a sense of homecoming and the return to some firm ground after unruly years at sea. At the end of the novel's trajectory that spans June 16, 1904, Molly returns to her memories, and Leopold Bloom returns to their home in 7 Eccles Street, Dublin.

For Bloom as for Homer's returning Odysseus, however, home is not initially welcoming. It has lost some of its comfort, and has become oddly unfamiliar. Bloom has difficulty entering his house having misplaced his key, and unlike Penelope, Molly has not remained faithful to her husband to whom familiar objects such as the bed no longer promise any shelter. When Bloom lies down and notices "the imprint of a human form, male, not his" (17, 601), he poignantly becomes aware of the fact that his marital bed is anything but a safe haven. At the end of *Ulysses*, therefore, the promise of stability and fulfilment is undermined by the unsettling sense of unfamiliarity and the abiding notion of a desire that remains unfulfilled.

This ambivalence is pervasive in the differential structure of Molly's numerous yeses that frame the episode and punctuate her phrases in what sometimes seems to replace a full stop. On the one hand, the yeses provide affirmation and rest, and on the other, they harbour an element of doubt and raise new questions. They mark a circular pattern of departure and return, and create a point of reference for the speaker, who in bringing one strand of meaning to an end, immediately starts off another one. In Molly's repeated yeses, every beginning and every ending therefore remains temporary when the desire to reach an ultimate affirmation or to come to an end is constantly challenged by the desire to continue narrating, or to start all over again. Molly's yeses are not fixed in space and time, but become part of the dynamic movement of the text. The sheer number of repetitions of the yeses in different contexts creates a dialectical structural dynamics that at the same time suggests and defers closure.

---

1 All references to *Ulysses* are to: Gabler, H.W., W. Steppe and C. Melchior (eds.) (1984): *Ulysses*. The corrected text, with a new preface by R. Ellmann. London: Bodley Head.

The enigmatic occurrence and multiple meanings of the *yes* have made it a source of research questions in Joyce scholarship, and 'Joyceans' have examined its numerous occurrences and provided taxonomies of the varied implications and contexts of the *yes*:

> "Yes, yes, but which yes are we talking about? There is a large spectrum of resonances in yes, before we even encounter the intricate universe of *Ulysses'* yeses. A cursory review would pass through the yes of acknowledgement; the yes of acquiescence; the yes of subscription; the questioning yes; the suspicious yes; the irritated yes; the impatient yes; the pensive yes; the reassuring yes; the yes of surrender; the yes of concession; the yes of triumph; the promising yes; the yes of 'yes, but…'; the yes of surprise; the reparative yes; the yes of jouissance. Let us not forget some of the most remarkable dramatizations of yes: the yes of ideological interpellation ('Hey, you there! Yes?'); the yes of the military scene (Yes, sir!); the yes of racial hierarchy (Ralph Ellison's Yassuh, yassuh, yassuh); the yes of the marriage ceremony ('Yes, I do'). At the other end of the spectrum there is the revolutionary, eventual yes."[2]

No scholar has made his own fascination with the occurrence of the *yes* in *Ulysses* so prominent as Jacques Derrida in the opening address that he delivered at the Ninth International James Joyce Symposium in Frankfurt 1984,[3] where he studies the interplay of the written and the spoken *yes*, or rather the French "oui".

Molly's first words, however, are not just *yes*, but *yes because*, and in this essay I intend to explore Derrida's interpretation of the *yes*, both in its roots in deconstruction and in his analysis of the *Ulysses* text itself. I would like to show that Molly's *yes because*, in the "Penelope" episode carries a particular significance because it does not entirely fit into the categories that Derrida lays out for the *yes* and also because this particular kind of *yes* is an answering to an internalised other that includes the reader and introduces a dialogic element into her soliloquy. I will first look at what in Joyce may have inspired Derrida in the first place, and then at what Derrida claims about the yeses, particularly in the "Penelope" episode. With this background in mind, in the second part of this essay I would like to show why not only the *yes* but also the *yes because* is unique and how understanding this latter uniqueness can enrich an interpretation of the *yes* in general in *Ulysses*, and especially in the "Penelope" episode.

---

2 Parvulescu, A. (2010): To Yes-laugh Derrida's Molly. *Parallax* 16: 16–27, 17.

3 It was published under the title 'Ouï-dire de Joyce' together with a previous essay on *Finnegans Wake*, in: "*Ulysse* gramophone: Deux mots pour Joyce" (1987) and translated into English as 'Hear say yes in Joyce' (1992: 252–343).

I

Joyce profoundly inspired Derrida's work,[4] and Derrida, who remained a lifelong reader and admirer of works like *Ulysses* and *Finnegans Wake* describes how Joyce's spectre accompanies his thought "every time I write, and even in the most academic pieces of work, Joyce's ghost is always coming on board".[5]

Upon encountering one of Derrida's texts one may likely wonder how this spectre materializes in his writing, and in answering this question one must first look at the larger project of deconstruction, with which Derrida greatly concerned himself over the course of his lifetime.[6] His seminal paper, titled "Structure, Sign and Play in the Discourse of the Human Sciences", which Derrida delivered at the Johns Hopkins University in 1966, marked a turning point in his own thinking as well as a milestone in the project of deconstruction itself. In this essay, Derrida focuses on the idea of centeredness and structure as well as on what he describes as "two interpretations of interpretation, of structure, of sign, of play".[7]

Derrida begins the essay by highlighting what he cautiously terms an "event" in the history of the concept of structure. This event marked the beginning of a new way of interpreting structure, which was no longer bound to the idea of a centre. Derrida writes: "Perhaps something has occurred in the history of the concept of structure that could be called an 'event', if this loaded word did not entail a meaning which it is precisely the function of structural – or structuralist – thought to reduce or to suspect [...]. What would this event be then? Its exterior form would be that of a *rupture* and a redoubling."[8]

Before this event, according to Derrida, the concept of structure or "the structurality of structure" which he claims is "as old as western science and western philosophy", has always been involved in a process of giving it a centre or referring it to a "point of presence", or what he terms "a fixed origin". The function of this centre, Derrida claims, was to "orient, balance, and organize" the structure, but most importantly to limit what he calls the free play of this structure.[9]

The centre, Derrida goes on to explain, is the point at which the substitution of contents, elements, or metaphors is no longer possible. Here is where Derrida makes an interesting turn. He claims that because "the center is at the centre of the totality", yet because the centre is not part of the totality, "the totality *has its center elsewhere*". This means, according to

---

4 Roughley, A. (1999): *Reading Derrida Reading Joyce.* Gainesville et al.: University of Florida Press

5 Derrida, J. (1984): Two Words for Joyce, transl. G. Gennington. In: D. Attridge and D. Ferrer (eds.), *Post-structuralist Joyce: Essays from the French.* Cambridge: Cambridge University Press, 149.

6 van Boheemen, C. (1988): Deconstruction after Joyce. In: B. K. Scott (ed.), *New Alliances in Joyce Studies: "When It's Aped to Foul a Delfian".* Newark: University of Delaware Press, 1988, 29–36.

7 Derrida, J. (1978): Structure, Sign, and Play in the Discourse of the Human Sciences. In: J. Derrida (ed.), *Writing and Difference*, transl. by Alan Bass. London: Routledge, 292.

8 Derrida, J. (1978): Structure, Sign, and Play in the Discourse of the Human Sciences. In: J. Derrida (ed.), *Writing and Difference*, transl. by Alan Bass. London: Routledge, 278.

9 Ibid., 278.

Derrida, "the center is not the center".[10] Thus the centre in western thought represents both a coherence and a contradiction. He then claims philosophy to be a kind of archaeology in that it is an accomplice of this reduction of the "structurality of structure" and always attempts to think of structure on the basis of an origin, "which is beyond play".[11]

Assuming this contradiction inherent in the origin, Derrida continues his discussion of origins or centres by claiming that the history of the concept of structure, before the event he spoke of, is best thought of as a series of substitutions of centres, which would receive different names and forms over time. Derrida goes so far as to claim that the "history of metaphysics, like the history of the West, is the history of these metaphors and metonymies."[12] He then gives examples of what metaphors have served for the centre over time, and these include essence, existence, substance, subject, truth, transcendentality, consciousness, God and man.[13]

Now, according to Derrida, there can be two interpretations of the turning toward the metaphors for the centre. This division arises from the event that Derrida began describing. The first of these interpretations is the "thematic of broken immediateness is thus the sad, negative, nostalgic, guilty, Rousseauist facet of the thinking of free play." The second is the Nietzschean "*affirmation*, that is the joyous affirmation of the play of the world and of the innocence of becoming, the affirmation of a world of signs without fault, without truth, and without origin which is offered to an active interpretation. *This affirmation then determines the noncenter otherwise than as a loss of the center*."[14] This means that the "event" Derrida spoke of produces a new interpretation that allows for a new focus on a noncenter rather than on the metaphor of a centre, or the nihilistic absence of a centre.

In conclusion to his essay, Derrida writes, "there are thus two interpretations of interpretation, of structure, of sign, of play". The first kind, the one that still relies on the centre, "seeks to decipher, dreams of deciphering, a truth or an origin which is free from free play and from the order of the sign, and lives like an exile the necessity of interpretation." The other, which is not focused on "the origin, affirms play and tries to pass beyond man and humanism, the name of man being the name of that being who, throughout the history of metaphysics or of ontotheology – in other words, throughout his entire history – has dreamed of full presence, the reassuring foundation, the origin and end of play."[15] This second interpretation of interpretation, the assertive embrace of the loss of origin that Derrida credits Nietzsche with discovering is very much in line with Derrida's own thinking as it focuses on the operations of language that is unrestrained from a transcendentally signified or the notion of an originary truth lying hidden behind appearances.

Derrida thus conceives of language and difference in a similar vein. On one occasion, when discussing difference as it pertains to the text, specifically to a philosophic text, Derrida writes that the text, although it is always written, includes the project of "effacing itself

10 Ibid., 279.
11 Ibid., 279.
12 Ibid., 279.
13 Ibid., 279–280.
14 Ibid., 292.
15 Ibid., 292.

in the face of the signified content which it transports and in general teaches".[16] He goes on to claim that the entire history of texts, and within it the history of literary forms in the West, should be studied from this point of view. Reading, Derrida claims, should be aware of this project of self-effacement, even if it intends to expose the project's failure.[17] Difference then, "is recognized as the obliterated origin of absence and presence," that is, the affirmation of the absence of the origin and the opening of the free play of metaphor: "Differance produces what it forbids, makes possible the very thing that it makes impossible."[18] Difference can be termed then as the disposition of the second kind of interpretation that affirms free play. For Derrida, thus language constitutes meaning through a play of differences, which is "permitted by the lack or absence of a center or origin", it is "the movement of *supplementarity*".[19]

It is easy to see then, given the project illustrated in "Structure, Sign and Play in the Discourse of the Human Sciences", why modernist literature would be of particular interest to Derrida. With its programmatic break with previous structures of the novel and its affiliation with non-centred movements in art and philosophy such as Dadaism and Existentialism, modernism opens itself up, more than any period before it, to the free play of the exchange of metaphors for the center. As part of the general anti-metaphysical drive of modernism, writers such as James Joyce and Virginia Woolf expressed a critique of language, and especially that of realism. Instead, they explored the inherent playfulness of language that was no longer attached to a referent outside the context of the narrative.

Modernist texts hence foreground their own processes of creation and mark immanence as a characteristic of their aesthetic dimension. They privilege the transient, the banal and the everyday, and, in doing so, they attest to the seemingly meaningless object a unique aesthetic value. Joyce's texts, in particular, experiment with language that is freed from the traditional protocols of mimesis and does not refer in some stable and predictable way to the world outside of it or to a metaphysical ground, but rather designates its own relationships of intertextuality and internal difference.

In Joyce, Derrida found not only a writer who prolifically experimented with a diversity of styles, narrative modes, and grammatical structures, but also one who in *Ulysses* created a work of art that criticized, questioned and redefined previous conceptions of the novel precisely by creating a new genre for itself. The work's complex web of relations with other texts, languages and traditions that far exceeds mere reference therefore finds a meaningful base in itself.

Even though *Ulysses* ventures into the "Heart of the Hibernian metropolis", as well as into the innermost workings of the minds of his many characters, the idea of a stable centrality from which to deduce meaning is readily jettisoned in the novel. Instead of a static moment within an epistemological schema, it is the continuum of material transformations of lan-

---

16 Derrida, J. (1976): That Dangerous Supplement. In: *Of Grammatology*, transl. by G. Chakravorty Spivak. Baltimore: Johns Hopkins University Press, 160.

17 Ibid., 160.

18 Ibid., 143.

19 Derrida, J. (1978): *Writing and Difference*, translated by Alan Bass. London: Routledge, 289.

guage, of hitherto unrealized linguistic and imaginary possibilities that lays the foundation for its poetic creation.[20]

In the "Penelope" episode, likewise, the notions of an unmoveable centre or a fixed origin that authorizes all attempts to define it appear doubtful, indeed.[21] Instead, the novel depicts any kind of return to an origin as inherently difficult, if not impossible. In many instances, *Ulysses* evokes the notion of origin, home, stability and centre only to undermine them. At the very beginning of *Ulysses*, Stephen Dedalus returns to Dublin from Paris only to find his family disintegrated and himself out of place even in the society of his friends. Bloom, likewise, experiences the deceptive opacity of everyday appearances, and for him, too, the sense of home from which the narrative departs and towards which it gravitates has become increasingly unfamiliar.

Central to the "Penelope" episode is, quite literally, a seemingly banal everyday object: the Blooms' bed, that, as the preceding "Ithaca" episode describes it, stands for the beginning and the end of life: "the bed of conception and of birth, of consummation of marriage and of breach of marriage, of sleep and of death" (17, 601). This centre to which Bloom attempts to return, however, is no longer a fixed centre of stability, but a dialectical entity that consists of opposites: life and death, love and betrayal, in which states of being that appear similar are in fact vastly different.

When pondering the bed and its varied occupants, that is the series of Molly's lovers, Bloom cannot help but notice that the return to an origin is impossible, that in fact an origin does not exist: "whereas he is neither first nor last nor only nor alone in a series originating in and repeated to infinity" (17, 601). Bloom uneasily orchestrates himself into this textual display of the potential infinity of play and substitution, and responds with equally "antagonistic sentiments" such as "envy, jealousy, abnegation, equanimity" (17, 602) only to gradually drift into sleep and indulge in a phantasy of travel to the land of milk and honey that evokes his Jewish roots and, at the same time, replaces and complements one narrative of origin by another.

II

A prominent example of dialectics that occurs in the language of *Ulysses* into which we will now investigate is that of the *yes* in the Penelope episode. In "*Ulysses* Gramophone: Hear Say Yes in Joyce," Derrida explores the occasion of this word in particular depth, highlighting especially its frequency and changing modality in the text, its *a priori* status in metalinguistics and its function as an answer to an "other". One peculiar characteristic of the *yes*" in the last chapter of *Ulysses* that Derrida emphasizes is the frequency in which it occurs. He writes, "I had even tried casually counting them; more than 222 *yeses* in the so-called original version [...] I came up with this no doubt approximate figure after an initial count-

---

[20] Olk, C. (2008): Ah the Soap: Objekt und Materie im *Ulysses*. *Poetica* 40, 169–188.

[21] Norris, M. (1974): *The Decentered Universe of 'Finnegans Wake': A Structuralist Analysis*. Baltimore: Johns Hopkins University Press.

ing up, which took into consideration only the *yeses* in their explicit form."[22] This means that there are also other versions of the *yes* in *Ulysses*, which may occur covertly, for example in the word "yesterday", "eyes", "jessamine", "jest", or "ay". These too, seem to count for Derrida. Also, more than a quarter of these 222 "yeses" Derrida says to have counted in *Ulysses*, occur in the "Penelope" chapter. He claims that there are "at least 79 [...] in Molly's so-called monologue"[23] (in my count I came up with 87). This amount in itself indicates that the *yes* has particular importance in this last chapter, and it, at the same time, parodies empirical attempts at providing objective, statistical proof. The catalogue of yeses and their variations rather displays the arbitrariness of seemingly objective systems of classification.

After counting up the various yeses, Derrida then attempts to organize them into categories or modalities, of which he lists ten.[24] He gives these example modalities in what he considers a hypothesis, and is sure to say that the list should remain open. The modalities of the *yes* he lists are: "the *yes* of question form, the *yes* of rhythmic breathing in the form of monologic self-approbation, the *yes* of obedience, the *yes* of making an agreement on fact, the *yes* of a passionate breathing of desire, the *yes* of exactly calculated and precise breathing, the *yes* of absentminded politeness, the *yes* of emphatic confirmation, the *yes* of open approval, and the *yes* of insisted confidence."

The ambivalence and double meaning of the yes becomes all the more clear when Derrida notes that in French 'Joyce's yes saying' and 'hear say in Joyce' is a homonym whose meaning can only be understood and 'received' by looking at the text because it depends on whether there is a single dot over the 'I' or the double one of a dieresis: l'ouï-dire de Joyce, 'Joyce's hear say': "*Yes* in *Ulysses* can only be a mark at once written and spoken, vocalized as a grapheme and written as a phoneme, yes, *in a word, gramophoned*".[25] Derrida here turns to the relation between speech and writing. He demonstrates that the signifier is as important as the signified, explaining that this homonymy cannot be translated but only heard rather than read with the eyes - a word that also contains *yes*.

A second characteristic of the *yes* according to Derrida, is its *a priori* status in metalinguistics. In the beginning of "*Ulysses* Gramophone", he writes that in the beginning there must have been some phone call, meaning that "in the beginning" was a question or request. The *yes* he places in a special category, preceding not only the answer, but also the asking of the question. According to Derrida: "The minimal, primary yes, the telephonic 'hello' or the tap through a prison wall, marks, before meaning or signifying 'I-here,' listen, answer, there is some mark, there is some other. Negatives may ensue, but even if they completely take over, this yes can no longer be erased."[26]

In this sense, the "yes" is always primary; it is in fact what is necessary for a conversation to ensue, precisely because it indicates that there is another voice. This is how Derrida

22 Derrida, J. (1992): *Ulysses* Gramophone: Hear Say Yes In Joyce. In: D. Attridge (ed.), *Acts of Literature*. New York: Routledge, 266.

23 Ibid. 306.

24 Ibid., 306–308.

25 Ibid., 267.

26 Ibid. 298.

justifies calling the *yes a priori*.[27] It is not a performative speech act in Austin's sense, but rather has pre-performative weight.

Despite these claims about the "yes", Derrida still maintains that it is difficult to say something definite and metalinguistic about the "yes", which:

> "names nothing, describes nothing, whose grammatical and semantic status is most enigmatic, it seems at least possible to affirm the following: it must be taken for an answer. It is always in the form of an answer. It occurs after the other, to answer a request or a question, at least implicit, of the other, even if this is the other in me, the representation in me of another speech. *Yes* implies, as Bloom would say, an 'implicit believer' in some summons of the other. *Yes* always has the meaning, the function, the mission of an *answer*, even if this answer, as we shall also see, sometimes has the force of an originary and unconditional commitment".[28]

This implicit believer is for whom the *yes* exists and is the reason behind its existence. Without the other the *yes* would have no meaning, it would be directed towards nothing. It is important here to recognize that for Derrida the other can also be oneself, presumably in another state or time. It is to the idea of this other, on whose answer the *yes* depends, that we now turn.

A third and last characteristic of the *yes* is that of it being an answer to another. Derrida writes that a "yes" never comes alone, and we never say this word alone.[29] This would imply both that we never say it without saying something in addition, and that we never say it without the possibility and acknowledgement of another potential yes-sayer on the other side. This becomes important when looking at the "Penelope" chapter because Molly is solitary in her thoughts, and this would justify that the chapter is called a monologue. Also, this is where the implication of the other becomes very prominent, because the frequency of the *yes* is so prevalent in this chapter. However, according to Derrida, from the moment there is a *yes*, a break occurs in the monologue,[30] making it not a monologue at all, but rather a dialogue between her and some other. This other, the one addressed by the initial, *a priori yes*, becomes central to the deconstructionist interpretation of the *yes* in *Ulysses*. That is, whatever their modality, whatever category or context, the *yes* always presupposes and precedes the existence of, or possibility of, some other.

In the event in the concept of structure, which I explored at the beginning of this paper, there occurred a rupture in interpretation that eventually allowed for a new kind of interpretation that affirmed the free play of metaphors for the centre. Here it is the *yes* in the "Penelope" chapter that inspires Derrida because of its immediate general affirmation, and because of its affirmation of something which is open to a free play of interpretation that is, the other. In his essay "*Ulysses* Gramophone" Derrida wrote that the signature of the *yes* is

---

27 Ibid., 276.
28 Ibid., 265.
29 Ibid., 288.
30 Ibid., 266.

one of reversal and that it holds open the circle it institutes,[31] thus affirming its own paradox. Derrida writes:

> "This situation is one of reversal, stemming from the paradox of the *yes* [...] So this is the paradox: just when the work of such a signature gets going – some might say submits itself, at any rate restarts *for itself*, so that it might return to itself – the most competent and reliable production and reproduction machine, it simultaneously ruins the model".[32]

This paradox in the *yes* of answering to oneself a question posed by oneself, is an instance of what Derrida terms 'difference' in "Structure, Sign, and Play in the Discourse of Human Sciences", in that it functions as "the obliterated origin of absence and presence."[33] The *yes* therefore, in its answering to the other in oneself, is the most pure example of the affirmation of the *yes's* paradox in *Ulysses*.

There is something, however, very peculiar to one particular kind of *yes* in the Penelope chapter, and this is something that Derrida neglects to point out. This *yes* is namely the *yes because*. Not only is it peculiar in that it represents the first *yes* and the most frequent kind of *yes* in the Molly chapter[34], but it is also peculiar because this kind of *yes*, more than any other kind, indicates the special, and in fact paradoxical nature, of the *yes* that is calling or referring to an other in oneself. This is supported by the fact that Molly, in her answering with *yes because* is answering a *yes* in its question form: "Yes because he never did a thing like that before as ask to get his breakfast in bed" (18, 608). Yet the other in her case, both since she is alone and because she initiated the question with her initial *Yes* in the chapter, is she herself or an internalized other that includes the reader. Here, the *yes because* that Derrida does not explicitly mention is particularly fitting to the project of deconstruction in making explicit the other in oneself in that it closes and completes the paradox of the *yes*.

On another occasion, Molly's answering to herself is a way of reassuring herself about what she knew all along – mostly about men: "yes because theyre so weak and puling when theyre sick they want a woman to get well if his nose bleeds youd think it was O tragic " (18, 608).

Based on this knowledge, she uses the *yes because* to convince herself about Bloom's potential betrayal when she recalls finding him writing a letter to his girlfriend Martha: "if they only knew him as well as I do yes because the day before yesterday he was scribbling something a letter when I came into the front room" (18, 609). It is this evidence that leads her to casually observe that: "yes because he couldnt possibly do without it that long so he must do it somewhere" (18, 609).

In matters of marital faithfulness or deceit, the *yes because* creates a parallel between Molly and Leopold and unites the seemingly different and incompatible when it is not only used in contexts where Molly seeks to convince herself about Bloom's weaknesses, but where it also serves her to defend her own flirtatiousness: "yes because I felt lovely and

---

31 "*Ulysses* Gramophone", 302.
32 Ibid., 282.
33 Derrida, J. (1976): That Dangerous Supplement. In: *Of Grammatology*, 143.
34 The "yes because" occurs a total of seven times in the last chapter of *Ulysses*.

tired myself and fell asleep" (18, 611). Molly's view of Leopold and her view of herself therefore both contradict and complement each other.

Throughout the "Penelope" episode, Molly clearly enjoys telling herself as well as other people details about her affairs and, in doing so, causing their curiosity and jealousy: "youre always in great humour she said yes because it grigged her because she knew what it meant because I used to tell her a good bit of what went on between us" (18, 612). Her taking pleasure in elaborating on episodes in her love life does not only include herself and other characters, but she also addresses the reader when she makes him privy to her emotional and erotic experiences: "yes because theres a wonderful feeling there so tender all the time" (18, 626). The *yes because* is not only a mode of Molly doubling her view of herself in answering to herself, but also an instance where the text introduces a double perspective in which the reader finds himself both inside and outside of Molly.

In cases like these, the *yes because* also has the character of a rationalization or explanation, and the next question then is what is at stake in her question, such that it requires an explanation? Given the important function of the *yes* in the "Penelope" chapter, both to the chapter itself and to how well it serves the deconstructive project, a special case of the *yes* such as the *yes because*, has significant importance to the meaning of the text. One important unanswered issue left remaining then, is the meaning and function of the *yes because* to the chapter, or more provocatively put, what is at stake for Molly in her *yes because*?

My take on this theme stems from a quote from Derrida's "*Ulysses* Gramophone" when he says that the *yes* is at once an "I am" and an "I will".[35] One might assume that what Derrida was probably trying to highlight here was the *a priori* status of the *yes*, but there is a profounder possible meaning. It seems to me to be the case that once the *yes* is given in the dialogue there must be a certain gravity given to an outcome. That is, something begins to matter to the speaker with the advent of the *yes* because the existence of something has been stated and put into play.

Throughout the novel there is always the implicit believer in Bloom, waiting for Molly's yes to come forth, and ultimately, at the end of the last chapter, it does. Yet, in her *yes because*, Molly is not answering the believer in Bloom, but rather the implicit believer in herself. The *yes because* in these cases does not establish a logical causality, but rather a deliberate pseudo-causality in which she rationalizes her actions to herself and the reader. Part of Molly is always waiting for the outcome of her decision, the part to which the outcome has meaning and weight. If Molly's *yes* is in fact both an "I am" and "I will", then her *yes because* is an answer to the why of her willing and being. The *yes* here functions as a changeable point of reference for the willing and meaning of Molly's presence. Molly, therefore, in the *yes because* is giving reasons for why she chooses one centre over another – she is, in a sense, rationalizing the free play of answers, in which all outcomes are possible ("and I thought well as well him as another" (18, 643-644)), but it is important to her that it is not random or without sense and meaning. She does this because what is at stake in the *yes* as within all instances of free play, is meaninglessness because of a randomly chosen, or simply not well considered, metaphoric centre. Her choice, her will, her life and her yes, must in some way matter, at least to the other in herself, and this is what the *yes because* indicates.

---

35 "*Ulysses* Gramophone", 290.

The processes of justification, rationalization and explanation that emerge in the *yes because* hence remain anchored in her dialogical self. Her being answers to herself, creates meaning for herself and in its dialogic performativity it acknowledges the paradox of identity in difference, both in her relation with other characters, with the reader and in her relation to herself. It is therefore only in this mode of difference, paradox and contradiction that Molly remains identical to herself.

In the course of her soliloquy, its shifting perspectives and its structural movement of departure and return, Molly produces herself from within herself in a process that goes beyond what is conventionally labelled the stream of consciousness technique. In her *yes* as both an "I am" and an "I will", Molly's language and identity become one. As Derrida has observed about the literary figures of Rousseau "we have access to their so-called 'real' existence only in the text and we have neither any means of altering this, nor any right to neglect this limitation",[36] Molly's *yes* likewise constitutes her differential being-as-text.

As Molly is given the last word, and her soliloquy is positioned at the end of the novel, *Ulysses*, as many critics have noted, closes on a language that can be identified as female. Indeed, Molly, in her final *yes because* once again addresses another when she gives reasons why the world would be better off if women ruled it:

> "itd be much better for the world to be governed by the women in it you wouldnt see women going and killing one another and slaughtering when do you ever see women rolling around drunk like they do or gambling every penny they have and losing it on horses yes because a woman whatever she does she knows where to stop" (18, 640).

Molly's text stops where it started, or it almost does so, when it ends on the famous last words "yes I will Yes" (18, 644). Molly's being and her willing become one when she goes back to an original moment of choice, the *yes* of marriage that started her life with Bloom. The sense of affirmation and closure provided by this final capitalized *Yes* is, as it were, countersigned by Joyce's line "*Trieste-Zürich-Paris,* 1914-1921" that complements the textual odyssey and reintroduces the notion of the shifting origins of the novel itself and its many travels through space and time. At the end of Ulysses, therefore, the novel's own coming into being is juxtaposed to Molly's textual presence. Molly's paradoxical *yes* is again part of the self-constituting textual multiplicity of heterogeneous, partial and contingent perspectives. It is both an answer and a question, and as such creates a potentially infinite occasion for narrative of a being that is not separate from language.

Bibliography

Derrida, J. (1976): That Dangerous Supplement. In: J. Derrida (ed.), *Of Grammatology*. Baltimore: Johns Hopkins Press, 141–164.

Derrida, J. (1978): Structure, Sign, and Play in the Discourse of the Human Sciences. In: J. Derrida (ed.), *Writing and Difference*. London: Routledge, 278–294.

[36] Derrida, J. (1976): That Dangerous Supplement. In: *Of Grammatology*, 158.

Derrida, J. (1984): Two Words for Joyce. In: D. Attridge and D. Ferrer (eds.), *Post-structuralist Joyce: Essays from the French*. Cambridge: Cambridge University Press, 145–161.

Derrida, J. (1992): *Ulysses* Gramophone: Hear Say Yes in Joyce. In: D. Attridge (ed.), *Acts of Literature*. New York: Routledge, 252–343.

Joyce, J. (1984): *Ulysses*. The corrected text, H. W. Gabler, W. Steppe and C. Melchior (eds.), and with a new preface by R. Ellmann. London: Bodley Head.

Norris, M. (1974): *The Decentered Universe of* Finnegans Wake: *A Structuralist Analysis*. Baltimore: Johns Hopkins University Press.

Olk, C. (2008): Ah the Soap: Objekt und Materie im *Ulysses*. *Poetica* 40, 169–188.

Parvulescu, A. (2010): To Yes-laugh Derrida's Molly. *Parallax* 16: 16–27.

Roughley, A. (1999): *Reading Derrida Reading Joyce*. Gainesville et al.: University of Florida Press.

van Boheemen, C. (1988): Deconstruction after Joyce. In: B. Kime Scott (ed.), *New Alliances in Joyce Studies: "When It's Aped to Foul a Delfian"*. Newark: University of Delaware Press, 29–36.